# Cooking Along the Ganges

# Cooking Along the Ganges

## The Vegetarian Heritage of India

*Malvi Doshi*
*with Neil Doshi and Bella Doshi*
*Foreword by Michele Anna Jordan*
*Illustrations by Sonya Quayle*

Writer's Showcase
New York  Lincoln  Shanghai

# Cooking Along the Ganges
## The Vegetarian Heritage of India

Writer's Showcase
an imprint of iUniverse, Inc.

For information address:
iUniverse
2021 Pine Lake Road, Suite 100
Lincoln, NE 68512
www.iuniverse.com

ISBN: 0-595-24422-X

Printed in the United States of America

***A Depiction of the Ganesha Statue that Stood in The Ganges Restaurant,
San Francisco, CA.***
Hindus revere the elephant-headed Ganesha as the remover of obstacles. Son of Shiva,
Ganesha is worshipped at the commencement of Hindu ceremonies. He is regarded as a
joyous and jovial, but infinitely wise deity.

**To**

My loving husband Arun, and my parents Indumati and Ramanlal.

Your patience, guidance and love continue to carry me.

With love and gratitude,

Malvi.

# Contents

Foreword ...................................................................................xi

Acknowledgements ..................................................................xiii

Introduction ...............................................................................1

The Basics of Indian Cooking ..................................................7

Indian Dairy Basics ................................................................53

Chutneys, Relishes, *Raitas* and Pickles ...............................63

Appetizers, Snacks or One-Dish Meals ................................128

Vegetables ..............................................................................185

Rice, Bulgur and Other Grains ............................................295

*Dals*: Beans, Peas and Lentils ..............................................334

Indian Breads ........................................................................395

Desserts and Sweetmeats ......................................................439

Beverages ...............................................................................481

Glossary .................................................................................503

About the Author ..................................................................505

Index .....................................................................................507

# FOREWORD

My meals at *The Ganges* are among my most treasured culinary memories. The bright flavors dance in my mind's eye like little fireflies of taste: fresh pineapple chutney, fiery green chili fritters, rich potato curry, an extraordinary banana stuffed with cilantro, jalapeños, and coconut. How fine and true Malvi Doshi's cooking is, how generous both of spirit and of taste.

It may have been the deliciousness of my first meal that drew me back a second time to the charming little Victorian house in an out-of-the-way neighborhood of San Francisco, but it was Malvi Doshi herself who made *The Ganges* feel like home and who made me long to return again and again and again.

One visit in particular stands out, an evening with my friend Richard, who was dazzled by Malvi's cooking. We sat like pampered felines on floor cushions at a low table in the upper dining room as a beautiful young waitress, clad in traditional Indian dress, brought dish after savory dish to our table. We sipped hot *chai*, made in Malvi's tiny kitchen and not poured from a box as so much *chai* is today. Time receded, the day's struggles eclipsed by Malvi's gentle hospitality and robust cooking.

Malvi Doshi's style is both traditional and unique, shaped as it was by the devout vegetarian orthodoxy of her Vaishnavite home and one very simple yet profound variation. Most Vaishnavs do not eat garlic or onions, but Malvi's mother believed they were good for you. These two ingredients add a depth of flavor and a richness to Malvi's cooking, and I raise a cup of spicy *chai* to her father for deferring to his wife's wisdom.

It is no surprise that Malvi, with her generosity of spirit, is as wonderful a teacher as she is a cook. She presents her recipes in clear, accessible language that allows both the novice and the accomplished cook to achieve authentic flavors again and again. And she is refreshingly articulate about the philosophical foundations that shape her style. My copy of her first book, *A Surti Touch*, has that tattered and torn look that all well-used cookbooks should have; this new one will take its place nearby and soon it, too, will be stained with the colorful spices of this wonderful cuisine.

I like to imagine that in some parallel universe, Richard and I are still at *The Ganges*, slowly savoring each luscious bite until we collapse back into the deep billowy cushions, sated and happy. Malvi is still cooking, her beloved husband Arun at her side lending a hand. In this other world, *The Ganges* lives on forever, as it does within these fine pages.

*Michele Anna Jordan*

An award-winning chef and writer, Michele Anna Jordan is the author of 14 cookbooks to date, including such critically acclaimed titles as *The New Cook's Tour of Sonoma* (Sasquatch Books, 2000), *Salt and Pepper* (Broadway Books, 1999), and *California Home Cooking* (Harvard Common Press, 1997). Jordan also writes for a number of national publications, including *Wine Enthusiast*, *Bon Appetit*, and *Cooking Light*. She is currently at work on four new books, including *Learning to Taste*, a memoir of her father, and *Love's Table: Changing the World, One Meal at a Time*. Jordan lives in Sonoma County, where she hosts two radio shows on KRCB-FM.

# ACKNOWLEDGEMENTS

Opening and running a restaurant is not an easy task. Human resources are the essential ingredients, necessary for success. Many thanks to my first employee in the kitchen, Manu Patel-Desai, who provided me with invaluable help, during those difficult first days. I would also like to thank Parvati, Jaya, Sandhya, Sonu, Yogi, Utkala, Sunila, Ameeta, Ragini, Sujata, Tanuja, Pushpa and Gulab, all of whom were wonderful to work with. To those other restaurant staff members who worked with me over the years, so numerous that I cannot list their names here, I offer my sincere gratitude.

I would like to convey thanks to the musicians, Teed Rockwell, Diana Stork, Lakhwinder Grewal, Ben Cunin, Ramadhan, Ross, Kenny Annis, Erse, Paul and others for providing live Indian music every weekend at my restaurant.

I would like to acknowledge my husband's family, his mother Mankuvar, and his sisters Chandra and Sushila for their support. My sisters Ramila, Mayuri and Anjani provided me with much needed encouragement. Family members Rajni, Arvind, Ashok, Kiran, Kamlesh, Umesh, Rohini, Madeline, Meenaxi, Bhanu, Kaumudi and Rati all contributed suggestions and ideas for this book. My other family, Josephine and Lawrence Thibeaux also merit prominent mention here. They have acted as parents and mentors to my children, and as inspirational, devoted friends to me.

If it weren't for my children Bella and Neil, this book may not have been possible. Neil helped me throughout; he even took leave from his graduate work to assist. My daughter Bella wrote several of the chapters in this book, and I am proud of her for succeeding me in the line of Indian cooks in my family, all while excelling in her medical career. I owe gratitude to Sonya

Quayle, who provided beautiful illustrations for this book, to Rodwin Pabello, who designed a fantastic book-cover, to Monica Gandhi, who assisted in checking the desserts and beverages chapters, and to my son-in-law Jong Yoon, who tasted and approved all of the *dal* recipes! Special thanks also go to Michele Anna-Jordan, for writing the foreword to this book, to Arun Kamat, for providing front and back cover images, and to Catherine Lee for her kind support.

Other friends, for whom simple mention here cannot approximate my thanks are: Russ Wesp, Tom McReynolds, Susan Zemsky, Ann and the late A. T. Ganesan, Jeanne and Bill Whitesell and John Gilmore. My friend from my graduate student days in New York, Ted Jacobs, advised me about the self-publishing route.

Most significantly, however, I would like to remember my late husband Arun who I know would be smiling now, if he could hold this book in his hands. *The Ganges* restaurant was our "baby," and this book is as much his as it is mine.

In closing, let me recognize the talented writers and reviewers in the Bay Area, who made *The Ganges* so popular. And last, but certainly not least, to the innumerable patrons of *The Ganges*, I extend my deepest regards and appreciation.

# Introduction

## I.

Centerpiece of my grandmother's garden in the Gujarati city Surat, the beautiful *Parijat* or Coral Jasmine Tree figured importantly in my exposure to the concept of coexistence with nature, a central tenet in the Hindu vegetarian philosophy. A delicate, star-shaped flower, the *Parijat* is creamy-white in color and has a bright orange center. The flower buds open in the late evening and fall to the ground at daybreak, spreading their magnificent fragrance in the humid, tropical air.

Each morning, as I prepared to go into the garden to play and to gather fruits, my grandmother would warn me not to step on the fallen flowers. A small, stooped figure in her soft, cotton sari, she would follow me outside and gently gather the *Parijat* in her cupped hands. Taking them inside, she would give some to the neighbors who were drawn to our home by the drifting perfume of the tiny buds. With the remainder, she would adorn the silver idols she worshipped in her daily *puja* rituals.

Extending profound respect for life towards all creation, Grandmother Jadav interpreted *dharma*, the Hindu code of conduct, to its fullest extent. In Hindu mythology, all plants are said to grow from the hair of Brahma, Lord of Creation. Plants nourish and sustain humans. For these reasons, according to my grandmother, they merit the respect of human beings. To her, the tiny *Parijat* flower embodied all that nature gives to humans: beauty, life, and the means to pursue one's own spirituality.

The idea of respecting nature while using what it offers for survival leads to a principle at the heart of Hinduism, one that is also present in

1

both Buddhism and Jainism. Called *ahimsa,* or love, this notion establishes the unity of all life. *Ahimsa* is the foundation of non-violent practice, and it suggests that human beings should abstain from eating meat.

Hindu teachings suggest that a diet of animal flesh distorts the human senses, drawing the believer off of the path to spiritual perfection. This perfection, or *adhyatmik jivan,* is only achieved when the devotee learns to live in harmony with nature. For the vast agrarian community in India, the cow maintains this balance between human activity and the Earth. The traditional Indian villager relies on the cow as an aid in small-scale agricultural efforts, and as a provider of milk and of dung for fuel and fertilizer.

The *Bhagavata Gita*, the Hindu religious scripture which also instructs in the practice of Hindu vegetarianism, divides food into three categories: *sattvic, rajasic,* and *tamasic.* Foods grouped in the first (*sattvic*) category (dairy products, fruits, vegetables, and grains) are deemed pure foods that allow a person to open the soul to an understanding of inner spirituality. *Rajasic* foods (meat, fish, eggs and alcohol), or those that are pungent, bitter, salty, sour or hot are believed to overly-stimulate the nervous system, thereby clouding the mind of the individual seeking enlightenment. Foods in the *tamasic* category comprise leftovers or spoiled food and are considered impure.

In India, groups such as the *Vaishnavs*—devotees of Lord Vishnu, Sustainer of the Hindu triumvirate—discourage the consumption of the *rajasic* foods, garlic and onion. Although we are *Vaishnav,* my family nevertheless believes in the healing properties of these two foods and we accept them in our diet. In fact, the majority of Hindus do not fully abide by all of the scriptural limitations discouraging the consumption of the wonderful flavorings that distinguish Indian cooking, such as garlic, onions, sharp peppers and tamarind. The message however, persists: food affects both the character and spirituality of an individual; a diet including many vegetables, fruits and grains contributes to a healthy mind and body. It is a fascinating corroboration, many centuries old, for the current emphasis on complex carbohydrates, fiber, and whole grains, advocated by nutritionists and physicians.

## II.

While the Hindu philosophy of vegetarianism—as I have cursorily described my version of it above—has been the primary spiritual inspiration behind this book, Gujarati cooking has been the major culinary influence. This is not to say, however, that the cuisines of other regions are absent. Prior to Indian independence in 1947, my father worked for the British Railways. Consequently, my family moved frequently, sometimes as often as every two-and-a-half years. In many of the remote villages where we were stationed, our house was the only one within a several mile radius, and large selections of vegetables were often unavailable. It was sometimes even difficult to obtain milk. Eventually, my father decided to keep a cow who, enjoying a whole carriage to herself, traveled with us in style! Gradually, we started traveling to more populated areas. Moving between various locales, we met many extraordinary people. Originating from Goa (near Bombay), South or North India, friends and neighbors introduced us to new combinations of spices. Living in North India, notably, exposed my sister and me to the many variations in vegetarian cooking styles in the sub-continent.

Friends and coworkers in New York also taught me much about the diversity of Gujarati cooking and Indian cuisine in general. While pursuing graduate study at New York University I served as a staff member in the Indian Consulate, and was often charged with cooking for official parties. Once, I was even required to cook for India's Finance Minister, Mr. Morarji Desai, who was a strict vegetarian. Given a list of all *sattvic* vegetables and ingredients that he could eat, I prepared lunch to his requirements. So great was his surprise when served his meal, that he immediately asked to congratulate the cook.

I was further able to explore my interest in extending the boundaries of my cooking when I married Arun and traveled to Kenya with him. Having lived in London for over ten years, Arun had become accustomed to a diet of primarily meat and starch. I strove to invent new recipes in order to spark his interest in Indian vegetarian food.

## III.

In 1975, after twelve years in Kenya, Arun and I elected to leave for America, and to seek out better opportunities for both our children and ourselves. Not long after our arrival in the States, we settled in San Francisco. Arun and I opened *The Ganges* Restaurant in 1985.

Referring to the river, of course, I chose the name *The Ganges* for its evocative quality. For me, mention of the Ganges conjures up images of devotees bathing at its *ghats* (steps leading to the river), vast, fertile plains nourished by its waters and the numerous Hindu myths that feature the great river. One such story interests me in particular:

Hindu mythology holds that the deity Lord Krishna left Mathura to establish his capital in the Gujarati city of Dwarka. One day, he and his consort Rukmini received the sage Durvasa Muni. Upon reception of the guest, Rukmini became extremely thirsty and turned to Krishna, who obligingly struck his foot on the earth, opening a fountain from which Ganges water flowed. Watching Rukmini slake herself with the water, Durvasa Muni—known for his temperament—grew extremely angry, for timeless Indian etiquette holds that a host should not eat or drink until the guest has been served. The rest of the story, where Durvasa Muni curses Rukmini, is less important to me than this pivotal moment that captures the importance of hospitality in Hindu tradition. For my husband Arun and I, running *The Ganges* involved not only the work of preparing food, but also the practice of receiving guests as though they were visiting our home.

From its first day, *The Ganges* was strictly vegetarian. Over the years, the preferences of our patrons changed my approach to cooking. In addition to diversity, I considered the nutritional value of foods to be an extremely important factor in daily menus. I reduced the amount of oil, butter and salt used in dishes, and I prepared vegetables in such a manner that their texture and nutrients were retained. I developed dairy-free menus for our vegan customers, as well as easy shortcuts for more complicated dishes.

I sold *The Ganges* in October 2000, and the restaurant closed in May 2002. For those who visited the restaurant, whom I was lucky enough to meet, I will hope that they remember the restaurant equally for both its distinctive, vegetarian menu and its focus on fresh, quality ingredients. Freshness is that first, important step to the healthful, creative cooking which celebrates India's incredibly varied culinary tradition.

# THE BASICS OF INDIAN COOKING

Dumplings—*vadi*
Spice Mixture-1—*garam masala*-1
Spice Mixture-2—*garam masala*-2
Vegetable *Masala*—*shakno masalo*
Flour *Masala* Mix—*lotwalo masalo*
Coriander and Cumin Mix—*dhania jeera*

## The Basics of Indian Cooking

Indian cooking is not as difficult as it may seem. In fact, most American and/or Asian markets carry the basic, often-used ingredients and spices. Turmeric, fenugreek seeds, coriander and cumin seeds, chili power, cloves, cinnamon, etc. can all be found in the spice and condiment area of the grocery. If you are adventurous and wish to use authentic ingredients though, a trip to an Indian food store is prerequisite to purchase such ingredients as *ajwain*, asafoetida (*hing*) and black mustard seeds.

Refer to local telephone directories for names of Indian restaurants or stores. Call these establishments and use them as sources if you have trouble locating certain ingredients. I used to answer such inquiries at *The Ganges* and sometimes even gave callers what they needed. It should be mentioned, however, that there are a number of recipes in this book that do not require special, hard to find ingredients. Exotic ingredients alone do not define well-cooked Indian meals.

## Herbs and Spices

As both skilled cook and practitioner of the ancient Indian system of medicine, the *Ayurveda*, my mother passed on to me a keen awareness of the curative, medicinal properties of spices and herbs. I remember my mother as a "walking encyclopedia" on all manner of natural cures, and I thank her for granting me awareness of how spices and herbs can make dishes appetizing, aromatic and healthful.

The art of mixing and interchanging spices is one that may seem difficult to master. But the challenge does not arise from complexity, rather, it is a question of quantity: the combinations of ingredients that can be added to a vegetarian dish are innumerable. With a rudimentary knowledge of flavorings, however, even a novice cook can experiment and almost always be assured of success.

The following is a selection of herbs and spices particular to Indian cooking. One should exercise caution when purchasing spices in any quantity. Hints for shopping, cleaning and storing spices, wherever necessary, are included in this chapter. As a general rule, if purchasing spices whole and not ground, I always recommend picking over them in order to ensure cleanliness. Please note that if I have included information below about the ayurvedic properties of spices, it is, in this context, for interest/informational purposes only.

**A Note on Toasting Spices:**

Toasting spices enhances their flavor and prevents them from spoiling; it is best carried out by placing ingredients in a wok or a frying pan over very low heat, stirring well every few minutes until the ingredient changes color and exudes an aroma. Spices can also be toasted in an oven on very low heat, stirring well every few minutes, or in a microwave. Let cool completely before grinding or storing.

**Ajwain (*ajwain*):** Called Bishop's Weed in English, this is an important ingredient in recipes made with fresh beans such as green beans or lima beans; if not available locally, a visit to an Indian store may be necessary. When purchasing, buy in small quantities, and look for clean stock that is free of tiny rocks. Especially for small children, this is one of the best ayurvedic remedies for the common cold.

If *ajwain* is unavailable, Italian Oregano may be used as a substitute.

**Anise (*chhoti saunf*):** Stronger and smaller than its sister herb, fennel (*saunf*), anise is toasted and eaten as a mouth-freshener. It is considered good for eye diseases, and the seeds are regarded as being a deterrent of urges related to both the appetite and alcoholic beverages.

In some Gujarati spice mixtures, star anise (*badiyan*)—which has an even stronger aroma—is used. Neither anise nor its stronger varieties are universal favorites. Use fennel if you prefer a milder flavoring.

If purchasing anise in any quantity from bins in an Indian store, watch for loose straws attached to the seeds, which will need to be separated and discarded. As the recipes in this book call for anise in only small amounts, it is best to purchase only a few ounces at a time.

**Asafoetida (*hing*):** Asafoetida is a dried gum resin that has a lingering odor—avoid touching it with your bare hands. In Persian *asa* means gum and *foetid,* in Latin, means odiferous. Once cooked, however, asafoetida exudes a pleasant aroma.

Available in powder and rock forms, asafoetida is usually used in small quantities. As a powder, it is traditionally stored in tin containers. In its rock form, it is sold in larger quantities and is most often used as a preservative.

Four varieties of asafoetida are available. The first type, *Khada hing*, most always found in rock form, may be used for cooking, but is tedious to grind in small quantities on a daily basis. When grinding in large quantities, remember that the unpleasant odor permeates. *Khada hing* is bright yellow when fresh and turns dark brown as it ages.

The second, most pungent form is *Rasayan hin*g, which I use in pickles. A third variety, yellow *hing* is the least strong of the four varieties—it's mild flavor is partially due to the fact that it is usually sold mixed with wheat and rice flours. Most Indian cooks prefer to use this form, though I prefer a fourth type, brown *hing*, which is just slightly stronger than the yellow variety.

In my recipes I shall refer to asafoetida by its Indian name, *hing*.

**Basil (*tulsi* or *tulasi*):** In Hindi, basil is referred to by *tulasi*, meaning matchless, or by *Vrinda* (less common), meaning cluster. The most widely used varieties are *Ram tulsi*, characterized by lighter green leaves and *Krishna tulsi*, identified by its dark green leaves with purple tinges. Considered an effective remedy for numerous ailments including cold and flu, *tulsi* is often added to Indian tea.

The *Krishna tulsi* plant has the unique property of curbing thirst. In former times, it was commonly grown outside the temples, which then also served as guesthouses. By placing a few leaves under the tongue, the thirsty traveler could temporarily satisfy his thirst for water. In time, the plant acquired religious significance and became essential in the worship of Hindu Gods and Goddesses, especially *Vishnu*. According to the *Padma Purana*, a Hindu scripture, even soil where this plant is grown is considered holy. Devout Hindus continue to believe that the *tulsi* plant brings happiness to families.

**Bay Leaves (Indian *tejpatta*):** Indian bay leaves are slightly stronger than the supermarket variety, though the latter will serve the purpose. When purchasing them loose and not pre-packaged, be sure that the leaves are not broken into too many pieces.

Bay leaves are used in rice or vegetable dishes and are ground into some *masalas*, or spice mixtures.

**Black Pepper:** see **Pepper**

**Black Salt:** see **Salt**

**Brown Sugar:** see **Jaggery**

**Camphor (*kapoor* or *karpoor*):** Two varieties are available in India. One variety, called "Baras" in India, is edible, has strong flavor and is used in very small quantities in Indian sweets. (I haven't used it in any recipe in this book.) The other, inedible variety is used for religious ceremonies. It is burnt during *pooja* rituals in order to purify the air.

**Caraway Seeds (*gunyan*):** Do not confuse this ingredient with cumin or *ajwain*. Kashmiri cooks often use these seeds in their bread or curries, and Gujaratis mainly use them in savory snacks.

**Cardamom (*elchi* or *elaichi*, *elcha*):** The three varieties are: green, black and white. Indians use the more flavorful green cardamom in most of their sweets. Black or large cardamoms (*elcha*) are used in certain spice mixtures, curries or pilafs. Although sometimes used, the white variety tends to be the least preferred. Be cautious when purchasing pre-packaged cardamom seeds; in my experience they are not always clean. When small quantities are called for, I recommend purchasing green cardamom in pods. A quick spin in the coffee grinder will soften the pods for peeling. Remove the skin and use the seeds as required. Save the peels for use in preparing Indian tea.

Large black cardamoms are known as *badi elaichi* or *elcha*. These cardamoms are difficult to peel, and it is best to slightly heat them in an oven or a microwave before peeling. Be warned to only heat the cardamom—do not burn it. Black cardamoms can be added whole (and unpeeled) to pilafs and curries.

**Chilies, Green (*hari mirch*):** The recipes in this book mainly call for serrano or jalapeño varieties of chili. Generally, the smaller and the thinner the chili, the hotter it is. Be aware that chilies tend to be spicier at the stem end, and that more than the flesh or skin, chili seeds contribute to the spiciness of the dish into which they are added.

When less expensive, I recommend buying chilies in large quantities and grinding them in a food processor with added salt. For 1 cup trimmed chilies, add 1 teaspoon salt (no additional water is needed). The ground chilies can be frozen, will retain their color, and can be scooped with a spoon. When using this ground chili mixture, compensate for added salt by cutting down on quantities called for in a recipe.

**Red Chili Peppers (dried)—Whole (*sabut lal mirch*):** I have used these in some recipes, though you may substitute other varieties—fresh or dried—if preferred. Store the dried, red variety in a tightly covered jar.

**Chili Powder (*lal mirch*):** A great variety of chili powder is available in the United States. On some packages, the spiciness of the chili is even given a rating. Select a variety of chili according the level of spiciness that you wish to attain. Available in some Indian stores in America, the "Reshampatti" brand of powder remains especially popular in Gujarat and Maharashtra for making pickles. A rock of *hing* is an effective preservative for chili powders bought in large quantities.

**Cilantro or Chinese Parsley (*hara dhania*):** Available in most supermarkets and produce stores, cilantro is a common ingredient in Indian cuisine. The herb lends a fresh flavorful taste to recipes and it is also an excellent garnish for vegetables, *dals*, *raitas* and pilafs. When using, do not discard the stems, as they can be used in recipes or for making chutneys. If cilantro is not available in your area, you may grow your own using coriander seeds. I recommend washing cilantro at least twice before use, as the leaves and stems can sometimes bear traces of sand or mud. If bought in large quantities, cilantro can be cut, washed and frozen for future use. Though frozen cilantro darkens in color, it returns to a more natural shade of green when warmed.

**Cinnamon (*dalchini* or *taj*):** Available in all supermarkets and grocery stores, cinnamon is an important ingredient in Indian cooking. Indian cinnamon tends to be both thinner and easier to grind than the supermarket variety. A main ingredient in *garam masala*, cinnamon is also used in rice, vegetable and *dal* recipes, as well as in non-vegetarian dishes. While ground cinnamon is widely available, I recommend toasting and grinding cinnamon yourself when making spice combinations such as *garam masala*. Ayurveda holds that cinnamon combats bacteria.

**Citric Acid (*nimbuka sat* or *limbuna phool*):** Sold in Indian stores, citric acid is a very good souring agent for recipes that require a dry texture. I have used citric acid in a few recipes in this book in order to cut the liquid content of the recipe. When purchasing from Indian stores, I recommend asking for this by either of its Indian names.

**Cloves (*laung* or *lavang*):** Cloves are mostly used in *garam masala*, pilafs and *dals*. Always look for the larger variety and pick over before use. My mother used to tell us to keep a few cloves on our person while traveling or when visiting a sick person, as the spice is believed to ward off bacteria. Along with black pepper, cloves may be used as a preservative for certain ingredients such as nuts or white poppy seeds (which quickly go stale).

**Coconut (*nariyel*):** Coconut is called *Narikela* or *Suphala* in Sanskrit. (*Narikela* derives from the root word *Narik*, meaning water.) Whether green and fresh or dry on the outside, coconut has high water content. Coconut water is clean and fit to cook with if clear, rather than cloudy. In Gujarat, as in much of India, no Hindu ceremony is completed without the coconut, which is a symbol of fertility. In some parts of India, coconuts are thrown into the sea at the close of the monsoon in order to augur good luck.

Dried whole coconut is readily available in America. When purchasing a coconut, shake it well to make sure there is water inside. Breaking one open can be a difficult task. I recommend soaking the coconut in water for several hours or equally, placing one in an oven at 300 °F for 30 minutes before attempting to break open.

The inside meat can be separated with a knife, the brown skin can be peeled and the meat can be ground to extract the juice. For those not inclined to undertake such a time consuming task, I suggest purchasing canned coconut milk. Both coarsely grated coconut and powdered coconut are available, though I prefer coconut powder, which is most commonly found at Indian grocers. To make dried coconut powder or coarsely grated coconut look fresh, combine a couple of tablespoons with an equal amount of either water or milk and set aside for several minutes. Mix well before use. Many Indians like to garnish their preparations with freshly grated coconut and cilantro.

**Coriander Seeds** (*dhania*): When purchasing either small or large coriander seeds check carefully in order to ensure that what you purchase is clean. Loose straws and tiny rocks can be removed by picking over the seeds, but avoid buying seeds with holes in them. Toast coriander lightly before storing.

To prepare cracked coriander, called for in a few recipes in this book, begin by toasting the seeds lightly in a frying pan over a stove, or on a tray in an oven until they exude a nice aroma and are slightly brown. Stir while toasting to prevent burning. When the seeds have cooled, give them a few spins in a coffee grinder or a food processor fitted with a metal blade. Cracked or ground coriander may be stored for later use.

Mixed ground coriander and cumin powder is often called for in Indian cooking. Make your own following the recipe (p. 26), or buy it ready-made in an Indian store. When storing coriander and/or cumin, place a *hing* rock, as a preservative, into the same container. You may toast and grind both coriander and cumin seeds separately and use as required. Alternatively, prepackaged coriander and cumin powders are available and may be used separately, as I have done in this book.

**Cumin Seeds** (*jeera* or *safed jeera*): Whole, ground or toasted, cumin seeds are a common ingredient in Indian cooking. Whole or ground varieties may be found in Indian stores. If buying whole seeds, purchase the variety with full, plump-looking seeds. Pick over before use, removing loose straws, tiny rocks or any other foreign objects, and store in a tightly covered jar. As with ground coriander, use a *hing* rock as a preservative when storing large quantities of ground cumin (no *hing* rock is required when storing whole cumin seeds).

**Black Cumin Seeds** (*kala jeera* or *shah jeera*): This expensive, less common variety of cumin is particular to Kashmiri cooking, though some Gujarati cooks have begun to use it as well. Mellow in flavor, black cumin exudes a sweeter aroma than the more common variety described above.

*Curry* Leaves (*limdo* or *limdana paan*): Fresh *curry* leaves are available in Indian stores. Indians commonly purchase the leaves in large quantities and store them in the refrigerator. A *Limdo* tree grew in my grandmother's yard, and I fondly recall gathering the sweet smelling leaves in my cupped hands.

The name "*curry*" leaves can be rather misleading. Although the leaves are indeed flavorful, somewhat akin to Bay leaves, I would like to stress that they are in no way prerequisite to any curry. A curry is defined by the mixture of multiple spices that enhance the dish as a whole. If added in the correct proportions, even the simplest of ingredients such as coriander-cumin powder and turmeric can be combined to create delicious main dishes. The variety of spices that may be added into curries is only limited by the imagination of the cook.

*Dals*—Beans, Peas and Lentils: See *Dals* Chapter, page (334).

Dates (*khajur*): Dates available in India tend to be drier than the preferable, American variety. Always purchase pitted dates. Date-chutney is extremely popular in India, as is *Khajur Pilla* (p. 476), a dessert that includes among its ingredients, dates, pistachio nuts, almonds and cardamom.

Dumplings (*vadi* or *badi*) Several varieties of *vadi* are made in India. They may be sun-dried, boiled in water, steamed or added directly into a recipe. I discuss sun-dried *vadi* here—for other varieties refer to the section on vegetables.

*Vadi* can be prepared from a variety of grains including rice. Rice *vadi* can be fried and eaten as snack. Ones made from split chickpeas (*chana dal*), split Indian black beans (*urid dal*), split mung beans (mung *dal*) or black-eyed peas are more popular and are used in a variety of recipes. Pre-prepared, sun-dried *vadi* are available in some Indian stores, in large and small sizes. In my experience, however, the varieties imported from India tend not to be fresh and I prefer to make my own.

Spices used in sun-dried *vadi* vary, though the most commonly used spices are salt, turmeric and *hing*. Ground or chopped fresh green garlic, chopped, fresh fenugreek leaves, cilantro, grated green mangoes or mango powder, number among the many ingredients that may be added into *vadi* recipes. Coarsely ground cumin seeds, chilies and black pepper may also be added, to taste. While homemade *vadi* can be stored for longer periods of time, the store-bought variety should be used immediately.

## Dumplings—*vadi*

Though the recipe given here is made with mung *dal*, you may equally use common black-eyed peas. In order that the *vadi* dry faster, use little or no water when grinding the soaked grain.

*Vadi* can be used to add exotic flavors and unusual textures to vegetable dishes. There is no limit to the number of combinations of spices that may be added into *vadi* recipes.

| | |
|---|---|
| 2 cups | split mung beans (mung *dal*), soaked overnight |
| 4 | serrano chilies, chopped with seeds |
| 2 teaspoons | toasted, coarsely ground cumin seeds |
| 1 ¼ teaspoons | salt, or to taste |
| ½ teaspoon | *hing* (asafoetida) |

Pick over, wash (see note, p. 336) and soak *dal* overnight. Drain and grind *dal* and chilies in a food processor fitted with a metal blade. When smooth, remove to a bowl and add the remaining ingredients. Using your hands mix well.

Line a large tray with foil. With your fingers, drop about 1 heaping teaspoon mixture for each *vadi* onto the tray. Continue, leaving a little space in between each *vadi*. Place the tray in direct sunlight, or leave in a warm area such as the kitchen or near a heater. Turn the *vadi* after about 2 days and continue to dry thoroughly for another day or so. Store in a jar with a tightly covered lid.

**Fennel Seeds** (*variali* or *badi saunf*): While fennel is mainly used as a mouth freshener, it can also replace anise or star-anise in different recipes where milder flavors are desired.

**Figs** (*anjeer*): see section on **Fruits** (p. 33)

**Fenugreek Leaves and Seeds** (*methini bhaji* or *methi*): Fenugreek leaves or greens can be grown from seeds: the herb grows as easily as cilantro and can be used in pilaf, stuffed vegetables recipes or in Indian breads. While only fenugreek leaves are normally used in preparations, the stems can also be added if they are soft and not stiff. Both fresh and dry leaves are available in most Indian grocers. Fresh leaves can also be obtained in some produce markets.

Fenugreek seeds are an important ingredient in Indian pickles. Prior to use, they are toasted lightly and cracked in a coffee grinder. Note that pre-packaged cracked seeds that are available in Indian stores are rarely pre-toasted, and toasting the seeds prior to use releases their distinct flavor. Cracked seeds are called *methi na kuria*. My mother advocated ingesting sprouted *methi* seeds for arthritis, diabetes or for general health. Fenugreek seeds lose their bitter taste when they are sprouted—a relatively simple process.

**Garlic** (*lasun* or *lasan*): Garlic was an essential ingredient in my parents' cooking. When buying garlic, look for pods with large cloves, as they take less time to peel. To make cloves easier to peel, some cooks prefer to rub the cloves with oil and to broil them in an oven for a short while. At *The Ganges*, we would immerse the cloves in hot water for a few minutes in order to make them easier to peel. Peeled garlic may be stored in an airtight container and refrigerated for a couple of weeks. Ground garlic will keep for a few weeks.

**Green Garlic** (*hara lasun* **or** *lilu lasan*): While easily purchased in produce stores, I find that I can grow much stronger green garlic at home.
When home-growing green garlic, note that the blades that sprout can be
clipped without replanting. If the clove itself is used, of course, the garlic
must be replanted.

*Garam Masala* **and Other Spice Mixtures:** In Indian, *garam* means hot
and *masala* means spices. *Garam masalas* tend to be warm and strong in
flavor, but not spicy-hot. Indians use a great variety of spice mixtures, and
I have tried to include the most popular combinations in this book. The
proportions of each ingredient in a recipe may be changed to suit individual tastes. When time is limited, however, store-bought, pre-prepared
*garam masala* will suffice.

## Spice Mixture-1—*garam masala-1*

This is the basic recipe that I used most of the time at *The Ganges*. I prepare this in large quantities. Note that spices like coriander and cumin are added separately into recipes.

| | |
|---|---|
| 9 three–inch sticks | cinnamon |
| 3 tablespoons | black pepper |
| 3 tablespoons | cloves |
| 2 teaspoons | cardamom seeds |

Toast the above spices in an oven at 300 °F, or on low heat, in a shallow pan on top of stove, stirring frequently until they change color. Let cool and grind into fine powder using a coffee grinder or a grinding mill. Store in a tightly covered jar. Use as desired. 4 or 5 bay leaves can be added to the above mixture as a variation.

## Spice Mixture-2—*garam masala-2*

At times, I like to combine this *masala* with the previous version of the recipe, prior to adding into a dish. Note that ironwood, a spice reminiscent of the clove, is an optional ingredient in this recipe; it is extremely hard to find it in the United States.

| | |
|---|---|
| 4 cups | coriander seeds |
| 1 cup | cumin seeds |
| 10 three–inch sticks | cinnamon |
| ½ cup | cloves |
| ½ cup | black pepper |
| ½ cup | ironwood, (*dagadful*) (optional) |
| ½ cup | black cumin seeds |
| ¼ cup | star anise (*badian*) |
| ¼ cup | large cardamoms, peeled (p. 11) |
| 1 tablespoon | ground mace |

Toast coriander and the next 8 ingredients including cardamom seeds in an oven at 300 °F, or on low heat, in a shallow pan on top of stove, stirring frequently until they change color. Spices can also be heated in a microwave. Let cool and, using a coffee grinder or a mill, grind into fine powder. Add mace and mix well. Store in a tightly covered jar. Use as desired.

## Vegetable *Masala*—*shakno masalo*

This spice combination can be made ahead of time and may be used in stuffing-mixes for vegetables. You may add it into any vegetable recipe for added flavor and texture.

| | |
|---|---|
| 2 cups | unsweetened, grated coconut |
| 2 teaspoons | oil |
| ½ teaspoon | *hing* (asafoetida) |
| ¼ cup | dried, whole red chili peppers |
| 4 three–inch sticks | cinnamon, broken |
| 1 tablespoon | cloves |
| 1 tablespoon | black pepper |
| 12 | large cardamoms, peeled (p. 11) |
| 3 tablespoons | coriander seeds |
| 2 tablespoons | cumin seeds |
| 1 tablespoon | fennel seeds |
| 1 tablespoon | pomegranate seeds (optional) |
| 2 tablespoons | white poppy seeds (optional) |
| ¼ cup | sesame seeds |
| ½ cup | toasted peanuts, peeled (p. 37) |

In a frying pan, over low heat, toast coconut, stirring well, until slightly golden. Remove to the bowl of a food processor fitted with a metal blade. In the same frying pan, heat oil and add *hing*. When the *hing* turns brown, add peppers and fry on low heat until peppers are dark red in color. Remove to a bowl and set aside. Again, in the same frying pan, gently toast cinnamon and the next 7 ingredients, including pomegranate seeds, stirring well, until they change color, about 15 minutes. Remove with peppers and allow to cool.

In the same frying pan, gently toast poppy and sesame seeds. They will change color shortly. Remove onto a cutting board.

Using a coffee grinder, grind the pepper mixture until fine and add to the coconut, in the bowl of the food processor. In the same coffee grinder, grind peanuts and add to coconut mixture. Briefly spin the food processor to thoroughly combine ingredients, and to grind any remaining large particles in the mixture. Remove to a large bowl. Using a rolling pin, grind or crush the poppy and sesame seeds on the cutting board. Add to ground spice mixture. Mix well and store in a tightly covered jar.

## Flour *Masala* Mix—*lotwalo masalo*

This is a favorite spice mixture of mine that I like to use for dry vegetables. If you are preparing a vegetable dish that contains little stock, try adding a small amount of this mixture to that dish as it cooks.

| | |
|---|---|
| 2 cups | split Indian black beans (*urid dal*) |
| ½ cup | split chickpeas (*chana dal*) |
| ¼ cup | dried, whole red chili peppers |
| 10 three–inch sticks | cinnamon, broken |
| 2 tablespoons | cloves |
| 2 tablespoons | black pepper |
| 10 | large cardamoms, peeled (p. 11) |

Toast all the ingredients in an oven on low heat until they change color, about 25 minutes. Let cool and finely grind the mixture in a coffee grinder. Store in a covered jar.

## Coriander and Cumin Mix—*dhania jeera*

This mixture is commonly used in Indian cooking. Though many Indian stores sell it ready made, I have included the recipe below for those who prefer to make it themselves. You may also use *dhania* and *jeera* powders separately in your cooking.

| | |
|---|---|
| 1 pound | coriander seeds |
| ¼ pound | cumin seeds |

Pick over both the seeds, removing foreign objects, and toast together in a large frying pan or a saucepan on low heat, stirring frequently until they change color and emit a nice aroma. Alternatively, they can be toasted in an oven at 250 °F, stirring every few minutes, until they change color. Let cool, and finely grind in a mill or a coffee grinder. Store in a tightly covered jar. A *hing* rock may be added to the powder as a preservative.

**Ginger—Fresh (*adrak* or *aadu*) and Powdered (*sonth*):** Ginger is an ingredient that is often used in Indian cooking. I have used both the fresh and dry varieties in this book. As dry ginger is extremely difficult to grind, I recommend buying ground powder.

Rounded, smooth-skinned, smaller pieces of fresh ginger are the preferable variety as they are less fibrous than longer fingers of ginger. The fresh root is always peeled, and then grated, ground or chopped before use in vegetables or *dals*. To store fresh, ground ginger in large quantities, add a little salt (2 teaspoons of salt for each pound of ginger) while grinding, and freeze for future use. If using frozen ginger in a recipe, correspondingly reduce the amount of salt called for. For other varieties of fresh roots see turmeric.

**Jaggery (*gor* or *good*):** Jaggery is known as "Indian brown sugar." A pure form of sugar, it may be consumed by vegetarians who refrain from processed foods. The softer the jaggery, the better is the quality. Unfortunately, varieties available here are not as consistently good as those available in India. Jaggery is an important and essential ingredient in many Indian sweets. When it is called for in vegetables or other non-dessert recipes, grocery store varieties of brown sugar can serve as an adequate substitute. Vegetarians should maintain a level of caution: methods utilized to process brown sugar—which sometimes call for animal products—are not always clearly indicated on packaging.

**Lemon Grass (*leeli chai*):** Gujaratis use lemon grass mainly in tea. It is not commonly used in Indian dishes. *Leeli chai* is easily grown in moderate climates and may even be cultivated indoors. For those who wish to try to grow it themselves: be aware that once the blades of the stalk are cut, the lemon grass will have to be replanted. The herb Citronella is to be distinguished from lemon grass, the two are quite different.

**Mace (*javitri* or *javantri*):** Mace is the red membrane that grows around the nutmeg seed. More delicately flavored than nutmeg, ground mace is easily obtained in almost any supermarket or Indian store.

**Mango Powder (*amchoor*):** Made from the unripe, tart mango, *amchoor* is used as a souring agent in some Indian recipes. It is not as popular in Gujarat as it is in North India. *Amchoor* does not spoil, and can be purchased in any Indian store.

**Mint (*fudino* or *pudino*):** Mint is used throughout India in a variety of recipes including chutneys, appetizers and even Indian tea. It is available in most stores and is also very easy to grow. When purchased in large quantities, grind the mint when fresh, and freeze for later use.

**Mustard Seeds—Black or Reddish-Brown (*rai* whole and cracked):** Though I prefer the reddish-brown to the black variety, I have used black mustard in this book, since the other may not be available everywhere. Either variety may be used.

Mustard seeds exude a wonderful, nutty flavor when cooked in a little bit of oil. Called *rai na kuria*, cracked mustard seeds are available in some Indian stores and are used mainly in pickles. Mustard seeds can be ground using a rolling pin. Wet the mustard seeds lightly before grinding so they do not scatter under the rolling pin.

*An Indian Mortar and Pestle—the perfect tool for grinding or crushing dry spices in small quantities.*

**Nutmeg** (*jayful* or *jaiphal*): If purchasing nutmeg in whole, nut-form, crack open and discard the shell, and then grind or grate the nut prior to adding to the recipe. Nutmeg is used in some *garam masalas* and in a few desserts.

**Pepper—Black, White and Fresh Green:** (*kala mari, safed mari* and *leela mari*): Indians use all varieties of pepper. One of the ingredients in *garam* *masala*, black peppercorns are used in cut, cracked, ground or whole forms. Ground white peppercorns are used when a brightly colored dish is preferred. Fresh green peppercorns are used for pickling. Cut black peppers are available in some stores, and should be used when either these or coarsely ground black peppers are called for. When cut black pepper is required, you may also coarsely grind whole black peppercorns in a coffee grinder.

**Pomegranate Seeds (*anardana* or *darukhatta*):** The dried kernels of wild pomegranate fruit, these are used as a souring agent, like tamarind, lemon or *amchoor*. Unlike normal pomegranate, the seeds and not the fruit of the wild pomegranate are edible.

**Poppy Seeds (*khus khus*):** These creamy white seeds are much smaller than the blue gray variety used to decorate cakes and breads in this country. Prior to use, the seeds are lightly toasted and then ground with a rolling pin. Unless preparing *garam masala*—in which case the seeds should be kept dry—a small amount of water is normally sprinkled onto the seeds prior to grinding, in order to keep them together. The seeds stale easily, and it is best to store them in a cold corner or in the refrigerator, mixed with few black peppercorns as a preservative.

**Toasted Split Chickpeas (*dalia*):** Most Indian stores carry this delicious, nutty flavored, toasted *dal*. Buy in small quantities if available, as the *dalia* become stale after a few months.

**Saffron (*kesar*):** Saffron is the stigma collected from crocus flowers. This is the most expensive ingredient in Indian cooking. Spanish saffron is reputed to be the best, although Daniel Roulland, a Parisian friend of mine who is a fabulous chef, swears by the Moroccan variety. It is best to grind saffron in desired quantities. If purchased in large quantities, I recommend storing it in the freezer. If the saffron is damp or soft, heat it lightly in a dry frying pan or in a microwave before crushing.

**Salt (*namak*)—unrefined, Kosher, Sea Salt (*sindhav*), Black Salt (*kala namak*):** Three varieties of salts are common in India; the most common is regular salt, which is available unrefined in India, and which I have found to be stronger than what I get in the United States.

The second variety is black salt, which smells unpleasant, but loses its odor when cooked. It is often used in *chat masala*. Black salt is also used in some recipes for distinct taste. My mother would heat this variety of salt in rock form over an open flame and then place the hot rock in rose water. She would then administer small doses of this water in order to treat stomach ailments.

The third variety is *sindhav*, a sea salt that is used on religious days.

Though I have used table salt in all my recipes, you may use any other variety, as desired.

**Sesame Seeds (*til* or *tal*):** Most commonly, two varieties are available in the stores. One is unpolished and slightly golden in color and the other is polished and white. Either may be used, according to preference. When purchasing, look closely to ensure that there are no lumps in the seeds. The rolling pin is an ideal tool for grinding these seeds. Besides the two varieties used in cooking, a third variety, *kala tal*, or black sesame seeds, is available in some stores. This variety is mostly used in *puja* rituals.

**Silver or Gold Leaves (*varak* or *vark*):** These delicate, micro-thin leaves are used as decoration on desserts. They are edible and considered good for the health, if pure. The best and most reliable place to buy these is any Jain temple in India, however, some Indian grocery stores in the United States also carry them.

**Sugar (*sakkar* or *khand*):** The unrefined sugar that is widely used in India tends to be sweeter than that is available in the United States. Unrefined sugar is considered pure and therefore suitable for strict vegetarians. I have used table sugar in this book since natural sugar products are not available in all areas. Feel free to substitute, though proportions may need to be altered, depending on the sweetness of the substitute that is used.

**Tamarind (*aamli* or *imli*):** Slabs and Concentrate: The name originates from the Persian word Tamar-i-Hind meaning Indian date. The Sanskrit name for this is *Amlika* which means sour. Common folklore has it that the Tamarind tree is the home of spirits, thus travelers are advised not to sleep under it. One grew in our front yard, when my father was stationed at Bulsar in Gujarat, and we were strictly forbidden to approach it after dark. To obtain fruit, we had but to throw a tiny stone at any one of the monkeys inhabiting the tree. In retaliation, the monkeys would throw back tamarind fruit, which are delicious when fresh.

The fruit is sour when fresh or dried. Only dried tamarind is used in Indian cooking. It is available in this country in either slabs or concentrate. The color of fresh dried tamarind is brownish red; however what is available in this country is often black (meaning the stock is old). Unfortunately, I have not yet found a way of obtaining fresh stock here. Watch for sand and tiny rocks when using either slab or concentrate forms. When using a tamarind slab, soak the needed portion in hot water in a bowl for about 30 minutes, squeeze the tamarind using your fingers, and discard the fibers and seeds. Pour off the tamarind water into another bowl and discard the sand and tiny rocks that settle to the bottom.

Most Indians prefer using tamarind slabs, as the slabs give the recipe texture and thickness.

***Tulsi* Seeds or Sweet Basil Seeds (*tukmaria*):** Available at Indian grocers, these seeds are normally soaked in water prior to use. Ayurveda holds them as "cooling," and as being beneficial for digestion. I have used them in my *falooda* recipe (p. 499).

**Turmeric (*haldi* or *haldar*):** Powdered turmeric or "poor man's saffron" can impart the color of saffron but not the flavor to recipes in which it is added. Throughout Asia, turmeric has long been used as a spice, medicine and as a ceremonial coloring.

Turmeric is also considered good for skin. Mixed with a small amount of oil, it is applied to the face and arms of a bride-to-be and then washed off, as it lends a golden glow to the skin. Devout Hindus believe in applying a dab of turmeric to the forehead as a symbolic gesture towards the Goddess Lakshmi, (the Goddess of Wealth) who is the God Vishnu's consort.

**Turmeric—Fresh (*leeli haldar*):** Fresh turmeric roots are available in most Indian stores, and is often served as a condiment prepared in the following fashion: Peel these roots and cut into thin slices that resemble matchsticks. Combine with mango turmeric (below), peeled and sliced the same way, add a little salt and lemon juice to taste.

**Turmeric—Mango (*amba haldar*):** These off-white roots are to be distinguished from turmeric. Both fresh and mango turmeric are considered good for the blood.

# Fruits

Commonly used fruits in Indian cooking include bananas, apples, guava, chickoo, lemons, limes, mangos, pineapples, ber (a type of berry), carambolas (star fruits) and custard apples. Below, I have listed fruits that are commonly used in Indian cooking.

**Apple** (*safarjan*): Although the apple is perhaps considered the most popular table fruit in the world, its commercial cultivation in India is extremely limited. Choose your favorite variety when preparing recipes that call for apples.

**Apricot** (*jardalu*): In Indian cuisine, fresh apricots are often cooked, stuffed with various spice mixtures and served as a vegetable dish. Dried apricots may be used in chutneys, or alternatively, they may be added to different vegetable and pilaf recipes.

**Banana** (*kela*): Hindu mythology reveres the banana plant as an incarnation of the Goddess Parvati (who bore two sons even though she had no mate). Similarly, the plant fertilizes itself without cross-pollination. Although referred to as growing on a tree, the banana actually grows on what is more like an oversized plant. All parts of the banana plant are used in India. For example, the leaves are folded into eating plates and are also used in religious and in marital ceremonies. The water obtained from banana bark is considered pure, free of any bacteria, and when available, it is used to make dough for *papadum*. The wild banana tree is used to border crop fields as it repels termites, and the seeds of the wild fruit are given to children once a year to ward off chickenpox and measles.

Two varieties of bananas are available in the market, a large, green banana for cooking, and the other—yellow bananas—for eating as a fruit. For recipes in the book, I have used yellow bananas.

**Ber or Berries—Indian Plum or Jujube tree (*bor*):** *Badari* or *Badara* in Sanskrit, ber are known as Oriental figs or Oriental dates in English. According to Hindu legend, a grove of *badari* trees at the foot of the Himalayas was chosen as the site of the hermitage of the two great saints, *Nara* and *Narayana*, the latter being an incarnation of *Vishnu*. The site is now called *Badrinath* and is a sacred pilgrimage center for Hindus.

Several varieties of the fruit are available, ranging from the small red berries called *chania bor* to the cultivated, longer yellow-green variety called *bor*, which may be found locally in some farmer's markets.

In some regions of India, it is considered unlucky to plant a ber tree near the house, as it is believed to incite domestic quarrel.

**Carambola or Star Fruit (*kamrakh*):** Delicious chutney may be made from this fruit (p. 85), which turns from greenish yellow to yellow as it ripens. This fruit may also be used in cooking as a souring agent.

**Cherry (Cherry):** Of the many cherries available in markets, I have used the bing variety in a spicy-sweet pickle recipe (p. 123).

**Chickoo or Sapola (*chickoo*):** Though chickoo resembles a kiwi, it has a distinct taste. I fondly remember picking chickoo off of the fruit tree that grew in my grandparents' backyard. I would let the fruit ripen on the tree, and at one point, even constructed a scarecrow in order to frighten the voracious raccoons. Chickoo *Halwa* is a popular dessert in Gujarat.

**Fig (*anjeer*):** Most figs are allowed to fully ripen and at least partially dry on the tree. Among the varieties of figs available in the States, Black Figs are the more common. Figs are regarded as being good for stomach problems. I prefer to use either Greek or Indian figs.

**Lemon (*limbu*):** Thin-skinned, yellow varieties of lemons are preferred when making lemon pickle (p. 120). Lemon chutney (p. 84) was a favorite of customers at *The Ganges*.

**Mango (*aam*):** Called *Amra* in Sanskrit, the mango has been cultivated in India for over 4000 years. Ripe mangoes are commonly used for their juice or served sliced. Green, unripe or slightly ripe mangoes are used in chutneys and pickles.

Hindu mythology holds the Mango tree as a wish-granting tree and as a symbol of humility, love and devotion. As my mother often advised me, humans should measure their success with modesty just as the mango tree stoops with the weight of its succulent fruit.

**Papaya (*paw paw* or *papayee*):** This tropical plant is native to Mexico and arrived India in the 16th century. Today, the papaya is considered beneficial for stomach ulcers, diphtheria and even cancer. The raw fruit is used to make vegetables, relishes and chutney and is also considered an excellent tenderizer. Papain made from raw papaya is a very useful medicinal product.

**Pineapple (*ananas*):** Native to Brazil, the pineapple did not reach India until the mid-sixteenth century. I have used this fruit in relishes or chutneys.

# Nuts

Nuts are considered a nutritious part of the Indian diet, if consumed in small quantities. In fact, Mahatma Gandhi advocated a diet consisting primarily of nuts and fruits. Almonds, cashews and pistachios are the most commonly used nuts in Indian cooking: almonds and cashews in both main dishes and desserts, and pistachios mostly in desserts. Chironjia and walnuts are also used in some desserts.

**Almonds—Dried and Fresh (*badam*):**
  **Dry Almonds:** When buying almonds look for clean, preferably new stock. If buying in quantity, toast almonds lightly or add some cloves before storing. If buying in small quantities for immediate use in recipes, look for chipped or broken almonds, which will be less expensive.

  I find it more economical to blanch or sliver almonds myself. To sliver almonds, place almonds in water and bring it to a full boil. After 10 seconds remove from heat. When cool, peel the almonds and using a sharp knife, cut each into thin slices. Unused slivered almonds may be refrigerated for a few days at most.
  **Fresh Almonds:** Fresh almonds resemble green, tiny mangoes. They are mainly used in pickles.

**Cashews (*kaju*):** In markets where cashews are sold in large batches out of containers, it may be worthwhile to inquire if cheaper, broken nuts are available. Either is suitable for grinding. Whole nuts appear more elegant when used as a garnish, although chipped or broken ones serve the purpose.

**Chironjia (*charoli*):** These small, round nuts are commonly used in Indian desserts. These nuts stale easily, they are difficult to import and are inconsistently available in Indian stores. When purchased, I recommend that they be stored in the refrigerator with a few cloves added to the batch in order to maintain freshness.

**Peanuts** (*moogphali* or *bhoyphali*): Available shelled or unshelled, peanuts are used in some recipes in this book. After purchasing raw unshelled peanuts, many Indians prefer to boil them in lightly salted water before eating. Shelled peanuts can be toasted either in an oven or in a frying pan over the stove, on low heat (heating lightly until the nuts turn slightly brown). Such methods of preparing peanuts are relatively simple and are more healthful than frying.

Toasted peanuts stale when kept for long periods and I don't recommend toasting in bulk. Toasted or raw peanuts can be coarsely ground in a coffee grinder or a food processor fitted with a metal blade.

**Pistachios** (*pista*): Unsalted pistachio nuts are often used in desserts. They are normally ground or sliced before use, and are rarely added whole into recipes. Prior to storage, I suggest placing them in an oven for few minutes at 250 °F, and let cool. Store with a few cloves added in order to preserve freshness.

**Walnuts** (*akhrot*): Used in some desserts, walnuts are often eaten as a snack. If purchasing in large quantities, store in a cool place with a few cloves added as with pistachios.

# Root Vegetables

An excellent source of potassium, roots such as *sakkaria, suran* or *ratalu* are a common item in the Indian diet, and are added to *dals* and vegetable dishes. Interestingly, these roots are also traditionally eaten twice a month on the religious day *Ekadesi*.

Maintaining the belief that roots continue to live after being pulled from the ground, Indian Jains refrain from consuming roots altogether.

**Beets (*beet*):** Both the root and greens are used in cooking. Beet greens can be used like any variety of greens.

**Carrots (*gajar*):** Aside from the common carrot available in the states, a second, deep red variety is also available in India. Dishes made with this second variety acquire the beautiful red shade of the vegetable. I have yet to see this type of carrot easily available in the United States.

**Elephant's Foot or Bulbous Root (*suran*):** On Hindu religious days, this root, considered to be *sattvic* or pure, is consumed, cooked with butter, green chilies, salt, ginger and lemon juice. I have only very rarely seen it sold fresh in America, though it can more often be found canned.

**Onions (*kanda* or *pyaz*):** Onions are considered poor man's musk. While religious vegetarians abstain from eating onions, they were ubiquitous in my family's kitchen. My mother so firmly believed in their medicinal properties that she was willing to disregard any notion of religious taboo. In both Indian folklore and *Ayurveda*, onions are purported to be beneficial to humans. In the state of Gujarat, for example, some farmers make a habit of eating onions and jaggery with meals in order to reduce fatigue.

I have observed that onions in this country tend to have higher water content than their Asian counterparts. Consequently, onions purchased here take longer to brown. While certain cooks tend to use additional oil to induce faster browning, I prefer to brown onions well ahead of time and not to add more than a minimum amount of oil. Browned onions will keep in the refrigerator for several days.

Dried onion flakes or granules are ideal for recipes requiring onion flavor without the added moisture of fresh onion.

**Potatoes (*bateta*):** Potatoes are extremely common fare in Indian cooking. In this book, I have used either Idaho or red potatoes, though you may substitute any variety, according to preference—do note that in stuffed potato recipes, smaller potatoes, such as red potatoes, are required. When purchasing any variety, choose potatoes that are clean, firm and regularly shaped. Potatoes should be stored in dark, cool, dry and well-ventilated areas; refrigeration is not recommended.

**Radish (*mula*):** Red Daikon or White: The white variety, called *mula*, is served as a vegetable in Indian cuisine. Grated, it may also be used in certain breads (p. 409).

**Sweet Potatoes (*sakkaria*):** In India, yams and sweet potatoes are regarded as two completely different varieties of roots. While Indian yams are white or purple inside with a tough grayish skin, *sakkaria* are white inside and have a dark red skin. When purchasing sweet potatoes in this country, I look for those that are white or off-white inside and dark red on the outside: in my opinion, these tend to be the sweetest. In some produce stores, they are called Japanese sweet potatoes.

**Yam (*ratalu*):** *Ratalu* means purple in our language; the name of this root referring to its color. I have discovered that varieties purchased in Asian, Mexican or Latino groceries are white inside but more or less taste the same as the Indian yam. Yams may be used in vegetables or made into *pakora*.

# Grains and Flours

When I first came to the United States, Indian stores generally carried only wheat, whole-wheat and chickpea flour, called *chana atta* or *besan*. A larger selection is available today, making it easy and enjoyable to prepare the entire variety of Indian breads and appetizers.

For those who abstain from consuming wheat or fat, dense, chewy Indian breads made with millet and sorghum flours are a hearty substitute. Corn or rice flours may also be used.

**Amaranth** (*rajagaro*): This grain is now widely available in the United States. Mainly used on *Ekadesi* in Gujarat, it can be popped like popcorn and eaten with milk, or combined with jaggery to make sweet snack/dessert squares called *chiki*.

**Amaranth Flour** (*rajagarano lot*): Amaranth flour is used to make breads that are often consumed on religious days, when wheat or rice products are forbidden to the devotee. High in protein, iron, calcium, phosphorous and fiber, Amaranth is extremely nutritious.

**Arrow Root Flour** (*tapkir no lot*): This flour is used as a binding agent. It resembles starch but can be used for cooking on religious days when corn-starch and certain flours are prohibited.

**Bulgur** (*lapsi*): Bulgur is also known as cracked wheat. In Indian stores it is available in different grades (small, medium and/or large). To retard spoilage, warm lightly in a dry pan or microwave and let cool prior to storing.

**Buckwheat Flour** (*fafar atta*): Buckwheat flour is available in health-food or Indian stores. Indians use this on religious days. This flour gets very sticky while cooking, but once cooked, cooled and reheated, the flour assumes a slightly grainy but smooth texture. Buckwheat has high fiber content and is rich in protein. *Halwa* (p. 473) made with this flour is delicious.

*Chapati* **Flour** (*atta*): see Wheat Flour

**Chickpea Flour or Gram Flour** (*besan, chanano lot*): Do not confuse this with garbanzo flour, available in some health-food stores. Although one type may substitute for the other, the two flours have a different taste. In the event that either flour is unavailable, soak dry garbanzo beans overnight and grind for immediate use. When replacing either type of flour with ground garbanzo beans, reduce the amount of water called for in the recipe in order to compensate for the water content of the soaked beans.

**Khaman Flour:** Coarsely ground *chana dal.* Available in Indian stores.

**Corn** (*makkai*): In India, white corn is more popular than yellow. Roasted over an open fire, it is often accented by a little bit of salt, red chili powder and lemon juice before being served as a snack.

**Corn Flour** (*makkaino lot*): Finely ground flour is available at Indian grocers, however corn meal or maize meal sold in supermarkets can also be used. Since this flour has no gluten, it must be cooked in water prior to use so that it will bind. It may also be mixed with wheat or chickpea flour in order to acquire a more sticky consistency.

*Dhokla* **Flour** (*dhoklano lot*): This is available in most Indian stores, however, you can make your own using three portions of rice and one portion of split chickpeas (*chana dal*). Some cooks prefer, as I do, to increase the proportion of split chickpeas to lend a nuttier flavor to the recipe.

*Dosa* **Flour** (*dosano lot*): This flour is normally available in Indian stores. If not at hand, four portions of rice and one portion of *urid dal* can be soaked, ground separately and combined for recipes calling for this flour.

**Farina—Cream of Wheat or Semolina** (*sooji* or *ravo*): The large grade of farina, called thick *sooji,* is more commonly known as Cream of Wheat and it is usually used in desserts. The smaller grade, called thin *sooji,* may be acquired in Indian stores and is used most often in dough preparations. When buying either grade of *sooji* in large quantities from an Indian store, make sure it is free from lumps and toast lightly prior to storage in order to retard spoilage. (Toast it in a frying pan, stirring well, until heated through but not browned.)

**Garbanzo Flour** (*chanano lot*): This flour may serve as a suitable substitute for chickpea flour. The color and flavor of the recipe will differ slightly but it will serve the purpose.

*Handva* **Flour** (*handvano lot*): This flour is available in most Indian stores. However, you may grind your own using three portions of rice and one portion of split chickpeas (*chana dal*). If unable to grind the flour from dry ingredients, soak rice and beans and grind separately before combining.

*Idlee* **Flour** (*idleeno lot*): Readymade *idlee* flour is available in most Indian stores, although you may grind your own by mixing four portions of rice and one portion of *urid dal.* Alternatively you may soak and grind rice and *urid dal* separately before mixing. Buying prepared *idlee* flour, of course, will save you time.

**Millet (*bajri*):** Indian millet is gray in color. It is mainly consumed during the winter months, as it is believed to warm the body. I have found that Indian food stores inconsistently carry whole millet.

**Millet Flour (*bajrino lot*):** Like the millet from which it is derived, this flour is gray in color. Bread made from this flour is particularly suitable for dieters: no oil need be added to this flour when making bread.

Millet flour is available in Indian stores. The flour stales easily and should be stored with a few whole cloves added to the batch in order to preserve freshness. Be sure to sift the flour before use, to remove the cloves.

**Rice (*chokha*):** Many varieties of rice are available in this country. While I occasionally like to use brown or wild rice when cooking, I generally prefer to use *basmati* for its nutty aroma.

**Rice Flour (*chokhano lot*):** Rice flour is available in most Indian and Asian stores. When buying this flour, make sure it is finely ground; I recommend buying in small quantities for infrequent use.

**Sorghum (*juwar*):** Coarsely ground sorghum can be used in place of rice in some *khichadi* recipes that are mixed with *dal*. Some Gujaratis also add coarsely ground sorghum to *handva*. Whole sorghum is available in some Indian stores and in some specialty groceries, and is said to be beneficial for health.

**Sorghum Flour** (*juwarno lot*): Like millet flour, breads made with sorghum flour do not require the addition of oil. The flour stales easily and should be stored with a few whole cloves added to the batch in order to preserve freshness. Be sure to sift before use, to remove the cloves.

**Tapioca** (*sabudana*): *Sabudana* is sold in two or three grades in some stores. I prefer the medium grade. *Sabudana* flour is used as a binding agent in some recipes. *Sabudana* is easily digested and when mixed with milk, boiled and slightly sweetened to make *kanji*, it is regarded as a good food for the sick. Wafers made from *sabudana* are popular in Gujarat.

**Quinoa** (*kodri*): A roundish, sand colored grain, quinoa is available in polished and unpolished varieties. It is normally cooked in the same manner as rice. Nutty in taste, it has a light texture and is easy to digest. It is high in protein and is highly regarded for its nutritional value.

In some parts of India, cows are fed *ghughari*, which is Gujarati for quinoa cooked with jaggery.

*Papad* **Flour** (*papadno lot*): Now carrying an assortment of *papad* flour, Indian stores in this country have begun to cater to the needs of Indians wishing to make their own *papadams*.

**Wheat** (*ghaun*): In this country, wheat is available in both red and yellow varieties. Wheat grass can be grown using either. The grass grows very quickly—I have succeeded in growing the grass in one week.

**Wheat Flour** (*ghaunno lot*): A large variety of wheat flour is available in Indian stores. Be precise when purchasing. Ask for *chapati* flour.

**Coarsely Ground Wheat Flour (*ghavno kakario lot*):** This flour, used in some appetizers and breads, is also available in most Indian stores.

**Split Black Bean (*urid dal*) Flour (*adadno lot*):** *Urid* flour is used for making *papadams*. It is combined with rice flour to make South Indian *dosa*, and with chickpea flour to make a variety of Indian snacks.

## Essences in Indian Cooking

The following are the most commonly used essences in Indian cooking, though many other varieties are available in Indian stores.

*Kewra* **Essence:** Also spelt *keora* at times, *kewra* is known in English as screw pine. Popular in North India, the flavoring is obtained from the tropical screw pine, whose blossoms are noted for their beauty and fragrance.

**Mango Essence:** The essence can be used to add extra flavor to recipes calling for mangoes.

**Rose Essence:** Prepared from pure rose oil, this essence is very commonly used in rose *sherbat* (p. 496). I also use it in *Gulab Jaman* (p. 450).

# Indian Cooking Utensils

While brass, earthenware or aluminum pots are the tools of the traditional cook, most modern-day Indians prefer stainless steel. Stainless steel utensils are a must when any souring agent is added to the recipe, as aluminum reacts with and changes color when exposed to certain agents. Earthenware continues to be used in remote India—foods cooked in earthenware acquire a unique, delicious taste.

Indian cooking does not require many special cooking gadgets or utensils. When frying, a wok or deep frying pan may adequately replace the *peni* or *karai*, and a shallow frying pan can substitute for the *tava* or Indian griddle.

Two convenient tools for the kitchen are the noodle press or *sevno sancho* (illus. p. 175) and an *idlee* maker (illus. p. 160). However, the two most desirable Indian cooking utensils are a stainless steel sieve (illus. p. 50) and the thinner, Indian-style rolling pin, both of which are available in Indian stores. The rolling pin is particularly useful as it may be used to grind cumin (in small quantities), poppy seeds and sesame seeds. For certain recipes in this book, a food processor, a blender and a coffee grinder are a must.

# Fats and Oils

In Surat, Gujarat, Indian sesame oil was the oil of choice. I fondly recall the numerous times my grandmother asked me to run to the *ghani* (the place where oil is processed) in order to fetch her more oil. A large wooden contraption powered by a bullock, the crude sesame press produced fresh, pure sesame oil. Reminiscing, I can recall the smell of the freshly crushed sesame wafting through the air.

I have cooked with corn oil for the past over 25 years. In certain recipes, for added variety and distinct flavors, I mix corn oil with mustard or olive oil. If preferred, olive oil may be used instead of corn oil in any recipe in this book. Though do note that olive oil will burn faster than corn oil.

Some desserts and sweets require unsalted butter or *ghee* (clarified butter). *Ghee* (p. 59) gives any dish a distinct, rich flavor.

## Cooking Without Oil

I often receive request for recipes without oil. Apart from some breads, oil can be eliminated from almost any recipe without significantly altering the taste of that dish.

In many recipes, a small amount of oil is heated along with dry spices. The spices impart their flavor to the oil, and both are subsequently added to a dish.

If concerned about oil or fats, be aware that ingredients such as cumin seeds, fenugreek seeds, cloves and cinnamon can all be dry toasted in a frying pan. Mustard seeds can also be dry toasted, but only in a covered frying pan, as the seeds tend to "pop" into the air when they are heated. After dry-toasting the spices, add little water and cook spices in the water for 1 minute before adding other ingredients. Like dry spices, *hing* can also be toasted in a frying pan on low heat, prior to being added to the recipe.

As for other seasonings, sliced onions, garlic and coconut can all be browned in small quantities, without oil, in a non-stick frying pan.

There are a few varieties of breads that can be made without oil (p. 432). If you wish to make bread using wheat flour, without oil, adding a little millet or chickpea flour will change the texture, resulting in a less chewy bread.

## Cooking Without Salt or Sugar

I have used table salt in many of my recipes; you may choose the variety you prefer, adding salt to your taste. If used in the proper quantities, salt enhances the flavor of the other spices it is cooked with. Because of nutritional concerns however, I strictly limit the amount that I use when cooking. Rather than increasing the sodium content of dishes I prepare, I sometimes replace salt with lemon juice; at times, I even use tomatoes.

I have added sugar (brown or white) into some recipes to balance the taste of lemon, tamarind or tomatoes. In these recipes, the sugar may be omitted. For many pickles or relishes, however, sugar is a must. Note that you may substitute dried, sweet fruit for sugar in many pickle (or relish) recipes, but that the taste will differ.

*Aloona*: *Loon* means salt, and *Aloona* means without salt. When I was about four years old, my Grandparents told me that I would have to perform *Aloona Vrat* for five days to ensure that when I grew older, I would find a good husband. Trained to be very religious and obedient, so I agreed. When the time came to do the *Vrat*, or fast, I was required to eat only one meal a day, consisting of foods made with rice and without salt. As required of girls performing *Aloona Vrat*, I visited the temple during those five days to worship Shiva and perform *puja* that involved "*gorma*"—a grass grown using five grains: wheat, rice, mung beans, barley, and sesame.

I fondly recall this experience, when all the little girls, dressed in beautiful clothes and jewelry, would go to the temple together. Our hands and feet were painted with henna for this occasion, and in the evening, we danced and sang about our future husbands.

In the first five years during which one performs this annual *Vrat*, one eats meals made only of rice, in the subsequent five years, the meals may be made with wheat. No vegetable except *luni bhaji*, similar to watercress, was allowed in our diet during this period of fasting. Religion, diet, marriage were woven into our upbringing from a very early age.

## Steaming

A special steamer called *dhokaliyu* is available in Gujarat and Maharashtra. I have used the same one for the last 30 years: it is slightly battered, but it still works. European steamers or even Asian steamers can be used, and a saucepan with a rack inside and a tightly fitted lid can also do the job. When a starving student in New York, I used a saucepan with a coffee can cut on both the sides to serve as a rack. If using a saucepan with a lid, note that a stainless steel sieve (illus. p. 50) can serve as a rack. Invert the sieve, and place it in saucepan. Add water to the saucepan until the level is halfway to the surface of the sieve upon which the food is placed.

For steaming large quantities of *dhokla*, you may use a very large mixing bowl instead of a saucepan. Invert the sieve in the bowl, and then place on top, a large stainless steel platter, about 16–inches in diameter, holding the *dhokla* batter for steaming. Cover the bowl with a large pizza plate. While steaming, the water level in the saucepan or a bowl should be halfway to the sieve or a rack.

When using a saucepan to steam any of the "kebabs" or stuffed potatoes described in this book, note that the items to be steamed may be placed directly upon the inverted sieve. As always, make sure that the water in the pan is filled half way to the top of the sieve, ensuring that no water touches the ingredients while steaming.

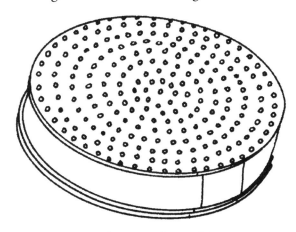

*An Indian, Stainless Steel Sieve*

# Recommendations: Preparing to Cook

1. Read the recipe thoroughly, reviewing the steps involved. If preferred, you may grind or puree ingredients, wherever required, before starting to cook.

2. For seasoned oil, heat the oil well, taking care not to overheat. If, for instance, you find that the spices added to the oil begin to burn, then immediately remove the pan from the heat to lower the temperature of the oil. The process of seasoning and adding the seasoned oil to the recipe is called *vaghar*, *tadka* or *chhowk*.

3. For deep-frying, I have mentioned to heat the oil to certain temperatures: this is just to give you an idea how hot the oil should be. Heat the oil, just barely to the point when it begins to smoke. Drop a small piece of dough into the oil. If it browns immediately, the oil is too hot. Lower heat slightly and wait a couple of minutes before beginning to fry. With little practice, you will be able to gauge the temperature of the oil without a thermometer.

4. Fresh beans and fresh spinach will change color if covered while cooking.

5. Pass a knife through potatoes, to make sure they are cooked. For all recipes but those using mashed potatoes, take care not to let the potatoes cook such that they fall apart.

6. While cooking recipes from the book, you may partially or fully cover the pan making sure the liquid does not boil over. You may maintain the heat on medium to prevent over boiling.

# Useful Hints

- Cut a lime into halves and leave it in the refrigerator, it will absorb all the smell. Cut lime or lemon and salt can also be used to clean counters.
- While cooking *dal*, add a little oil. This will prevent it from boiling over.
- To cook garbanzo or dried peas faster, add a few drops of coconut oil to the boiling water.
- To remove burned food from steel or aluminum pots/pans, boil chopped onions in water, in the utensil in which food has burnt.
- Dried leaves of mango trees will keep flies away.
- Wooden cooking tools can be cleaned with water and salt mixture.
- To keep fried snacks for longer periods, add a little clarified butter to the hot oil before frying.
- Do not discard water in which potatoes are boiled. You can shine silver, brass and stainless steel utensils with this water.
- Place lemons, oranges and mangoes in warm water for about 10 minutes before extracting juice. They will yield more juice.
- If your recipe with sauce gets too salty, peel and place halved potato or a little chickpea flour tied in a cheesecloth and simmer for few minutes. Remove potato or flour bundle before serving.

# INDIAN DAIRY BASICS

Yogurt—*dahi*
Thickened Yogurt—*maska*
Clarified Butter—*ghee*
Traditional Indian Cheese—*chenna* or *paneer*
Variation: Indian Cheese with Spices
Solidified Milk, Traditional Method—*khoya* or *mavo*
Solidified Milk, Shortened Method

# Indian Dairy Basics

All Indian children grow up hearing the tales of the Lord Krishna's pranks as a little boy. His playful attempts to steal *makhan*, or sweet churned butter made by his mother and other women in the village of Brindaban are celebrated in stories, music, classical and folk, dance and painting. These stories, so prevalent within Indian culture, illustrate the prominent place that dairy products enjoy in the daily menu of most Indians.

The *Vaishnavs*—the Hindu worshippers of Vishnu the Preserver— refrain from using water to prepare foods for religious offerings. Rather, *Vaishnavs* as well as Brahmins prepare *Panchamrat*, "five nectars," to bathe the images of their deities or to offer their gods in ritual daily prayers. A mixture of milk, yogurt, honey, *ghee* and sugar, *Panchamrat* is an all-*sattvic* or pure food, and is therefore considered nourishing and purifying. This practice is observed in homes as well as in temples. After the ritual is completed, leftover *Panchamrat* is distributed among the people as *prasadum*, offerings blessed by the gods.

*Ghee*, or clarified butter, yogurt and milk are essential ingredients to authentic Indian cooking. Their presence in the Indian diet is partly responsible for the reverence of cows, a vital element in Hinduism. As Mahatma Gandhi wrote (in the journal *Young India*): "The cow is enjoined to realize his identity with all that lives. Why the cow was selected for apotheosis is obvious to me. The cow was, in India, the best companion. She was the giver of plenty. Not only did she give milk, but she also made agriculture possible…She is the mother to millions of Indian mankind." I would note here that Veganism, or vegetarianism advocating abstinence from all animal products including dairy products, is more Western in practice.

Milk is considered to be the most perfect of all *sattvic* foods, providing the basis for yogurt or curd, and *ghee*, made from butter.

Fresh, homemade yogurt is superb: thick, with a cream-like consistency and mild tasting, it is unsurpassed by commercially produced varieties.

Most Indians consume the yogurt made each day, saving a small amount as a starter for the next batch. This habit ensures that the yogurt will not sour. Indians value yogurt for both the cooling contrast it offers to the spices in a meal and its efficacy in promoting digestion. In Indian folk medicine, yogurt with plain rice is known as an effective treatment for an upset stomach. In a vegetarian meal, yogurt provides protein to compliment those in *dals* and rice, as well as vitamins A and D, with the minerals calcium, phosphorus and potassium.

*Ghee* has a value praised since Vedic times. Prepared from butter, which is heated until its buttermilk content is separated, *ghee* is the clear, yellow butterfat separated and strained from milk protein solids to yield the purified product. Many Hindus believe that *ghee* aids in the development of the mind. My mother would tell us that, in the same way machines need to be oiled periodically to run smoothly, so the human machine needs *ghee* to maintain good health.

While I was growing up, my parents kept a cow to provide us with a daily milk supply. My daily routine was to go to the stable at milking time to enjoy a bowl of warm, fresh milk. When the cow had a calf, the first lot of her milk was cooked with jaggery and given to the cow. The second lot was used to make *bali*, a steamed, sweet cake similar to *dhokla* (p. 155), which is considered to be extremely healthy (I never liked it, but had to eat it!). I should add that in my family, we always left enough milk for the calf!

These carefree memories of my youth have yielded to concerns about nutrition and health-consciousness. While milk is rich in protein, vitamins and naturally obtainable fats, I am aware of the detrimental effects of a diet heavy in fats. I now use lowfat milk in most of my cooking and try to keep butter and *ghee* to a minimum. A few recipes included here call for extra rich milk or light cream, and I reserve such dishes for special occasions.

Basic dairy ingredients and the techniques for their preparation are discussed in the following pages. A few recipes using dairy products appear throughout the various chapters and are identified with the word "dairy" next to the recipe title.

## Yogurt—*dahi*

In Indian cooking, plain yogurt is used in a variety of ways. It develops a slightly tart taste when cooked with other foods. An important ingredient in many appetizers, breads and curries, it can be mixed with fruits, vegetables and seasonings. It is also used in several popular beverages and in desserts. *Raita* or yogurt mixed with chopped fruits or vegetables accompanies a meal, and buttermilk, made from yogurt is often served after lunch, the biggest meal of the day for most Indians.

Low fat milk yields a rich, creamy yogurt. The richness can be increased by using whole milk, or decreased with nonfat milk. When making yogurt for the first time, use commercial, plain yogurt for starter. Thereafter, a small amount, about 4 teaspoons from each prepared batch, can be used as a starter for the next. After five or six preparations of yogurt, the starter tends to become sour. At that point begin again with commercial yogurt for starter. Use the starter within the first two or three days of initial preparation. I usually made a supply of two gallons of yogurt every other day at *The Ganges*.

The key to perfect results lies in adding the starter when the scalded milk has reached the optimum temperature range for the bacteria in the starter to proliferate. When the temperature is too high, the bacteria die, and the milk does not set. Below the optimum range, the yogurt takes unnecessarily long to set. A candy thermometer and well-timed monitoring result in a sweet yogurt, adding incomparable richness to a menu.

| | |
|---|---|
| 1 quart | lowfat milk |
| 4 teaspoons | plain yogurt |

Rinse a large saucepan with cold water. Add milk to the saucepan and place over high heat. Bring to a full boil. As soon as the milk begins to rise, remove from heat and allow it to cool until the temperature reads 118 °F.

Add yogurt starter to milk, mixing thoroughly with a wire whisk. Cover pan with a lid and place in a warm place, such as an oven with a gas pilot light. If kept outside, you may cover the pan with a towel.

Check after four or five hours. Refrigerate immediately if set. For mild or sweet yogurt, refrigerate just before yogurt has set completely. This requires checking yogurt after about three hours. Test by giving yogurt a gentle shake; if set, refrigerate immediately.

Yogurt tastes best if used within 3 days. It will keep, refrigerated, about 5 days.

Yield: 1 quart.

## Thickened Yogurt—*maska*

*Shreekhand* (p. 452), made from drained, thickened yogurt, is possibly the most popular sweet pudding in Gujarat. As a child, I recall watching my mother at night, as she hung up a piece of cloth holding yogurt. The next morning, my father would add sugar and strain the yogurt through the same cloth in order to procure the thickened yogurt dessert. To the painstakingly obtained product, he added cardamom, saffron, slivered pistachios and (sometimes) rose essence.

For weddings and certain festive occasions, most Gujaratis, use newspapers, cheesecloth and a piece of net to carry out this process. After being drained for four or five hours, the yogurt is combined with sugar and then strained through the net, by two or three people at a time, into a large pot and then refrigerated until ready to use in a day or two. Drained of water, the yogurt acquires a sweet taste. The same method may be used to drain yogurt in small quantities.

Perhaps the simplest method to thicken yogurt is to line a colander with a cheesecloth, place the yogurt in it and stand the colander in a large bowl. Leave in the refrigerator overnight; the thickened yogurt will be ready in the morning. Either of the above methods will work effectively.

Note that thickened yogurt is also sometimes used to make dense *raitas*.

## Clarified Butter—*ghee*

1 pound.                          unsalted butter

Using a small saucepan, place butter on medium heat. As the butter starts to melt, lower the heat. Stir well when the butter has melted. Keep the heat low and continue to stir every few minutes. The melted butter will be frothy in the beginning and then the buttermilk part will start to separate into a white residue; maintain the heat on low. When the residue turns golden, remove from heat. It will continue to cook in the hot pan. When it stops to cook—in about 20 minutes—and while the melted butter is still clear, strain into a jar, and let cool completely before covering the jar. Discard the residue.

People making *ghee* in large quantities add a betelnut leaf to the boiling liquid. Removed when the *ghee* is strained, the leaf prevents *ghee* from turning rancid.

Yield: Approximately 1 ½ cups.

## Traditional Indian Cheese—*chenna* or *paneer*

Indians have prepared *paneer* since Vedic times. Whereas *Chenna* refers to milk curd that still contains whey; *paneer* is drained and pressed until firm. *Chenna* is used to make a variety of sweets and *paneer* is mainly used in savory recipes. Requiring only milk and lemon juice, this is a pure vegetarian recipe (it contains no animal rennet). Though some Indians use vinegar to curdle the milk, Gujaratis prefer not to, as vinegar is fermented and therefore not *sattvik*. Though extra-rich milk will make *chenna* or *paneer* smooth and creamy, I prefer to use lowfat milk in order to limit dietary fat intake.

| ½ gallon | milk |
| 4 tablespoons | lemon juice |

Bring milk to a full boil in a stainless steel saucepan over high heat. Lower the heat as it starts to rise and gradually add lemon juice. Stir well. The milk will separate within minutes. If all of it does not curdle, add 1 more tablespoon lemon juice and mix again. Remove saucepan from heat and set aside, covered, for about 10 minutes. Strain through double-folded cheesecloth and squeeze out most of the whey, the curdled milk in the cheesecloth is *paneer*. Save the whey to use in vegetables or any other preparation requiring water.

Cover a large tray or cutting board with several layers of paper towels. Spread the same piece of cheesecloth with *paneer* over this, and in the center, flatten the ball of *paneer* into a circle or square shape, keeping it about 1–inch thick. Fold the corners of the cheesecloth over to cover *paneer* completely, and cover again with paper towels. To squeeze out remaining liquid from *paneer*, fill a large saucepan with water, to weigh it down, and place it over paper towel-covered *paneer*.

**For desserts:**

If using *chenna* for *rasmalai* (p. 458), leave a little whey and knead as required.

**For vegetables and other dishes:**

As soon as whey is drained, add ¾ teaspoon salt and 1 teaspoon coarsely ground toasted cumin to *paneer*, and mix well. Press into a slab and place weight over it as per instructions above. After about three hours, remove and cut into 1–inch squares, use as required.

Ready-made *paneer* is now available at Indian grocery stores and it is quite firm and suitable for use in various recipes.

## Variation: Indian Cheese with Spices

Prepare *paneer* as in above recipe, add salt, coarsely ground cumin, finely chopped onions, finely cut bell peppers and garlic, finely chopped mint and cilantro, if preferred, and press and proceed as above. Cut into bite-size squares or diamonds and serve without frying.

Yield: Approximately 8 ounces.

## Solidified Milk, Traditional Method—*khoya* or *mavo*

Full cream milk can be used to prepare *khoya*. Half and half may be used to shorten preparation time.

| | |
|---|---|
| 1 quart | half and half |
| 2 tablespoons | lemon juice |

Bring half and half to a full boil in a medium saucepan over high heat. Maintain boiling, stirring well for 5 minutes. Gradually add lemon juice and keep stirring. Milk will curdle and it will solidify in about 25 minutes. The *khoya* will have an excellent "*danedar*," or grainy texture that is ideal for making Indian sweets.

## Solidified Milk, Shortened Method

The above recipe is high in calories; use part-skim ricotta cheese for a lighter version of *khoya*. In the microwave, ricotta will take about 30 minutes to solidify. Lightly cover the container to prevent splatter. Stir every 5 minutes so that the *khoya* does not brown on the sides. When dry, remove from heat, let cool and use as desired. Can be refrigerated for 4 or 5 days.

Alternatively, ricotta can be cooked on stovetop, on low heat, stirring the content frequently to prevent sticking or burning. Cook until all the moisture dries out.

# CHUTNEYS, RELISHES, *RAITAS* AND PICKLES

## Chutneys and Relishes

Raisin and Tamarind Chutney—*draksh aamlini chutney*
Cilantro Chutney—*kothmirni chutney*
Coconut and Split Chickpea Chutney—*koprune chana dal chutney*
Potato Chutney—*batetani chutney*
Coconut and Red Pepper Chutney—*koprune lal marchani chutney*
Tomato Chutney—*tametani chutney*
Garlic and Red Chili Chutney—*lasanni thikhi chutney*
Persimmon Chutney—persimmon *chutney*
Apricot Chutney—*jardaluni chutney*
Cranberry Chutney—*cranberry chutney*
Mango Chutney—*kerini chutney*-1
Cooked Mango Chutney—*kerini chutney*-2
Carrot Chutney—*gajarni chutney*
Green Garlic Chutney—*leela lasanni chutney*
Toasted Split Chickpea Chutney—*chana dal chutney*
Lemon Peel Chutney—*limbuni chutney*
Carambola or Star Fruit Chutney—*kamrukhni chutney*
Tomato and Onion Relish—*tametane kandani kachumber*
Cucumber Relish—*kakdini kachumber*
Mango and Onion Relish—*keri kandani kachumber*
Green Papaya Relish—*kacha papayani kachumber*
Variation: Spicy Green Papaya Relish—*papayani chhin*
Daikon Relish—*muli kachumber*
*Papadum* Relish—*papadni kachumber*
Mango Relish with Cumin—*chhundo*

Mango Relish with Cardamom—*murrabbo*
Carrot Relish—*gajarno chhundo*
Pineapple Relish with Cumin—*ananasno chhundo*
Cabbage Relish—*kobijnu kachumber*

## Raitas

Cucumber *Raita* with Green Chilies—*kakdinu raitu*
Carrot *Raita*—*gajarnu raitu*
Cauliflower *Raita*—*flowernu raitu*
Spinach *Raita*—*bhajinu raitu*
Cilantro *Raita*—*kothmirnu raitu*
Mint *Raita*—*fudinanu raitu*
Onion *Raita*—*kandanu raitu*
Dumpling *Raita*—*bundi raita*
Dry Fruit *Raita*—*suka mevanu raitu*
Banana *Raita*—*kelanu raitu*
Fresh Fruit and Nut *Raita*—*durbari raita*
Grains and Spice *Raita*—*methkoot*
Spicy Hot *Raita*—*tikhari*
Potato *Raita*—*batetanu raitu*

## Pickles

Pickling Spice-Basic—*athanano masalo*
Mango Pickle—*kerinu athanu or methia keri*
Sweet and Hot Mango Pickle—*kerinu galune tikhu athanu*
Sweet and Hot Carrot Pickle—*gajarnu athanu*
Sweet and Hot Lemon Pickle—*limbunu galu athanu*
Dry Fruit Pickle—*suka mevanu athanu*
Unripe Cherry Pickle—*cherinu athanu*
Fresh Carrot and Cucumber Pickle—*gajar kakdinu athanu*
Hot Chili Pickle—*marchanu athanu*
Hot and Sweet Chili Pickle—*marchanu tikhune galu athanu*
Raisin Pickle—*drakshnu athanu*

# Chutneys, Relishes, *Raitas* and Pickles

Chutneys, relishes, *raitas* and pickles are an integral part of the Indian meal. They accompany appetizers as well as main dishes and without them, the most elaborate feasts would be incomplete. Through my experience as a chef and a teacher, I have observed that the use and concept behind chutneys and other condiments remains a mystery to novices of Indian cooking.

Both chutneys and relishes are spiced sauces that are usually eaten with Indian appetizers such as *pakora* or *samosa*. Indians prepare both cooked and raw chutneys and relishes with a variety of herbs, fruits, vegetables and even split chickpeas. Prepared to various degrees of pungency and spiciness, and combined with raw/refined sugar or fruits, condiments can add a completely new dimension to traditional flavor combinations. The sweet or mellow component of a chutney instantly enhances the flavor of pepper or chilies, as well as the vegetables or snack the chutney accompanies.

In general, I distinguish between chutneys, which are ground, and relishes, which designate chopped or grated pieces of fruit or vegetable. *Raitas* are yogurt mixed with minced or grated vegetables or chopped fruits; aromatic spices; and piquant chilies, eaten with the main dishes of a meal. The yogurt base guarantees a source of protein and has the advantage of being one of the *sattvic* or pure foods. Mildly flavored yogurt *raitas* also counter-balance spicy chutneys. Pickles consist of fruits or vegetables allowed to season in oil with spices, lemon juice and occasionally sugar. Like chutneys, pickles are served to provide a spicy accent to the meal.

The choice of condiments served at a meal requires an understanding of the blending of different flavors, as well as an appreciation of the visual appeal of the color and the texture of main dishes and condiments. Used knowledgeably, chutneys, *raitas* and pickles become more than condiments or seasonings for food, but a component of the meal itself.

Each region of India boasts its own variation of *raitas*, pickles and chutneys. South Indians use more coconut and *dals* in their chutneys, which tend to have a thin consistency. Gujarati chutneys, by contrast tend to be thicker and to contain cilantro, mint and fruit. Gujarat and Maharashtra are in fact famous for the sheer variety of chutneys, *raitas* and pickles in their respective cuisines.

Tips on deciding which condiments work best with different dishes are included in the following pages, along with the ingredients traditionally used in preparation. After you have tried some of the recipes I hope that you will be inspired to experiment. Take the initiative to blend spices, fruits and vegetables in new combinations. Through intuition and experiment you can devise delicious complements to meals.

# Chutneys

Chutneys are prepared in a time-honored ritual in traditional Indian households. Each morning, before any other cooking begins, the ingredients of fresh chutneys are ground in stone mortars. This allows for the creation of thick pastes without the addition of water or lemon juice. As a child I loved the task of grinding spices and herbs on the grindstone. Chutneys prepared in such a way are redolent, fresh and exude a wonderful, earthy taste. The quantities I now prepare are made with blenders and food processors, making the once labor intensive tasks virtually effortless, although lacking in the extra special results of labor-intensive hand preparation.

Chutneys are meant to be eaten in small quantities. Indian families typically prepare limited amounts, and consume tiny portions of chutney with their meals. At *The Ganges*, the customers ate their way through almost one hundred pounds, monthly!

Fresh chutneys, especially those prepared with cilantro, green garlic and mint, should ideally be eaten within several hours of preparation. If refrigerated, however, these chutneys will keep for a maximum of seven days, but will darken in color. A small amount of lemon juice may be added so that ground or blended ingredients maintain their bright green color for at least one day. Alternatively, if storing the chutney is an issue, vinegar may be added to extend the life of the chutney an additional week (if refrigerated). Vinegar will not preserve the color of a chutney, but it will contribute to its longevity. (For one cup of chutney, use 1 tablespoon lemon juice, or 2 teaspoons of vinegar). No additional lemon juice or vinegar should be added into recipes in this chapter that already contain either of the ingredients.

In contrast to freshly ground chutneys, cooked chutneys can be stored safely for long periods of time. Adding flavor to the simplest of menus, cooked chutneys are generally prepared with fruits such as mangos and lemons. Tomatoes and carrots are sometimes used in cooked chutneys, but these do not keep for more than a week.

## Pairing Condiments and Foods

Appetizers made with yogurt, or those that are slightly sour or salty, blend well with sweet-hot, fresh chutneys. For example most Indians serve *pakora*, vegetables dipped in chickpea flour and deep fried, with raisin and tamarind chutney. The sweetness of raisins perfectly complements the spiced *pakora* batter. Since *pakora* usually go from cooking directly to the table, freshly ground, cool chutney provides a welcome contrast.

We always serve *urid dal* or mung bean patties dipped in yogurt, called *dahivada*, with sweet and sour raisin and tamarind chutney. The brown colored chutney livens the deep flavors of the patties, and contrasts pleasingly with the white yogurt, and the red-chili powder and cilantro garnish.

Steamed appetizers, like *dhokla*, are usually mild with a slightly sour aftertaste, and are served with cilantro chutney. The delicate sweet flavor of cilantro accents the peppery flavor of *dhokla*, which are made with split chickpeas (*chana dal*) or rice with split black-bean (*urid dal*) flours.

The chutneys used at festivals or important occasions are almost always cooked. More convenient to make and to serve in large quantities than fresh chutneys, these chutneys are often presented alongside spicy breads like *thepla* or *puri*. Also, their flavor pleasingly contrasts with *dhokla* and other dishes with slightly sour flavors, such as the rice and yogurt dish, *vagharelo bhat*.

A few of the recipes that I have included draw upon the sweet-hot or sweet-sour range of flavors. Such combinations add wonderful zest to the simplest of meals. The amount of sugar in a few of the recipes may seem excessive, but these chutneys are meant to be sweet and to be eaten only in small quantities with other foods. The sugar balances the spiciness, not only of the chutney, but also of the food it accompanies.

Note that to keep the recipes pleasantly spicy, I have kept the use of chilies to a minimum. The spiciness can be modified to taste.

# Raisin and Tamarind Chutney—*draksh aamlini chutney*

The tart tamarind combined with sweet raisins results in a bold taste that enlivens almost any dish. One of India's most popular chutneys, this version is moderately accented by the chili. Raisins, although more economical, may be replaced by dried currants when available.

| | |
|---|---|
| 2–inch square | tamarind slab |
| 2 cups | hot water |
| 2 cups | seedless black raisins |
| 2 teaspoons | salt, or to taste |
| 2 teaspoons | toasted, coarsely ground cumin seeds |
| ¼ teaspoon | chili powder |

In a medium-sized stainless steel bowl, combine tamarind and water and soak until soft, about 30 minutes. While tamarind is soaking, place raisins in a small bowl, cover with warm water, and allow to soak, draining the raisins and discarding the water after one hour. Using your hands, squeeze tamarind in the same water in which it is soaked. Strain liquid into a small bowl and discard fibers and seeds, if any.

Combine raisins, tamarind water and spices in a blender, and puree until mixture is smooth. Transfer to a glass bowl, cover and refrigerate. This will keep for about 10 days.

Yield: Approximately 4 cups.

## Cilantro Chutney—*kothmirni chutney*

A popular Indian condiment, this chutney has many uses. Along with raisin and tamarind chutney (p. 69), this chutney is always served with *bhel puri* (p. 178), a spectacular snack mix. The latest "fast food" trend in Bombay consists of grilled cilantro chutney sandwiches with cheese, tomatoes and thinly sliced steamed potatoes.

You can add this chutney to many vegetable dishes for a sharp, spicy flavor. Free of oil, coconut, and peanuts, this chutney is a good choice for those on restricted diets. Serve with steamed or fried appetizers.

| | |
|---|---|
| 4 cups | chopped cilantro, stems included |
| 1 tablespoon | lemon juice |
| 1 ½ teaspoons | salt, or to taste |
| 3 whole | serrano or jalapeño chilies |
| ¼ cup | water |

Place ingredients in the jar of a blender and grind until smooth. Transfer to a bowl and refrigerate until serving. Best used the same day, this chutney will keep for about one week in the refrigerator. Be aware that the next day, this chutney will change color in spite of the addition of lemon juice.

Yield: Approximately 1 cup.

**Note:** ½ cup mint leaves may be added to this chutney as a variation.

## Coconut and Split Chickpea Chutney
### —*koprune chana dal chutney*

This chutney can be served with *dosa* (p. 426), *idlee* (p. 159) or most deep-fried appetizers. Cilantro is not added in some parts of South India, though in Gujarat, it is commonly used for this recipe.

| | |
|---|---|
| ¼ cup | split chickpeas (*chana dal*) |
| 2 cups | water, or as required |
| 2 teaspoons | salt, or to taste |
| 2 cup | unsweetened, grated coconut |
| 4 | serrano or jalapeño chilies |
| 2–inch piece | fresh ginger, peeled, chopped |
| ½ cup | chopped cilantro |
| 5 | black peppercorns |
| 2 tablespoons | lemon juice, or to taste |
| 2 teaspoons | oil |
| 1 teaspoon | black mustard seeds |
| ½ teaspoon | *hing* (asafoetida) |
| 6 | *curry* leaves (optional) |

In a small frying pan over medium heat, toast split chickpeas, stirring well until slightly golden, about 7 minutes. Remove to a bowl, add 2 cups water and soak the *dal* for at least four hours. In a blender grind soaked *dal* with water together with the next 7 ingredients including lemon juice, until almost smooth. Remove to a bowl, set aside.

In the frying pan, heat the oil well over medium heat and add mustard. When mustard starts to crackle, add *hing* and *curry* leaves, if using any. Immediately add mixture to ground chutney, mix well, chill and serve. ½-cup buttermilk may be used in lieu of the lemon juice if a thinner consistency and a creamier taste are desired

Yield: Approximately 3 cups.

## Potato Chutney—*batetani chutney*

For this chutney, you may use potato scrapings from the cored potatoes used in the stuffed baby potato recipe (p. 200). Otherwise, peel, wash and chop potatoes before grinding. Your guests will never identify the main ingredient! The flavor of this chutney is similar to the seasonal Carambola chutney (p. 85).

| | |
|---|---|
| 2 medium | potatoes, peeled, chopped, washed |
| 3–inch piece | fresh ginger, peeled, chopped |
| 3 | serrano or jalapeño chilies |
| 2 cups | chopped cilantro |
| ½ cup | peanuts, unsalted |
| 2 teaspoons | salt, or to taste |
| 2 teaspoons | oil |
| 1 teaspoon | black mustard seeds |
| 1 teaspoon | cumin seeds |
| ½ teaspoon | *hing* (asafoetida) |
| 10 | *curry* leaves (optional) |
| 2 tablespoons | brown sugar or to taste |
| 2 teaspoons | tamarind concentrate (p. 31) |
| 2 cups | water |

Using a blender or a food processor fitted with a metal blade, grind until smooth the potatoes with the next 5 ingredients including salt. Remove to a bowl and set aside.

In a medium stainless steel saucepan, heat the oil over high heat and add mustard and cumin seeds. Add *hing* when mustard crackles and the cumin sizzle. Immediately add *curry* leaves, if using any. Lower the heat to medium, cook for 3 seconds and add the ground potato mixture.

Add brown sugar, tamarind and water, and cook the mixture, stirring well, for about 7 minutes. Remove to a glass or stainless steel bowl. Chill before serving. This chutney is best if used the same day, but will keep refrigerated for several days.

Yield: Approximately 4 cups.

## Coconut and Red Pepper Chutney
### —*koprune lal marchani chutney*

This normally hot chutney may be rendered less spicy by cutting down on the number of chilies to three-fourths or even one-half of the suggested quantity. Alternatively, add yogurt when serving. To give a spicy twist to your vegetable, *dal* or rice preparations, try adding a small amount of this chutney into the recipe. I like to serve this with more mild dishes such as *idlee* (p. 159)

| | |
|---|---|
| 2 cups | unsweetened, finely grated coconut |
| 2 tablespoons | oil |
| ½ teaspoon | *hing* (asafoetida) |
| 15 | dried, whole red chili peppers |
| 15 cloves | garlic, peeled, chopped |
| ¼ cup | sesame seeds |
| 2 tablespoons | fennel seeds |
| 1 tablespoon | cumin seeds |
| 2 teaspoons | salt, or to taste |

In a medium frying pan over medium heat, toast coconut until slightly golden. Remove to the bowl of a food processor fitted with a metal blade. In the same frying pan, heat oil over medium heat and add *hing*. Add peppers as soon as *hing* turns brown. Fry peppers, stirring well until they change color to dark red. Remove with a slotted spoon and add to the coconut.

In the same frying pan, add garlic and cook, stirring well until golden, remove with a slotted spoon and add to the coconut. Again in the same frying pan, without adding any more oil, fry sesame, fennel and cumin, stirring well, until they change color. Add to coconut mixture and grind chutney until slightly coarse. Remove to a bowl or a jar and let cool. This dry chutney will keep for an extended period of time.
Yield: Approximately 2 ½ cups.

## Tomato Chutney—*tametani chutney*

Use ripe, preferably roma tomatoes, for a brightly colored, savory mixture. This chutney should be made in small quantities and be used within three or four days. Serve with any meal or with fried appetizers such as *pakora* (p. 134).

| | |
|---|---|
| 1 cup | water |
| 6 | roma tomatoes |
| 4 teaspoons | oil |
| 1 three–inch stick | cinnamon |
| 6 | cloves |
| 1 tablespoon | sesame seeds |
| 3 | serrano or jalapeño chilies, ground |
| ¼ teaspoon | dry ginger powder |
| ½ teaspoon | chili powder |
| 3 tablespoons | brown sugar, or to taste |
| 2 teaspoons | salt, or to taste |
| 1 tablespoon | chopped cilantro, for garnish |

Place tomatoes and water together in a medium saucepan and cook over high heat. When the tomatoes become limp, use the back of a spoon to press the tomatoes against the side of the saucepan and extract the juice. Strain the tomato sauce, discard skin and seeds.

In a medium frying pan, heat the oil over medium heat and add cinnamon and cloves. When cinnamon starts to swell (after a few seconds), add sesame seeds. As soon as sesame changes color, add tomato sauce.

Add the next 5 ingredients including salt, mix well and cook until the chutney comes to a boil. Remove to a bowl and let cool before serving. Serve garnished with cilantro.

Yield: Approximately 1 ½ cups.

## Garlic and Red Chili Chutney—*lasanni thikhi chutney*

My daughter and son love to eat this chutney with *parotha* (p. 411). In this country a food processor and rolling pin replace the grinding stone that is traditionally used in India. Serve with any meal. This chutney keeps for a long time.

| ½ cup | garlic cloves, peeled |
| 2 tablespoons | red hot chili powder |
| ¼ cup | peanuts, toasted, peeled (p. 37) |
| 1 tablespoon | sesame seeds, crushed (p. 30) |
| 2 teaspoons | salt, or to taste |

Grind until smooth all the ingredients in a food processor fitted with a metal blade. If the food processor fails to finely grind the chutney, remove to a cutting board and grind further with a rolling pin. Remove and store in a jar. Will keep until finished!
Yield: Approximately ¼ cup.

## Persimmon Chutney—*persimmon chutney*

I have yet to see a persimmon in India, and this recipe is completely of my own making. The use of the fruit is unique, though all the ingredients are easily available. Serve as desired.

| | |
|---|---|
| 2 | ripe Hachiya persimmons, trimmed, cut |
| ½ teaspoon | salt, or to taste |
| 1 teaspoon | toasted, coarsely ground cumin seeds |
| 1 tablespoon | sugar, or to taste |
| 2 teaspoons | fresh lemon juice |

Trim, discard stems and cut persimmons into large pieces. In a blender or a liquidizer, grind all the ingredients until smooth. Chill before serving. You may garnish the chutney with chopped cilantro, if desired.
Yield: Approximately ½ cup.

## Apricot Chutney—*jardaluni chutney*

I have used dried apricots, available year-round, for this recipe. During the apricot season, you may use fresh fruit, reducing the quantity of water to ½ cup (you will not need to soak the fresh fruit). Flavored with cumin and chili, this chutney goes well with spicy appetizers.

| | |
|---|---|
| 2 cups | dried apricots |
| 2 cups | water or as needed |
| 1 ½ teaspoons | salt, or to taste |
| 1 teaspoon | chili powder |
| 2 teaspoons | lemon juice |
| 1 tablespoon | toasted, coarsely ground cumin seeds |
| 2 tablespoons | brown sugar, or to taste |

In a glass bowl, soak apricots in water for two hours. If required, add sufficient water such that apricots are immersed in water. Remove apricots with water to the jar of a liquidizer or blender, add remaining ingredients and grind until smooth. Remove to a bowl and serve as desired.
Yield: Approximately 3 cups.

## Cranberry Chutney—*cranberry chutney*

The large quantity of sugar called for in this preparation compensates for the tartness of the cranberries. Remember that chutneys are meant to be eaten in small quantities, and that therefore, one should not feel guilty eating this! This chutney goes very well with any meal.

| | |
|---|---|
| 3 cups | cranberries |
| 1 cup | water |
| ¾ cup | sugar |
| 1 ½ teaspoons | salt, or to taste |
| 4–6 | serrano or jalapeño chilies |
| 1 ½ teaspoons | toasted, coarsely ground cumin seeds |

Place cranberries, and the next 4 ingredients, including chilies in the jar of a liquidizer, and grind until smooth. Remove to a bowl, add cumin and mix well. Chill before serving. Will keep for several days in the refrigerator. Yield: Approximately 3 ½ cups.

## Mango Chutney—*kerini chutney-1*

This refreshing chutney made from unripe mangoes is best served with fried appetizers. Refrigerated, this chutney will keep for a few days.

| | |
|---|---|
| 6 (2 cups, cut) | unripe firm mangoes, peeled |
| 2 teaspoons | salt, or to taste |
| ½ teaspoon | chili powder |
| 3 tablespoons | jaggery or brown sugar, or to taste |
| 1 tablespoon | toasted, coarsely ground cumin seeds |

Peel mangoes and remove all flesh from the stone. Discard skin and stones. In a liquidizer or a blender, grind until smooth, mango with ingredients including cumin. Remove to a bowl and serve.

Yield: Approximately 1 ½ cups.

## Cooked Mango Chutney—*kerini chutney*-2

This cooked variety of mango chutney will keep for extended periods of time, as the vinegar acts as a preservative. Perhaps the easiest way to find good unripe, tender mangoes is to contact your local Indian store and ask for the unripe fruit to be saved for you. At times, Asian grocers also sell unripe mangoes. Serve with any appetizer or with any meal.

| | |
|---|---|
| 6–8 | unripe tender mangoes (about 2 pounds) |
| 1 teaspoon | turmeric |
| 1 tablespoon | salt, or to taste |
| 3 cups | sugar, or to taste |
| 4–inch piece | fresh ginger, peeled, ground |
| 2 teaspoons | ground cinnamon |
| 2 teaspoons | coarsely ground black pepper |
| 1 tablespoon | toasted, coarsely ground cumin seeds |
| 1 tablespoon | ground anise |
| 2 teaspoons | ground cardamom seeds |
| 1 tablespoon | black mustard seeds, ground (p. 27) |
| ½ cup | vinegar |

Wash mangoes and wipe until completely dry. Peel and coarsely grate the mangoes, discard skin and stones. In a stainless steel bowl, combine grated mangoes with turmeric and salt and set aside. After about one hour, squeeze and discard all the water from the mangoes.

Combine the mangoes and sugar in a stainless steel saucepan and place over medium-high heat. Add the next 6 ingredients including cardamom and cook until the sugar has dissolved. The mixture will thicken within minutes. Remove and add mustard and vinegar. Mix well, let cool and remove to a jar with a tight lid. Serve as desired.

Yield: Approximately 5 cups.

## Carrot Chutney—*gajarni chutney*

The added ginger complements the sweet flavor of carrots in this delicious chutney. Serve with any appetizer or with any meal.

| | |
|---|---|
| 4 | medium carrots |
| 5 | serrano or jalapeño chilies, chopped |
| 1–inch piece | fresh ginger, peeled, chopped |
| 2–inch piece | mango turmeric, peeled, chopped (p. 32) (optional) |
| 2 teaspoons | salt, or to taste |
| 3 tablespoons | lemon juice |
| ¼ cup | brown sugar, or to taste |
| ½ cup | water |
| ½ teaspoon | ground anise seeds |
| 2 teaspoons | oil |
| 1 teaspoon | black mustard seeds |
| ½ teaspoon | *hing* (asafoetida) (optional) |
| 8 | *curry* leaves (optional) |

Peel, trim and cut the carrots lengthwise into halves. Remove center white or green part and discard. Chop carrots and place in the jar of a blender. Add the next 8 ingredients including anise and blend until smooth. Remove to a glass bowl.

Heat the oil in a small frying pan, over medium heat, and add mustard seeds. When mustard starts to crackle, add *hing* and *curry* leaves, if any. Cook until *hing* changes color. Add mixture to chutney, mix well, chill and serve.

Yield: Approximately 2 cups.

## Green Garlic Chutney—*leela lasanni chutney*

As the green garlic available in stores is often excessively large and less flavorful, I prefer to grow my own (p. 19). This refreshing chutney goes well with any appetizer or meal.

| | |
|---|---|
| 2 cups | trimmed and cut green garlic |
| 2 tablespoons | peanuts, toasted, peeled (p. 37) |
| 6 | serrano or jalapeño chilies |
| 1 cup | chopped cilantro |
| 1 tablespoon | lemon juice |
| ½ cup | water |
| 1 ½ teaspoons | salt, or to taste |

In a liquidizer or a blender grind together garlic with all the ingredients including salt. Remove to a bowl, chill and serve.

Yield: Approximately 1 ½ cups.

# Toasted Split Chickpea Chutney—*chana dal chutney*

This chutney is a favorite among both Maharashtrians and Gujaratis. Sometimes served with Bombay *bhel* (p. 178), this chutney goes well with fried appetizers.

| | |
|---|---|
| ½ cup | split chickpeas (*chana dal*) |
| 2 cups | water |
| 1 teaspoon | salt, or to taste |
| 2 tablespoons | unsweetened, grated coconut |
| 5 | serrano or jalapeño chilies |
| 1–inch piece | fresh ginger, peeled |
| ½ teaspoon | black pepper, ground |
| ½ cup | chopped cilantro |
| 1 tablespoon | lemon juice |
| 2 teaspoons | sugar, or to taste |
| 2 teaspoons | oil |
| 1 teaspoon | black mustard seeds |
| ½ teaspoon | *hing* (asafoetida) |
| 4 | *curry* leaves (optional) |

In a small frying pan, toast the *dal* on low heat, stirring occasionally, until it exudes a nice aroma and turns golden, about 7 minutes. Soak *dal* in 2 cups water overnight.

The next morning using a liquidizer or a blender, grind *dal*, with the water in which the *dal* was soaked, together with the next 8 ingredients including sugar. If the mixture dries, losing its creamy consistency, add a little more water while grinding. Remove to a bowl.

In a small frying pan, over medium heat, heat the oil and add mustard. When mustard starts to crackle, add *hing* and *curry* leaves, if any. When *hing* turns brown, add mixture to chutney. Mix well, chill and serve.
Yield: Approximately 2 cups.

## Lemon Peel Chutney—*limbuni chutney*

This wonderful chutney can be made when one is left with lots of lemon peels or lemons. Lemons with thinner skins are preferable, although one may use what is available. My guests at *The Ganges* would request this chutney every day. This tart and sweet chutney goes well with fried appetizers such as *samosa* (p. 140), or with any meal.

| | |
|---|---|
| 6 | preferably thin-skinned lemons **or** |
| Peels | from 10 lemons |
| 8 cups | water |
| 2 teaspoons | salt, or to taste |
| 1 teaspoon | chili powder |
| ¼ teaspoon | turmeric |
| 2 teaspoons | coarsely ground cumin seeds |
| 2 ½ cups | jaggery or brown sugar, or to taste |

In a stainless steel saucepan, boil lemons in water until limp, about 45 minutes. Remove from water, cut in halves and remove seeds, leaving fruit intact. In a food processor fitted with a metal blade, grind lemons and ingredients including jaggery. Remove chutney to a stainless steel saucepan and cook until it begins to simmer. If using lemon peels, add 3 tablespoons lemon juice to the chutney. Remove, cool and serve as desired.

Leftovers will keep in the refrigerator for several days.

Yield: Approximately 3 cups.

# Carambola or Star Fruit Chutney—*kamrukhni chutney*

Of the many ways in which this chutney may be made, I prefer the following recipe. Although carambola is expensive, the preparation is well worth it. Pick ripe fruit that is deep yellow and slightly soft: the recipe will be less sour and will require less sugar. Can be served with any meal.

| | |
|---|---|
| 2 | carambola or star fruit, trimmed, cut |
| ½ cup | peanuts, toasted, peeled (p. 37) |
| 1–inch piece | fresh ginger, peeled, chopped |
| ¼ cup | chopped cilantro |
| ½ cup | unsweetened, finely grated coconut |
| 1 tablespoon | oil |
| ½ teaspoon | *hing* (asafoetida) |
| ½ cup | brown sugar or to taste |
| 2 teaspoons | salt, or to taste |
| 2 teaspoons | ground coriander seeds |
| 1 teaspoon | ground cumin seeds |
| 1 cup | water |

In a blender or food processor fitted with a metal blade, grind carambola until fine, remove to a bowl and set aside. Using the same blender or a processor, grind peanuts with the next 3 ingredients including coconut, remove with ground carambola. You may add little water while grinding.

In a small stainless steel saucepan over medium heat, heat oil and add *hing*. When *hing* turns brown, add carambola and peanut mixture, stir well. When it starts to simmer, add remaining ingredients including water, letting mixture come to a boil on medium-low heat. Remove to a bowl, let cool and serve.

Leftovers will keep in the refrigerator for several days.
Yield: Approximately 2 cups.

## Tomato and Onion Relish—*tametane kandani kachumber*

This recipe is simple, colorful and extremely tasty. I recommend that this relish be consumed on the same day as when it is prepared. If kept overnight, the onions wilt, and the relish assumes a watery consistency. When I am left with this relish, however, I add it to recipes the next day. Goes well with steamed appetizers, *khichadi* (p. 320), *dal dhokli* (p. 360) and with Indian breads.

| | |
|---|---|
| 1 cup | finely cut roma tomatoes |
| ½ cup | finely cut yellow onions |
| 1 teaspoon | salt, or to taste |
| 2 teaspoons | toasted, coarsely ground cumin seeds |
| 2 teaspoons | sugar, or to taste |
| 1 tablespoon | chopped cilantro, for garnish |

In a glass bowl, combine tomatoes with the next 4 ingredients including sugar. Garnish with cilantro and chill before serving.
Yield: 1 ½ cups.

## Cucumber Relish—*kakdini kachumber*

Fresh cucumbers and chilies combine in this recipe to create a cooling, refreshing relish with a slightly spicy aftertaste. Serve as an accompaniment to any meal.

| | |
|---|---|
| 3 medium | cucumbers, peeled, cubed ½–inch |
| 1 teaspoon | salt |
| 1 teaspoon | sugar, or to taste |
| 2 | serrano or jalapeño chilies, chopped, |
| 2 tablespoons | crushed cilantro |
| 1 teaspoon | toasted, coarsely ground cumin seeds |
| 2 tablespoons | coarsely ground *dalia* (p. 29) (optional) |
| 2 teaspoons | lemon juice |
| 2 tablespoons | chopped cilantro, for garnish |

Combine cucumber and salt and set aside for at least 10 minutes. Squeeze water from cucumber, discard water and remove cucumber to a bowl. Add sugar and the next 5 ingredients including lemon juice and mix well. Chill and serve garnished with cilantro.
Serves 6.

## Mango and Onion Relish—*keri kandani kachumber*

This relish is best made at the beginning of the mango season, when the fruit tends to be very tender. Goes well with any rice and *dal* preparation or with any meal.

| | |
|---|---|
| 3 small | unripe mangoes, peeled, grated |
| 1 teaspoon | salt, or to taste |
| ¼ cup | finely cut onions |
| 1 teaspoon | toasted, coarsely ground cumin seeds |
| 2 teaspoons | sugar, or to taste |
| 1 | serrano or jalapeño chili, seeded, chopped |
| ¼ teaspoon | chili powder |
| 2 tablespoons | chopped cilantro, for garnish |

Wash, wipe, peel and coarsely grate the mangoes. Add salt, mix well and squeeze all the water from the mango, discard water and place the fruit in a bowl. Add onions and the next 4 ingredients including chili powder. Mix well. Chill and serve garnished with cilantro.
Makes: Approximately 1 cup.

## Green Papaya Relish—*kacha papayani kachumber*

Unripe green papayas are available year-round. I recommend searching for them in Asian markets or in farmers' markets. I particularly enjoy this relish with snacks or crisp Indian breads such as Festive Surti *Puri* (p. 421).

| | |
|---|---|
| 1 medium | green unripe papaya |
| ½ cup | peanuts, toasted, peeled, coarsely ground (p. 37) |
| 2 teaspoons | grated mango turmeric (optional) |
| 1–inch piece | fresh ginger, peeled, finely chopped |
| 2 | serrano or jalapeño chilies, seeded, chopped |
| 2 teaspoons | sugar, or to taste |
| ½ teaspoon | black pepper |
| 2 teaspoons | lemon juice |
| 2 teaspoons | oil |
| ½ teaspoon | cumin seeds |
| ¼ teaspoon | fennel seeds |
| ¼ teaspoon | black mustard seeds |
| 2 tablespoons | chopped cilantro, for garnish |

Wash, peel and cut papaya into halves. Remove seeds, if any, and coarsely grate. Remove papaya to a bowl. Add peanuts and the next 6 ingredients including lemon juice. Mix well.

In a small frying pan, heat oil over medium heat, and add cumin, fennel and mustard. When cumin starts to sizzle and mustard crackle, add oil mixture to papaya and mix well. Chill and serve garnished with cilantro. Serves 6–8.

## Variation: Spicy Green Papaya Relish—*papayani chhin*

The following version of the above recipe includes chickpea flour, which yields a slightly drier, nuttier condiment.

| | |
|---|---|
| 1 small | green papaya |
| 3 tablespoons | oil |
| ½ teaspoon | black mustard seeds |
| ½ teaspoon | *hing* (asafoetida) |
| 4 | serrano or jalapeño chilies, chopped |
| ¼ cup | chickpea flour |
| ½ teaspoon | salt, or to taste |
| ½ teaspoon | turmeric |
| 2 tablespoons | water, or as required |

Peel papaya and cut into halves. Remove seeds, if any. Cut each half into quarters and each quarter, lengthwise, into two. Cut each segment into about 2–inch long and ½–inch thick slices. Set aside.

In a small saucepan over medium heat, heat oil and add mustard, add *hing* when mustard starts to crackle. Add chilies when *hing* turns brown. Cook for 1 minute and add papaya. Cook for 5 additional minutes.

Mix flour, salt and turmeric and add to papaya and mix well. Cook on low heat for 3 minutes, stirring well. Gradually add in the water. Stir while cooking, until almost dry. Serve with any meal.

Serves 4–6.

## Daikon Relish—*muli kachumber*

I offer this relish recipe here exactly as my mother prepared it. Fragrant fenugreek and daikon make this a delicious accompaniment for hot *parotha* (p. 411) or *chapati* (p. 404). As a child I often enjoyed eating this in place of vegetable dishes.

| | |
|---|---|
| 6 cups | chopped daikon with greens |
| 2 teaspoons | salt, or to taste |
| 2 teaspoons | oil |
| ½ teaspoon | fenugreek seeds |
| ½ teaspoon | *hing* (asafoetida) |
| 2 teaspoons | lemon juice |

Wash and drain daikon before cutting. Cut white part into tiny cubes and finely chop the greens. Combine cut cubes, greens and salt in a bowl. Set aside for about 20 minutes. Squeeze all the liquid from the daikon mixture. Discard liquid and place daikon in a bowl.

Heat oil in a medium frying pan over medium heat, and add fenugreek seeds. Add *hing* when fenugreek turns slightly brown. When *hing* turns brown, add daikon. Add lemon juice, mix well and serve warmed through. Serve with any Indian bread.

Serves: 4–6.

## *Papadum* Relish—*papadni kachumber*

When you are left with broken toasted or fried *papadum*, you can make an interesting relish combined with onions, coconut and green chilies. No extra salt is required for the recipe, since the *papadum* are already salted. Serve with any meal.

| | |
|---|---|
| 1 cup | crumbled *papadum* |
| ¼ cup | finely cut onions |
| 3 | serrano or jalapeño chilies, chopped finely |
| 2 tablespoons | unsweetened, finely grated coconut. |
| 2 tablespoons | chopped cilantro |

In a bowl, combine all the ingredients for relish and serve. Serves 4–6.

## Mango Relish with Cumin—*chhundo*

There are two ways to make this relish. In India, and especially Gujarat, during the mango season, it is cooked under the sun and is called *tadka, chhaya no chhundo*. The process takes about 15 days. More conveniently, this relish may be prepared on the stovetop. Once the mangoes are grated the cooking time is not long. Serve with any meal.

| | |
|---|---|
| 8–10 | unripe, firm mangoes, peeled, coarsely grated |
| 4 ½ cups | sugar, or as needed |
| 1 tablespoon | salt, or to taste |
| 2 teaspoons | toasted, coarsely ground cumin seeds |
| 1 teaspoon | chili powder |

Wash and peel the mangoes. Discard skin and coarsely grate the fruit, discarding stones (seeds), if any. Using your hands, squeeze the grated mangoes. The extracted liquid may be saved for use in recipes for dishes that require a tart taste. The grated mango should measure about 3 cups. Each cup of squeezed mango will require about 1 ½ cups sugar. Make sure to measure both the mango and the sugar.

In a stainless steel saucepan, combine mango and sugar and set aside for about 1 hour. During this time the sugar will melt partially. Place the saucepan on the stove over medium-high heat. Gently stir the mango and sugar. When the sugar melts completely, the syrup will start to thicken and mango shreds will turn transparent, about 10 minutes. Remove saucepan from heat and add remaining 3 ingredients. Mix well and let cool. Store in a tightly fitted jar. Will keep for several months, when stored at room temperature.

Yield: Approximately 5 cups.

## Mango Relish with Cardamom—*murrabbo*

This recipe is popular amongst fasting Gujaratis for whom salt and turmeric are proscribed on specific religious days. An aromatic, delicious recipe, this relish may be served with any meal—when young, my children would enjoy this with toast at breakfast.

| | |
|---|---|
| 8–10 | unripe, firm mangoes, peeled and coarsely grated |
| 4 ½ cups | sugar, or as needed |
| ¼ teaspoon | crushed saffron |
| 2 teaspoons | coarsely ground cardamom seeds |

Wash and peel the mangoes. Discard skin and coarsely grate the fruit, discarding stones (seeds), if any. Using your hands, squeeze the grated mangoes. The extracted liquid may be saved for use in recipes for dishes that require a tart taste. The grated mango should measure about 3 cups. Each cup of squeezed mango will require about 1 ½ cups sugar. Make sure to measure both the mango and the sugar. In a medium stainless steel saucepan, combine mango and sugar and set aside for about 1 hour.

Place the saucepan over medium-high heat and let the mixture come to a full boil, stir well. When the syrup begins to thicken and mango shreds look transparent—about 10 minutes—add saffron and cardamom and cook for about 1 minute.

Remove, let cool and store in a clean jar. Can be stored at room temperature.

Yield: Approximately 5 cups.

## Carrot Relish—*gajarno chhundo*

This easy to make relish can serve as a quick stand-in for mango relish when unripe mangoes are unavailable. I used to serve this at *The Ganges* when out of fruit chutney.

| | |
|---|---|
| 1 cup | sugar |
| ½ cup | water |
| 1 cup | finely grated carrots |
| 1 teaspoon | salt, or to taste |
| ¼ teaspoon | chili powder, or to taste |
| 2 teaspoons | toasted, coarsely ground cumin seeds |
| 1 tablespoon | lemon juice or vinegar |

Combine sugar and water in a medium saucepan and bring to a full boil. Lower the heat and let the syrup simmer for about 3 minutes.

Wash, peel and grate carrots and add to sugar syrup. Mix well and bring the mixture to a boil on high heat. Cook relish for 2 minutes. Remove, add the remaining ingredients, mix well and set aside to cool. Remove to a jar and refrigerate.

Yield: Approximately 2 cups.

## Pineapple Relish with Cumin—*ananasno chhundo*

In Gujarat, this relish is commonly prepared with mangoes rather than pineapple. I make this with either canned or fresh pineapple—either way, the results are wonderful. Cumin and chili powder accent the sweet pineapple in this assertive, strongly flavored relish.

Prepared with saffron, the fragrant relish makes a special homemade gift. Serve with any appetizer or any meal.

| | |
|---|---|
| 1 medium | fresh pineapple, peeled, cut into ½–inch cubes **or** |
| 3 (15-ounce) cans | cubed pineapple |
| 2 cups | sugar, or to taste |
| 1 cup | water |
| 1 teaspoon | chili powder |
| 1 tablespoon | toasted, coarsely ground cumin seeds |
| 2 teaspoons | salt, or to taste |
| ¼ teaspoon | saffron, crushed (optional) |

If using canned pineapple, strain and discard liquid from the pineapple and set the cubes aside. If using fresh, peel the pineapple, remove all the eyes and cut it into cubes, discarding the hard, core of the fruit. Strain the liquid and set the cubes aside. Retain pineapple juice for any other use.

Over high heat, bring sugar and water to a full boil in a medium stainless steel saucepan, stirring intermittently. Boil 12 minutes over high heat or until the syrup thickens. To test, cool a few drops of the syrup, and place a drop on the thumb. Press down with index finger, then slowly lift. Tiny threads should appear between the 2 fingers. Alternatively, place a drop of liquid on a small piece of flat, waxed paper; if the liquid does not spread, the syrup is ready.

Once the syrup has been prepared, add pineapple cubes and continue boiling. Add spices including saffron, and cook 10 minutes. Remove from heat and let cool.

Transfer to a glass jar with a tight fitting lid. The relish does not require refrigeration and will keep until finished!

Yield: Approximately 5 cups.

## Cabbage Relish—*kobijnu kachumber*

This preparation is quite common in Gujarat and Maharashtra. This condiment may be served as a vegetable.

| | |
|---|---|
| 1 medium head | cabbage, finely cut |
| 2 teaspoons | salt, or to taste |
| 2 teaspoons | oil |
| 1 teaspoon | black mustard seeds |
| ½ teaspoon | *hing* (asafoetida) |
| 2 | serrano or jalapeño chilies, finely chopped |
| ¼ cup | chopped cilantro, for garnish |

Discard top two layers of the cabbage. Cut the cabbage into halves, cut each half into a quarter and chop each quarter finely. Place chopped cabbage in a bowl and sprinkle over with salt. Mix well and set aside for about 20 minutes. Using your hands squeeze water from the cabbage, set aside, discard water.

In a medium saucepan, heat the oil over medium heat and add mustard seeds. When mustard starts to crackle, add *hing*, when *hing* turns brown, add cabbage. Stir briskly, remove pan from heat and add chopped chilies. Mix well and serve garnished with cilantro.

Serves 4–6.

## *Raitas*

*Raitas* can be made using any vegetable, fruit (fresh or dry) or nuts. The one exception to this is a variation included in this book for *methkoot* (p. 110), where I have used several grains and spices with yogurt. If vegetables such as cauliflower and potatoes are used to make *raitas*, they are cooked and chilled before they are added to yogurt. If using leafy greens, it is best to wash, chop and lightly cook the greens before adding to yogurt.

I take care to select appropriate *raitas* as accompaniments to specific dishes. For example, a host(ess) must take into consideration the fact that a cauliflower *raita* would not go well with a cauliflower or potato vegetable. *Raitas* using fruit can be offered with meals where fruit is neither used in any preparation nor offered at the end of the meal. While sugar is never added to a fruit *raita*, cumin seeds, green chilies and other spices are common ingredients. Clearly, the emphasis is on complex, contrasting flavors.

Generally, Indians prefer to use homemade yogurt for making *raitas* as this yogurt tends to be sweeter than store-bought brands. For certain *raitas*, the yogurt may be drained to obtain a thicker, sweeter yogurt.

## Cucumber *Raita* with Green Chilies—*kakdinu raitu*

This may well be India's most popular *raita*. I suspect each Indian knows a particular variation. It is a refreshing combination of textures and flavors and is especially pleasing as a complement to a spicy dish.

| | |
|---|---|
| 1 medium | cucumber, trimmed, peeled, grated |
| ½ teaspoon | salt, or to taste |
| 3 cups | yogurt |
| 3 | serrano or jalapeño chilies, ground |
| 1 teaspoon | toasted, coarsely ground cumin seeds |
| 2 tablespoons | chopped cilantro, for garnish |

Trim, peel and coarsely grate cucumber. Place grated cucumber in a bowl, sprinkle with salt, toss, and let sit for 20 minutes. Using your hands press out liquid from the cucumber, discard the liquid. Combine cucumber, yogurt and remaining 3 ingredients. Chill for about two hours before serving.

Serve garnished with cilantro.

Yield: Approximately 4 cups.

### Carrot *Raita*—*gajarnu raitu*

When using carrots, Indians prefer to remove the center greenish or white part. Prepared with red-orange carrots and white yogurt, this *raita* is attractive and tasty. For added color, garnish with cilantro. Serve with any meal.

| | |
|---|---|
| 5 medium | carrots, trimmed, coarsely grated |
| 3 cups | thickened yogurt (p. 58) |
| 1 ½ teaspoons | salt, or to taste |
| 1 teaspoon | black mustard seeds, ground (p. 27) |
| 1 teaspoon | sugar, or to taste |
| 2 tablespoons | chopped cilantro, for garnish |

Trim, peel and coarsely grate carrots. In a bowl, combine grated carrots with the next 4 ingredients including sugar and garnish with cilantro. Chill before serving.

Yield: Approximately 3 cups.

## Cauliflower *Raita*—*flowernu raitu*

This is a popular *raita* in most parts of India, only the ingredients vary. Do not use cauliflower stems for this recipe; save them for other dishes. Serve with any Indian meal when cauliflower is not on the menu.

| | |
|---|---|
| 2 cups | chopped cauliflower, steamed |
| 3 cups | plain yogurt |
| 2 teaspoons | salt, or to taste |
| 2 | serrano or jalapeño chilies, seeded, chopped |
| 2 tablespoons | crushed cilantro |
| 2 teaspoons | toasted, coarsely ground cumin seeds |
| 1 teaspoon | sugar, or to taste |
| 2 teaspoons | oil |
| 1 teaspoon | black mustard seeds |
| ½ teaspoon | *hing* (asafoetida) |
| 2 tablespoons | chopped cilantro, for garnish |

Wash the cauliflower before cutting. Steam cauliflower briefly, when cool combine cauliflower with yogurt and the next 5 ingredients including sugar. Heat oil in a small frying pan over medium heat, and add mustard seeds. When mustard starts to crackle, add *hing*. When *hing* turns brown, remove pan from heat and add oil mixture to cauliflower. Mix well, chill and serve garnished with cilantro.

Yield: Approximately 5 cups.

## Spinach *Raita*—*bhajinu raitu*

This recipe is slightly different from the one in my first cookbook. Featuring spinach cooked with mustard and sesame, both versions are delicious. Serve with Indian bread.

| | |
|---|---|
| 2 teaspoons | oil |
| 1 teaspoon | black mustard seeds |
| ½ teaspoon | *hing* (asafoetida) |
| 1 tablespoon | sesame seeds |
| 4 | *curry* leaves (optional) (p. 16) |
| 6 cups | finely cut spinach leaves, washed, drained dry |
| 3 cups | yogurt |
| 2 teaspoons | salt, or to taste |
| 2 tablespoons | chopped cilantro |
| 1 ½ teaspoons | sugar, or to taste |
| 2 | serrano or jalapeño chilies, ground |
| ½–inch piece | fresh ginger, peeled, ground |
| 1 tablespoon | grated carrots, for garnish |

In a medium saucepan, heat the oil over medium heat and add mustard seeds. When mustard starts to crackle, add *hing*, sesame seeds and *curry* leaves, if any. Immediately add spinach and lower the heat. Cook, stirring well, for about 3 minutes. Remove from heat and let cool completely.

In a bowl combine spinach with yogurt and the next 5 ingredients including ginger. Mix well and serve garnished with carrots.

Yield: Approximately 4 cups.

## Cilantro *Raita*—*kothmirnu raitu*

This *raita* is very refreshing and can be served with any meal. If mango turmeric (p. 32) is unavailable, add 1–inch extra of grated ginger.

| | |
|---|---|
| 5 cups | yogurt |
| 1 cup | very finely chopped cilantro |
| ½ cup | finely chopped pitted dates |
| 2 | serrano or jalapeño chilies, seeded, finely chopped |
| 2–inch piece | mango turmeric, peeled, finely chopped (optional) |
| ½–inch piece | fresh ginger, peeled, grated |
| 1 ½ teaspoons | salt, or to taste |

Thicken the yogurt following instructions on page (58). Combine thickened yogurt with all the ingredients including salt. Chill before serving. Yield: Approximately 3 cups.

## Mint *Raita*—*fudinanu raitu*

Mint leaves impart a delicate flavor to foods with which they are cooked. This pleasing *raita* goes well with both vegetarian and (God forbid!!) non-vegetarian curries.

| | |
|---|---|
| ¼ cup | mint leaves, minced |
| 3 cups | yogurt |
| 2 | serrano or jalapeño chilies, seeded, chopped |
| 1–inch piece | fresh ginger, peeled, grated |
| 1 teaspoon | salt, or to taste |

Finely mince mint leaves with a cleaver or chef's knife. Remove to a bowl. Combine mint with yogurt and the remaining ingredients including salt. Chill and serve.

Yield: Approximately 3 cups.

## Onion *Raita*—*kandanu raitu*

This *raita* was my father's favorite and was often served with *dal dhokli* (p. 360). It goes well with any rice and *dal* preparation. Do not make in excess, as the *raita* will become watery the next day.

| | |
|---|---|
| 3 cups | yogurt |
| ¾ cup | finely chopped onions |
| 2 teaspoons | toasted, coarsely ground cumin seeds |
| 1 teaspoon | salt, or to taste |
| 2 tablespoons | chopped cilantro, for garnish |

In a bowl, combine yogurt with onions, cumin and salt. Chill and serve garnished with cilantro.

Yield: 4 cups.

## Dumpling *Raita*—*bundi raita*

This *raita* is very popular with North Indians. Making *bundi* is time consuming but the *raita* is well worth the time. Serve with any meal.

### *Bundi:*

| | |
|---|---|
| 1 cup | chickpea flour |
| ¼ teaspoon | salt, or to taste |
| ½ teaspoon | chili powder |
| ¼ cup | water or as needed |
| Oil | for frying |

### Yogurt mix:

| | |
|---|---|
| 3 cups | yogurt |
| ½ teaspoon | salt, or to taste |
| 1 teaspoon | toasted, coarsely ground cumin seeds |
| 2 tablespoons | chopped cilantro, for garnish |

### *Bundi*:

In a bowl, combine chickpea flour with salt and chili powder. Add water to make a thick batter. Heat about 1–inch of oil in a frying pan over medium heat. Lower the heat and drop batter through a slotted spoon or an Indian sieve (illus. p. 50). The batter will form tiny drops, or *bundi*, which will float to the top of the oil as they fry. Cook for a few more seconds or until the *bundi* are golden yellow in color. Remove with a slotted spoon and drain on paper towels. Repeat until the batter is used up. Let cool.

### Yogurt Mix:

In a bowl, combine yogurt with *bundi,* salt and cumin. Serve garnished with cilantro. Can also be garnished with red chili powder.

Yield: Approximately 4 cups.

## Dry Fruit *Raita*—*suka mevanu raitu*

Any dry fruit available in the market can be used to make this *raita*. You may also add chopped nuts, if desired. I like to use dried, unsweetened papaya, dried apricots and chopped walnuts.

| | |
|---|---|
| 3 cups | yogurt |
| ¼ cup | dried apricots, chopped finely |
| ¼ cup | dried unsweetened papaya, chopped finely |
| 2 tablespoons | walnuts, chopped finely |
| 6 | serrano or jalapeño chilies, ground |
| ¼ cup | finely chopped cilantro |
| 1 ½ teaspoons | salt, or to taste |
| 1 teaspoon | toasted, coarsely ground cumin seeds |

Combine yogurt with all ingredients including cumin. Chill and serve. Yield: Approximately 3 ½ cups.

### Banana *Raita*—*kelanu raitu*

For this recipe, slightly mashed or sliced banana can be used. This sweet and spicy *raita* is among my favorites. It goes well with any spicy meal.

| | |
|---|---|
| 3 cups | yogurt, preferably thickened (p. 58) |
| 2 | bananas, peeled, sliced thin |
| 3 | serrano or jalapeño chilies, seeded, chopped finely |
| 2 teaspoons | salt, or to taste |
| 2 tablespoons | finely chopped cilantro |

If using thickened yogurt, drain plain yogurt following directions on page (58). Combine yogurt with all the ingredients including cilantro, chill and serve.

Yield: Approximately 4 cups.

## Fresh Fruit and Nut *Raita*—*durbari raita*

This version of *raita* lends itself to any combination of fruit and nuts. I like to use walnuts with bananas, apples, mangoes or kiwi. Sweet oranges and tangerines may also be used. The blend of sweet fruit and sharp, hot chilies is lively and refreshing. Serve this unique *raita* with any meal.

| | |
|---|---|
| 6 cups | yogurt |
| 1 teaspoon | salt, or to taste |
| 2 tablespoons | orange juice concentrate |
| 4 | serrano or jalapeño chilies, ground |
| 2 teaspoons | toasted, coarsely ground cumin seeds |
| 2 cups | fruit of your choice, peeled, cut into small pieces |
| ¼ cup | chopped nuts (of your choice) |
| 2 tablespoons | chopped cilantro, for garnish |

Thicken yogurt following directions on page (58). Mix thickened yogurt with the next 4 ingredients including cumin. Fold fruit and nuts into yogurt mixture. Chill and serve garnished with cilantro.
Serves: 6–8.

## Grains and Spice *Raita*—*methkoot*

Faced with a shortage of vegetables and fruit, mother came up with her own version of this recipe, which is popular in some areas of Gujarat. In fact, this *raita* balances meals in which many fruits and vegetables are served. Indians frequently make the grain mixture in large quantities, storing it in a tightly covered jar and using it whenever required.

I sometimes add this mixture to dry vegetable recipes (without sauce) to add texture—for example, cabbage or dry potato vegetables.

| | |
|---|---|
| 1-½ cup | split chickpeas (*chana dal*) |
| ¼ cup | split Indian black beans (*urid dal*) |
| ½ cup | split mung beans (mung *dal*) |
| ½ cup | cumin seeds |
| 1 cup | coriander seeds |
| 1 tablespoon | cardamom seeds |
| 8 | cloves |
| 2 teaspoons | black mustard seeds |
| 10 three–inch sticks | cinnamon, broken |
| 1 teaspoon | dry ginger powder |
| 2 teaspoons | chili powder |
| 2 teaspoons | turmeric (optional) |
| ¼ teaspoon | *hing* (asafoetida) (optional) |

**Grain Mix:**

In a medium frying pan over low heat, toast all the three *dals* together, stirring well, until they exude a nice aroma and turn slightly golden, about 15 minutes. Remove and set aside to cool.

In the same frying pan, add cumin and the next 5 ingredients including cinnamon. Toast on low heat, stirring well until they change color, about 15 minutes. Remove and let cool.

Using a coffee grinder or a mill, grind the toasted *dals* until slightly coarse and remove to a bowl. Using the same grinder, grind cumin seeds mixture and combine with ground *dals*. Add the remaining ingredients, mix well and store in a tightly covered jar. This grain and spice mixture may be stored for extended periods of time.

Yield: Approximately 2 cups.

### *Raita*:

| | |
|---|---|
| 2 cups | yogurt |
| 3 tablespoons | grain and spice mixture (preceding recipe) |
| ¾ teaspoon | salt, or to taste |
| 2 tablespoons | chopped cilantro, for garnish |

Combine yogurt with grain and spice mixture. Add salt and mix well. For a thicker consistency, add more grain and spice mix. Garnish with cilantro, chill and serve. Note that this *raita* will thicken as it cools.

Yield: Approximately 2 ¼ cups.

## Spicy Hot *Raita*—*tikhari*

Golden raisins and chili combine to yield a spicy-sweet accompaniment to any lightly-spiced meal. Alternatively, serve with a second, fruit or vegetable *raita* alongside a meal.

| | |
|---|---|
| 2 teaspoons | oil |
| 6 | dried, whole red chili peppers, toasted |
| 6 cloves | garlic, peeled |
| ½ cup | peanuts, toasted, peeled (p. 37) |
| 1 teaspoon | salt, or to taste |
| 1 tablespoon | golden raisins, chopped |
| 3 cups | yogurt |
| 2 tablespoons | chopped cilantro, for garnish |

In a small frying pan, heat oil and add red chili peppers. Fry until the peppers change color to dark red. Using a slotted spoon, remove to paper towels and let cool. In a liquidizer or a food processor fitted with a metal blade, grind until almost smooth chili peppers with the next 4 ingredients including raisins. Remove to a bowl, add yogurt and mix well. Garnish with cilantro, chill and serve.

Yield: Approximately 3 ½ cups.

## Potato *Raita*—*batetanu raitu*

Flavored with ginger and green chilies, this lively *raita* is simple and delicious. Serve with any meal.

| | |
|---|---|
| 3 large | potatoes, boiled, peeled, cubed small |
| 1–inch piece | fresh ginger, peeled, chopped |
| 2 | serrano or jalapeño chilies, chopped |
| ¾ teaspoon | salt, or to taste |
| ¼ teaspoon | chili powder or to taste |
| 2 cups | yogurt |
| 2 tablespoons | chopped cilantro, for garnish |

In a bowl, combine cubed potatoes with the next 5 ingredients including yogurt. Chill and serve garnished with cilantro.
Serves: 6–8.

# Pickles

Generally speaking, four main varieties of pickles are made in India, the flavors of which result from combinations of sweet, sour and hot ingredients. The varieties are hot; sweet and sour; sweet and hot; and sweet, sour and hot. Perhaps the most common pickles are either mango or lemon, though many households prepare a large variety of pickles using number of fruits and vegetables to last the year-round. While many pickling ingredients are prepared from scratch, some Indians also make extra pickling spice (p. 115), used for "instant pickles," such as the carrot and cucumber preparation (p. 124).

Indians prefer to use peanut or sesame oil in their pickles. They heat the oil to a smoking point and let it cool before adding to prepared pickles. Some Indians also use castor oil in the pickles to keep the fruit or vegetables crisp. I wish that this would also work for human beings! The ingredients for most of the recipes in this section are commonly available. I should mention that of all pickles, my guests at *The Ganges* preferred the sweet and hot mango (p. 118) and lemon preparations (p. 120).

## Pickling Spice-Basic—*athanano masalo*

This spice mixture is basic and very much Gujarati. Fennel, mustard seeds, coriander seeds and sometimes jaggery are added to make other varieties of pickles, popular in different regions of India. I make this mixture once a year and store it in the refrigerator. I have limited the amount of oil in the recipe, and have used castor oil, as it maintains the crispness of the pickled fruit or vegetables. However, any oil of your choice may be used.

I advise the use of a bright red chili powder, in order to add color to the recipe. Table salt may be used when the coarse variety is unavailable. Lastly, do note that you may proportionately reduce the quantity of the ingredients in order to make the amount of pickling spice you require.

| | |
|---|---|
| 1 ½ pounds | coarse salt, lightly toasted |
| ¾ pound | fenugreek seeds, toasted, coarsely ground |
| 4 tablespoons | corn oil |
| 2 tablespoons | castor oil (optional) |
| 1 ½ teaspoons | *hing* (asafoetida) |
| ¾ pound | chili powder (*reshampatti* brand preferred) (p. 12) |
| ½ pound | turmeric |

In a wok, toast salt on low heat, stirring well to make sure it does not burn. When heated through, remove from heat and let cool.

In a frying pan, toast fenugreek, on low heat stirring well until golden in color, about 10 minutes. Remove and let cool. In a food processor fitted with a metal blade coarsely grind fenugreek, remove with salt.

In a frying pan over medium-high heat, heat both the oils together (if not using castor oil, use total 6 tablespoons corn oil) and add *hing*. When *hing* turns brown, add the oil mixture to salt and fenugreek mixture. Let cool completely.

Add chili powder and turmeric and mix well. Remove to a jar and refrigerate. Use as desired.

Yield: Approximately 3 pounds

**Note:** Once the oil mixture has been added to the fenugreek and salt, it is important to let the mixture cool completely before adding chili and turmeric. Adding spices to hot mixture will change the color of chili.

## Mango Pickle—*kerinu athanu or methia keri*

This is perhaps the most famous Indian pickle, though the spices very from region to region. If preferred, you may substitute another oil of your choice. This pickle is made in large quantities at the beginning of the mango season, when young, tender mangoes without stones arrive on the market. In the United States, they are best in March. Indian stores are likely the best source. You may even call them and place your order.

Serve with any Indian meal.

| | |
|---|---|
| 6 | tender, unripe, firm mangoes, cubed |
| 2 cups | pickling spice (preceding recipe) |
| 1 cup | corn oil, or as required |

Wash and wipe mangoes completely dry. Trim the mangoes on the stem side, cut into halves and quarters and cut each quarter into small cubes, about 1–inch in size. Discard stones, if any. Combine cubes with pickling spice and remove the pickle to a jar. Cover tightly and set aside.

After 12 hours, lightly toss the pickle in the jar. In a saucepan, heat the oil well and set aside to cool. Pour cold oil over the pickle, cover and set aside. Next morning, press the mango pieces with the back of a spoon so the oil will float to the top; otherwise the pickle will be spoiled. Actually mango and the spice mixture have to be drowned in oil. Pickle will be ready in about a week. Each time after taking out the pickle, press the rest in the jar with the back of a spoon so the oil will float to the top.

Yield: Approximately 4 cups.

## Sweet and Hot Mango Pickle—*kerinu galune tikhu athanu*

This popular Gujarati pickle is also made in the beginning of the mango season, with unripe fruit. I have also made the same recipe with slightly ripe mangoes, and the results were delicious.

If you decide to make this in large quantities and want to keep it for a long time, immerse the mangoes and spices in oil as in the preceding recipe. Serve with any Indian meal.

| | |
|---|---|
| 6 | tender, unripe mangoes, peeled, cubed small |
| 2 teaspoons | salt |
| ½ teaspoon | turmeric |
| ¼ cup | pickling spice (p. 115) |
| ¼ cup | cracked coriander seeds (p. 15) |
| ½ cup | jaggery (p. 26) |
| 2 tablespoons | cracked black mustard seeds (p. 27) |

In a glass bowl, combine mangoes, salt and turmeric. Set aside overnight, covered in a corner free from draft. The next day, mix well again, re-cover and set aside for another day. On the third morning, drain and spread mango pieces on a tray lined with paper towels and cheesecloth. Discard the liquid. Let the mangoes dry completely, about six hours. Remove to a bowl. Add pickling spice and coriander seeds.

Using a knife, cut jaggery into fine pieces and add to mangoes. Add mustard and mix well. Set aside covered for a day or until the jaggery melts completely. Mix well and remove to a jar. Serve as desired.
Yield: Approximately 3 cups.

## Sweet and Hot Carrot Pickle—*gajarnu athanu*

This tasty pickle should be made in small quantities, as it doesn't keep for more than one week.

| | |
|---|---|
| 6 medium | carrots, trimmed, peeled, cubed ¼–inch |
| 1 cup | fresh lemon juice |
| 2 teaspoons | salt, or to taste |
| 1 tablespoon | cracked black mustard seeds (p. 27) |
| ½ cup | oil |
| ¼ teaspoon | turmeric |
| 1 tablespoon | jaggery or brown sugar, or to taste |

Peel, trim and cut carrots into halves, remove white or green part from the center. Cut into ½–inch cubes. In a bowl combine carrots with salt and lemon juice and set aside, covered, overnight.

In the morning drain and spread carrots to dry on a tray lined with paper towels and cheesecloth. Only the outer layer of the carrots has to be dry (approximately six hours). Discard the liquid.

In a small bowl, add a little cold water to mustard and mix, stirring in one direction for about a minute. This will make the mustard more pungent. Remove carrots to a bowl. Add mustard and the remaining 3 ingredients, mixing well. Cover and set aside in a corner overnight. Serve next day with any meal. Leftovers can be refrigerated.

Yield: Approximately 2 cups.

## Sweet and Hot Lemon Pickle—*limbunu galu athanu*

This pickle is made almost all over India with slight differences in spice combinations. It will keep for an extended period of time, provided the lemon pieces are covered with the sauce. It may be refrigerated and makes an excellent gift any time of the year. Indians prefer to use thin-skinned lemons as they limp easily; however, any yellow variety can be used for this pickle. This sweet, sour and hot pickle was a favorite of many of our customers. Serve with any meal.

**Lemons:**

| | |
|---|---|
| 24 | lemons, about 2–inches in diameter |
| ½ cup | salt |
| 1 ½ teaspoons | turmeric |

**Sauce:**

| | |
|---|---|
| 9 cups | sugar |
| 1 ½ tablespoons | red hot chili powder, or to taste |
| 1 ½ teaspoons | *hing* (asafoetida) |
| 1 ½ tablespoons | salt, or to taste |

**Lemons:**

Wash and wipe each lemon well. Cut each into about 6 to 8 cubes (do not peel the lemons). Put cubed lemons in a container, add salt and turmeric and mix well. Cover and set aside in a cool place.

Toss lemons every day until they are limp enough that they stick, and cannot be tossed without a spoon, about 1 week. Afterwards, stir lemons with a spoon once a day total for about 2 ½ to 3 weeks or until they look soft.

Drain lemons in a colander for about two hours. Most salt and turmeric will drain at this point. Discard liquid. Lemon pieces will measure about 6 cups. Remove to a large bowl.

**Sauce:**

Add sugar and the 3 remaining sauce ingredients including salt to the lemons and mix well.

Set aside covered for 3 days or until the sugar has dissolved. I keep the bowl near a pilot light, especially during winter. The sugar will melt and make an extremely tasty pickle. Remove to a clean jar and store in a cool place.

Yield: Approximately 1 gallon.

## Dry Fruit Pickle—*suka mevanu athanu*

This is one of my favorite recipes, which I like to bottle and offer as a gift.

| | |
|---|---|
| 4 ounces | dried apricots, cubed small |
| 4 ounces | dried Greek or Indian figs, cubed small |
| 4 ounces | whole cashew nuts |
| 3 tablespoons | seedless black raisins |
| 1 ½ cups | lemon juice |
| 1 teaspoon | salt, or to taste |
| 3 teaspoons | chili powder, or to taste |
| ½ teaspoon | *hing* (asafoetida) |
| 2 tablespoons | cracked coriander seeds (p. 15) |
| 1 tablespoon | cracked black mustard seeds (p. 27) |
| 1 tablespoon | oil |
| 1 ¼ cups | sugar |

Cut apricots and figs into ½–inch pieces. In a glass bowl, combine apricots and figs with next 4 ingredients including salt, cover and set aside in a corner for 24 hours. The fruit will soak up most of the lemon juice.

Remove fruit to a colander and let drain for 10 minutes. Discard juice. Line a tray with paper towels and cheesecloth on top. Spread fruit over the cheesecloth in the tray in a single layer. Let dry in any part of the kitchen for 24 hours, or under the sun for about two hours.

In a bowl, combine chili powder with the remaining ingredients including sugar. Add dried fruit and mix well. Remove mixture to a clean, heatproof jar, cover and set aside until the sugar dissolves, about 3 days, stirring once every day. Store the jar in a warm place free of draft (such as a gas stove with a pilot light), but do not cook. Serve when the sugar has dissolved completely.

Yield: Approximately 4 cups.

## Unripe Cherry Pickle—*cherinu athanu*

In some parts of India, especially in Gujarat, berries known as *bor* are used to make pickles. They are a little smaller than cherries and are soaked in salt water, drained and dried before using in pickles. In the United States in absence of finding *bor*, I use bing cherries. Serve with any meal.

| | |
|---|---|
| 1 cup | water |
| 1 cup | sugar |
| 2 pounds | washed and pitted bing cherries |
| 2 teaspoons | toasted, coarsely ground cumin seeds |
| 1 teaspoon | chili powder, or to taste |
| 1 ½ teaspoons | salt, or to taste |

In a medium saucepan over high heat, bring water and sugar to a full boil. As the mixture continues to boil, it will thicken in about 5 minutes. Add cherries and next 3 ingredients including salt and lower the heat. Let the mixture cook for 3 minutes. Remove from heat, let cool. Remove to a jar. Yield: Approximately 5 cups.

## Fresh Carrot and Cucumber Pickle—*gajar kakdinu athanu*

This colorful, crunchy pickle is slightly pungent. I regularly prepared this very popular condiment at *The Ganges*.

| | |
|---|---|
| 1 cup | carrots, peeled, very finely chopped |
| 1 cup | pickling cucumber, peeled, finely cubed |
| 2 tablespoons | pickling spice (p. 115), or to taste |

Combine ingredients in a small bowl and serve fresh. Leftovers will keep 3 to 4 days in the refrigerator, after which the pickle will become watery.

Yield: Approximately 2 cups.

## Hot Chili Pickle—*marchanu athanu*

This spicy pickle is a favorite of most Indians and can be made every few days. Since no extra oil is added to this, it does not keep for long. Serve alongside any meal.

| | |
|---|---|
| 20 pieces | chilies of your choice |
| 2 teaspoons | salt, or to taste |
| 2 tablespoons | cracked fenugreek seeds (p. 119) |
| 3 tablespoons | cracked black mustard seeds (p. 27) |
| ¼ teaspoon | turmeric |
| ½ teaspoon | citric acid (*limbuna phool*) (p. 13) **or** |
| 2 tablespoons | lemon juice |
| 2 tablespoons | oil |

Wash and wipe chilies, remove and discard stems. With a knife, place a long cut into each chili lengthwise. Do not remove seeds. Set aside.

Combine salt with ingredients including oil and stuff the chilies through the cut. Remove to a bowl and set aside. If any stuffing is left over, spread it over the chilies. Cover and refrigerate for a day before serving.
Yield: 20 chilies.

## Hot and Sweet Chili Pickle—*marchanu tikhune galu athanu*

This sweet, sour and hot pickle is delicious and can be served with any meal. You may use any variety of chili, except *habanero*, which are extremely hot. *Ancho*, *Mulato*, *Cascabel* or Anaheim chilies are preferable for pickling. Serve with any Indian meal.

| | |
|---|---|
| ½ pound | chilies of your choice |
| ½ cup | cracked black mustard seeds (p. 27) |
| 2 teaspoons | salt, or to taste |
| 2 tablespoons | oil |
| ½ teaspoon | *hing* (asafoetida) |
| ¼ teaspoon | turmeric |
| ½ cup | jaggery (p. 26) |
| ¼ cup | lemon juice |

Wash, trim and cut chilies into about ½–inch pieces. Add mustard and salt and mix well. Heat the oil in a frying pan over medium heat and add *hing*. As soon as *hing* turns brown, remove and set aside to cool. When cool, add oil to chilies, add turmeric, and mix well.

Using a sharp knife, cut jaggery into small pieces. Place jaggery in a small saucepan over very low heat; jaggery will start to melt. As soon as the jaggery has melted and starts to bubble, add chili mixture and stir well. When the mixture comes to a boil, remove from heat and let cool.

Add lemon juice and mix well. Remove to a jar and serve as desired. Leftovers can be refrigerated.

Yield: Approximately 3 cups.

## **Raisin Pickle**—*drakshnu athanu*

In this recipe, sweet raisins are offset by vinegar, cumin and chili, resulting in a delicious, sweet-sour and hot pickle. This simple recipe goes well with any meal. The ingredients for this recipe are easily available.

| | |
|---|---|
| 2 cups | golden raisins |
| ¼ cup | white vinegar |
| 1 ½ cups | water |
| 1 ½ cups | sugar |
| 1 tablespoon | toasted, coarsely ground cumin seeds |
| 1 teaspoon | chili powder, or to taste |
| 1 ½ teaspoons | salt, or to taste |

In a small glass bowl, combine raisins with vinegar and set aside. In a small saucepan over high heat, combine sugar and water and bring it to a boil. Lower the heat to medium after the sugar has dissolved. Cook the syrup for 5 more minutes.

Add raisins together with vinegar and cook for 3 minutes or until the raisins swell. Add remaining ingredients and cook for 1 minute. Remove, let cool.

Remove to a jar and serve as desired. Leftovers will keep refrigerated for a long time.

**Note:** This mixture may be finely ground into an exquisite chutney.
Yield: Approximately 4 cups.

# APPETIZERS, SNACKS OR ONE-DISH MEALS

## Fried Appetizers

*Pakora* Flour (Mix)—*pakora atta*
Fried, Battered Vegetables—*pakora* or *bhajia*
Chili *Pakora*—*mirch pakora*
Mashed Banana *Pakora*—*kela methi pakora* (dairy)
Triangular Pastry Stuffed with Vegetables—*samosa*
Variation: Traditional *Samosa*
Split Mung Patties—mung *dal kachori*
Mixed Bean Patties with Yogurt—*dahivada* (dairy)
Lentil Kebabs—*masoorna muthia*
Split Chickpea Patties—*chana dal vada*
Spicy Mashed Potato Rounds—*bateta vada*
*Papadum*-Lentil Wafers—*papadum* or *papad*
Rice Wafers—*papdi*

## Non-fried Appetizers

Steamed Savory Cake—*dhokla*
Cucumber Savory Cake—*kakdina dhokla*
Steamed Savory Rounds—*idlee* (dairy)
Variation: Black Bean and Rice Cake with Cracked Pepper—*idada*
Chickpea Flour Rolls—*khandvi* or *pilla patodi* (dairy)
Baked Savory Cake—*handvo* or *bhakhar*
Bean and Spinach Cake—*chola chanano handvo*
Spicy Spinach Squares—*bhajina dhokla* (no oil)

128

Savory Cabbage Cake—*kobijno bhakhar* (dairy)
Spinach Kebabs—*palakna muthia*
Steamed Spinach and Peas Rounds—*palak vatanana muthia*

## Snacks

Rice Flour Curls—*chakri* (dairy)
Chickpea Flour Noodles—*sev*
Stuffed Crispy Rounds—*mathdi* (dairy)
Bombay Snack Mix—*bhelpuri*
Cream of Wheat with Yogurt and Cashew Nuts—*upama* (dairy)
Butter Biscuits—*Surti khari biscuit* (dairy)
Cardamom Cookies—*nankhatai*
Toasted Almonds—*shekeli badam*
Toasted Peanuts—*shekeli shing or moongphali*

## Appetizers, Snacks or One-Dish Meals

Street-side food vendors are a common sight throughout India. Seated under canvas awnings on busy streets or in tiny alleys, they prepare and sell everything from steaming hot, spicy Indian tea or *chai*, fresh vegetable-filled *samosa*, to complete meals of *chapati*, vegetables, rice and *dals*. Morning, afternoon and evening, small crowds gather around these stands to savor the variety of food prepared over portable stoves. My son maintains that the best food to be eaten in India is from these stalls, though I would caution the adventurous to be aware of both hygiene and traveler's illnesses!

In this chapter, I have included a range of both fried and non-fried appetizers, snacks and one-dish meals. For the health-conscious, omitting oil can further reduce the fat content of the non-fried appetizers. In terms of food storage, fried snacks can generally keep for days or even weeks, and non-fried appetizers are generally consumed the same day they are made, though they will keep in the refrigerator for 3–4 days.

Chutneys and not *raitas* are generally served with appetizers, though yogurt can be added to hot chutneys to make them mild. When entertaining, I recommend complementing appetizers with more than one chutney.

# Appetizers—Fried and Non-fried

The concept of appetizers, or hors d'oeuvres is Western in character. Indians tend to refrain from appetizers before a meal except on very special occasions or at elaborate, formal dinners. What is an appetizer in Western cuisine is therefore an integral part of the Indian meal. In Indian cuisine, "appetizers" are intended to stimulate the appetite and are served in small portions, usually arriving with the meal itself. With the increased Western influences upon Indians, however, this has begun to change

The Gujarati term for appetizers, *farsan*, means "delicate, and refers to the care and attention that are devoted to the preparation of appetizers, a specialty of Gujarati and more generally, Indian cuisine.

When planning an Indian meal, the cook must consider the menu as a whole. The flavors of chutneys and appetizers must complement not only each other, but also the main dishes of the meal. Harmony of aroma and spices is a single goal in Indian cooking, for everything is served at once: "appetizer", vegetables, bread, *dal*, chutney, and a sweet dish. All are followed by rice and more *dal*.

Besides preparing complementary dishes, Indian cooks strive to present a variety of foods. They avoid serving two dishes with a common main ingredient, and also consider the comparative richness of foods. Rich appetizers and rich desserts are seldom paired together. For example, fried appetizers such as *pakora* (p. 134) or *samosa* (p. 140) would not be served with a dessert made with *paneer* (Indian cheese) or another heavy, milk product. *Shreekhand* (p. 452), a light, yogurt preparation, or *lapsi* (p. 477), sweetened bulgur with only a small amount of *ghee* are better accompaniments for fried foods. Conversely, steamed appetizers such as *dhokla*, which tend to be on the lighter side, go well with richer sweets such as *doodkpaak* (p. 444).

Another important consideration is the number of people for whom food is being cooked. For large groups, steamed appetizers require less effort, and moreover are very economical. (One cup of *dhokla* flour yields

15–20 one–inch squares and requires very little oil). For serving large groups of people, *pakora* are impractical without help with the frying. *Pakora* must be served immediately or the batter coating loses its crunchiness—the dish confines the cook to the kitchen until the demand subsides. Indians tend to serve *Pakora* and *samosa* with high tea, or as a light meal in themselves with rice and *dal*.

The above conventions are useful when serving Indian meals that are reasonably light. Again, the stress is on serving a variety of complementary foods without the predominance of a single flavor. If carefully planned, the most simple of recipes, when served together, can make for fantastic meals.

# Fried Appetizers

## *Pakora* Flour (Mix)—*pakora atta*

*Pakora* at *The Ganges* were quite famous. In the beginning, when we had but two appetizers on the menu, we ended up making hundreds of *Pakora* each day. In order to avoid having to repeatedly measure ingredients, and to save time, I would usually prepare the dry mix ahead of time and then add water when ready to prepare the batter.

The same mix is used for making *bateta vada* (p. 151), *puda* (p. 431) and even Asparagus in Yogurt Sauce (p. 210). Those allergic to wheat may substitute rice flour for all-purpose, or use only chickpea flour. The mix keeps for an extended period of time.

| | |
|---|---|
| 2 ½ cups | chickpea flour |
| ½ cup | all purpose or rice flour |
| 1 tablespoon | salt, or to taste |
| 1 ½ teaspoons | turmeric |
| ¾ teaspoon | *hing* (asafoetida) |
| ¾ teaspoon | chili powder |
| 1 ½ teaspoons | baking powder |

Combine both flours with salt, turmeric, *hing* and chili powder. Mix well, add baking powder and mix again. Never add turmeric and baking powder together as this will add a red tint to your recipe. It is best to add them separately. Remove dry *pakora* mix to a container with a lid. Use as desired.

Yield: Approximately 3 cups.

## Fried, Battered Vegetables—*pakora* or *bhajia*

*Pakora* may be made with a variety of vegetables (cut into large pieces), such as broccoli, cauliflower, eggplant, zucchini or potatoes. *Pakora* soften when they cool, and should be served while hot and crisp. This appetizer may also be half-fried ahead of time and refried when ready to serve. Serve with raisin and tamarind chutney (p. 69) or cilantro chutney (p. 70).

| | |
|---|---|
| 3 cups | *pakora* flour (p. 133) |
| 2 ½ cups | water or as needed |
| 40–45 pieces | potatoes, cauliflower, broccoli etc. |
| Oil | for frying |

In a bowl, combine *pakora* flour and water, the consistency of the batter should be that of thick pancake batter. Set aside.

Wash all the vegetables before cutting.

Slice potatoes without peeling, keeping slices about ¼–inch thick.

If using cauliflower, remove stem and separate florets, cut florets into large pieces.

If using broccoli, remove large stems and discard or use in other recipes. Cut broccoli into large pieces.

Eggplant can be cut into two halves and then cut it into about ¼–inch thick wedges. Zucchini and carrots can be cut into long, thick slices.

Heat about 3–inches of oil in a *karai* or a wok until the temperature reaches approximately 375 °F. Immerse several vegetable pieces in the batter. With salad tongs, grip a piece of vegetable and turn it in the batter, ensuring that it is completely coated. Lift and gently place into the oil, dropping several pieces of vegetable at a time (making sure not to let the tongs touch the oil). The temperature of the oil will drop a few degrees at this point but it will rise again in a few seconds. When the *pakora* start to swell, the vegetables will start to cook. Maintain the temperature at 375 °F.

To half-fry the *pakora* ahead of time (so that cooking prior to serving will take less time), then fry evenly on both sides until slightly golden. Remove with a slotted spoon and drain on paper towels. Repeat until all are ready. To refry *pakora*: heat the oil to 375 °F again and fry *pakora* until golden all around, remove and drain on paper towels.

If you decide not to refry, fry *pakora* until they are golden and crisp all around.

Serve hot.

Yield: Approximately 45.

## Chili *Pakora*—*mirch pakora*

This spicy appetizer was a favorite of my customers at *The Ganges*. When I find fresh red chilies, I like to combine a few of them with the green, as this adds visual appeal to the recipe.

Chili *pakora* can be served with any sweet chutney, though a few of my guests preferred either cucumber *raita* (p. 99) or cilantro chutney (p. 70).

| | |
|---|---|
| 1 cup | chickpea flour |
| 1 cup | rice flour |
| 2 tablespoons | coriander seeds, toasted, cracked |
| 2 teaspoons | salt, or to taste |
| ¼ teaspoon | turmeric |
| ½ teaspoon | baking soda |
| 2 cups | serrano or jalapeño chilies, coarsely chopped |
| 2 cups | finely chopped onions |
| 1 cup | chopped cilantro |
| Oil | for frying |

In a bowl combine both the flours with coriander, salt and turmeric. Add baking soda and mix again.

In a food processor fitted with a metal blade, coarsely chop chilies. Just a few spins would do the job, make sure they do not grind. Add chopped chilies to flour mixture and mix well. Add onions and cilantro and mix again. Do not knead. The mixture will be crumbly yet damp. If not, add 2 or 3 tablespoons water. Mix again.

Heat 3–inches of oil in a *karai* or a wok until the temperature reaches 375 °F. Using your hands, scoop about 3 tablespoons of mixture for each *pakora*. Making a fist, shape it into slightly oblong shape. Making sure the *pakora* is firm, slide it into the oil. Slide several at a time. To half-fry, cook *pakora* until they are slightly golden all around. Remove with a slotted spoon and drain on paper towels.

When all *pakora* are ready, set aside covered with a paper towel. Half-fried *pakora* can also be refrigerated for about 5 days and refried when required.

To refry *pakora*: heat the oil to 375 °F again and fry *pakora* until deep golden all around, remove and drain on paper towels.

Yield: Approximately 30.

## Mashed Banana *Pakora*—*kela methi pakora* (dairy)

Seemingly contrasting flavors of banana, fenugreek, yogurt and chilies, blend quite harmoniously in this recipe. The batter can be prepared and refrigerated ahead of time. If using next day, the top layer might discolor, mix again before making *pakora*. Serve with cilantro chutney (p. 70) or any hot chutney.

| | |
|---|---|
| 2 ½ cups | chickpea flour |
| ½ cup | wheat flour |
| 1 tablespoon | coarsely ground black pepper |
| ½ cup | chopped, fresh fenugreek leaves **or** |
| 2 teaspoons | toasted, coarsely ground fenugreek seeds |
| 2 tablespoons | toasted, cracked coriander seeds |
| 8 | very ripe bananas, peeled, mashed |
| 2 tablespoons | oil |
| ½ cup | plain yogurt |
| 6 | serrano or jalapeño chilies, ground |
| 3–inch piece | fresh ginger, peeled, ground |
| 1 tablespoon | chili powder, or to taste |
| 1 tablespoon | salt, or to taste |
| ½ teaspoon | baking soda |
| Oil | for frying |

In a bowl, combine both of the flours with all the ingredients including baking soda. Heat about 3–inches of oil in a *karai* or a wok, until the temperature reaches 355 °F. Using your hands, drop about 1 tablespoon of the *pakora* mixture into the oil; drop several at time. Stir well and fry until they are medium-brown all around. Cooking over low heat is very important, as otherwise *pakora* will crisp quickly on the outside, but will remain dough-like in the center. Drain and serve hot.
Yield: Approximately 60.

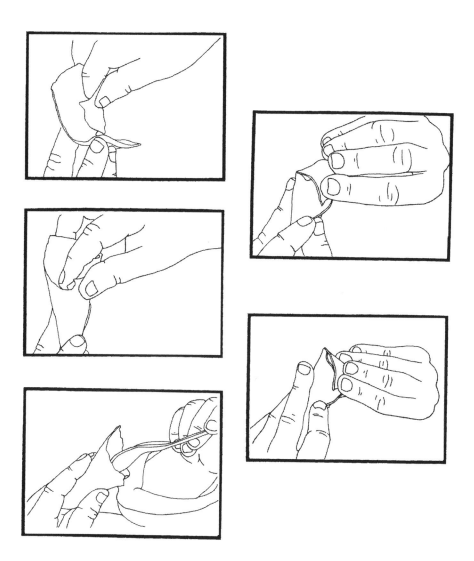

*Preparing Samosa; Shortcut Using Flour Tortillas*

## Triangular Pastry Stuffed with Vegetables—*samosa*

*Samosa* at *The Ganges* were very popular, and at times, guests would forgo main dishes entirely, only to order several of these. The stuffing, which in this recipe calls for potatoes, carrots, peas and onions, may vary from place to place in India. Serve with raisin and tamarind chutney (p. 69) or any chutney of your choice. Note that I have described two methods for preparing *samosa* casing. The first uses tortillas as a shortcut, and the second, traditional method (p. 142) involves making the dough from scratch.

**Stuffing:**

| | |
|---|---|
| 4 cups | grated potatoes, washed |
| 1 cup | grated carrots |
| 2 tablespoons | oil |
| 1 teaspoon | black mustard seeds |
| ½ teaspoon | cumin seeds |
| ½ cup | frozen green peas |
| 2 ½ teaspoons | salt, or to taste |
| ¼ teaspoon | turmeric |
| 1 tablespoon | *garam masala*-1 (p. 21) |
| 2 teaspoons | chili powder or to taste |
| 1 tablespoon | lemon juice |
| 2 tablespoons | sugar, or to taste |
| 1 medium | onion, finely sliced |

**Casing:**

| | |
|---|---|
| 3 tablespoons | all purpose flour |
| 2 tablespoons | water or as required |
| 3 twelve–inch | flour tortillas |
| Oil | for frying |

**Stuffing:**

Wash potatoes well and coarsely grate without peeling. Wash the grated potatoes again to avoid discoloration, drain well, squeeze lightly and set aside. Trim and coarsely grate the carrots, set aside, separate from the potatoes.

In a medium saucepan, heat oil and add mustard and cumin seeds. When mustard starts to crackle and cumin sizzle, add peas and cook for 5 minutes, stirring well. Add drained potatoes and mix well. Cook the mixture for 7 minutes. Add carrots, stir well and cook on low heat for about 1 minute.

Add next 6 ingredients including sugar. Mix well and cook for 5 more minutes. Add sliced onions, stir well and cook on low heat just for few seconds. Remove the mixture from heat and allow to cool.

**Casing:**

In a small bowl, combine flour and water and prepare a thick paste.

Cut tortilla into half and then into quarters. Hold each quarter in your hands with pointed side up. Turn one round side half way, apply little paste on the edge. Turn other round side on top of the first one to form a cone (illus. p. 139). Making sure that the edges are joined properly with the paste, fill the cone with potato mixture. Apply paste on the top and fold the pointed edge to close the cone. Secure with paste, set aside. Repeat until all are ready.

In a *karai* or a wok, heat about 3–inches of oil to 375 °F. Gently slide 2 or 3 *samosa* and fry on both the sides until golden. Remove with a slotted spoon to a tray lined with paper towels. You may half-fry the *samosa*, until the edges are slightly golden, cool and refry later before serving. You may even freeze half-fried *samosa* for later use (defrost in a microwave or in an oven before refrying).

To refry *samosa*: heat the oil to 375 °F and fry *samosa* until golden all around. Remove to a tray lined with paper towels.

Serve hot.

Yield: 12.

## Variation: Traditional *Samosa*

For those who prefer not to use tortilla as directed above, I here include instructions for traditional casing, made from *chapati* flour.

**Casing:**

| | |
|---|---|
| 1 ½ cups | *chapati* flour |
| ½ teaspoon | salt |
| 3 tablespoons | oil |
| ½ cup | warm water |

Prepare stuffing as directed in preceding recipe (p. 141).

**Casing:**

In a mixing bowl, combine flour, salt and oil. Gradually add water and prepare a smooth, stiff dough. Knead well. Divide into twelve portions; shape each portion into a smooth round patty.

Roll a single patty into a 4–inch circle and cut into two halves. Holding one half in your hand, make a cone by joining the straight edges together, one overlapping the other by ¼–inch (illus. p. 143). Press edges together. If the dough is too stiff, and if the edges do not adhere, moisten edges with water. Fill cone with stuffing, leaving ¼–inch seam free at top. Join upper seam and press shut. Set aside, covered with paper towels. Repeat with remaining semi-circle, and continue with other patties. .

Heat oil and fry as directed in the preceding recipe (p. 141).

Yield: 24 small *samosa*.

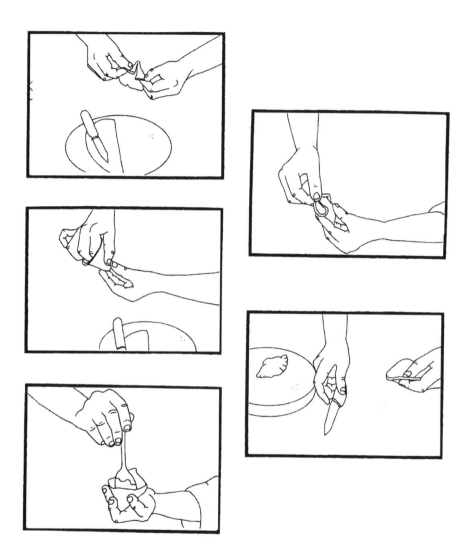

*Preparing Samosa; Traditional Method*

## Split Mung Patties—*mung dal kachori*

There are various types of stuffing for this recipe and various ways of making them. In some parts of India it is called *kachowdi* while others call it *kacholi*. *Kachori* from the Gujarati city of Jamnagar are quite famous and are exported all over the world. Here, I have made up my own version of the recipe. Serve alone, or with any sweet or hot chutney.

**Stuffing:**

| | |
|---|---|
| 2 cups | split mung beans (mung *dal*), soaked four hours |
| 3 tablespoons | oil |
| ½ teaspoon | *hing* (asafoetida) |
| ¼ cup | chickpea flour |
| 2 teaspoons | salt, or to taste |
| 1 teaspoons | ground anise |
| 2 teaspoons | chili powder |
| ¼ teaspoon | turmeric |
| 1 teaspoon | *aamchoor* (p. 27) |
| ½ teaspoon | black salt (p. 30), (optional) |
| ¼ cup | golden raisins, chopped |
| ¼ cup | chopped cilantro |

**Casing:**

| | |
|---|---|
| 2 cups | wheat flour |
| 4 tablespoons | oil |
| 1 teaspoon | salt |
| 2 tablespoons | cornstarch |
| 3 tablespoons | lemon juice |
| ¼ cup | water, or as required |

**Stuffing:**

Pick over and wash mung *dal* (see note, p. 336). Soak mung *dal* for four hours.

Drain and steam mung *dal* (p. 50) until soft, but not mushy. If you decide not to use a steamer, cook drained mung *dal* on low heat, adding ½ cup water, or as needed (be careful not to let the *dal* dry and burn, add the minimal amount of water, letting the *dal* cook until soft). Set aside. Note: if you find that the *dal* slips through the holes in your steamer, you may spread cheesecloth over the steamer before placing the *dal*.

In a large frying pan, heat oil and add *hing*. Add chickpea flour when *hing* turns brown. Lower the heat and stir well. When the flour starts to get frothy, add mung *dal* and remaining 8 ingredients for stuffing including cilantro. Cook on low heat, stirring well, for about 3 minutes. Remove and allow to cool.

**Casing:**

In a bowl, combine wheat flour with oil. Add salt, cornstarch and lemon juice and mix well. Gradually add water and prepare stiff yet smooth dough. Divide into 40 portions. Shape each portion into a smooth round patty. Roll each into a circle about 3 ½–inches in diameter; place 2 tablespoons stuffing mixture in the center. Gather up the edges and pinch the edges shut (illus. p. 425). Gently press the patty, making it slightly flat and set aside covered. Repeat until several are ready.

Heat about 3–inches of oil in a *karai* or a wok. When the temperature reaches about 375 °F, drop several patties in the oil and fry, turning once, until golden on both the sides. Remove and drain on paper towels. Repeat until all are ready. *Kachori* may be half-fried ahead of time, refrigerated and refried when ready to serve. Serve hot.

Yield: Approximately 40.

## Mixed Bean Patties with Yogurt—*dahivada* (dairy)

This unique recipe is quite popular all over Gujarat, though different versions are popular all over India. Whereas some Indians use only split Indian black beans—*urid dal*, others use black-eyed peas or even a mixture of a variety of beans to make this recipe. Garnish with raisin and tamarind chutney (p. 69) and cilantro.

**Vada Crust:**

| | |
|---|---|
| 1 cup | split mung beans (mung *dal*), soaked four hours |
| ½ cup | split black beans (*urid dal*), soaked four hours |
| 3 slices | white bread, crusts trimmed |
| 1 teaspoon | salt, or to taste |
| 2 teaspoons | cracked black pepper |
| Oil | for frying |

**Stuffing:**

| | |
|---|---|
| 1 teaspoon | oil |
| ½ teaspoon | *hing* (asafoetida) |
| 2 cups | green peas, coarsely ground |
| 2 | serrano or jalapeño chilies, finely chopped |
| 2–inch piece | fresh ginger, peeled, finely chopped |
| ½ teaspoon | salt, or to taste |
| ½ teaspoon | white poppy seeds (optional) |
| 2 tablespoons | finely chopped cilantro |
| 1 tablespoon | golden raisins, chopped |

**Yogurt Sauce:**

| | |
|---|---|
| 3 cups | plain yogurt |
| ½ cup | raisin tamarind chutney (p. 69) |
| 1 teaspoon | chili powder |
| 1 teaspoon | toasted, coarsely ground cumin seeds |
| ¼ cup | chopped cilantro, for garnish |

***Vada* Crust:**

Pick over both the *dals* and wash them separately (see note, p. 38). Soak both the *dals* for four hours.

In a food processor fitted with a metal blade, drain and grind both the *dals* separately until slightly coarse. Remove both *dals* to a bowl and mix well. Cut bread into small pieces and add it to ground *dals*, add salt and black pepper and mix well, making sure the bread pieces have combined well. Divide into 20 portions, set aside.

**Stuffing:**

In a frying pan, heat oil and add *hing*. Lower the heat when *hing* turns brown. Add peas and next 6 ingredients including raisins. Mix well and cook for 7 minutes. Set aside to cool. This mixture can be made ahead of time and refrigerated. Divide into 20 portions.

Take 1 portion of *vada* crust (bean mixture) and shape into a cup, place 1 portion of pea mixture in the cup and cover it, making it into a smooth round patty, prepare several and set aside.

In a *karai* or a wok, heat about 3–inches of oil to 375 °F. Gently slide about 6 patty and fry on both sides until golden brown. Alternatively these patties can be flattened more and fried in a non-stick frying pan using very little oil, until golden on both sides. Remove and drain on paper towels. Set aside to cool.

On one side of each patty, place single vertical and horizontal cuts, like a "plus" sign. Arrange patties on a platter, the cut-sides facing up.

**Yogurt Sauce:**

Using a whisk, beat yogurt until smooth and spoon over patties. Spread chutney over the patties. Sprinkle chili powder and cumin over the *dahivada* and serve garnished with cilantro.

Yield: Approximately 20.

## Lentil Kebabs—*masoorna muthia*

The mixture for these hearty kebabs may be made ahead of time and refrigerated for four-five days. Serve hot with lemon wedges and sliced, raw onion.

| | |
|---|---|
| 1 cup | whole brown lentils, soaked overnight |
| 5 | serrano or jalapeño chilies |
| 5–7 cloves | garlic, peeled |
| 1 cup | chopped cilantro |
| 1 tablespoon | chopped mint |
| 1 teaspoon | salt, or to taste |
| ¼ teaspoon | chili powder |
| ¼ cup | dry onion flakes or granules (p. 38) |
| 1 teaspoon | *garam masala*-1 (p. 21) |
| ¼ teaspoon | ground cloves |
| 2 teaspoons | coarsely ground cumin seeds |
| ½ teaspoon | baking soda |
| 1 teaspoon | ground cinnamon |
| Oil | for frying |
| 1 medium | onion, peeled, cut into thin rings |
| 1 lemon | cut into wedges |

Pick over, wash (see note, p. 336) and soak lentils overnight.

Drain lentils and set aside. In a food processor fitted with a metal blade, grind until coarse, chilies, garlic, cilantro and mint. Add lentil and grind the mixture until almost smooth. Remove to a bowl. Add salt and the next 7 ingredients including cinnamon and mix well.

In a *karai* or a wok, heat 3–inches of oil to 375 °F. Take about 4 table-spoons mixture in your hand, make a fist, shaping it into an oblong "kebab," and drop it gently into the oil. Drop several at a time.

You may use a chopstick to shape the kebab and gently remove the stick to keep a hollow in the center. Fry on low heat until they are brown all around. Remove with a slotted spoon and drain on paper towels. Serve hot with onion rings and lemon wedges.

Yield: Approximately 12.

**Note:** Instead of frying, lentil kebabs may also be steamed for 20 minutes as in the *muthia* recipe (p. 169).

## Split Chickpea Patties—*chana dal vada*

In this recipe, the combination of whole, coarse, and slightly coarse *chana dal* imparts the recipe with a pleasing, crunchy texture. Serve with either sweet or hot chutneys.

| | |
|---|---|
| 3 cups | split chickpeas (*chana dal*), soaked four hours |
| 8 cloves | garlic, peeled |
| 8 | serrano or jalapeño chilies |
| 2 ½ teaspoons | salt, or to taste |
| 1 teaspoon | chili powder, or to taste |
| 2 teaspoons | ground anise |
| ½ teaspoon | turmeric |
| 1 large | red bell pepper, seeded, finely cut |
| ¾ cup | dried onion flakes or granules (p. 38) |
| ½ teaspoon | *hing* (asafoetida) |
| ¼ cup | all purpose flour |
| ¼ cup | chickpea flour |
| ¼ cup | chopped cilantro |
| Oil | for frying |

Pick over, wash (see note, p. 336) and soak *dal* for four hours. Drain the *dal* well, remove ½ cup soaked *dal* to a bowl and set aside.

In a food processor fitted with a metal blade, grind garlic and chilies until coarse. Add remaining *dal* and grind for 10 seconds. Remove about 1 cup mixture and add to the whole *dal* saved earlier in the bowl.

Grind remaining *dal* until slightly coarse but not smooth, about 3 minutes. Remove with the mixture in the bowl. Add salt and the remaining 9 ingredients including cilantro and mix well.

In a *karai* or a wok, heat 3–inches of oil to 375 °F. Scoop about 3 tablespoons of the *dal* mixture in your hand and shape in to a patty. Slide into the hot oil, dropping several at a time. Fry turning once or twice until golden brown on both the sides. Remove with a slotted spoon and drain on paper towels. Serve hot or at room temperature.

Yield: Approximately 30.

## Spicy Mashed Potato Rounds—*bateta vada*

Flavored with fresh cilantro, this slightly tart appetizer can be made fairly quickly once the potato mixture is prepared. The mixture can be made ahead of time, shaped into rounds and refrigerated for up to 2 days. Serve with either cilantro chutney (p. 70) or raisin and tamarind chutney (p. 69).

| | |
|---|---|
| 3 large | potatoes, boiled, peeled and mashed (app 1 ½ cups) |
| 1 tablespoon | lemon juice, fresh preferred |
| 1 ½ teaspoons | salt, or to taste |
| 5 | serrano or jalapeño chilies, ground |
| ½ cup | cilantro, chopped |
| 2 cups | *pakora* flour (p. 133) |
| 1 ¼ cups | water or as needed |
| Oil | for frying |

In a bowl combine mashed potatoes with lemon juice, salt, chilies and cilantro. Divide mixture into walnut-sized portions, and using your hands, shape portions into smooth rounds. The recipe should make about 15 balls.

Add water to *pakora* flour. Mix well to prepare a thick batter—if batter is lumpy, add more water as required and mix well. Note that the batter should not be watery.

Heat about 3–inches of oil, in a *karai* or a wok, to 375 °F.

Drop several potato balls in the batter. Using your hands, salad tongs or a soup spoon, cover each ball thoroughly with the batter, lift and gently slide it into the hot oil. Drop several at a time. Using a slotted spoon, gently turn *bateta vada* after about one minute. Fry until each *bateta vada* is golden brown all around. Remove and drain on paper towels. Serve hot, as soon as they are sufficiently drained.

Yield: Approximately 15.

**Note:** The same recipe may be followed using Jersey or Japanese sweet potatoes.

## *Papadum*-Lentil Wafers—*papadum* or *papad*

I have included a recipe for making *papadum* in my first book. Since making *papadum* is such a labor-intensive effort, I recommend buying them ready-made; they are available "flavored" with a variety of seasonings.

*Papadum* may be toasted or fried as follows.

**To Toast**:

With a pair of tongs hold *papadum* over a low open flame or place it on a diffuser over electric stove. Turn (rotate) it round quickly, and flip. *Papadum* will lighten in color and become flecked with tiny, light brown spots. It will be ready when whole of the *papadum* is toasted. Place on flat surface and quickly and gently flatten each *papadum* with your palms, taking care not to break the rounds. Stack as they cook.

**To Deep-Fry**:

Heat about 1–inch oil in a wok or frying pan, place *papadum* and fry all around, turning with a tong. Remove and drain on paper towels. To shape it into a triangle, quickly place a spoon in the center. Holding it firm, fold with a tong, making *papadum* into a half-circle. Repeat and fold again making it a quarter-circle—looking like a triangle. Remove on paper towels. Serve hot or let cool and store covered tightly until ready to serve.

# Rice Wafers—*papdi*

A couple of our regulars at *The Ganges*, having remarked that we served *papadum* daily, once jokingly inquired where the "*mamadum*" was that accompanied the *papadum*. For them, I fried *papdi*, telling them that this was the "*mamadum*." Actually in Gujarati, *papadum* or *papad* is a masculine word and *papdi* is feminine. Made with rice flour, sesame and cumin, this is a delicious snack.

| | |
|---|---|
| ¾ cup | water |
| ½ teaspoon | salt, or to taste |
| 2 teaspoons | serrano or jalapeño chilies, ground |
| 2 teaspoons | sesame seeds |
| ½ teaspoon | cumin seeds |
| 1 cup | rice flour |
| Few drops | oil for rolling |

In a small saucepan over high heat, heat water and add the next 4 ingredients including cumin; mix well and bring the mixture to a full boil.

Place the rice flour in a bowl, and gradually add boiled water with spices and mix well using a spoon. When it is slightly less hot, knead the dough well using your hands. Knead until smooth, and then divide the dough into 2 portions and shape each into a large donut with a hole in the center.

Prepare a steamer (p. 50) and steam the donuts for about 30 minutes. Remove from steamer and immediately cut the donuts into large pieces with a knife. Right away, start to knead the pieces together. Though the dough will be hot, you will be able to touch it comfortably within a few seconds. If the dough sticks, wet your hands with little water and proceed. When smooth, divide the dough into 9 portions. Shape each into a smooth patty and roll *papdi* into a circle about 6–inches in diameter.

Spread the *papdi*, in a single layer, in a large tray lined with paper towels. Set the tray aside and allow the *papdi* to dry. Store in a jar when dry and crisp. Toast or fry *papdi* as you would *papadum*. You will not be able to fold *papdi* while frying.

Yield: 9.

# Non-Fried Appetizers

## Steamed Savory Cake—*dhokla*

Once you know how to make one variety of *dhokla*, the many variations of this recipe will become easy. Many Gujarati's use Eno's fruit salt in order to make this recipe "instant."

The recipe in my first book differs from this in that in the older book, I recommend using yeast. Here, I use club soda. Serve with cilantro chutney (p. 70).

| | |
|---|---|
| 1 cup | *khaman* flour (p. 42) |
| ¾ cup | club soda |
| 2 tablespoons | lemon juice |
| ½ teaspoon | salt, or to taste |
| 4 | serrano or jalapeño chilies, ground |
| 1 ½–inch piece | fresh ginger, peeled, ground |
| 1 tablespoon | oil |
| 1 teaspoon | black mustard seeds |
| ½ teaspoon | *hing* (asafoetida) |
| 2 tablespoons | chopped cilantro, for garnish |

Place a 9–inch cake pan over the rack or the sieve of a prepared steamer (p. 50). Cover the steamer, letting the cake pan warm while you prepare the batter.

In a bowl, combine flour with the next 5 ingredients including ginger and mix well. Open the steamer and pour batter into the cake pan. Cover and steam *dhokla* for about 20 minutes. Just before the *dhokla* finish steaming, prepare the spiced oil as follows.

In a small frying pan, heat oil over medium heat and add mustard seeds. Add *hing* when mustard starts to crackle. As soon as the *hing* turns brown, open the steamer and pour seasoned oil all over the *dhokla*. Remove cake pan from the steamer and, using a spatula, gently spread the mustard seeds around the pan, over the *dhokla*. Set aside to cool.

Cut *dhokla* into about 1 ½-inch squares. Using a spatula, remove *dhokla* to a serving platter. Garnish with cilantro and serve.
Serves 4–6.

## Cucumber Savory Cake—*kakdina dhokla*

Cucumbers are equally delicious when warmed, as in this recipe, which is infused with chili and ginger. No oil is used in the batter, making this recipe particularly low fat. If desired, however, seasoned oil may be drizzled on these *dhokla* before serving (see previous recipe).

| | |
|---|---|
| 1 medium | cucumber, peeled, grated |
| ½ cup | yellow cornmeal |
| ½ cup | wheat flour |
| 1 teaspoon | salt, or to taste |
| 3 | serrano or jalapeño chilies, ground |
| 2–inch piece | fresh ginger, peeled, ground |
| 2 teaspoons | sugar, or to taste |
| ½ teaspoon | baking soda |
| 1 tablespoon | lemon juice |
| ¼ teaspoon | turmeric |
| ½ cup | club soda |
| 2 tablespoons | chopped cilantro, for garnish |
| 1 tablespoon | oil (optional) |
| 1 teaspoon | black mustard seeds (optional) |

Place a 9–inch cake pan over the rack or the sieve of a prepared steamer (p. 50). Cover the steamer, letting the cake pan warm while you prepare the batter.

Combine cucumber with cornmeal and the next 7 ingredients including lemon juice. Add turmeric and mix well (note that if baking soda and turmeric are added at the same time, the recipe will assume a reddish tint). Add club soda and mix again—stirring the mixture in one direction. Open the steamer and immediately pour the batter into the cake pan. Cover the steamer and steam *dhokla* for about 20 minutes or until done— checking as you would a cake. Remove cake pan from steamer, let cool for few minutes. Cut into about 1 ½–inch squares. Using a spatula, gently remove *dhokla* to a serving platter. Serve garnished with cilantro.

Optional: To season, heat oil in a frying pan over medium heat and add mustard seeds. When mustard starts to crackle, remove from heat and pour oil with mustard all over the *dhokla* before cutting.

Serves 4–6.

## Steamed Savory Rounds—*idlee* (dairy)

This South Indian preparation is extremely popular in Indian restaurants. We made it at *The Ganges* using a cocktail *idlee* stand (illus. p. 160) that makes much smaller *idlee* than the regularly sized mould. We would serve these smaller *idlee* with *sambhar* (p. 376). You may, however, use a regular *idlee* maker or even an egg poacher. *Idlee* can also be served as a snack with cilantro chutney (p. 70).

| | |
|---|---|
| 2 cups | *idlee* flour (p. 42) |
| ½ cup | buttermilk |
| 1 cup | water, or as needed |
| 3 | serrano or jalapeño chilies, ground |
| 2–inch piece | fresh ginger, peeled, ground |
| 1 teaspoon | salt, or to taste |
| 2 tablespoons | oil |
| ½ teaspoon | baking soda |

Combine flour, buttermilk, and water to form a thick paste. Set aside for at least six hours.

Add the next 4 ingredients including oil and mix well, stirring in one direction. Add baking soda and more water as needed to achieve a thick pouring consistency. Apply a little oil to the *idlee* moulds and pour a little mixture into each mould, leaving little space for *idlee* to rise. Set aside.

Fill a large saucepan about 2–inches high with water, and bring to a boil over high heat. Place the *idlee* stand in the saucepan, cover and steam for about 15 minutes. Remove the stand from the steamer, gently lift the *idlee* and serve hot. Repeat until all the batter is used up. Leftover *idlee* can be reheated in a steamer or in a microwave.

Yield: Approximately 12–16 regular-size *idlee*.

**Note:** *Idlee* may be made non-dairy using all water and no buttermilk.

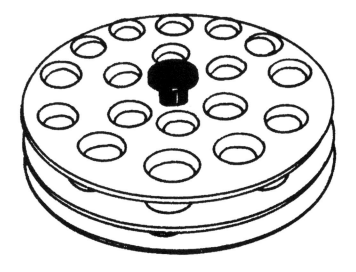

*Cocktail Idlee Maker*

## Variation: Black Bean and Rice Cake with Cracked Pepper—*idada*

Whenever I visited India, my mother would have this made for me on the first day of my arrival. Use either ready-made white *dhokla* flour (p. 41) or *idlee* flour when preparing this recipe. Serve with cilantro chutney (p. 70).

**Ingredients:** As in the preceding recipe.

**Procedure:** As in *dhokla* recipe (p. 155). Sprinkle cracked black pepper over the batter before steaming.

Serves 4–6.

# Chickpea Flour Rolls—*khandvi* or *pilla patodi* (dairy)

This unique Gujarati recipe is deceptively difficult—it becomes much easier after one time through the recipe. Note that prior to making the rolls, the cooked mixture must be spread very quickly, as it will be harder to manipulate as it cools. Reheating the dough, unfortunately, does not work.

*Khandvi* batter can also be cooked in a microwave for 12 minutes, stirring, 2 or 3 times in between. If cooking in microwave, add ¼ cup more buttermilk to the batter. Serve this delicate preparation as an elegant, unique appetizer.

| | |
|---|---|
| 1 cup | chickpea flour |
| 2 ½ cups | buttermilk |
| ½ teaspoon | salt, or to taste |
| ½ teaspoon | turmeric |
| 2 | serrano or jalapeño chilies, ground |
| 1–inch piece | fresh ginger, peeled, ground |
| 1 tablespoon | oil |
| 1 teaspoon | cumin seeds |
| 1 teaspoon | black mustard seeds |
| ¼ cup | chopped cilantro, for garnish |

To prepare this you will need three large pizza plates or a very large flat tray.

In a thick stainless saucepan, combine flour with buttermilk and the next 4 ingredients including ginger. Place the pan on medium-high heat and stir well constantly: the mixture will thicken in a few minutes. In about 12 minutes, it will almost be ready to spread. Lower the heat to very low and with a spatula, spread a tiny bit of the mixture on the pizza plate and try to lift it off in one piece. If it lifts easily, the mixture is ready. If not, cook the mixture for a couple of minutes longer. When the mixture is ready, quickly pour about one sixth of the mixture on the pizza plate and quickly spread it with a spatula.

Wearing a disposable glove (to prevent burning your palm), spread the mixture further into a very thin layer, about one-sixteenth inch thick, all around the plate. Flip the plate over, pour some mixture on the backside of the plate and spread in a similar manner. Repeat on other plates until the batter is used up. Set aside for about 5 minutes.

Cut the layers, starting with the reverse of each plate, into long, approximately 2–inch wide strips. Roll each strip lengthwise—as you would roll up paper—into a *khandvi* and set aside on a serving platter. Repeat until all are ready.

Heat the oil in a small frying pan, over medium heat, and add cumin and mustard. When the cumin starts to sizzle and mustards crackle, remove pan from heat and with a spoon, drizzle a little oil mixture with seeds on each roll. Garnish with cilantro and serve at room temperature. Leftovers, if any, may be refrigerated.

Serves 8–10.

**Note**: A non-dairy version of this recipe can be made using water and lemon juice instead of buttermilk. Use two and a quarter cup plus 2 tablespoons water and 2 tablespoons lemon juice. To make *khandvi* **oil free**, dry toast cumin and mustard seeds (p. 27) and sprinkle over *khandvi* before serving.

# Baked Savory Cake—*handvo* or *bhakhar*

*Handva* flour is available in most Indian stores, or you can grind your own following the recipe in this book (p. 42). Alternatively, you can soak rice and *dal* separately following the recipe below to make *handvo*. The proportion of rice and *dal* varies with different cooks; using more *dal*, however, makes it moister. Some Indians also add vegetables and fresh beans to this dish.

This spectacular savory cake topped with mustard and sesame seeds can be served hot or at room temperature. Sweet and hot mango relish (p. 93) goes well with this dish.

| | |
|---|---|
| 1 cup | split chickpeas (*chana dal*) soaked four hours |
| ¼ cup | *basmati* rice, washed, soaked four hours |
| 1 cup | grated zucchini |
| 10 cloves | garlic, peeled, chopped |
| 1 teaspoon | chili powder or to taste |
| 2 teaspoons | salt, or to taste |
| ¼ teaspoon | turmeric |
| 4 tablespoons | oil |
| 2 teaspoons | black mustard seeds |
| ½ teaspoon | *hing* (asafoetida) |
| 1 tablespoon | sesame seeds |

Pick over, wash (see note, p. 336) and soak *dal* for four hours. Also wash and soak rice separately for four hours.

Preheat oven to 400 °F.

Drain and grind *dal* and rice separately until slightly coarse. Remove both to the same bowl. Add zucchini and the next 4 ingredients including turmeric and mix well. Pour mixture into a greased, 9–inch cake pan.

Heat oil in a small frying pan, over medium heat, and add mustard. When mustard starts to crackle, add *hing* and sesame seeds. When sesame changes color, remove and spread the oil over the rice and *dal* mixture. Place the pan in the preheated oven and bake *handvo* for 30 minutes, or until the top turns slightly golden and toothpick inserted in the center comes out clean. Cut as you would a cake and serve hot. Can also be served at room temperature.

Leftovers can be refrigerated and served either cold or reheated the next day.

Serves 4–6.

## Bean and Spinach Cake—*chola chanano handvo*

This is another variation of the Gujarati specialty *handvo*. Spinach adds moisture and flavor to this nutritious, tasty dish. Serve either at room temperature or hot (the dish may be prepared ahead of time and reheated). As part of a light meal, serve with any green salad.

| | |
|---|---|
| 2 cups | black-eyed peas, soaked overnight |
| 1 cup | garbanzo beans, soaked overnight |
| 2 ½ teaspoons | salt, or to taste |
| ½ teaspoon | chili powder |
| 6 | serrano or jalapeño chilies, ground |
| 3–inch piece | fresh ginger, peeled, ground |
| ½ teaspoon | turmeric |
| 2 tablespoons | lemon juice |
| 10 cloves | garlic, peeled, chopped |
| 4 tablespoons | oil |
| 3 cups | finely chopped, fresh spinach |
| 1 cup | water |

Pick over, wash (see note, p. 336) and soak both peas and beans separately overnight. In the morning drain separately and set aside for few minutes.

Preheat oven to 400 °F.

In a food processor fitted with a metal blade, grind black-eyed peas until slightly coarse. Remove to a bowl. Grind garbanzo beans in the same manner and remove together with the ground peas.

Combine ground peas and beans with all remaining ingredients including water and mix well. Pour mixture into an approximately 8 by 5–inch baking pan, brushed with a small amount of oil. Bake for 35 minutes or until the knife inserted into the center comes out clean. Alternatively, microwave at high heat for the same amount of time or until done. Cut into desired sized pieces and serve.

Serves 8–10.

## Spicy Spinach Squares—*bhajina dhokla* (no oil)

Made without any oil, this unique, light appetizer is extremely low in fat. It can be made ahead of time and reheated before serving. For a slightly spicy-sweet variation, add ½ cup raisin and tamarind chutney (p. 69) to the batter. Serve with any sweet or hot chutney.

| | |
|---|---|
| 1 ¼ cups | chickpea flour |
| 6 cups | chopped, fresh spinach |
| 1 ½ teaspoons | salt, or to taste |
| 6 | serrano or jalapeño chilies, ground |
| ½ teaspoon | chili powder, or to taste |
| 3–inch piece | fresh ginger, peeled, ground |
| 1 tablespoon | lemon juice |
| 1 tablespoon | brown sugar, or to taste |
| ¼ teaspoon | turmeric |
| ¼ teaspoon | baking soda |
| 2 cups | water |

Preheat oven to 375 °F

Combine all the ingredients including water in a mixing bowl and pour the mixture into a medium, non-stick baking tray. Bake the *dhokla* for 35 minutes, or until the top is golden brown. The *dhokla* may alternatively be microwaved on high heat for about 15 minutes. Cut into desired pieces and serve hot as an appetizer.

Serves 4–6.

**Note:** In absence of chickpea flour, you may use soaked and ground garbanzo beans (p. 41).

## Savory Cabbage Cake—*kobijno bhakhar* (dairy)

This simple yet delicious recipe is easy to prepare and can make a very satisfying meal. Leftovers taste even better the next day. Serve with a cup of tea (p. 485).

| | |
|---|---|
| 1 cup | yellow or white cornmeal |
| 1 cup | chickpea flour |
| 4 tablespoons | oil |
| 1 ½ teaspoons | salt, or to taste |
| 6 | serrano or jalapeño chilies, ground |
| 3–inch piece | fresh ginger, peeled, ground |
| ½ teaspoon | *hing* (asafoetida) |
| ¼ teaspoon | turmeric |
| ¼ cup | yogurt |
| ¼ cup | buttermilk |
| 2 teaspoons | toasted, ground coriander seeds |
| 6–8 tablespoons | boiling water |
| ½ teaspoon | baking soda |
| 2 cups | finely chopped cabbage |

Preheat oven to 350 °F.

Combine cornmeal with chickpea flour, 2 tablespoons oil and salt. Add chilies and the next 6 ingredients including coriander and mix well. Add 6 tablespoons boiling water and mix again. The consistency should be like that of thick pancake batter. Add more water if needed. Add baking soda and cabbage and mix well, stirring the mixture in one direction.

Heat 1 tablespoon of oil in a medium frying pan over medium heat. When hot, gently turn the pan so as to coat the cooking surface with oil. Pour the mixture in the frying pan, spread it to make the layer about 1 ½–inch thick, lower heat, cover and cook for about 7 minutes or until the top changes color to deep yellow. By this time the bottom side will be firm and slightly golden.

Using a spatula, gently unstick the cake from the pan. Invert a round baking dish over the frying pan and turn the cake into the baking dish. This way the bottom side will be facing you. Spread remaining oil around the baking dish and bake in the oven for 20 minutes. If a crispy texture is preferred, turn it again and brown both the sides evenly.

Remove to a serving plate and cut into eight pieces as you would a cake and serve.

Serves 4–8.

## Spinach Kebabs—*palakna muthia*

These appetizers take their name from the Gujarati word, *muthi*, meaning fist, referring to the particular technique employed in shaping individual portions. Savory, mild, and light in texture, their flavor is enhanced if brushed with a little oil before serving. A favorite of spinach lovers, they are delicious and lowfat.

Alone, these kebabs make a satisfying light meal. In my restaurant, I served this dish with onion and tomato relish (p. 86). The combination is visually appealing, and the sharp onions and sweet tomatoes balance the hearty, dense flavors of the dish.

| | |
|---|---|
| 1 cup | chickpea flour |
| 1 cup | coarsely ground wheat flour or Cream of Wheat |
| 2 tablespoons | oil |
| ½ teaspoon | baking soda |
| 1 teaspoon | salt, or to taste |
| 10 cloves | garlic, peeled, chopped |
| 5 | serrano or jalapeño chilies, ground |
| ¼ teaspoon | turmeric |
| 2 teaspoons | ground coriander |
| 2 teaspoons | sugar, or to taste |
| 1 tablespoon | sesame seeds |
| 1 bunch | spinach leaves, washed, finely chopped |

Prepare a steamer (p. 50). Combine both flours, oil and baking soda. Add the next 7 ingredients including sesame seeds and mix well. The mixture will be slightly crumbly.

Add spinach. As the spinach is mixed in, the dough should become slightly lumpy. If not sprinkle little water and mix well, do not knead. Place about 4 tablespoons of dough in the palm of one hand, and close your fingers over it, pressing lightly. This action gives the kebab its oblong shape. Set aside. Use all the dough in this manner.

Place the kebabs in the steamer tray leaving space between each, as they will swell while cooking. Cover the steamer and cook 20 minutes or until a knife, inserted into the center of a kebab, comes out clean. If the steamer cannot hold all kebabs at one time, steam in batches.

Remove kebabs from the steamer, slice and serve immediately when they are hot.

Yield: Approximately 15 kebabs

## Steamed Spinach and Peas Rounds
### —*palak vatanana muthia*

This appetizer was extremely popular at *The Ganges*. I recall that when I first prepared this for my customers, the whole batch sold within one hour. Serve with chutney of your choice.

| | |
|---|---|
| 1 ½ cups | *handva* flour (p. 41) |
| 1 teaspoon | salt, or to taste |
| 8 | serrano or jalapeño chilies, ground |
| 3–inch piece | fresh ginger, peeled, ground |
| 3 tablespoons | oil |
| 1 cup | green peas, frozen |
| 1 ½ cups | chopped spinach |
| ¼ teaspoon | turmeric |
| 3 cups | water |

In a medium saucepan, combine flour and all the ingredients including water. Place the pan over medium heat.

Cook stirring well, until the mixture thickens, about 10 minutes. Lower the heat to very low and cook for 1 minute. Remove from heat.

Prepare a steamer (p. 50). Taking about ¼ cup cooked mixture in your hands, make a fist and shape into a thick, oblong kebab. Gently place the kebab in the steamer. Repeat with remaining mixture, keeping a little space between each kebab, as the pieces will swell while steaming. Steam for about 25 minutes. Remove the steamer from the heat, let cool for few minutes. Remove kebabs, gently cut into rounds and serve. Can also be served whole, without cutting, garnished with cilantro. Leftovers may be refrigerated and reheated in a microwave before serving.

Yield: Approximately 10.

# Snacks

Indians are known for their hospitality; in fact, a Sanskrit saying tells us that "Atithi Devo Bhava," meaning that guests are like Gods. When Indians receive unexpected visitors, they will often offer the guest a glass of water, a drink (tea), and refreshments.

In most Gujarati homes, several snacks are made frequently. As I mentioned earlier, snacks that are to be kept for several days or for weeks are deep fried, whereas steamed or stovetop cooked snacks are served fresh.

## Rice Flour Curls—*chakri* (dairy)

Requiring an Indian noodle press (p. 175) to prepare, this crunchy snack is as addictive as pretzels or potato chips. Chilies, ginger and cumin enhance the slight sour taste of buttermilk. If you decide to serve this with cocktails, make sure you have enough, as the tray will empty quickly. Leftovers may be stored in a tightly covered jar and will keep for several weeks.

| | |
|---|---|
| 6 cups | rice flour, fine |
| 6 tablespoons | butter, melted |
| 2 ½ teaspoons | salt, or to taste |
| 4 cups | buttermilk |
| 15 | serrano or jalapeño chilies, ground |
| 6–inch piece | fresh ginger, peeled, ground |
| 3 tablespoons | sesame seeds |
| 2 tablespoons | toasted, coarsely ground cumin seeds |
| Oil | for frying |

In a large mixing bowl, mix together flour, butter and salt. The mixture will be crumbly. In a small bowl, combine buttermilk with the next 4 ingredients including cumin. Add to the flour and mix well. The dough should be soft enough to drop it through the press. If it is too stiff, add little more buttermilk and mix well.

In a wok or a *karai*, heat about 4–inches of oil over medium-high heat to about 365 °F. Insert a star-shaped disc into the Indian noodle press and fill with the dough. Cover tightly with the lid with handle and tighten firmly. With one hand hold the press over the oil (illus. p. 175). Turn the handle with the other hand, while simultaneously rotating the press in 2 or 3 small circular motions to drop several *chakri* rounds in the oil. Fry evenly, turning 2 or 3 times, until slightly golden. Remove and drain on paper towels.

Fill the press again, when the first batch is frying. One batch should make about 18 *chakri*. Repeat until the dough is finished. Let cool and store in a jar with a lid.

Yield: Approximately 150.

## Chickpea Flour Noodles—*sev*

This snack is available in most Indian stores. However, if you have the required, Indian noodle press, and a lot of patience, you can make your own. Some cooks add a pinch of turmeric and white chili powder to the flour. When used as a garnish, *sev* can liven up many steamed or stovetop cooked appetizers. Stored in an airtight container, *sev* will keep for several weeks.

| | |
|---|---|
| 2 cups | chickpea flour |
| ½ teaspoon | salt, or to taste |
| 10 tablespoons | water, or as needed |
| Oil | for frying |

In a small bowl, combine flour and salt, add water and prepare soft dough. If the dough is stiff, add a little more water to make it soft enough to press through the tiny holes on the disc.

In a wok, small saucepan or *karai* heat about 3–inches of oil. Lower the heat to 375 °F. Place a portion of dough into an Indian noodle press— *sevno sancho*—fitted with a disc with tiny holes. Cover the press tightly with the lid/handle and tighten firmly. With one hand hold the press over the oil (illus. p. 175). Turn the handle with the other hand, while simultaneously rotating the press in 2 or 3 wide circular motions over the oil to press *sev* through, into the hot oil. Fry *sev* until crisp, turning it once, in between. Remove and drain on paper towels. When cold, crumble lightly and remove to a container with a lid.

Yield: Approximately 6 cups.

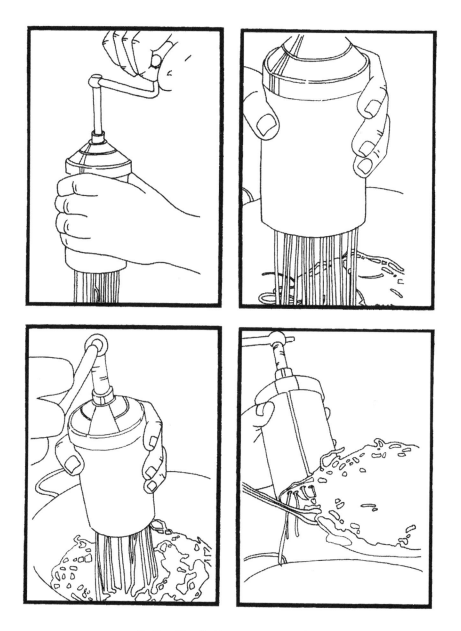

*Indian Noodle Press—sevno sancho*

## Stuffed Crispy Rounds—*mathdi* (dairy)

This snack has various names in India, the most common being *mathdi* or *matthi*. This is a delicious appetizer that I enjoy serving with high tea. Leftovers will keep for several weeks.

**Pastry:**

| | |
|---|---|
| 2 cups | all purpose flour |
| 4 tablespoons | butter |
| 1 tablespoon | coarsely ground, cumin seeds |
| ¾ teaspoon | salt, or to taste |
| ¾ cup | warm milk |
| Oil | for frying |

**Stuffing:**

| | |
|---|---|
| 1 cup | chickpea flour |
| 1 tablespoon | oil |
| ½ teaspoon | salt, or to taste |
| 1 tablespoon | cracked or cut black peppers (p. 28) |
| 2–3 tablespoons | water |

**Pastry:**

In a medium bowl, mix flour and butter, add cumin and salt and mix well again. Gradually add milk and prepare stiff dough. Knead for a minute to make it smooth. Divide into 50 portions and shape each into a smooth round patty. Cover and set aside.

**Stuffing:**

In another bowl mix chickpea flour with oil, add salt and black pepper and mix well. Gradually add water and prepare stiff dough. Divide into 25 portions and shape each into round patty slightly smaller than those made with the all purpose flour. Set aside.

Placing one chickpea flour round in between two white ones, press the edges of the white patties so that they join and envelope the yellow. Repeat until all are ready. Set aside.

On a cutting board, roll each stuffed patty into a circle about 3–inches in diameter. Prick the circle with a fork so that they will not puff while frying. Set aside,

When several rounds are rolled, over medium-high heat, heat about 3–inches oil, in a wok or a *karai* and lower the heat to 355 °F. Gradually slide 3 or 4 rounds in the oil, and fry on low heat until slightly golden, turning once to fry both the sides evenly. Remove with a slotted spoon and drain on paper towels. Roll others when the first batch is frying. Allow to cool and store in a tightly covered container. Serve as desired. Yield: 25 rounds.

## Bombay Snack Mix—*bhelpuri*

No visit to Bombay is complete without visiting the street side vendor at the Churchgate Station who, from his portable stand, sells the meal-sized snack *bhel puri*. Throughout India, Bombay is known for its *bhel*. It is a heavenly mixture comprised of toasted puffed rice; lightly spiced *sev*—crisp chickpea flour noodles; broken, crunchy *puri*—a cracker-like version of one of India's favorite breads; onions; chopped mangoes (when available); boiled and chopped potatoes; sweet and hot raisin chutney; and a spicy cilantro and green-chili chutney. Adeptly mixing the ingredients for you, the vendor or *bhelwala* of this Gujarati-Maharastrian specialty serves *bhel* in a bowl folded out of paper.

Here, I have simplified the recipe by using rice krispies instead of puffed rice, and crumbled tortillas instead of crisp *puri*. Once you prepare *sev* (p. 174) or buy it readymade, the rest of the preparations including the chutneys are not that difficult. Though some Indian restaurants in the United States do serve this, I recommend making your own.

| | |
|---|---|
| 4 cups | rice krispies |
| 1 cup | *sev* (p. 174) |
| 2 | tortillas |
| 2 medium | potatoes, boiled, peeled, cubed small |
| 1 small | onion, finely chopped |
| ½ cup | toasted split chickpea chutney (p. 83) (optional) |
| 1 ½ cups | raisin tamarind chutney (p. 69) |
| ¼ cup | cilantro chutney (p. 70) |
| 1 small | fresh unripe mango, peeled, finely cut (optional) |
| ½ cup | finely chopped cilantro |
| Salt | as required |
| Red Chili powder | as required |

In a bowl combine rice krispies and *sev* and set aside. Dry toast tortillas in a frying pan or fry using very little oil, until crisp. Crumble tortillas and add to rice krispie mixture. This is your basic *bhel* mix.

Normally, guests are invited to serve themselves, taking as much of any *bhel* ingredient as they like. On a table place basic *bhel* mix in a large serving bowl, and arrange rest of the ingredients in small bowls. Guests should be instructed to mix the ingredients well before eating. Add extra salt and chili or any chutney—some people prefer garlic and red chili chutney (p. 75)—to taste.

Serves 3–4.

## Cream of Wheat with Yogurt and Cashew Nuts
### —*upama* (dairy)

This popular South Indian dish is traditionally made from semolina, a grainy wheat product, known as *sooji* in Hindi or *ravo* in Gujarati. Cream of Wheat or farina, a similar wheat product processed differently from semolina, is a convenient substitute, which I prefer since it is clean, readily available and cooks quickly. Resembling Italian polenta in consistency, this dish is a spicy version of the dessert, *sheera* (p. 472). Partially cooked cashews and *urid dal* retain their flavor, and amplify the sharp, nutty aroma of the mustard seeds. Chilies and fresh ginger add an additional, flavorful bite. A very satisfying snack or light meal, it may be served hot or at room temperature.

| | |
|---|---|
| 2 tablespoons | oil |
| 2 teaspoons | black mustard seeds |
| ½ teaspoon | *hing* (asafoetida) |
| 2 teaspoons | *urid dal* (optional) |
| 10 | cashew nuts, broken |
| 1 cup | Cream of Wheat |
| 1 cup | buttermilk |
| 1 cup | water |
| 1 ½ teaspoons | salt, or to taste |
| 4 | serrano or jalapeño chilies, chopped finely |
| 2–inch piece | fresh ginger, peeled, chopped finely |
| ¼ cup | chopped cilantro, for garnish |

Heat oil in a saucepan, over high heat, and add mustard. When mustard starts to crackle, add *hing* and *urid dal*, if using any. Add cashew nuts and lower the heat. Cook for 1 minute until cashew nuts are evenly golden. Add cream of wheat and cook, stirring well, until slightly golden.

Add the next 5 ingredients including ginger, and mix well. Cook over low heat, stirring occasionally, until mixture thickens, about 7 minutes. Serve garnished with cilantro.

Serves 3–4.

**Note:** For a **non-dairy** version, substitute 1 cup of water for buttermilk and add 2 tablespoons lemon juice.

**Oil-free:** Heat the saucepan over high heat. Once the saucepan is hot, remove from heat and add mustard, cover immediately. When seeds crackle, remove lid and add *hing* and cashew nuts. Return the saucepan to the stovetop, over low heat, and cook stirring well for 10 seconds. Immediately add cream of wheat and proceed with the recipe as above.

## Butter Biscuits—*Surti khari biscuit* (dairy)

My assistant *Manu* shared this recipe with me at *The Ganges*. I had been looking for the recipe, which is a specialty from the Gujarati city Surat. Serve with tea.

| | |
|---|---|
| ½ cup | all purpose flour |
| ½ cup | self-rising flour |
| 8 tablespoons | unsalted margarine or butter, melted |
| 3 tablespoons | plain yogurt |
| 1 teaspoon | caraway seeds |
| 3 tablespoons | milk or as required |

Preheat oven to 250 °F.

In a bowl, combine both the flours and margarine or butter. Add the remaining 3 ingredients including milk and mix well to make a soft dough. Divide into about 35 portions. Shape each portion into a smooth round and place it on a baking tray. Repeat until finished, leaving little space between each round. Place the tray in the oven and bake until biscuits rise and turn light golden, about one hour. Turn off the oven and let the tray sit in the oven for another hour. Remove, store in a container with a tight lid.

Yield: 35 biscuits.

## Cardamom Cookies—*nankhatai*

This Surti specialty is a wonderful accompaniment to tea. It is non-dairy and therefore suitable for vegans.

| | |
|---|---|
| ½ cup | melted vegetable shortening |
| ½ cup | sugar |
| 1 cup | all purpose flour |
| ½ teaspoon | cardamom seeds |
| ¼ teaspoon | ground nutmeg |

Preheat oven to 250 °F.

Melt shortening before measuring. In a food processor fitted with a metal blade, process shortening and sugar until the sugar has dissolved. We did it by hand when we did not have a food processor or a liquidizer.

Add flour and process again until well mixed. Remove to a bowl, add cardamom seeds and nutmeg and mix well. Divide into 35 portions. Shape each portion into a round and place it in a baking tray. You may gently press, couple of slivered almond on top, making the round slightly flat. Repeat until all the *nankhatai* are placed in the tray, leaving little space between each. Place the tray in the oven and bake until cookies rise and turn light golden, about one hour. Turn off the oven and let the tray sit in the oven for another hour. Remove, store in a container with a tight lid.

Yield: 35 cookies.

## Toasted Almonds—*shekeli badam*

Toasted almonds may be served at cocktails as a snack. ½ teaspoon garlic or onion powder may be added to the salt. Though the recipe may seem somewhat mundane, the results are surprisingly good.

| | |
|---|---|
| 4 cup | almonds |
| 3 tablespoon | salt, or to taste |
| 3 tablespoon | water |

Place almonds in a baking tray. In a small bowl combine salt and water. Add it to almonds and mix well, coating all of the almonds with the salted water. (Much of the salt will not adhere to the almonds as they toast.) Cover with paper towels and set aside for three hours or overnight to dry.

Preheat oven to 300 °F. Place the tray in the oven and toast almonds stirring frequently. After about 20 minutes, lower the temperature to 250 °F to prevent almonds from burning. Toast until crisp, about 30 minutes. Serve hot or let cool and store in a jar.

Yield: 4 cups.

## Toasted Peanuts—*shekeli shing* or *moongphali*

Toasted peanuts may be either served as a snack or used in recipes in this book. They are easy to prepare, and store for a few weeks. Note that much of the salt that is called for will fall off into the oven tray as the peanuts toast.

| | |
|---|---|
| 1 ½ cups | peanuts, picked over |
| 1 tablespoon | salt |
| 2 tablespoons | water |

Place peanuts in a clean baking tray. Combine water and salt and apply to peanuts. Set aside for about two hours. After two hours, sprinkle water over the peanuts and mix again. Set aside for another two hours, or overnight.

Preheat oven to 250 °F. Place tray with peanuts in the oven, and toast stirring frequently, until lightly golden. When the skins easily peel from the peanuts, the nuts are ready. Turn off the oven, let the tray rest in the oven for 5 minutes before removing. When cool, store in a tightly covered jar.

Yield: 1 ½ cups.

# VEGETABLES

## Dumplings

Mock Potatoes—*labaad aaloo*
Spinach Dumplings—*palak vadi*
Ajwain Dumplings—*ajmani vadi*

## Onions

Basic Sauce: Onions with Tomatoes and Spices
Onions with Potatoes—*kanda bateta*
Onions with Chickpea Flour and Yogurt—*pitla* (dairy)

## Potatoes and Sweet Potatoes

Spicy Potatoes with *Garam Masala*—*suki bhaji*
Potatoes with Peanuts—*batetane shing*
Stuffed Potatoes in Onion and Yogurt Sauce—*dum bateta* (dairy)
Stuffed Potatoes in Coconut-Onion Sauce—*kandana rasama bharela bateta*
Stuffed Potatoes in Spinach and Coconut Sauce—*bhaji koprama bateta*
Sweet Potatoes, Potatoes, and Peas with Onions—*sakkaria bateta, vatana*
Sweet Potatoes and Potatoes with Peanuts—*sakkaria bateta*

## Asparagus

Asparagus with Potatoes—asparagus *bateta*
Asparagus in Yogurt Sauce—*dahiwala* asparagus (dairy)

185

## Cauliflower

Cauliflower in Coconut Sauce—*koprana doodhma gobi*
Cauliflower with Potatoes—*aaloo gobi*
Creamy Cauliflower with Potatoes and Peas—*moglai gobi* (dairy)
Cauliflower with Spicy Yogurt Sauce—*gobi korma* (dairy)

## Green Beans and Long Beans

Green Beans with Potatoes—*fansi bateta*
Green Beans with Dumplings—*fansi dhokli*
Long Beans with Eggplant—*choli vengan*

## Indian Lima Beans and Cluster Beans

Indian Lima Beans with Fresh Spices—*papdinu shak*
Indian Lima Beans with Dumplings—*papdi dhokli*
Indian Lima Beans with Spinach Kebabs—*papdi muthia*
Indian Lima Beans with Eggplant—*papdi vengan*
Cluster Beans with Coriander and Cumin—*guwarnu shak*
Cluster Beans with Yogurt—*dahiwali guwar* (dairy)

## Eggplant

Eggplant with Peas—*vengan vatana*
Eggplant with Split Indian Lima Beans—*vengan valni dal*
Stuffed Eggplants in Spicy Sauce—*ravaiya vengan*
Stuffed Eggplants in Cilantro Sauce—*kothmirma ravaiya*
Stuffed Eggplants with Peas—*vatana bharela vengan*
Roasted Eggplant with Onions—*bharta-1*
Roasted Eggplant with Yogurt—*bharta-2* (dairy)
Sliced Eggplants with Onions and Chickpea Flour—*khalva*
Eggplant with Nuts and Yogurt—*badshahi baigan* (dairy)

# Cabbage

Cabbage with Potatoes and *Garam Masala*—*kobi bateta*
Cabbage with Chickpea Flour—*kobij khalva*
Spicy Cabbage, Stir-Cooked with Mustard Seeds—*vaghareli kobij*

# Tomatoes

Tomatoes with Potatoes—*tameta bateta*
Sweet and Spicy Green Tomatoes—*kacha tameta khalva*

# Green Peas and Fresh Pigeon Peas

Green Peas with Potatoes—*vatana bateta*
Peas and Paneer in Raisin Sauce—*drakshawala matar paneer* (dairy)
Fresh Pigeon Peas—*leeli tuver*

# Bottle Gourd and Ridge Gourd

Bottle Gourd with Potatoes—*doodhi bateta*
Bottle Gourd with Split Chickpeas—*doodhi chana*
Bottle Gourd *Kofta* in Onion Sauce—*doodhina kofta*
Ridge Gourd with Mustard and Lemon—*turia*
Ridge Gourd with Cucumber and Yam—*turia kakdi*

# Zucchini, Pumpkin and Spaghetti Squash

Zucchini with Peas and Tomatoes—zucchini *vatana*
Stuffed Zucchini—*bhareli* zucchini
Pumpkin with Peas and Tamarind—*kohlu vatana*
Pumpkin with Split Lima Beans and Spinach—*kohlu, valdalne palak*
Spaghetti Squash with Dumplings—spaghetti squash *ne vadi*

## Bitter Gourd and Tinde (Ivy Gourd)

Stuffed Bitter Gourd with Anise—*saunfwale karele*
Sweet and Sour Bitter Gourd with Onions and Potatoes—*karela, kan-dane bateta*
Tinde, or Ivy Gourd, with Potatoes—*tindora bateta*
Tinde, or Ivy Gourd, with Spicy Potatoes and Onions—*tindora, bateta, kanda*

## Mushrooms

Mushroom with Green Onions—*pyazwali gucchi*
*Masala* Mushrooms with Spinach—*gucchi palak*
Zucchini with Mushrooms—zucchini *gucchi*

## Spinach, Collard and Amaranth Greens

Spinach and Potato "Curry"—*palak aaloo*
"Curried" Spinach with *Paneer*—*palak paneer* (dairy)
Spiced Spinach with Sesame—*bhaji ragad* (dairy)
Spinach with Split Chickpeas—*palak moglai* (dairy)
Spinach with Carrots—*sai bhaji*
Collard Greens with Onions—collard *saag*
Collard Green with Split Bengal Grams—collard *patalbhaji*
Amaranth Greens with Cumin—*cholai*
Amaranth Greens with Onions—*kandane cholai*

## Okra

Stuffed Okra—*bhindi masala*
Okra with Onions—*Punjabi bhindi*
Vegetarian "Gumbo"—*bhinda, kandane paneer* (dairy)

## Mixed Vegetables

Vegetable Casserole—*dum shak*

## Fruits as Vegetables

Stuffed Bananas with Fresh Spices—*bharela kela*
Stuffed Bananas with Chickpea Flour and Spices—*kelana ravaiya*
Honeydew Melon with Green Peas—*khadbucha vatana* (no oil)
Mango Vegetable—*kerinu shak*
Persimmon with Cumin—*jeera* persimmon

# Vegetables

While the *tandoor* or clay oven is a trademark of North Indian cooking, a typically Gujarati meal is distinguished not by the vessel in which it is cooked, but rather, by the manner in which it is served: in a *thali*, or large round stainless steel plate. A 1–inch vertical rim lines the edge of the *thali*, permitting several small bowls to line the edge of the plate. Usually, these bowls hold a vegetable; a typical Gujarati *dal* made of beans, peas or lentils; and at times, a *kadhi*, a soup-like yogurt sauce for rice. Daily bread, rice and chutneys are placed directly on the *thali*.

The number of dishes served varies with the occasion. A large or festive occasion requires a complex menu while a meal at home may consist of one or two vegetables, *dal* or *kadhi,* rice and *chapati*. In some homes, however, two vegetables are made each day, out of which one is often a potato vegetable—the potato is common and popular fare in Indian cooking.

The abundance of greens and vegetables available in India makes it easy and satisfying to be a vegetarian. Indian vegetables such as fresh lima beans, fresh pigeon peas, tinde or ivy gourd, snake gourd, etc. have become widely available in the U.S. over the past few years. I look for these vegetables in areas like San Francisco's Chinatown or at bi-weekly farmer's markets. Since many of these vegetables are available only during the summer months, many Indians purchase them in bulk, then clean, peel, cut, blanch and freeze them for later use.

**Low Fat Cooking:**

Any of these recipes can be made without the addition of oil. To omit oil, dry toast spices, mix with a little water and boil for a few seconds prior to adding to the vegetable (p. 47). Those on sodium-free diets should keep in mind that salt may also be deleted from any recipe (p. 48). Coconut may be omitted, except when used in the sauce-base of a recipe.

I encourage readers of this book to experiment: once you have tried making a few of the recipes here, try to develop ideas about which vegetables you may substitute for recipes, for added variety.

The selection of vegetable recipes included here are the more popular dishes among the 200 various vegetable preparations I served at one time or another at *The Ganges*.

# Dumplings

## Mock Potatoes—*labaad aaloo*

Spiced with *ajwain*, these simple dumplings resemble tiny baby potatoes. Made without oil, they are light and provide a flavorful twist to any recipe to which they are added. They can be cut or added whole to any recipe. One evening at *The Ganges*, I prepared a dry vegetable with green onion and potatoes; for half of the evening not a single consumer expressed interest in ordering the dish. I decided to add some of these dumplings to the vegetable, and quickly revised the menu describing specials of the day. Before long, all that I had prepared was gone.

The dumplings may be prepared ahead of time and refrigerated in a covered container for 4–5 days.

| | |
|---|---|
| 16 cups | water for boiling |
| 2 cups | chickpea flour |
| 1 teaspoon | salt, or to taste |
| ½ teaspoon | chili powder |
| ¼ teaspoon | turmeric |
| 1 teaspoon | *ajwain* (p. 9) (optional) |
| ½ teaspoon | baking soda |
| ½ cup | water, or as needed to prepare the dough |

In a large saucepan over high heat, bring water to a full boil. Meanwhile, mix flour and the next 5 ingredients including baking soda. Gradually add water and, using your hands, prepare a stiff, smooth dough.

Divide the dough into about 60 portions—note that the uncooked dumplings will be tiny, and that they will swell as they cook. Shape each portion into a smooth ball and set aside. When all the balls are ready, drop them, one at a time, into the boiling water. Boil for about 15 minutes.

Remove, drain and allow to cool. Use as dumplings in any recipe of your choice. I particularly like to add them into dishes made with beans, or even into light, non-dry *dals* such as Split Peas with Garlic and Cloves (p. 375). Yield: 60.

## Spinach Dumplings—*palak vadi*

The dough for this oil-free variety of dumplings is made with ground spinach, which adds flavor and moisture to the recipe. Below, I have described ways in which these dumplings may be steamed, cut and added to a cooked vegetable recipe, or alternatively, added directly to any non-dry vegetable dish as it cooks.

| | |
|---|---|
| 2 cups | chopped spinach |
| ¾ teaspoon | salt, or to taste |
| ½ teaspoon | chili powder |
| ½ teaspoon | baking soda |
| ¼ teaspoon | turmeric |
| 2 teaspoons | chopped garlic |
| 2 cups | chickpea flour |

In a food processor, fitted with a metal blade, grind spinach together with the next 5 ingredients including garlic. Add flour, and continue processing to form a ball of dough. Remove to a bowl.

**Steamed:**

Prepare steamer as directed on page 50.

Divide the dough into 4 portions. Dusting your hands with flour to prevent sticking, shape each portion into a long cylinder about 1–inch thick. Carefully arrange portions in the steamer in a circular fashion, leaving at least ½–inch in between the rolls. (Cook in batches if the steamer cannot accommodate all the rolls.) Cover the steamer and cook for about 20 minutes. Remove, allow to cool, and cut each roll into 1–inch pieces. Use as dumplings in recipes of your choice.

**Directly cooked:**

Using your hands take about 2 teaspoons dough, shape into a round ball and add to the boiling sauce of a vegetable dish 20 minutes prior to end of cooking. Note that any dish containing dumplings should be stirred gently, so as not to break the *vadi*.

Yield: Approximately 80.

## Ajwain Dumplings—*ajmani vadi*

I like to steam these dumplings and to add them to dry vegetable dishes, as well as dishes with sauces.

| | |
|---|---|
| 2 cups | chickpea flour |
| ½ teaspoon | salt, or to taste |
| 1 teaspoon | *ajwain* (p. 9) |
| ¼ teaspoon | turmeric |
| ½ teaspoon | baking soda |
| ½ cup | water, or as required |

In a bowl combine flour with the next 3 ingredients including turmeric. Add baking soda and mix again (note that if baking soda and turmeric are added at the same time, the recipe will assume a reddish tint). Prepare dumplings following directions in the preceding recipe. Use in any vegetable dish, adding approximately 20 minutes prior to the end of cooking time.

Yield: Approximately 60.

# Onions

## Basic Sauce: Onions with Tomatoes and Spices

This is a basic sauce for making a variety of "curry" recipes calling for browned onions and tomatoes. Use this basic sauce in recipes included in this book, or create your own "curry" by adding one or more of the following ingredients: anise, fresh ginger, basil, green chilies, mint, cilantro, extra *garam masala* or coconut. You may make the base in large quantities and freeze in small batches for future use. This sauce also keeps in the refrigerator for several days.

| | |
|---|---|
| 4 tablespoons | oil |
| 3 three–inch sticks | cinnamon |
| 10 | cloves |
| 5 | cardamom pods |
| 8 cups | finely sliced onions |
| 10 large cloves | garlic, peeled, chopped |
| 2 teaspoons | salt, or to taste |
| 3 tablespoons | tomato paste |
| 2 teaspoons | chili powder, or to taste |
| ½ teaspoon | turmeric |
| 2 teaspoons | *garam masala*-1 (p. 21) |
| 4 tablespoons | ground coriander seeds |
| 1 tablespoon | ground cumin seeds |

Heat oil in a medium, stainless steel saucepan, over high heat. Add the next 3 ingredients including cardamoms pods. When cinnamon starts to swell, add onions and cook, stirring well until brown but not burned, about 30 minutes. Add the remaining 8 ingredients including cumin. Lower the heat to medium-low and cook, stirring well, for 7 minutes. Remove from heat, and use as called for in recipes.
Yield: Approximately 3 cups.

## Onions with Potatoes—*kanda bateta*

This simple dry vegetable recipe was a favorite of many customers at *The Ganges*. At times, to add a bit of variety to the recipe, I added 1 teaspoon *garam masala* 2 (p. 22) and ¼ cup potato flakes. Leftovers will keep for a couple of days in the refrigerator. Serve with rice and *dal* (p. 358), or *khichadi* (p. 320).

| | |
|---|---|
| 2 tablespoons | oil |
| 1 teaspoon | fenugreek seeds |
| 2 medium | onions, finely cut or sliced |
| 3 medium | potatoes, boiled, peeled, cubed 1–inch |
| 1 ¼ teaspoons | salt, or to taste |
| ¼ teaspoon | turmeric |
| 1 teaspoon | chili powder |
| 2 tablespoons | ground coriander seeds |
| 2 teaspoons | ground cumin seeds |
| 1 tablespoon | brown sugar, or to taste |
| 1 teaspoons | *garam masala*-1 (p. 21) |
| 3 tablespoons | vegetable *masala* (p. 23) (optional) |
| ¼ cup | chopped cilantro, for garnish |

In a medium saucepan, heat oil on medium-high heat and add fenugreek. When fenugreek turns brown, lower the heat to medium and add onions. Cook onions for about 3 minutes, stirring frequently. Add potatoes and the next 7 ingredients including *garam masala*. Add vegetable *masala,* if using, and mix well. Cook, stirring gently for 3 more minutes. Serve garnished with cilantro.
Serves 6.

# Onions with Chickpea Flour and Yogurt—*pitla* (dairy)

A typical Gujarati and Maharastrian preparation, this recipe was a great family favorite, which my mother would make at least once a week when we were young. *Pitla* can be served with any Indian bread.

| | |
|---|---|
| 1 tablespoon | oil |
| 1 medium | onion, chopped |
| ½ cup | yogurt |
| 2 cups | water |
| ½ cup | chickpea flour |
| ¾ teaspoon | salt, or to taste |
| ¼ teaspoon | turmeric |
| 1 teaspoon | chili powder |
| ¼ cup | chopped cilantro, for garnish |

Heat oil in a medium stainless steel saucepan over high heat. Add onions. Cook for 1 minute, stirring well. Reduce the heat to low.

In a small bowl, mix yogurt and the next 5 ingredients including chili powder, and add to onions. Cook stirring well, until the mixture thickens, about 7 minutes. Serve garnished with cilantro.

Serves 4–5.

## Potatoes and Sweet Potatoes

### Spicy Potatoes with *Garam Masala*—*suki bhaji*

This dry recipe is often served with *puri* (p. 420), with rice and *dal*, or with rice and *kadhi* (p. 393).

| | |
|---|---|
| 3 tablespoons | oil |
| 2 teaspoons | black mustard seeds |
| ½ teaspoon | *hing* (asafoetida) |
| 4 large | potatoes, boiled, peeled, cubed |
| 2 teaspoons | salt, or to taste |
| 1 teaspoon | chili powder |
| ½ teaspoon | turmeric |
| 3 tablespoons | ground coriander seeds |
| 2 teaspoons | ground cumin seeds |
| 2 teaspoons | *garam masala*-1 (p. 21) |
| 2 tablespoons | brown sugar, or to taste |
| ¼ cup | chopped cilantro, for garnish |

Heat oil in a large frying pan over high heat. Add mustard seeds. Add *hing* when mustard starts to crackle. When *hing* turns brown, add potatoes and lower the heat to medium. Stir well.

Add the next 7 ingredients including brown sugar, and mix well. Cook for about 5 minutes, occasionally stirring gently. Serve garnished with cilantro.

Serves 6.

## Potatoes with Peanuts—*batetane shing*

The addition of peanuts lends this simple recipe a pleasing, crunchy texture. Serve with any meal.

| | |
|---|---|
| 2 tablespoons | oil |
| 2 teaspoons | black mustard seeds |
| ½ teaspoon | *hing* (asafoetida) |
| 3–4 large | potatoes, boiled, peeled, cubed 1–inch |
| 2 teaspoons | salt, or to taste |
| ½ teaspoon | turmeric |
| 1 teaspoon | chili powder, or to taste |
| 1 tablespoon | brown sugar (optional) |
| 3 tablespoons | ground coriander seeds |
| 2 teaspoons | ground cumin seeds |
| 1 cup | peanuts, toasted, peeled, coarsely ground (p. 37) |
| ¼ cup | chopped cilantro, for garnish |

In a large frying pan, heat oil and add mustard seeds. Add *hing* when mustard starts to crackle. When *hing* turns brown, add potatoes and the next 7 ingredients including peanuts. Mix well and cook on medium heat for about 5 minutes.

Serve hot garnished with cilantro.

Serves 4–6.

## Stuffed Potatoes in Onion and Yogurt Sauce
### —*dum bateta* (dairy)

Stuffed potato dishes, popular in Gujarat and Maharashtra, are often served during the summer months, when certain other vegetables are unavailable. When I would prepare this dish at *The Ganges*, the wafting, mouth-watering fragrance of onions cooking in yogurt turned the heads of many passers-by. Serve with any Indian bread.

20 (2–inches diameter) red potatoes, peeled, cored

**Stuffing:**

| | |
|---|---|
| ½ cup | chickpea flour |
| 1 ½ cups | chopped cilantro |
| ½ cup | unsweetened, finely grated coconut (optional) |
| 1 teaspoon | salt, or to taste |
| ½ teaspoon | baking soda |
| ¼ teaspoon | turmeric |
| 1 teaspoon | *garam masala*-1 (p. 21) |
| 2 teaspoons | ground cumin seeds |
| 3 | serrano or jalapeño chilies, ground |
| ½ teaspoon | chili powder |
| 2 teaspoons | sugar, or to taste |

**Sauce:**

| | |
|---|---|
| 3 tablespoons | oil |
| ½ teaspoon | *hing* (asafoetida) |
| 2 cups | finely chopped onions |
| 1 cup | water |
| ½ cup | yogurt |

With a peeler, peel and scoop out the center of each potato in order to form "cups" for stuffing (illus. p. 202). Place potatoes in a bowl of water to prevent discoloration.

**Stuffing:**

Combine chickpea flour, 1 ¼ cup cilantro (save ¼ cup for garnish) and the next 9 ingredients including sugar. Drain potatoes well, and stuff each potato with the stuffing mixture; set aside. Keep leftover stuffing mix, if any, for later use.

**Sauce:**

Heat oil in a medium stainless steel saucepan over high heat and add *hing*. When *hing* turns brown, add onions and sauté for 2 minutes. Lower the heat to medium, and add potatoes. Mix well, cover and cook for about 10 minutes, stirring two or three times to prevent burning.

Combine water, yogurt and remaining stuffing mix, if any. Add mixture to potatoes, stir well; cover and cook on very low heat until the potatoes are done, about 10 minutes. A toothpick or a knife should pass easily into each potato when fully cooked. If further cooking is required, cover and cook for a few more minutes.

Serve garnished with the remaining ¼ cup cilantro.

Yield: 20 baby potatoes.

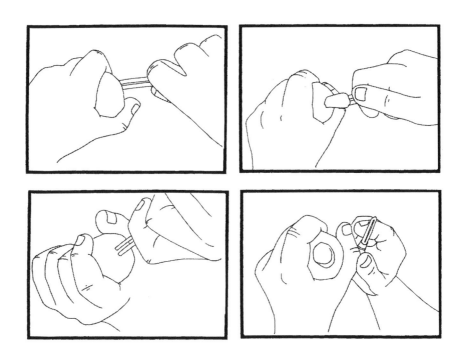

*Method for Coring Potatoes for Stuffing*

# Stuffed Potatoes in Coconut-Onion Sauce
## —*kandana rasama bharela bateta*

The potatoes in this flavorful vegetable dish are cooked and stuffed with the same ingredients, yielding a boldly flavored recipe. Lightly cooked, ground onions lend the dish a smooth texture. Serve with any meal.

20 (2–inches diameter) red baby potatoes, peeled, cored (p. 202)
**Sauce:**

| | |
|---|---|
| 3 tablespoons | oil |
| 6 cups | chopped onions |
| 5 cups | water |
| 1 cup | chopped cilantro |
| 3–inch piece | fresh ginger, peeled, ground |
| 5 | serrano or jalapeño chilies, ground |
| 2 teaspoons | salt, or to taste |
| ½ cup | chickpea flour |
| ½ cup | unsweetened, finely grated coconut |
| 1 tablespoon | sugar, or to taste |

**Stuffing:**

| | |
|---|---|
| 1 ½ cups | unsweetened, finely grated coconut |
| ½ teaspoon | baking soda |
| 1 ½ teaspoons | sugar (optional) |
| 5 | serrano or jalapeño chilies, ground |
| 3–inch piece | fresh ginger, peeled, ground |
| 1 ½ teaspoons | salt, or to taste |
| 2 tablespoons | lemon juice |
| ½ cup | chickpea flour |
| 1 cup | chopped cilantro |

With a peeler, peel and scoop out the center of each potato in order to form "cups" for stuffing (illus. p. 202). Place potatoes in a bowl of water to prevent discoloration.

**Sauce:**

Heat oil in a medium saucepan over high heat and add onions. Cook onions, stirring well for 5 minutes. Remove the pan from heat. Remove onions with a slotted spoon and grind them in a blender or a food processor fitted with a metal blade. Return ground onions to the same saucepan; add the remaining 8 sauce ingredients including sugar, and mix well.

Place the saucepan on low heat and stir well while cooking to prevent flour from sticking to the bottom of the pan.

**Stuffing:**

Combine all 9 ingredients including ¾ cup cilantro, saving ¼ cup for garnishing.

Drain the potatoes, and stuff each with the stuffing mix. Save the remaining stuffing mix, if any. Add stuffed potatoes to the boiling sauce. Mix well, cover and cook over low heat for 20 minutes or until the potatoes are done. A toothpick or knife can be easily inserted into the potatoes when done. Add the remaining stuffing, if any, to the boiling sauce, and mix well. Cook for 1 more minute and remove from heat.

Garnish with remaining ¼ cup cilantro and serve.

Yield: 20 baby potatoes.

**Note**: For a fancy touch, add 2 tablespoons ground almonds and ¼ teaspoon crushed saffron during the last 2 minutes of cooking. You may also substitute 2 tablespoons golden raisins for the sugar.

# Stuffed Potatoes in Spinach and Coconut Sauce
## —*bhaji koprama bateta*

Though it combines complex flavors, this dish is unbelievably simple. My loyal customers have waited patiently for this recipe. Serve with any Indian bread or rice.

| | |
|---|---|
| 20 (2–inches diameter) | red baby potatoes, peeled, cored (p. 202) |
| **Stuffing:** | |
| ½ cup | unsweetened, finely grated coconut |
| 1 ½ cups | chopped cilantro |
| ½ teaspoon | baking soda |
| 6 | serrano or jalapeño chilies, ground |
| 3–inch piece | fresh ginger, peeled, ground |
| ½ cup | chickpea flour |
| 1 ½ teaspoons | salt, or to taste |
| **Sauce:** | |
| 1 (15-ounce) can | coconut milk |
| 2 tablespoons | chickpea flour |
| 3 cups | water or as required |
| 2 (10-ounce) packets | frozen chopped spinach |
| 3–inch piece | fresh ginger, peeled, ground |
| 4 | serrano or jalapeño chilies, ground |
| 1 ½ teaspoons | salt, or to taste |
| 2 tablespoons | chopped cilantro, for garnish |

With a peeler, peel and scoop out the center of each potato in order to form "cups" for stuffing (illus. p. 202). Place potatoes in a bowl of water to prevent discoloration.
**Stuffing:**
Combine all 7 stuffing ingredients. Drain potatoes, stuff each of them and set aside. Save leftover stuffing mix, if any.

**Sauce:**

In a medium saucepan, combine coconut milk with chickpea flour. Add water, frozen spinach, and the remaining 3 ingredients, including salt. Add stuffed potatoes and place pan over high heat. Cook, stirring frequently, until the mixture comes to a boil. Lower the heat to medium-low.

Spinach will defrost and start to cook with the potatoes. Stir frequently to make sure the flour does not stick to the bottom. By the time spinach dissolves completely, potatoes will be almost cooked.

Add remaining stuffing mixture to the sauce, if any. Cook on low heat, stirring every few minutes until the potatoes are done, about 20 minutes. Check with a toothpick or a knife for doneness.

Serve hot, garnished with cilantro.

Makes: 20 baby potatoes.

# Sweet Potatoes, Potatoes, and Peas with Onions
## —*sakkaria bateta, vatana*

This spicy recipe is simple to prepare. Featuring green peas, it is attractive as it is tasty. Serve with any meal.

| | |
|---|---|
| 4 cups (2 medium) | boiled, peeled, cubed sweet potatoes, cubed 1–inch |
| 3 cups (2 large) | boiled, peeled, cubed potatoes, cubed 1–inch |
| 3 tablespoons | oil |
| 1 cup | chopped onions |
| 2–inch piece | fresh ginger, peeled, ground |
| 4 | serrano or jalapeño chilies, ground |
| 2 ½ teaspoons | salt, or to taste |
| 2 teaspoons | *garam masala*-2 (p. 22) |
| 3 tablespoons | ground coriander seeds |
| 2 teaspoons | ground cumin seeds |
| 2 cups | green peas; defrosted, if using frozen |
| ¼ cup | chopped cilantro, for garnish |

Boil sweet potatoes and potatoes separately. Cook them until a knife passes easily into the potato, but take care not to overcook the potatoes such that they fall apart. Peel and cut both potatoes into about 1–inch cubes, set aside.

Over high heat, in a medium saucepan, heat oil, add onions and cook for 3 minutes or until the onions are translucent. Add next 4 ingredients including *garam masala*, and cook the mixture, stirring well, for about 2 minutes.

Add sweet potatoes, potatoes, coriander and cumin; gently mix well and cook on low heat for about 3 minutes, stirring two or three times in between. Add peas, and mix well. Cook until the vegetable is heated through.

Serve garnished with cilantro.

Serves 6–8.

## Sweet Potatoes and Potatoes with Peanuts
### —*sakkaria bateta*

This simple yet unusual combination was a favorite at *The Ganges*. This dish is traditionally served on *Ekadesi* or religious days, and is made with rock salt and *ghee*. Serve with any meal or with Amaranth Flour Bread (p. 438).

| | |
|---|---|
| 4 cups (2 medium-large) | sweet potatoes, boiled, peeled, cubed 1–inch |
| 4 medium | potatoes, boiled, peeled, cubed 1–inch |
| 2 tablespoons | oil |
| 2 teaspoons | cumin seeds |
| 6 | serrano or jalapeño chilies, ground |
| 3–inch piece | fresh ginger, peeled, ground |
| 3 tablespoons | lemon juice |
| 1 cup | peanuts, toasted, peeled, coarsely ground (p. 37) |
| 2 teaspoons | salt, or to taste |
| 2 tablespoons | chopped cilantro, for garnish |

Boil sweet potatoes and potatoes separately. Cook them until a knife passes easily into the potato, but take care not to overcook the potatoes such that they fall apart. Peel and cut both potatoes into about 1–inch cubes, set aside.

Heat oil in a medium saucepan, over high heat, and add cumin. When cumin starts to sizzle, add chilies, ginger and lemon juice. Lower the heat to medium, and mix well.

Add both the potatoes, peanuts, and salt. Mix again and cook, stirring very gently, for 5 minutes, or until heated through. Serve hot, garnished with cilantro.

Serves: 4–6.

# Asparagus

## Asparagus with Potatoes—asparagus *bateta*

Featuring an unusual pairing of ingredients, this invention of *The Ganges* kitchen, was popular among restaurant regulars. As with all asparagus recipes, I take care not to overcook asparagus. Serve with *parotha* (p. 411) or any Indian bread.

| | |
|---|---|
| 2 bunches | asparagus |
| 8 cups | water plus 2 teaspoons salt, for boiling |
| 1 tablespoon | oil |
| ½ teaspoon | *hing* (asafoetida) |
| 2 medium | potatoes, boiled, peeled, cubed |
| 1 ½ teaspoons | salt, or to taste |
| 1 tablespoon | vegetarian *masala* (p. 23) |
| ¼ teaspoon | turmeric |
| 1 teaspoon | chili powder |
| 3 tablespoons | ground coriander seeds |
| 2 teaspoons | ground cumin seeds |
| 1 ½ teaspoons | sugar, or to taste |
| 2 teaspoons | lemon juice |
| 2 tablespoons | chopped cilantro, for garnish |

Trim and discard the hard stems of the asparagus. Cut asparagus into 2-inch pieces. Add to salted water and bring to a boil over high heat. When water comes to a boil, remove and drain asparagus; discard water.

Heat oil in a medium saucepan over high heat and add *hing*. As soon as *hing* turns brown, add asparagus, potatoes and the remaining 8 ingredients including lemon juice, lower heat, and mix well. Cook until heated through. Serve hot, garnished with cilantro.
Serves 4–6.

## Asparagus in Yogurt Sauce—*dahiwala* asparagus (dairy).

A popular dish among my patrons, this recipe frequently featured on *The Ganges* restaurant menu. Note that no added salt is required, since the *pakora* flour is already seasoned.

| | |
|---|---|
| 1 bunch | asparagus, trimmed |
| 6 cups | water plus 1 teaspoon salt, for boiling |
| 1 cup | *pakora* flour (p. 133) |
| 3 cups | buttermilk |
| 1 cup | water |
| 2 teaspoons | oil |
| 1 teaspoon | black mustard seeds |
| ¼ cup | chopped cilantro, for garnish |

Cut trimmed asparagus into 2–inch pieces, add to a medium saucepan and bring to boil in 6 cups salted water over high heat. When the water comes to a boil, remove from heat. Drain asparagus and discard water.

In a medium stainless steel saucepan, combine *pakora* flour with buttermilk and water, and mix well using a whisk. Cook the mixture on low heat, stirring well, until it thickens, about 10 minutes. When the sauce thickens, add boiled asparagus. Mix well, remove and set aside.

Heat oil in a small frying pan over medium heat, and add mustard. When mustard starts to crackle, add the mixture to asparagus; mix well. Serve garnished with cilantro.

Serves 4–6.

# Cauliflower

## Cauliflower in Coconut Sauce—*koprana doodhma gobi*

Coconut milk-based sauces are very popular in Gujarat, Maharashtra and in South India. Coconut milk is delightful and sweet when fresh, but obviously more readily available in cans.

Serve this with *bhakhari* (p. 408) or any Indian bread.

| | |
|---|---|
| 6 | serrano or jalapeño chilies |
| 3–inch piece | fresh ginger, peeled |
| 8 | mint leaves |
| 6 cloves | garlic |
| ½ cup | chopped cilantro |
| 2 (15-ounce) cans | coconut milk |
| 1 ½ teaspoons | salt, or to taste |
| ½ cup | wheat or chickpea flour |
| 1 medium | cauliflower, cut into florets, washed |
| 1 cup | fresh or frozen green peas (optional) |
| 1 | diced carrot, for garnish |

Using a blender or a liquidizer, grind together until smooth, chilies with the next 4 ingredients including cilantro. Set aside.

In a medium saucepan combine coconut milk with salt and flour. Cook over medium heat, stirring well, until the mixture starts to thicken, about 7 minutes. Add cauliflower and fresh peas. (If using frozen peas, add later, with the fresh, ground spices.) Lower heat, and cook for 2 minutes, stirring well.

Add ground chili mixture (and peas, if using frozen) to cauliflower. Stir well. Cook until heated through, and cauliflower is cooked to desired texture.

Serve hot, garnished with diced carrots.

Serves 6–8.

## Cauliflower with Potatoes—*aaloo gobi*

The combination of cumin, *garam masala*, onions and cilantro is tantalizing. For a more colorful recipe, add a quarter cup frozen green peas to the recipe with the water.

Note that, in this recipe, the cauliflower is meant to be slightly undercooked to preserve its crunchy texture. Serve with any Indian bread and rice.

| | |
|---|---|
| 2 tablespoons | oil |
| 2 teaspoons | cumin seeds |
| ½ teaspoon | *hing* (asafoetida) |
| 1 small head | cauliflower, cut into large pieces |
| 3 medium | potatoes, boiled, peeled, cubed 1–inch |
| 2 teaspoons | salt, or to taste |
| ¼ teaspoon | turmeric |
| 2 teaspoons | *garam masala*-1 (p. 21) |
| ½ teaspoon | chili powder |
| 3 tablespoons | ground coriander seeds |
| 2 teaspoons | ground cumin seeds |
| 1 cup | dried onion flakes or granules (p. 38) |
| 2 tablespoons | brown sugar, or to taste |
| ½ cup | water |
| ¼ cup | frozen green peas (optional) |
| ¼ cup | chopped cilantro, for garnish |

Heat oil in a medium saucepan over high heat, and add cumin. When cumin starts to sizzle, add *hing*. Immediately add cauliflower, stir for 1 minute and then lower the heat to medium. Add potatoes and the next 9 ingredients including water and mix well. (Add peas at this point, if desired.) Cook until the water is absorbed, about 5 minutes. The cauliflower will remain slightly undercooked and crunchy.

Serve hot, garnished with cilantro.

Serves 4–6.

## Creamy Cauliflower with Potatoes and Peas
### —*moglai gobi* (dairy)

This extremely flavorful dish goes well with *naan* (p. 422), *parotha* (p. 411) or *puri* (p. 420).

| | |
|---|---|
| 5 | serrano or jalapeño chilies |
| 1 cup | chopped cilantro |
| ¼ cup | unsweetened, grated coconut |
| 10 | mint leaves |
| 2–inch piece | fresh ginger, peeled, chopped |
| 3 cloves | garlic, peeled |
| 3 tablespoons | cashew nuts |
| ½ cup | light cream |
| 2 tablespoons | oil |
| 2 teaspoons | cumin seeds |
| ½ teaspoon | *hing* (asafoetida) |
| 1 small | cauliflower, cut into florets |
| 2 teaspoons | salt, or to taste |
| 2 cups | peas |
| 2 medium | potatoes, boiled, peeled, cubed |
| ¼ cup | chopped cilantro, for garnish |

In a liquidizer or a food processor fitted with a metal blade, grind together the chilies with the next 7 ingredients including cream. You may add a ¼ cup water to facilitate grinding. The mixture should be smooth in consistency, like pancake batter. Set aside.

Heat oil in a medium saucepan over high heat, and add cumin seeds. When cumin starts to sizzle, add *hing*. When the *hing* turns brown, add cauliflower and salt. Mix well and lower the heat to medium. Cook for about 5 minutes, or until the cauliflower is cooked to your taste. Add peas and potatoes, mix well, and lower heat to medium

Add the ground spice mixture to the cauliflower, stir well, and cook for 3 more minutes.

Serve garnished with cilantro.

Serves 6–8.

## Cauliflower with Spicy Yogurt Sauce—*gobi korma* (dairy)

The addition of both sliced and ground onions to this dish lends the recipe consistency, texture and flavor. This simple recipe goes well with any meal. Vegans may substitute 2 tablespoons lemon juice for the yogurt.

| | |
|---|---|
| 1 medium | cauliflower, washed, cut into 1–inch pieces, washed |
| ½ cup | plain yogurt |
| 2 medium | onions, quartered |
| 1 ½–inch piece | fresh ginger, peeled |
| 3 cloves | garlic, peeled |
| 1 ½ teaspoons | salt, or to taste |
| 3 tablespoons | oil |
| ½ cup | finely sliced onions |
| 6 | cloves |
| 2 teaspoons | ground cumin seeds |
| 1 cup | green peas, fresh or frozen |
| ¼ cup | water |
| ¼ cup | chopped cilantro, for garnish |

Combine cauliflower with yogurt and set aside while preparing onion mixture.

In a liquidizer or a food processor, fitted with a metal blade, grind quartered onions with the next 3 ingredients including salt. Combine the ground mixture with cauliflower and yogurt, and set aside for 10 more minutes.

Heat oil in a medium, stainless steel saucepan over high heat. Add sliced onions and sauté for 3 minutes. Add cloves, and fry the mixture until onions are slightly golden, about 7 minutes. Add cauliflower mixture, cumin and peas, if using fresh. Add water, and cook until cauliflower is done to taste.

If using frozen peas add after cauliflower is done, and simmer until the vegetable is heated through.

Serve hot, garnished with cilantro.

Serves 4–6.

# Green Beans and Long Beans
## Green Beans with Potatoes—*fansi bateta*

While this recipe may take slightly long to cook, it is simple and satisfying. Instead of green beans, you may substitute long beans, which are available in most Asian produce stores.

| | |
|---|---|
| 2 tablespoons | oil |
| 1 teaspoon | cumin seeds |
| 1 teaspoon | *ajwain* (p. 9) |
| ½ teaspoon | *hing* (asafoetida) |
| 2 tablespoons | sesame seeds |
| 1 pound | green beans, trimmed, cut into ¼–inch pieces |
| 2 medium | potatoes, peeled, cut into ½–inch cubes |
| 2 teaspoons | salt, or to taste |
| 1 teaspoon | chili powder |
| ¼ teaspoon | turmeric |
| 2 tablespoons | ground coriander seeds |
| 2 teaspoons | ground cumin seeds |
| 2 tablespoons | lemon juice |
| 2 teaspoons | sugar, or to taste |
| 2 tablespoons | chopped cilantro, for garnish |

Heat oil in a medium frying pan over high heat. Add cumin and *ajwain*. Add *hing* when cumin starts to sizzle. When *hing* turns slightly brown, lower the heat to medium-low and add sesame seeds. Sesame seeds will turn golden brown within seconds.

Add beans and potatoes, stir well, and cook for 2 minutes. Add salt and stir well again. Cook the mixture for about 10 minutes, stirring 2 or 3 times in between. Add chili powder and the next 5 ingredients, including sugar, mixing well. Maintaining low heat, cook for 5 more minutes, or until the vegetables are done to your taste. Garnish with cilantro and serve.
Serves 4–6.

## Green Beans with Dumplings—*fansi dhokli*

This is a delicious variation of the recipe included in my first cookbook, *A Surti Touch*. A satisfying preparation, it may be served as a one-dish meal.

### Dumplings:

| | |
|---|---|
| 1 cup | chickpea flour |
| 1 tablespoon | oil |
| ½ teaspoon | salt, or to taste |
| ¼ cup | finely chopped cilantro |
| ½ teaspoon | *ajwain* (p. 9) |
| ½ teaspoon | turmeric |
| ¼ teaspoon | chili powder |
| ¼ cup | water, or as needed |

### Beans:

| | |
|---|---|
| 2 pounds | fresh green beans, trimmed, cut into ½–inch pieces |
| 6 cups | water |
| ½ teaspoon | baking soda |
| 1 tablespoon | oil |
| 1 teaspoon | *ajwain* |
| 2 teaspoons | salt, or to taste |

### Spice Mixture:

| | |
|---|---|
| 1 cup | chopped cilantro |
| 2 tablespoons | unsweetened, grated coconut |
| 1 tablespoon | chopped mint leaves |
| 3 | serrano or jalapeño chilies |
| 2–inch piece | fresh ginger, peeled |
| 6 cloves | garlic, peeled |

### Dumplings:

Combine flour with the next 6 ingredients including chili powder, in a bowl. Gradually add water, mixing well to prepare a stiff yet smooth dough. Divide dough into 40 portions. Press each portion into a patty, and set aside.

**Beans:**

Trim stems off of beans and cut into ½–inch long pieces. In a medium saucepan, combine beans with water and the next 4 ingredients including salt. Bring to a boil over high heat. When the mixture comes to a boil, lower the heat, and simmer for 10 minutes.

**Spice Mixture:**

While the beans are cooking, using a blender or a liquidizer, grind into a fine paste cilantro together with the next 5 ingredients including garlic. If necessary, add a ¼ cup water to facilitate grinding.

Add the ground mixture to the beans and raise the heat to medium-high. When mixture comes to a boil, reduce heat to low and drop dumplings into the beans, one at a time. Raise heat again to bring the mixture to a full boil. Reduce heat to low, bring to a simmer and cook until the beans are done, about 10 minutes. Dumplings will also be cooked by this time. Do not cover while cooking, or the beans will lose their color.

Serve hot.

Serves 4–6.

## Long Beans with Eggplant—*choli vengan*

Long beans are readily available in Asian produce stores. Serve with rice and any *dal*.

| | |
|---|---|
| 1 pound | long beans, trimmed, cut into ¼–inch pieces, washed |
| 1 medium | eggplant, cut into small cubes |
| 2 tablespoons | oil |
| ½ teaspoon | *hing* (asafoetida) |
| 1 ½ teaspoons | salt, or to taste |
| 6 | serrano or jalapeño chilies, ground |
| 3–inch piece | fresh ginger, peeled, ground |
| 6 cloves | garlic, peeled, ground |
| 2 cups | water |
| ¼ cup | chopped cilantro |

Trim stems from beans and cut into ¼–inch long pieces. Trim and discard stem from eggplant, and cut into ½–inch cubes.

In a medium saucepan heat oil over medium heat and add *hing*. Add beans and eggplant as soon as *hing* turns brown.

Add the next 5 ingredients, including water, and half of the cilantro (save ½ cup for garnish). Mix well and cook on low heat until the beans and eggplants are cooked, about 30 minutes.

Serve garnished with the remaining cilantro.

Serves 4–6.

# Indian Lima Beans and Cluster Beans

## Indian Lima Beans with Fresh Spices—*papdinu shak*

Fresh Indian lima beans (p. 340) can be found in most farmers' markets and in some Indian stores during the summer months. If unavailable in your area, soak dry lima beans (p. 340)—commonly sold in Indian stores—and substitute into the recipe below. Serve with any Indian bread, or rice and *kadhi* (p. 393).

| | |
|---|---|
| 2 pounds | fresh Indian lima beans, trimmed, washed |
| 1 tablespoon | oil |
| 1 teaspoon | *ajwain* (p. 9) |
| ½ teaspoon | *hing* (asafoetida) |
| ½ teaspoon | baking soda |
| 2 teaspoons | salt, or to taste |
| 3 cups | water |
| 6 | serrano or jalapeño chilies, ground |
| 3–inch piece | fresh ginger, peeled, ground |
| 6 cloves | garlic, peeled, ground |
| 1 cup | chopped cilantro |
| 2 tablespoons | unsweetened, finely grated coconut (optional) |
| 2 teaspoons | sugar, or to taste |

Trim and prepare Indian lima beans as indicated on page 340; rinse beans (and pods, if any) thoroughly.

Add beans (and pods) to a small saucepan with the next 9 ingredients including garlic. Mix well and cook on high heat until the beans are soft, about 15 minutes. Add ¾ cup cilantro (saving ¼ cup for garnish), coconut and sugar. Cook for 2 more minutes, or until the beans are done. Remove, and serve garnished with the remaining cilantro.

Serves 4–6.

## Indian Lima Beans with Dumplings—*papdi dhokli*

This traditional Gujarati preparation may be served as a one-dish meal. I do not recommend substituting dry lima beans for the fresh variety called for below.

**Dumplings:**

| | |
|---|---|
| 1 ½ cups | chickpea flour |
| 1 tablespoon | oil |
| ¾ teaspoon | salt, or to taste |
| ½ teaspoon | baking soda |
| 1 teaspoon | *ajwain* (p. 9) |
| ½ teaspoon | chili powder |
| ¼ teaspoon | turmeric |
| ¼ cup | water, or as needed |

**Beans:**

| | |
|---|---|
| 2 pounds | fresh Indian lima beans, trimmed, washed |
| 2 tablespoons | oil |
| ½ teaspoon | baking soda |
| 1 teaspoon | *ajwain* (p. 9) |
| 6 cloves | garlic, peeled, ground |
| 6 | serrano or jalapeño chilies, ground |
| 4–inch piece | fresh ginger, peeled, ground |
| 1 ½ teaspoons | salt, or to taste |
| 4 cups | water |
| ½ cup | chopped cilantro |

**Dumplings:**

In a bowl, combine flour with the next 6 ingredients including turmeric. Gradually add water and prepare a smooth, stiff dough. If the dough becomes too sticky to work with, apply a little oil on your palms. Knead for about 1 minute, until the dough is smooth. Divide the dough into about 40 tiny portions. Shape each portion into a smooth round patty and set aside.

**Beans:**

Trim and prepare Indian lima beans as indicated on page 340. Wash beans and pods—if any—and transfer to a medium saucepan. Add oil and the next 7 ingredients including water. Bring the mixture to a full, over high heat. When the mixture comes to a boil, add half of the chopped cilantro, saving ¼ cup for garnishing.

After about 5 minutes, drop the dumplings into the beans, one at a time so that they do not stick to one another. Gently stir after dropping in a few dumplings to ensure that they do not clump together. Boil the mixture until the beans and dumplings are cooked through, about 12 minutes.

Serve hot, garnished with the remaining cilantro. Leftovers can be refrigerated.

Serves 4–6.

# Indian Lima Beans with Spinach Kebabs—*papdi muthia*

Fragrant *ajwain* is combined with fresh spices and green lima beans in this traditional Gujarati recipe. I find that this dish tastes better the next day, heated through or cold. Note that the spinach "kebabs" in this recipe may be substituted with steamed spinach dumplings–*palak vadi* (p. 193).

**Beans:**

| | |
|---|---|
| 2 pounds | fresh Indian lima beans (p. 340), trimmed, washed |
| 2 tablespoons | oil |
| 2 teaspoons | *ajwain* (p. 9) |
| ½ teaspoon | baking soda |
| 6 | serrano or jalapeño chilies, ground |
| 3–inch piece | fresh ginger, peeled, ground |
| 6 cloves | garlic, peeled, ground |
| 2 teaspoons | salt, or to taste |
| 4 cups | water |
| ½ cup | chopped cilantro |

**Kebabs:**

| | |
|---|---|
| 1 ½ cups | chickpea flour **or** wheat flour |
| ½ teaspoon | baking soda |
| 1 ½ teaspoons | salt, or to taste |
| 1 teaspoon | chili powder |
| ¼ teaspoon | turmeric |
| 1 tablespoon | oil |
| 6 cloves | garlic, peeled, chopped |
| 3 cups | chopped spinach, washed, drained |

**Beans:**

Trim and prepare Indian lima beans as indicated on page 340; rinse beans and pods (if any) thoroughly.

In a medium saucepan, add lima beans and next 8 ingredients including water as well as half of the cilantro (save ¼ cup for garnish). Place the pan over low heat and mix well.

**Kebabs:**

While beans are cooking, in a mixing bowl, combine flour with the next 6 ingredients including garlic. Add spinach and mix thoroughly with your hands, so that the moisture from the spinach binds the dough. If the dough remains dry, sprinkle a little water and continue to mix. Be careful to only mix but not knead the dough, as kneading it will make it too soft. This dough will not need much water, as the spinach will release moisture as the dough is mixed.

Scoop approximately 2 tablespoons of dough in your hands and make a fist, shaping the dough into an oblong kebab, about 1–inch long. Set aside. If the dough is sticky, apply a little oil to your palms. Repeat until all are kebabs are shaped. This recipe will make about 40 kebabs.

By the time all the kebabs are ready, the lima beans should have started to boil. If not, raise the heat and start dropping the kebabs, one at a time into the saucepan. Gently stir the saucepan after dropping a few, so that the kebabs do not stick together. You will have about 40 kebabs to drop. Boil for 5 minutes after all of the kebabs have been added.

Lower the heat to medium-low and cook for 10 more minutes, or until the lima beans and kebabs are cooked—check for doneness by tasting. Kebabs should be even-textured and uniform in color on the inside. The beans should be soft, but not soggy (overcooked).

Remove and serve hot, garnished with the remaining cilantro.

Serves 4–6.

## Indian Lima Beans with Eggplant—*papdi vengan*

This vegetable dish is commonly made in Gujarati homes. I find that the recipe tastes best if the eggplant is cooked until very soft—which is in fact, what many Indians prefer. Serve with any Indian meal.

| | |
|---|---|
| 1 pound | Indian lima beans, trimmed, washed |
| 1 medium | eggplant, cut into small cubes |
| 3 cups | water |
| 1 tablespoon | oil |
| 2 teaspoons | *ajwain* (p. 9) |
| 2 teaspoons | salt, or to taste |
| 1 teaspoon | chili powder, or to taste |
| 3 | serrano or jalapeño chilies, ground |
| 6 cloves | garlic, peeled, chopped finely |
| 3–inch piece | fresh ginger, peeled, ground |
| 2 teaspoons | sugar, or to taste |
| 2 tablespoons | chopped cilantro, for garnish |

Trim and prepare lima beans as indicated on page 00; rinse beans and pods (if any) thoroughly. Add lima beans, eggplant and the next 8 ingredients, including ginger to a medium saucepan over high heat. Mix well. Lower the heat to medium when the mixture comes to a boil. Cook, stirring intermittently, until the eggplant and lima beans are done, about 20 minutes

Add sugar and cook for 2 more minutes. Mix well and serve garnished with cilantro.

Serves 4–6.

# Cluster Beans with Coriander and Cumin—*guwarnu shak*

A favorite of many of long-time customers at *The Ganges*, this recipe calls for brown sugar, which may be omitted according to preference, though I think that the slight sweetness enhances the recipe. Goes well with either *chapati* (p. 404) or *rotla* (p. 434).

| | |
|---|---|
| 1 ½ pounds | cluster beans, trimmed, cut into ½–inch pieces |
| 1 tablespoon | oil |
| 1 teaspoon | *ajwain* (p. 9) |
| 1 ½ teaspoon | salt, or to taste |
| ½ teaspoon | baking soda |
| 3 cups | water |
| ½ teaspoon | turmeric |
| 2 tablespoons | ground coriander seeds |
| 2 teaspoons | ground cumin seeds |
| ½ teaspoon | chili powder, or to taste |
| 2 tablespoons | brown sugar, or to taste |
| 2 tablespoons | chopped cilantro, for garnish |

Trim and discard stems from beans. Cut beans into ½–inch long pieces.

In a medium saucepan over high heat, combine beans with the next 5 ingredients including water. When the mixture comes to a boil, lower the heat to medium and cook for 5 minutes. Add turmeric and the next 4 ingredients including sugar, and cook the vegetable for 10 more minutes or until the beans are soft. Stir once or twice as the beans cook.

Serve hot, garnished with cilantro.

Serves 3–4.

## Cluster Beans with Yogurt—*dahiwali guwar* (dairy)

My grandfather's cooking inspires this recipe, which is a variation of a traditional Gujarati dish. Serve with either *chapati* (p. 404) or *parotha* (p. 411).

| | |
|---|---|
| 1 ½ pounds | cluster beans, trimmed, cut into ½–inch pieces |
| 2 tablespoons | oil |
| ½ teaspoon | *hing* (asafoetida) |
| ½ teaspoon | *ajwain* (p. 9) |
| 1 ¼ teaspoons | salt, or to taste |
| 1 teaspoon | chili powder |
| ¼ teaspoon | turmeric |
| 3 cups | water |
| ½ cup | plain yogurt |
| 2 tablespoons | chickpea flour |
| 2 tablespoons | chopped cilantro, for garnish |

Trim and discard stems from beans. Cut beans into ½–inch long pieces.

Heat oil in a medium stainless steel saucepan over high heat and add *hing*. When *hing* turns brown, add beans and the next 5 ingredients including water. Cook on high heat until the beans are soft but not overcooked, about 10 minutes. Stir once or twice as the beans cook.

In a small bowl, combine flour and yogurt, and add to the beans. Mix well and lower the heat. Cook stirring well for 5 more minutes, or until the sauce thickens. Serve garnished with cilantro.

Serves 4–6.

# Eggplant

## Eggplant with Peas—*vengan vatana*

This recipe takes only minutes to prepare once the required ingredients have been gathered. Serve with rice and any *dal*.

| | |
|---|---|
| 1 medium | eggplant, trimmed, cut into small cubes |
| 1 tablespoon | oil |
| ½ teaspoon | *hing* (asafoetida) |
| 1 ¼ teaspoons | salt, or to taste |
| 4 | serrano or jalapeño chilies, ground |
| 2–inch piece | fresh ginger, peeled, ground |
| 2 cloves | garlic, peeled, ground |
| 3 cups | water |
| 1 cup | green peas, fresh or frozen |
| 2 tablespoons | chopped cilantro, for garnish |

Trim and discard stem from eggplant and cut into small cubes.

Heat oil in a medium saucepan, over medium heat, and add *hing* . As soon as *hing* turns brown, add eggplant, salt and the next 4 ingredients including water. Cook until the eggplant is half done, about 12 minutes.

If using fresh peas, add now and continue to cook until the eggplant is soft, about 10 minutes. If using frozen peas, cook eggplant until soft, add the frozen peas and cook until the mixture is heated through. Mix well and remove from heat. Serve hot, garnished with cilantro.
Serves 4–6.

## Eggplant with Split Indian Lima Beans—*vengan valni dal*

This mixture of eggplant, split lima beans and garlic is a family favorite. If left unpeeled, the eggplant will darken the hue of the split lima, though the taste of the dish will be unchanged. Peel the eggplant if the appearance of the dish is a concern. Serve with *parotha* (p. 411), or rice and *kadhi* (p. 393).

| | |
|---|---|
| 1 cup | split Indian lima beans (*valni dal*), soaked four hours |
| 1 medium | eggplant, trimmed, cut into small cubes |
| 2 tablespoons | oil |
| 5 cloves | garlic, peeled, chopped |
| ½ teaspoon | *hing* (asafoetida) |
| ½ teaspoon | chili powder |
| 3 cups | water, or as required |
| 1 ¼ teaspoons | salt, or to taste |
| ¼ teaspoon | turmeric |
| ¼ cup | chopped cilantro, for garnish |

Pick over and wash split Indian lima beans (see note p. 336). Soak for four hours.

Trim and discard stem from eggplant and cut into ½–inch cubes. Place cubes in a bowl and cover with water to prevent discoloration. Set aside.

Heat oil in a medium saucepan over medium heat and add garlic. Add *hing*, when garlic turns golden. After 5 seconds, add chili powder. Raising the heat to high, continue to cook the mixture for an additional 5 seconds.

Drain and add split lima beans, water, salt and turmeric. Stir to mix. Maintaining the high heat, cook for 5 minutes or until the lima beans are half-cooked.

Drain and add eggplant and more water if the recipe appears dry, i.e. if you cannot see water bubbling in the pan, add enough water to barely cover the ingredients. Cook until the eggplant is done, about 15 minutes.

Remove from heat, garnish with cilantro, and serve hot.

Serves 4–6.

# Stuffed Eggplants in Spicy Sauce—*ravaiya vengan*

My grandmother provided me with this version of the classic Gujarati recipe. While coconut is a wonderful addition, it is not essential and may be omitted, if desired. Serve with any flat bread or with *khichadi* (p. 320).

**Eggplants:**

| | |
|---|---|
| 4–6 cups | water |
| ½ teaspoon | baking soda |
| 1 ½ teaspoons | salt, or to taste |
| 1 tablespoon | oil |
| 3–4 | Japanese eggplants **or** |
| 8 | small Indian eggplants, stems trimmed |

**Stuffing:**

| | |
|---|---|
| ¾ cup | chickpea flour |
| 1 teaspoon | salt, or to taste |
| ½ teaspoon | baking soda |
| 1 tablespoon | oil |
| ½ teaspoon | chili powder |
| ¼ teaspoon | turmeric |
| 4 tablespoons | ground coriander seeds |
| 1 tablespoon | ground cumin seeds |
| 3 tablespoons | brown sugar, or to taste |
| 4 tablespoons | unsweetened, finely grated coconut (optional) |
| 1 teaspoon | *garam masala*-1 (p. 21) |
| ½ cup | chopped cilantro |

**Eggplants:**

In a medium saucepan, combine water, baking soda, salt and oil; place the saucepan over low heat.

Trim the stems off of the eggplants. If using Japanese eggplant, slice cross-wise, into about 2 ½–inch thick rounds. On one flat surface of each piece, place 2 perpendicular cuts, one vertical and one horizontal, about 1 ½–inch deep (illus. p. 259), making a cross. If using Indian eggplants or any other tiny variety, place two perpendicular cuts on the stem side. Keep eggplants immersed in a bowl of water to prevent discoloration while preparing the stuffing.

**Stuffing:**

In a bowl, combine chickpea flour with the next 10 stuffing ingredients, including *garam masala*, and half of the cilantro (save ¼ cup cilantro for garnish). Remove eggplants from water. Gently fill the cuts of each eggplant piece with approximately 2 tablespoons stuffing mixture. When all the eggplants pieces are stuffed, place them in the saucepan with water mixture, and raise the heat to high. Save the remaining stuffing mixture, if any, for later use.

When liquid in the saucepan becomes frothy and starts to rise, reduce heat to low, and cook eggplants until done, approximately 15 minutes. The eggplants should be tender—insert a knife and check for doneness as you would a potato. If a softer textured eggplant is preferred, cook for an additional 3 minutes.

Combine remaining stuffing mixture with enough water to make a thick sauce and add it to the eggplant. Stir gently and simmer for 5 more minutes. Remove from heat. Serve hot, garnished with the remaining cilantro.

Serves 4–6.

# Stuffed Eggplants in Cilantro Sauce—*kothmirma ravaiya*

Coarsely ground cilantro and crunchy onions combine here to make an attractive, unusual and elegant dish. Serve with any flat bread or rice and any *dal*.

### Eggplants:

| | |
|---|---|
| 5 cups | water |
| ½ teaspoon | baking soda |
| 1 teaspoon | salt, or to taste |
| 1 tablespoon | oil |
| 4 | Japanese eggplants, trimmed, cut into 2 ½–inch pieces **or** |
| 10 | small Indian eggplants, stems trimmed |

### Stuffing:

| | |
|---|---|
| 2 cups | chopped cilantro, coarsely ground |
| ½ cup | chickpea flour |
| 1 ½ teaspoons | salt, or to taste |
| 2 tablespoons | brown sugar, or to taste |
| ½ teaspoon | baking soda |
| 6 | serrano or jalapeño chilies, ground |
| 6 cloves | garlic, peeled, chopped |
| 3 tablespoons | ground coriander seeds |
| 2 teaspoons | ground cumin seeds |
| 2–inch piece | fresh ginger, peeled, ground |
| ½ cup | finely cut onions |

### Eggplants:

Combine water with baking soda, salt and oil in a medium-sized saucepan and place over low heat.

Trim and discard the stems of the eggplants. If using Japanese eggplant, slice cross-wise, into about 2 ½–inch thick rounds. On one flat surface of each piece, place 2 cuts, one vertical and one horizontal, about 1 ½–inch deep (illus. p. 259), making a cross. If using Indian eggplants or any other tiny variety, place two perpendicular cuts on the stem side. Keep eggplants immersed in a bowl of cool water to prevent discoloration while preparing the stuffing.

**Stuffing:**

In a food processor fitted with a metal blade, coarsely grind cilantro, and remove to a bowl. Add the remaining 10 ingredients for stuffing, including onions, and mix well. Remove eggplants from water. Gently fill the cuts of each eggplant piece with approximately 2 tablespoons stuffing mixture. Save the remaining stuffing mixture for later use. When all the eggplants pieces are stuffed, place them in the saucepan with water mixture, and raise the heat to high.

When liquid in the saucepan becomes frothy and starts to rise, reduce heat to low, and cook eggplants until done, approximately 15 minutes. The eggplants should be tender—insert a knife and check for doneness as you would a potato. If a softer textured eggplant is preferred, cook for an additional 3 minutes.

When the eggplants are soft add remaining stuffing mix, stir gently and simmer for 2 minutes. Serve hot.

Serves: 4–6.

# Stuffed Eggplants with Peas—*vatana bharela vengan*

Though this recipe takes longer to prepare than other stuffed eggplant recipes in this section, it is worth the time and effort. The recipe combines many of the flavors for which Gujarati cooking is renowned.

**Stuffing:**

| | |
|---|---|
| 1 tablespoon | oil |
| ½ teaspoon | *hing* (asafoetida) |
| ¼ cup | finely chopped onions |
| 2 cups | fresh or frozen green peas, coarsely ground |
| 1 teaspoon | salt, or to taste |
| ½ teaspoon | baking soda |
| 3 | serrano or jalapeño chilies, ground |
| 2–inch piece | fresh ginger, peeled, ground |
| 4 cloves | garlic, peeled, chopped |
| 1 cup | chopped cilantro |
| 2 tablespoons | unsweetened, finely grated coconut (optional) |

**Eggplants:**

| | |
|---|---|
| 6–8 | small Indian eggplants **or** |
| 2–3 | Japanese eggplants, trimmed, cut into 2 ½–inch pieces |
| 2 tablespoons | oil |
| ¾ cup | water |

**Stuffing:**

Heat oil in a small frying pan over medium heat and add *hing*. When *hing* turns slightly brown, add onions, mix well and lower the heat.

As the onions cook, coarsely grind peas in a food processor fitted with a metal blade. Add to onions. Add the remaining 7 ingredients for the stuffing mixture including cilantro and coconut (optional) and mix well. Maintaining the heat on low, cook the mixture until almost dry, about 5 minutes. (If using frozen peas, the mixture will take longer to dry.) Remove from heat and set aside to cool.

**Eggplants:**

Trim and discard the stems of the eggplants. If using Japanese eggplant, slice cross-wise, into about 2 ½–inch thick rounds. On one flat surface of each piece, place 2 cuts, one vertical and one horizontal, about 1 ½–inch deep (illus. p. 259), making a cross. If using Indian eggplants or any other tiny variety, place two perpendicular cuts on the stem side. Keep eggplants immersed in a bowl of water to prevent discoloration.

Removing each eggplant piece from the water, gently fill the cuts with approximately 2 tablespoons stuffing mixture. Save the remaining stuffing mix, if any, for later use.

Heat oil in a deep, medium (preferably non-stick) frying pan on high heat. Gently place stuffed eggplants in the pan. Cover and cook on medium heat for about 3 minutes.

Uncover the frying pan and spread any remaining stuffing mix on top of the eggplant. Lower the heat, cover and cook for 7 more minutes. Uncover again, add water, and cook for 3 more minutes. Gently turn the eggplants, cover and cook for about 5 minutes, or until the eggplants are soft.

Serve hot.

Serves 3–4.

## Roasted Eggplant with Onions—*bharta*-1

Containing no butter or cream, this is a lighter version of the dish usually served in Indian restaurants. Roasting an eggplant on a gas stove imparts a rich, smoky flavor to the vegetable—though the cooking technique should be practiced with care. Eggplant may also be barbecued or roasted in an oven.

| | |
|---|---|
| 1 medium | eggplant |
| 2 tablespoons | oil |
| 1 cup | finely sliced onions |
| 2 medium | tomatoes, chopped |
| 3–inch piece | fresh ginger, peeled, ground |
| 1 teaspoon | chili powder, or to taste |
| 1 teaspoon | salt, or to taste |
| 2 tablespoons | chopped cilantro, for garnish |

Wash and wipe eggplant. Stand eggplant with stem side up, on gas stove over a low flame. Cook until the bottom of the eggplant is well charred, about 5 minutes. Using a pair of tongs, lay eggplant on its side over the flame and roast all around turning every few minutes until the eggplant is soft and blistered, about 15 minutes. Alternatively, wrap the eggplant loosely in aluminum foil and bake in an oven preheated to 500 °F for 20 minutes, or until soft. Let the roasted or baked eggplant cool for few minutes, remove skin and mash vegetable meat with a fork. Set aside.

Heat oil in a medium saucepan over medium heat and add onions. Cook onions, stirring well until they are light brown, about 7 minutes. Add tomatoes and cook, stirring well for 3 minutes. Mix in ginger, chili and salt and cook for 2 minutes. Add eggplant, mix well and cook for 3 more minutes.

Remove and serve, garnished with cilantro.
Serves 4.

## Roasted Eggplant with Yogurt—*bharta*-2 (dairy)

Made with nonfat yogurt, without the addition of any oil, this recipe is a good choice for those watching their dietary fat intake.

| | |
|---|---|
| 1 medium | eggplant |
| 8 ounces | nonfat plain yogurt |
| 2–3 | serrano or jalapeño chilies, ground |
| 2–inch piece | fresh ginger, peeled, ground |
| 2 cloves | garlic, peeled, finely chopped |
| ½ cup | green peas, cooked |
| 1 ½ teaspoons | salt, or to taste |
| 2 tablespoons | chopped cilantro, for garnish |

Wash and wipe eggplant. Stand eggplant with stem side up, on gas stove over a low flame. Cook until the bottom of the eggplant is well charred, about 5 minutes. Using a pair of tongs, lay eggplant on its side over the flame and roast all around turning every few minutes until the eggplant is soft and blistered, about 15 minutes. Alternatively, wrap the eggplant loosely in aluminum foil and bake in an oven preheated to 500 °F for 20 minutes, or until soft. Let the roasted or baked eggplant cool for few minutes, remove skin and mash vegetable meat with a fork. Set aside in a bowl and let cool.

Add yogurt and next 5 ingredients including salt, mix well and serve garnished with cilantro.

Serves 4.

**Note:** A non-dairy version of this recipe may be prepared by substituting 2 tablespoons lemon juice for the yogurt.

# Sliced Eggplants with Onions and Chickpea Flour—*khalva*

My mother's version of this recipe omitted onions and called for additional oil. When making this at *The Ganges*, however, I elected to reduce the amount of oil needed and to add sliced onion for extra moisture. This dry "curry" has no sauce. Serve with another vegetable with sauce and *chapati* (p. 404), or with rice and *dal* for a balance of textures.

| | |
|---|---|
| 2–3 | Japanese eggplants, trimmed, sliced thin |
| 3 tablespoons | oil |
| 1 medium | onion, sliced thin |
| 1 cup | chickpea flour |
| 6 cloves | garlic, peeled, ground |
| 2 teaspoons | chili powder, or to taste |
| 1 ½ teaspoons | salt, or to taste |
| ¼ teaspoon | turmeric |
| 4 tablespoons | ground coriander seeds |
| 2 teaspoons | ground cumin seeds |
| ½ teaspoon | baking soda |
| 2 tablespoons | chopped cilantro, for garnish |

Trim and discard stems from eggplants. Thinly slice eggplants into approximately ½–inch thick pieces. Set aside.

Heat oil in a medium frying pan over high heat. Add eggplants and onions. Cook, stirring frequently for about 3 minutes. Lower the heat to medium.

In a bowl, combine flour with next 7 ingredients including baking soda. Add to eggplant and mix well. Cover and cook on low heat, stirring every few minutes until the eggplant is soft and the flour mixture changes color to a deep yellow, about 20 minutes. If the texture of the vegetable is too dry for your taste, you may drizzle about 3 tablespoons water over the dish and heat through. Remove and serve garnished with cilantro.
Serves 4–6.

## Eggplant with Nuts and Yogurt—*badshahi baigan* (dairy)

| | |
|---|---|
| 3 medium | Japanese eggplants, trimmed |
| ½ teaspoon | salt (optional) |
| 3 tablespoons | oil |
| 2 tablespoons | broken cashew pieces |
| 1 tablespoon | golden raisins |
| 1 small | onion, finely sliced |
| ½ cup | finely chopped onions |
| 1 teaspoon | chili powder |
| 2 teaspoons | *garam masala*-1 (p. 21) |
| 1 tablespoon | ground coriander seeds |
| 1 teaspoon | ground cumin seeds |
| ¼ teaspoon | turmeric |
| 1 ½ teaspoons | salt, or to taste |
| 2–inch piece | fresh ginger, peeled, finely chopped |
| 4 cloves | garlic, peeled, finely chopped |
| 3 | tomatoes, preferably roma, chopped |
| ½ cup | nonfat plain yogurt |
| ¼ cup | chopped cilantro, for garnish |

Trim and discard eggplant stems. Thinly slice eggplant and set aside. If a denser textured recipe is desired, lightly salt the slices of eggplant and set aside for 30 minutes. The salt will draw out the moisture from the eggplant.

Heat the oil in a large, nonstick frying pan over medium heat and fry cashews until golden-brown, about 1 minute. Remove with a slotted spoon, and set aside on paper towels. In the same oil fry raisins until plump, remove and set aside together with the cashews.

Into the remaining oil in the frying pan, add sliced onions and fry until golden, about 7 minutes. Remove with a slotted spoon and set aside to drain on paper towels.

Again in the same frying pan, add chopped onions, and cook for 3 minutes. If you salted the eggplant slices, gently squeeze them at this point (to remove excess water), and add to onions. If eggplant was left unsalted, add directly to onions. Cook, stirring well for 5 minutes.

Add the next 9 ingredients including tomatoes, and cook until the eggplants are tender, about 10 minutes. Add yogurt, mix well and cook for 3 more minutes.

Serve garnished with cashews, raisins, browned onions, and cilantro. Serves 4–5.

# Cabbage

## Cabbage with Potatoes and *Garam Masala*—*kobi bateta*

This is a simple, quick and tasty recipe that makes up one of the many low-preparation time dishes that my son likes to make for himself. Serve with any flat Indian bread, rice and any *dal*.

| | |
|---|---|
| 2 tablespoons | oil |
| 1 ½ teaspoons | black mustard seeds |
| ½ teaspoon | *hing* (asafoetida) |
| 1 medium head | cabbage, finely sliced |
| 2 large | potatoes, boiled, peeled, cubed |
| 1 ½ teaspoons | salt, or to taste |
| 1 teaspoon | chili powder |
| ¼ teaspoon | turmeric |
| 3 tablespoons | ground coriander seeds |
| 1 tablespoon | ground cumin seeds |
| 1 ½ teaspoons | *garam masala*-1 (p. 21) |
| 2 tablespoons | brown sugar, or to taste |
| 2 tablespoons | chopped cilantro, for garnish |

Heat oil in a medium saucepan over high heat and add mustard. When mustard starts to crackle, add *hing*. When *hing* turns brown, after just a few seconds, add cabbage and cook for 3 minutes, stirring well.

Add potatoes, and the next 7 ingredients including brown sugar, and mix well. Lower the heat and cook for 2 minutes, or until the cabbage is done to desired texture. (Note: cooking for 2 minutes will leave a slight crunch; if a softer texture is desired, cook for 5 minutes.)

Serve hot, garnished with cilantro.

Serves: 4–6.

## Cabbage with Chickpea Flour—*kobij khalva*

This dry recipe (without stock) pairs well with rice, *kadhi* (p. 393) and any flat Indian bread. Serve on the same day it is made, as the cabbage loses its texture if kept overnight.

| | |
|---|---|
| 2 tablespoons | oil |
| 2 teaspoons | black mustard seeds |
| ½ teaspoon | *hing* (asafoetida) |
| 2 tablespoons | sesame seeds |
| 1 small head | cabbage, finely sliced |
| ½ cup | *khaman* flour (p. 41) |
| 1 teaspoon | salt, or to taste |
| ¼ teaspoon | turmeric |
| 3 tablespoons | ground coriander seeds |
| 2 teaspoons | ground cumin seeds |
| 1 teaspoon | chili powder |
| 1 tablespoon | brown sugar, or to taste |
| ¼ teaspoon | ground anise seeds |
| ¼ cup | chopped cilantro, for garnish |

Heat oil in a medium saucepan over high heat and add mustard. When mustard starts to crackle, add *hing* and sesame seeds. Stir in cabbage when sesame turns slightly golden.

In a medium bowl, combine flour with the next 7 ingredients including anise; add flour mixture to cabbage. Mix well, lower the heat, and cook for 7 minutes or until the flour mixture is cooked. The color of the flour will change to a deep yellow when done.

Serve hot, garnished with cilantro.

Serves 4–5.

## Spicy Cabbage, Stir-Cooked with Mustard Seeds
### —*vaghareli kobij*

The cabbage in this recipe is quickly stir-cooked; the brief cooking time allows the cabbage to retain its crunch yet still enabling it to absorb the flavors of the mustard seeds and green chilies. For a light meal, serve with any Indian bread.

| | |
|---|---|
| 1 medium head | cabbage, finely sliced |
| ¾ teaspoon | salt, or to taste |
| 2-3 | serrano or jalapeño chilies, ground |
| 3–inch piece | fresh ginger, peeled, ground |
| 1 tablespoon | oil |
| 1 teaspoon | black mustard seeds |
| ½ teaspoon | *hing* (asafoetida) |
| 1 tablespoon | flour *masala* (p. 25) (optional) |
| 2 tablespoons | chopped cilantro, for garnish |

In a medium-sized bowl combine cabbage with salt, chilies and ginger; set aside. Heat oil in a small saucepan, over medium heat, and add mustard seeds. When mustard starts to crackle, add *hing*. Immediately add flour masala, if using. Cook stirring well for few seconds and remove the pan from the heat. Let cool 2 minutes.

Add cabbage and mix well. Heat thoroughly approximately for about 2 minutes, over medium heat, before serving. Serve, garnished with cilantro. Serves 4.

# Tomatoes

## Tomatoes with Potatoes—*tameta bateta*

A large part of my childhood was spent moving from place to place in India, as my father was transferred often during the course of his work for the British railways. In many isolated regions of India, fruits and vegetables other than potatoes, onions and bananas were difficult to obtain, especially during the summer months. It was therefore a treat to be served a vegetable dish that contained tomatoes. I can still recall visions of my mother preparing this simple dish, and my rising anticipation of the moment when we would sit down to eat.

Add peas to the dish for additional color. Serve with any Indian bread.

| | |
|---|---|
| 3 | medium potatoes, peeled, sliced |
| 2 tablespoons | oil |
| 2 teaspoons | black mustard seeds |
| 1 teaspoon | cumin seeds |
| 1 three–inch stick | cinnamon, broken |
| ½ teaspoon | *hing* (asafoetida) |
| 2 | dried, whole red chili peppers |
| 4 cups | tomatoes, preferably roma, chopped |
| 2 cups | water |
| ¼ cup | chickpea flour |
| 2 teaspoons | salt, or to taste |
| ½ teaspoon | turmeric |
| ½ teaspoon | *garam masala*-1 (p. 21) (optional) |
| 2 tablespoons | brown sugar, or to taste |
| ½ cup | frozen green peas (optional) |
| 2 tablespoons | chopped cilantro, for garnish |

Peel, wash and slice potatoes into about ¼–inch thick slices. Immerse potato slices in a bowl of cool water to prevent discoloration.

Heat oil in a medium, stainless steel saucepan over high heat. Add mustard and cumin seeds. When mustard starts to crackle and cumin begins to sizzle, lower the heat to medium. Add cinnamon, and after few seconds add *hing*. When the *hing* turns slightly brown, drain and add potatoes. Mix well, reduce the heat to very low and cover the saucepan. Cook the potatoes for 5 minutes. Uncover saucepan, add tomatoes and mix well. Cover the saucepan again, and cook for 2 minutes.

In a small bowl, mix water and chickpea flour until smooth. To the water mixture, add the next 4 ingredients including brown sugar, stirring well. Add to vegetable and mix well. Though I prefer this dish on the dry side, you may make more stock by adding, at this point, ½ cup water and more chili and salt to taste. Lower the heat, add peas if desired, and cook the vegetable for 5 more minutes, or until the sauce thickens.

Serve hot, garnished with cilantro.

Serves 4–6.

## Sweet and Spicy Green Tomatoes—*kacha tameta khalva*

This typical Gujarati recipe is traditionally made with unripe, green tomatoes—it was a favorite of many of my guests at *The Ganges*. Since it is dry, meaning that it has no stock, I recommend serving it as part of a meal with Indian rice and any *dal*.

| | |
|---|---|
| 2 tablespoons | oil |
| 1 teaspoon | cumin seeds |
| 1 teaspoon | black mustard seeds |
| ½ teaspoon | *hing* (asafoetida) |
| 4 medium | unripe, green tomatoes, sliced thin |
| 2 teaspoons | salt, or to taste |
| 2 teaspoons | chili powder |
| ¼ teaspoon | turmeric |
| 3 tablespoons | ground coriander seeds |
| 2 teaspoons | ground cumin seeds |
| 1 ½ cups | chickpea flour |
| ½ teaspoon | baking soda |
| 3 tablespoons | brown sugar, or to taste |
| 2 tablespoons | chopped cilantro, for garnish |

Heat oil, in a medium frying pan, over high heat. Add cumin and mustard seeds. When mustard starts to crackle, add *hing*. As soon as *hing* turns slightly brown, add sliced tomatoes and the next 5 ingredients including cumin. Mix well, cover, and continue to cook on high heat, stirring intermittently, for about 7 minutes, or until tomatoes soften.

Add flour, baking soda and brown sugar, and mix well; lower the heat to medium. Cover and cook for 7 more minutes, or until the flour turns deep yellow in color, signifying that it is cooked. Serve hot, garnished with cilantro Serves 6.

## Green Peas and Fresh Pigeon Peas

### Green Peas with Potatoes—*vatana bateta*

This simple vegetable goes well with *parotha* (p. 411), rice and any *dal.*

| | |
|---|---|
| 4 | serrano or jalapeño chilies, chopped |
| 2–inch piece | fresh ginger, peeled, chopped |
| 4 cloves | garlic, peeled, chopped |
| ½ cup | chopped cilantro |
| 1 tablespoon | chopped mint leaves |
| 2 teaspoons | lemon juice |
| 2 tablespoons | oil |
| ½ teaspoon | *hing* (asafoetida) |
| ½ cup | sliced onions |
| 3 medium | potatoes, boiled, peeled, cubed |
| 1 (10-ounce) packet | frozen green peas |
| 1 ½ teaspoons | salt, or to taste |
| 1 | carrot, diced, for garnish |

In a blender or a liquidizer, grind together chilies with the next 5 ingredients including lemon juice, adding just enough water to facilitate grinding the mixture into a fine, thick paste. Set aside.

Heat oil in a medium saucepan over medium heat, and add *hing*. In a few seconds, the *hing* will turn brown. Add onions and fry, stirring well, for about 2 minutes. Add potatoes, peas and salt, mix well and cook for 2 minutes.

Add ground spice mixture, mix well, lower the heat and cook for 5 more minutes.

Serve hot, garnished with carrots.

Serves 4–6.

# Peas and *Paneer* in Raisin Sauce
## —*drakshawala matar paneer* (dairy)

This unique recipe is one of my children's' favorite. Alas, (sadly!) my son would prefer that I substitute something non-vegetarian for the peas and *paneer*.

| | |
|---|---|
| 6 | whole, dried red chili peppers, cut, seeded |
| 1 ½ cups | water |
| 1 cup | black seedless raisins, rinsed |
| 6 cloves | garlic, peeled, chopped |
| 2–inch piece | fresh ginger, peeled, chopped |
| 2 teaspoons | coarsely ground cumin seeds |
| 1 ½ teaspoons | salt, or to taste |
| 1 teaspoon | coarsely ground black pepper |
| 1 tablespoon | oil |
| 3 | tablespoons tomato paste |
| 1 cup | *paneer* pieces (p. 60) |
| 2 cups | frozen green peas, thawed |
| 2 tablespoons | chopped cilantro, for garnish |

Soak cut peppers in ½ cup hot water. Rinse raisins, and then soak in remaining 1 cup water. Set aside for about 30 minutes.

In a blender or a liquidizer, combine peppers and raisins (including the water in which they were soaked), and the next 5 ingredients including black pepper. Grind until smooth. Set aside.

In a large frying pan, heat oil over medium heat, and add the ground mixture. Cook for 5 minutes stirring well. Add tomato paste and an additional ¼ cup water, if the sauce appears very thick (you may add additional water as necessary, if a thinner consistency is desired). Cook for 2 more minutes.

Add *paneer* pieces, mix well and simmer for 1 minute. Add peas and cook until the vegetable starts to boil. Serve hot, garnished with cilantro. Serves 4–5.

## Fresh Pigeon Peas—*leeli tuver*

Available at farmer's markets during the summer months, whole, fresh pigeon peas are also available frozen, in many Indian stores. Fresh peas or any fresh bean, in the same proportions, may substitute for pigeon peas. This is an exceedingly simple and tasty dish that takes only minutes to prepare. Serve with rice, *kadhi* (p. 293) and *chapati* (p. 404) or with any Indian meal.

| | |
|---|---|
| 2 pounds | fresh or frozen pigeon peas (*leeli tuver)* |
| 1 tablespoon | oil |
| ½ teaspoon | *hing* (asafoetida) |
| 1 ¼ teaspoons | salt, or to taste |
| 1 cup | water |
| 4 | serrano or jalapeño chilies, ground |
| 3–inch piece | fresh ginger, peeled, ground |
| 2 tablespoons | unsweetened, finely grated coconut |
| ½ cup | chopped cilantro |

Shell pigeon peas, if using fresh, and set aside.

Heat oil in a medium saucepan over medium heat, and add *hing*. Add *tuver* when *hing* turns slightly brown. Add salt and water. Cook, stirring well, until *tuver* is soft, about 10 minutes.

Add remaining 4 ingredients, including cilantro, and cook for 2 more minutes. Serve hot.

Serves: 6.

# Bottle Gourd and Ridge Gourd
## Bottle Gourd with Potatoes—*doodhi bateta*

Bottle Gourd is commonly available in Asian produce markets. Of the many variations to this dish, I have provided one of the more common recipes below. Served with Indian bread, rice and *dal* (p. 358), this vegetable makes a satisfying meal.

| | |
|---|---|
| 1 medium | bottle gourd, trimmed, peeled, cut |
| 2 tablespoons | oil |
| 1 ½ teaspoons | cumin seeds |
| ½ teaspoon | *hing* (asafoetida) |
| 2 medium | potatoes, peeled, cubed ½–inch |
| 2 teaspoons | salt, or to taste |
| ¼ teaspoon | turmeric |
| ½ teaspoon | chili powder |
| 2 tablespoons | ground coriander seeds |
| 2 teaspoons | ground cumin seeds |
| 3 cups | water |
| 1 tablespoon | sugar, or to taste |
| 2 tablespoons | chopped cilantro, for garnish |

Trim and discard the stem from the bottle gourd. Peel and cut gourd lengthwise into half. Slice halves lengthwise and then cut slices to make ½–inch cubes.

Heat oil, in a medium saucepan, over medium heat, and add cumin seeds. Add *hing* when cumin starts to sizzle. When *hing* turns brown, add bottle gourd, potatoes and the next 5 ingredients including ground cumin. Mix well, cover, and reduce heat to low. After 2 minutes add water, return cover to saucepan, and cook the mixture until potatoes are done, about 15 minutes.

Add sugar and mix well. Simmer uncovered for 1 minute.

Serve garnished with cilantro.

Serves 6.

## Bottle Gourd with Split Chickpeas—*doodhi chana*

This recipe may also be made with any summer squash, in the same proportions described below. Serve with rice and *kadhi* (p. 293 or *parotha* (p. 411).

| | |
|---|---|
| 1 cup | split chickpeas (*chana dal)*, soaked four hours |
| 1 medium | bottle gourd, trimmed, peeled, cubed ½–inch |
| 6 cups | water, or as needed |
| 2 ½ teaspoons | salt, or to taste |
| ½ teaspoon | *garam masala*-1 (p. 21) |
| 1 teaspoon | *garam masala*-2 (p. 22) |
| 2 teaspoons | ground coriander seeds |
| ½ teaspoon | turmeric |
| 2–inch piece | fresh ginger, peeled, finely chopped |
| 4 | serrano or jalapeño chilies, chopped |
| 2 tablespoons | chickpea flour |
| 2 tablespoons | oil |
| 2 teaspoons | cumin seeds |
| 6 cloves | garlic, peeled chopped |
| ¼ teaspoon | *hing* (asafoetida) |
| ½ teaspoon | chili powder |
| ¼ cup | chopped cilantro, for garnish |

Pick over, wash (see note, p. 336) and soak *dal* for four hours.

Trim and discard the stem from the bottle gourd. Peel and cut gourd
lengthwise into half. Slice halves lengthwise and then cut slices to make
½–inch cubes. Set aside.

Drain split chickpeas and discard water. Combine chickpeas with water
and salt in a medium saucepan. Place over high heat, and cook for 7 minutes, until chickpeas are almost cooked.

Add bottle gourd, both *garam masala* variations, and the next 4 ingredients including chilies. Cover and cook until chickpeas are soft and squash is done to desired texture, about 7 minutes.

In a separate small bowl, combine chickpea flour with ¼ cup water, and add to the vegetable. Mix well and reduce heat to low.

Meanwhile, heat oil in a small frying pan over medium heat, and add cumin. When cumin starts to sizzle, add garlic. When garlic is slightly golden, add *hing* and chili powder. Cook the mixture for 5 seconds, and then add it to the vegetable. Mix well, return cover and simmer for 1 minute.

Serve garnished with cilantro.

Serves 6–8.

## Bottle Gourd *Kofta* in Onion Sauce—*doodhina kofta*

For this widely popular recipe, I have tried to combine the various ingredients that I have observed being used in various regions of India. Truly, this is a pan-Indian dish. In the absence of *khaman* flour, add an additional ¾ cup wheat flour. Serve with Indian bread and rice.

*Kofta:*

| | |
|---|---|
| 2 small | bottle gourds, peeled, grated coarsely, squeezed |
| ¾ cup | wheat flour |
| ¾ cup | *khaman* flour (p. 41) |
| 3 | serrano or jalapeño chilies, ground |
| 1 ½ teaspoons | salt, or to taste |
| 6 cloves | garlic, peeled, chopped |
| ½ teaspoon | baking soda |
| 1 teaspoon | chili powder |
| 1 teaspoon | ground anise seeds |
| 2–inch piece | fresh ginger, peeled, ground |
| 1 tablespoon | ground coriander seeds |
| 2 teaspoons | ground cumin seeds |
| 4 teaspoons | sugar, or to taste |
| ¼ teaspoon | turmeric |
| Oil | for frying |

**Sauce:**

| | |
|---|---|
| 2 cups | basic sauce (p. 195) |
| 1 teaspoon | salt, or to taste |
| 1 teaspoon | *garam masala*-1 (p. 21) |
| 4 cups | water |
| ¼ cup | chopped cilantro, for garnish |

*Kofta*:

Peel and grate bottle gourd. Squeeze and discard all the water out of grated bottle gourd, set aside.

Combine both flours with *kofta* ingredients through turmeric. Add squeezed bottle gourd and gently, thoroughly mix with your hands. Do not knead otherwise the dough will get very soft.

Heat about 3–inches of oil in a *karai* or a wok to 375 °F.

Scooping about 2 tablespoons of dough in your hand, form a round ball slightly bigger than a walnut. Make several and drop them gently into oil. Fry until golden brown all around, remove with a slotted spoon and drain on paper towels. Repeat with remaining dough. You will have about 32 *kofta*.

**Sauce:**

Add 2 cups of basic sauce (p. 195) to a medium saucepan over high heat. Immediately add salt, *garam masala* and 4 cups water. Mix well and bring to a boil. Add *kofta* and return mixture to a full boil. Reduce heat to low and simmer for 10 minutes or until the *kofta* are soft. Remove from heat, and serve garnished with cilantro.

Serves 10.

## Ridge Gourd with Mustard and Lemon—*turia*

Lemon, mustard seed and ginger combine in this recipe to yield an extremely tasty entrée. Serve with hot *chapati* (p. 404) for an exquisite meal.

| | |
|---|---|
| 5 medium | ridge gourds, peeled, trimmed, cubed |
| 1 tablespoon | oil |
| 1 teaspoon | black mustard seeds |
| ½ teaspoon | *hing* (asafoetida) |
| ½ cup | water or as desired |
| 4 | serrano or jalapeño chilies, ground |
| 2–inch piece | fresh ginger, peeled, ground |
| 1 teaspoon | salt, or to taste |
| 2 teaspoons | lemon juice, or as desired |
| 2 tablespoons | chopped cilantro, for garnish |

Trim and discard the stems from gourds. Using a peeler, scrape the ridges from and lightly peel gourds. Cut into ½–inch cubes, rinse and set aside.

In a medium saucepan over medium heat, heat oil and add mustard seeds. When mustard starts to crackle, add *hing*. After a few seconds, when *hing* turns brown, add ridge gourd. Reduce heat to low and add next 4 ingredients including salt, mix well. Cover and cook until gourd is soft to desired consistency, about 7–10 minutes. Add lemon juice, mix well, and serve garnished with cilantro.

Serves 4–6.

**Note:** If desired, add 10–12 Steamed Spinach Squares (p. 116) to this vegetable and heat through before serving.

## Ridge Gourd with Cucumber and Yam—*turia kakdi*

Ridge gourd is easily found in produce markets and in Asian stores, where it is sold under the name *sin qua*. A common vegetable for Gujaratis, it is light, very tasty and goes well with any meal. I prefer to serve it somewhat crunchy, rather than cooking it until soft.

| | |
|---|---|
| 2 pounds | ridge gourd, trimmed, peeled, cubed |
| 2 medium | cucumbers, trimmed, peeled, cubed |
| 1 medium | yam, trimmed, peeled, cubed |
| 2 tablespoons | oil |
| 2 teaspoons | black mustard seeds |
| 1 teaspoon | cumin seeds |
| ½ teaspoon | *hing* (asafoetida) |
| 2 teaspoon | salt or to taste |
| 3–inches | fresh ginger, peeled, ground |
| 6 | jalapeño or serrano chilies, ground with seeds |
| 3 tablespoons | unsweetened, finely grated coconut |
| ½ cup | chopped cilantro |
| 2 teaspoons | sugar (optional) |
| 1 tablespoon | lemon juice |

Trim and lightly peel the ridge gourd, leaving some of the green skin on. Cut gourd into about ½–inch cubes, rinse and set aside.

Trim ends from, peel and cut cucumbers and yam into ½–inch cubes.

Heat oil in a medium saucepan over high heat, and add mustard and cumin. When mustard starts to crackle and cumin sizzle, add *hing*. As soon as *hing* turns brown, add cut gourd, cucumber and yam. Add salt and the next 3 ingredients including coconut. Stir well, cover and cook the vegetables for 7 minutes. If you do not like yam undercooked, add it first and cook for few minutes prior to adding gourd and cucumber.

Add cilantro, sugar and lemon juice, mixing well. Cook briefly, uncovered. Serve hot.

Serves 8

## Zucchini, Pumpkin and Spaghetti Squash

### Zucchini with Peas and Tomatoes—zucchini *vatana*

This extremely colorful recipe is very simple and quickly made. It goes well with any Indian bread, rice and *dal* or any yogurt-based dish.

| | |
|---|---|
| 1 tablespoon | oil |
| 1 teaspoon | cumin seeds |
| ½ teaspoon | *hing* (asafoetida) |
| 6 medium | zucchini, washed, trimmed, cubed |
| 1 ½ teaspoons | salt, or to taste |
| 1 teaspoon | chili powder |
| ¼ teaspoon | turmeric |
| 2 tablespoons | ground coriander seeds |
| 1 teaspoon | ground cumin seeds |
| 2 teaspoons | sugar, or to taste |
| 1 cup | chopped roma tomatoes |
| ½ cup | water |
| 2 cups | green peas |
| ½ cup | chopped cilantro |

Heat oil in a medium saucepan, over high, and add cumin. When cumin starts to sizzle, add *hing*. When *hing* turns brown, add zucchini and the next 8 ingredients including water.

If using fresh green peas add them now, if not, add peas as soon as the zucchini is cooked to your taste. Mix well and cook for 2 minutes.

Add half of the cilantro (save ¼ cup for garnish), mix well and cook for few seconds.

Serve garnished with the remaining cilantro.

Serves: 4–6

## Stuffed Zucchini—*bhareli* zucchini

At *The Ganges*, we featured this spicy preparation almost every evening. Extraordinarily popular, the dish features tender pieces of zucchini stuffed with a tantalizing combination of coconut, peanuts and chickpea flour.

Interestingly, zucchini is not widely available in India; the closest Indian relative to the squash being *chibhada*, which differs slightly in texture and in taste.

Serve this dish with any Indian bread or rice.

| | |
|---|---|
| 5 | tender zucchini |
| ¼ cup | chickpea flour |
| 4 tablespoons | ground coriander seeds |
| 2 teaspoons | ground cumin seeds |
| 1 ½ teaspoons | salt, or to taste |
| ½ cup | unsweetened, finely grated coconut |
| ½ cup | unsalted, raw peanuts, coarsely ground (p. 37) |
| ½ teaspoon | chili powder |
| 2 | serrano or jalapeño chilies, ground |
| 2 tablespoons | brown sugar, or to taste |
| 2–inch piece | fresh ginger, peeled, ground |
| 6 cloves | garlic, peeled, ground |
| 1 teaspoon | *garam masala*-1 (p. 21) |
| 2 tablespoons | oil |
| 1 ¼ cups | chopped cilantro |
| 2 cups | water, or as desired |

Wash and trim zucchini. Cut each into about 2 ½–inch long pieces. You will have about 10 pieces. On one side of each piece place 2 perpendicular cuts, one horizontal and one vertical, looking like a plus sign about 1 ½–inches deep (illus. p. 259). Set aside.

In a bowl combine chickpea flour with all the ingredients through oil and 1 cup cilantro (save ¼ cup cilantro for garnish). Mix well, and gently stuff zucchini filling the cuts well. Set aside remaining stuffing mix. Place stuffed zucchini in a medium saucepan, and pour water over it. Cover the saucepan and cook on high heat.

As soon as the zucchini starts to boil, lower the heat to medium-low, open the saucepan and spread the remaining stuffing mixture over the zucchini, do not stir. Cover and cook for 5 more minutes or until the zucchini is cooked to your taste. Remove from heat, mix well and serve hot, garnished with remaining cilantro.

Serves: 5–6.

**Note:** Yellow ripe bananas or small white onions may be used in lieu of zucchini in the above recipe.

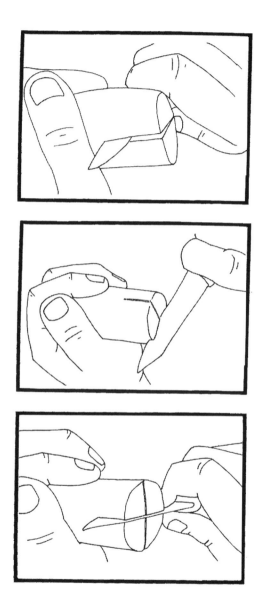

*Method for Preparing a Variety of Fruits and Vegetables (bananas, zucchini, Japanese eggplant…) for Stuffing*

## Pumpkin with Peas and Tamarind—*kohlu vatana*

The addition of tamarind and jaggery in the following recipe results in a mild sweet and sour flavored dish. I have added peas for both color and flavor. Serve with *chapati* (p. 404) or *parotha* (p. 411).

| | |
|---|---|
| 8 cups (1 med.) | peeled, cubed pumpkin |
| 2 tablespoons | oil |
| 1 teaspoon | fenugreek seeds |
| ½ teaspoon | *hing* (asafoetida) |
| 3 cups | water |
| 2 teaspoons | salt, or to taste |
| 1 teaspoon | chili powder |
| ¼ teaspoon | turmeric |
| 2 teaspoons | tamarind concentrate |
| 3 tablespoons | jaggery, or brown sugar |
| 1 cup | green peas, frozen |
| 2 tablespoons | chopped cilantro, for garnish |

To peel and cube the pumpkin, I recommend first removing the stem, and then cutting the pumpkin into halves. After removing the seeds, cut each half into slices. Finally, peel and cube each slice into approximately ½–inch pieces.

Heat oil in a medium stainless steel saucepan, over high heat, and add fenugreek. Add *hing* when fenugreek starts to turn brown. Immediately add pumpkin, water and the next 5 ingredients including brown sugar. Cook until the pumpkin is soft, about 10 minutes. Add peas and cook until it starts to boil. Serve hot, garnished with cilantro.
Serves 4–5.

# Pumpkin with Split Lima Beans and Spinach
## —*kohlu, valdalne palak*

Pumpkin with split lima beans is a family favorite. This flavorful dish may be served with rice, *parotha* (p. 411), and *kadhi* (p. 293).

| | |
|---|---|
| 1 cup | split lima beans, soaked four hours |
| 6 cups | peeled and cubed pumpkin |
| 2 tablespoons | oil |
| 6 cloves | garlic, peeled, chopped |
| ½ teaspoon | *hing* (asafoetida) |
| ½ cup | finely chopped onions |
| 1 ½ teaspoons | salt, or to taste |
| ¼ teaspoon | turmeric |
| 1 teaspoon | chili powder or to taste |
| 2 cups | water |
| 1 bunch | spinach, chopped, washed |

Pick over, wash (see note, p. 336), and soak *dal* for four hours.

To peel and cube the pumpkin, I recommend first removing the stem, and then cutting the pumpkin into halves. After removing the seeds, cut each half into slices. Finally, peel and cube each slice into approximately ½–inch pieces.

Heat oil in a medium saucepan over medium heat, and add garlic. Add *hing* when garlic turns slightly golden. Add onions after 2 seconds, when *hing* turns brown. Cook onions for 2 minutes, drain and add split lima beans, salt and the next 3 ingredients including water. Reduce heat to low, cover and cook the mixture until the split lima is cooked, about 10 minutes.

Add spinach and pumpkin and mix gently. Simmer the mixture on low heat until pumpkin is cooked to desired texture, about 10 minutes. Serve hot.

Serves 6–8.

## Spaghetti Squash with Dumplings—spaghetti squash *ne vadi*

My daughter Bella's friend Chris Hartley once brought us green garlic and about 20 large spaghetti squash from his farm. From this fresh produce was born a new recipe, accented with spinach dumplings. Do not overcook the squash when preparing this recipe. Serve with any Indian bread or rice.

| | |
|---|---|
| 8 cups | spaghetti squash, trimmed, peeled, cubed |
| **Dumplings:** | |
| 2 cups | chickpea flour |
| ½ teaspoon | baking soda |
| 1 teaspoon | salt, or to taste |
| ¼ teaspoon | turmeric |
| ½ teaspoon | chili powder |
| 3 cups | finely chopped spinach |
| ¼ cup | green garlic, trimmed, minced |
| **Sauce:** | |
| 2 tablespoons | oil |
| 2 teaspoons | cumin seeds |
| ½ teaspoon | *hing* (asafoetida) |
| 6 cups | water |
| 4 | serrano or jalapeño chilies, ground |
| 2–inch piece | fresh ginger, peeled, ground |
| 2 teaspoons | salt, or to taste |
| ¼ cup | chopped cilantro, for garnish |

Trim and discard stems from squash. Peel and cube squash into about 1–inch pieces, set aside.

**Dumplings:**

Using your hands, combine chickpea flour with baking soda and salt. Add turmeric and chili powder and mix well. Add spinach and garlic, and mix just long enough to prepare a stiff dough. Take care not to knead too much, else the dough will become very soft. The dough should not require water, as the inclusion of the spinach will add moisture. If the dough is dry and flaky, however, add a few drops of water and mix well.

Shape approximately 2 teaspoons of the dough into a ball, and repeat with remainder of the dough. If the dough sticks to your hands, rub a few drops of oil on your palms and proceed.

**Sauce:**

Heat oil in a medium saucepan, over high heat, and add cumin seeds. When cumin starts to sizzle, add *hing*. Immediately pour water into saucepan and add the next 3 ingredients including salt. Bring the mixture to a full boil, lower heat to medium.

Drop dumplings one at a time into the water mixture and cook for 10 minutes. Add squash, raise the heat and bring to a full boil. Cook over high heat until squash is soft but not overcooked, about 7 minutes.

Remove, garnish with cilantro, and serve hot.

Serves 6–8.

**Note:** Any squash, in the same proportions, can be used for the above recipe.

# Bitter Gourd and Tinde (Ivy Gourd)

## Stuffed Bitter Gourd with Anise—*saunfwale karele*

Indian bitter gourd or bitter melons are smaller and more acrid than those available domestically, in America. When using either the American or the Indian variety, note that the squash will mellow in flavor when cooked. Serve with hot *chapati* (p. 404), or *parotha* (p. 411).

**Bitter Gourd:**

| | |
|---|---|
| 4 medium | bitter gourds, trimmed, scraped |
| 1 ½ teaspoons | salt for rubbing bitter gourds |

**Onion-Potato Mixture:**

| | |
|---|---|
| 4 tablespoons | oil |
| 2 cups | very finely cut onions |
| 2 teaspoons | coarsely ground anise seeds |
| ½ teaspoon | turmeric |
| 3 tablespoons | ground coriander seeds |
| 1 tablespoon | ground cumin seeds |
| 1 ½ teaspoons | chili powder |
| 2 teaspoons | sugar, or to taste |
| 1 tablespoon | *garam masala*-1 (p. 21) |
| 1 ½ teaspoons | salt, or to taste |
| 4 medium | potatoes, peeled, halved, sliced ½–inch thick |
| 2 tablespoons | water |
| 2 tablespoons | chopped cilantro, for garnish |

Trim and discard stems from gourd. Using a peeler, scrape the ridges from and lightly peel the gourds, leaving on some of the skin. Slit each gourd lengthwise, taking care not to halve the gourd, cutting only to the center. Next, slice each gourd into 2–inch thick rounds. Remove and discard seeds from the rounds. Thoroughly rub salt into the rounds and set aside for 30 minutes. After 30 minutes, wash gourd rounds and wipe them free of water.

Heat 2 tablespoons oil in a small frying pan over medium heat (save 2 tablespoons for later use). Add onions and cook until golden brown, about 20 minutes. Add anise and the next 7 ingredients including salt and cook the mixture on low heat for about 5 minutes. Remove from heat. Divide onion mixture into two portions. Using one portion of the mixture, stuff gourd rounds through the cuts, pressing the rounds closed.

Heat the remaining oil in a large frying pan, over medium heat. Combine potatoes with remaining onion mixture and arrange with stuffed bitter gourds in a single layer in the frying pan. Cover and lower the heat. After about 10 minutes, remove the lid and gently turn the potatoes and gourds. Drizzle 2 tablespoons water over the potatoes and gourds. Cover again and cook until the potatoes and gourds are soft, about 10 minutes.

Serve hot, garnished with chopped cilantro.
Serves 4–6.

## Sweet and Sour Bitter Gourd with Onions and Potatoes
### —*karela, kandane bateta*

The addition of brown sugar and lemon juice to this recipe adds a sweet, tangy twist to the earthy flavor of the cooked bitter gourd. Serve with any Indian bread.

| | |
|---|---|
| 2 medium | bitter gourds, trimmed, scraped |
| 2 teaspoons | salt for rubbing bitter gourds |
| 2 tablespoons | oil |
| ½ teaspoon | *hing* (asafoetida) |
| 2 cups | sliced onions |
| 2 medium | potatoes, peeled, halved, sliced ¼–inch thick |
| 1 teaspoon | salt, or to taste |
| ½ teaspoon | turmeric |
| 1 teaspoon | chili powder |
| 4 tablespoons | ground coriander seeds |
| 1 tablespoon | ground cumin seeds |
| ½ teaspoon | lemon crystals (p. 13) **or** |
| 2 tablespoons | lemon juice |
| 2 tablespoons | brown sugar, or to taste |
| 2 tablespoons | chopped cilantro, for garnish |

Trim and discard stems from gourd. Using a peeler, scrape the ridges off of and lightly peel the gourds, leaving on some of the skin. Cut each bitter gourd into approximately 2–inch thick rounds. Cut each round into halves, making semi-circles, and then slice each half lengthwise into ¼–inch thick pieces. Rub salt into the slices and set aside for about 10 minutes. Squeeze after 10 minutes, discarding juice and large seeds, if any. Set aside.

Heat oil in a frying pan over medium heat and add *hing*. After a few seconds, when the *hing* turns brown, add bitter gourd, onions, potatoes and next 5 ingredients including cumin. Lower the heat, cover and cook, stirring frequently, until the potatoes are soft and bitter gourd is cooked, about 15 minutes.

Add lemon juice and sugar. Mix well and cook for 2 more minutes.

Serve garnished with cilantro.

Serves 4–6.

## Tinde, or Ivy Gourd, with Potatoes—*tindora bateta*

Resembling a tiny, oblong watermelon, this gourd is referred to by its proper name, "Ivy Gourd" or a derivative of its Indian name, "tinde." A seasonal vegetable, tinde can be bought in quantity, washed, sliced and frozen in small batches for future use (if using frozen, defrost prior to use). Serve with any Indian bread.

| | |
|---|---|
| 2 tablespoons | oil |
| ½ teaspoon | *hing* (asafoetida) |
| 1 ½ pounds | tinde or ivy gourd, trimmed, cut into ¼–inch slices |
| 2 medium | potatoes, peeled, halved, cut into ¼–inch slices |
| 1 ½ teaspoons | salt, or to taste |
| ¼ teaspoon | turmeric |
| 1 teaspoon | chili powder |
| 3 tablespoons | ground coriander seeds |
| 2 teaspoons | ground cumin seeds |
| 2 tablespoons | chopped cilantro, for garnish |

Trim and discard stems from tinde. Cut lengthwise into halves, and then cut each half lengthwise, into ¼–inch thick slices. Heat oil in a medium frying pan over medium heat and add *hing*. When *hing* turns brown, add tinde, potatoes and salt and mix well. Lower the heat, cover and cook, stirring occasionally, until the tinde and potatoes are done, about 12 minutes.

Add turmeric, and next 3 ingredients including cumin. Mix well and cook for 3 more minutes. Serve hot, garnished with cilantro.
Serves 4–6.

# Tinde, or Ivy Gourd, with Spicy Potatoes and Onions
## —*tindora, bateta, kanda*

Serve this dry vegetable with any Indian meal.

| | |
|---|---|
| 2 tablespoons | oil |
| ½ teaspoon | *hing* (asafoetida) |
| 1 ½ pounds | tinde or ivy gourd, trimmed, cut into ¼–inch slices |
| 2 medium | potatoes, peeled, cut into ¼–inch slices |
| 2 medium | onions, sliced thin |
| 2 teaspoons | salt, or to taste |
| 1 teaspoon | chili powder |
| ½ teaspoon | turmeric |
| 2 tablespoons | ground coriander seeds |
| 2 teaspoons | ground cumin seeds |
| 1 teaspoon | *garam masala*-2 (p. 22) |
| 3 tablespoons | chickpea flour |
| ¼ cup | chopped cilantro, for garnish |

Trim and discard stems from tinde. Cut gourd into ¼–inch slices. Heat oil in a large frying pan over high heat, and add *hing*. When *hing* turns brown, after a few seconds, add tinde, potatoes and onions. Mix well, lower the heat to medium and add salt. Mix again. Cover and cook until the potatoes and tinde are cooked, about 12 minutes.

Uncover frying pan, add chili powder and next 5 ingredients including flour. Mix well, cover again, and cook on low heat for 7 more minutes, stirring two or three times in between.

Serve hot garnished with cilantro.

Serves 4–6.

# Mushrooms

## Mushroom with Green Onions—*pyazwali gucchi*

The flavors of onions and mushrooms complement each other in this simple yet exotic recipe. Serve with any meal.

| | |
|---|---|
| 6 cups | mushrooms, trimmed, sliced |
| 2 tablespoons | oil |
| 1 large | onion, finely chopped |
| 4 cloves | garlic, chopped |
| 2–inch piece | fresh ginger, peeled, ground |
| 4 | serrano or jalapeño chilies, ground |
| 2 teaspoons | salt, or to taste |
| 3 cups | finely cut green onions |

Wash mushrooms, trim and discard stems, and slice thinly. Set aside.

In a large frying pan, over medium heat, heat oil and add onions. Cook onions, stirring well for 2 minutes. Add the next 4 ingredients including salt and cook on low heat for 5 minutes.

Add mushrooms, mix well and cook stirring frequently for about 3 more minutes. Add green onions. Cook until the green onions soften or are cooked to desired texture. Serve hot.

Serves 4–6.

## *Masala* **Mushrooms with Spinach**—*gucchi palak*

This simple and unique preparation combines the flavors of spinach, mushroom and cumin. Serve with any Indian bread or rice.

| | |
|---|---|
| ½ pound | mushrooms, trimmed, sliced |
| 2 tablespoons | oil |
| 2 teaspoons | cumin seeds |
| ½ teaspoon | *hing* (asafoetida) |
| 1 cup | finely sliced onions |
| 1 (10-ounce) packet | frozen spinach, chopped |
| 2 cups | water |
| 1 ¼ teaspoons | salt, or to taste |
| 1 tablespoon | vegetable *masala* (p. 23) |

Wash mushrooms, trim and discard stems and slice into ¼–inch pieces. Heat oil in a medium saucepan over medium heat and add cumin. Add *hing* when cumin starts to sizzle. After a few seconds, when *hing* turns brown, add onions. Cook onions until limp, about 2 minutes. Add spinach, water and salt and cook until the spinach is cooked to desired texture.

Add vegetable *masala* (p. 23) and mushrooms, mix well and cook for 3 more minutes. Serve hot.

Serves 3–4.

## Zucchini with Mushrooms—zucchini *gucchi*

Mushrooms and zucchini are particularly delicious when seasoned with cumin and fenugreek. Moisture from both vegetables results in a spiced, light stock. Serve with any Indian meal.

| | |
|---|---|
| ½ pound | mushrooms, trimmed, cut |
| 1 tablespoon | oil |
| ½ teaspoon | fenugreek seeds |
| ½ teaspoon | cumin seeds |
| ½ teaspoon | *hing* (asafoetida) |
| 2 | dried, whole red chili peppers |
| 3 pounds | zucchini, trimmed, cubed |
| ½ teaspoon | salt, or to taste |
| ¼ teaspoon | turmeric |
| 2 teaspoon | coarsely ground cumin seeds |
| 3 tablespoons | ground coriander seeds |
| 2 tablespoons | chopped cilantro, for garnish |

Wash mushrooms, trim and discard stems and slice into ¼–inch pieces. Heat oil in a medium saucepan over high heat, and add fenugreek and cumin. Within a few seconds, the fenugreek will turn brown and the cumin will sizzle. Immediately add *hing* and red chili peppers. When the *hing* and red chili peppers have darkened in color, add zucchini and mushrooms. Stir well, lower the heat to medium-low and cook the mixture for 3 minutes.

Add salt and next 3 ingredients including coriander. Stir well and cook for 10 more minutes. Serve garnished with cilantro.
Serves 4–6.

# Spinach, Collard and Amaranth Greens
## Spinach and Potato "Curry"—*palak aaloo*

This simple recipe does not take long to prepare and goes well with any meal. The addition of chickpea flour to the recipe imparts the dish with a smooth texture. If desired, substitute either any flour of your choice or soaked and ground garbanzo beans (p. 41). Serve with any flat Indian bread.

| | |
|---|---|
| 2 tablespoons | oil |
| 1 teaspoon | cumin seeds |
| ½ teaspoon | fenugreek seeds |
| ½ teaspoon | *hing* (asafoetida) |
| 2 medium | potatoes, peeled, cubed |
| 2 cups | water, or as needed |
| 1 ½ teaspoons | salt, or to taste |
| 2 (10-ounce) packets | frozen, chopped spinach |
| 2 tablespoons | ground coriander seeds |
| 2 teaspoons | ground cumin seeds |
| ¼ teaspoon | turmeric |
| ½ teaspoon | chili powder |
| 2 tablespoons | chickpea flour |

Heat oil in a medium saucepan over medium heat, and add cumin and fenugreek. Add *hing* when fenugreek turns brown and cumin sizzles. Add potatoes, water and salt. Cover and cook until the potatoes are just about half-cooked, about 3 minutes.

Add spinach and next 4 ingredients including chili powder and cook uncovered on low heat until the potatoes are done.

Combine chickpea flour with ¼ cup water and add it to the vegetable. Cook for about a minute and remove. Serve hot.
Serves 6.

# "Curried" Spinach with *Paneer*—*palak paneer* (dairy)

This was by far one of the most popular dishes on the menu at *The Ganges*. The *paneer* and basic sauce can be made ahead of time. Serve with any flat Indian bread or as desired.

| | |
|---|---|
| 2 (10-ounce) packets | frozen chopped spinach |
| 2 teaspoons | salt, or to taste |
| 2 cups | water or as required |
| ¼ cup | chickpea flour |
| 2 cups | basic sauce (p. 195) |
| 2 teaspoons | *garam masala*-1 |
| ¾ cup | *paneer* pieces (p. 66) |

　　Place spinach, salt and water in a medium saucepan over high heat, and cook until the spinach is soft, about 20 minutes. Note that the spinach must be completely soft for pureeing. Add chickpea flour, mix well and cook the mixture for 5 more minutes. Remove from heat and let cool.

　　Using a food processor fitted with a metal blade, grind spinach until smooth. Remove to the same saucepan in which it was cooked. Add basic sauce, *garam masala* and *paneer*, mix well and cook on medium heat for about 5 minutes. Serve hot.

Serves 6.

## Spiced Spinach with Sesame—*bhaji ragad* (dairy)

If you have trouble obtaining chickpea flour, replace with soaked and ground garbanzo beans (p. 41). Serve with any Indian bread or rice.

| | |
|---|---|
| 1 tablespoon | sesame seeds |
| ¼ cup | peanuts |
| 1 tablespoon | oil |
| ½ teaspoon | cumin seeds |
| ½ teaspoon | black mustard seeds |
| ½ teaspoon | *hing* (asafoetida) |
| 2 | dried, whole red chili peppers |
| 4 cups (app. 1 bunch) | fresh spinach, chopped, washed |
| 1 ½ teaspoons | salt, or to taste |
| ¼ cup | yogurt |
| 1 cup | water |
| 2 tablespoons | chickpea flour |

Crush sesame seeds with a rolling pin and set aside. Toast, peel and coarsely grind peanuts (p. 37) and set aside.

Heat oil in a medium stainless steel saucepan over medium heat, and add cumin and mustard. When mustard starts to crackle, add *hing*. Immediately add red chili peppers and cook for a few seconds, until the peppers change color to dark red.

Add spinach and lower the heat to medium. Add crushed sesame seeds and coarsely ground peanuts. Mix well and let simmer over very low heat.

Using a whisk, mix yogurt, water and flour until smooth. Add the mixture to spinach and maintaining heat on low, cook stirring well until the mixture thickens and spinach is cooked, about 3 minutes. Serve hot. Serves 3–4.

## Spinach with Split Chickpeas—*palak moglai* (dairy)

The Hindi name of this dish belies its mogul origins. Generally rich with nuts and cream, this style of cuisine was brought into the South Asian subcontinent by the Turkic/Persian Mughals (Moguls) in the 16th century.

I prefer to make this dish with light cream; the dish retains its rich texture, yet it is not high in calories. Garbanzo beans may be substituted for split chickpeas. (If using garbanzo, soak the beans for at least eight hours and cook until soft before adding spinach.)

Serve with any Indian bread.

| | |
|---|---|
| 1 cup | split chickpeas (*chana dal*), washed |
| 2 tablespoons | oil |
| 1 cup | chopped onions |
| 8 cloves | garlic, peeled, chopped |
| 3 whole | red hot peppers, broken into several pieces, seeded |
| 3 cups | water |
| 1 (10-ounce) packet | frozen chopped spinach |
| 1 ½ teaspoons | salt, or to taste |
| ¼ teaspoon | turmeric |
| ½ cup | cream, light if preferred |

Pick over and wash *chana dal* (see note, p. 336). Set aside.

Heat oil in a small saucepan over medium heat. Add onions and cook for 3 minutes, stirring occasionally. Add garlic and peppers. Mix well. Cook until peppers change color to dark red, or about 5 minutes.

Add split chickpeas and water. Cook until the chickpeas are half done, about 15 minutes. Add spinach and cook for 10 minutes, stirring occasionally.

Stir in salt and turmeric and simmer until chickpeas are soft and spinach is cooked but not overcooked. Add cream, mixing well. Cook for 2 minutes, remove and serve hot.

Serves 4–6.

## Spinach with Carrots—*sai bhaji*

This recipe is typically *Sindhi,* meaning that it originates from a North-Indian region incorporated into Pakistan during partition. Serve with any Indian bread.

| | |
|---|---|
| 1 tablespoon | oil |
| ½ teaspoon | *hing* (asafoetida) |
| 6 cups | loosely packed fresh spinach, washed |
| 1 large | onion, chopped |
| 2 cloves | garlic, peeled, chopped |
| 1 teaspoon | salt, or to taste |
| ¼ teaspoon | turmeric |
| 1 ½ cups | water |
| 2 | serrano or jalapeño chilies, chopped |
| 2 medium | carrots, peeled, diced |

Heat oil in a saucepan over medium heat, and add *hing.* As soon as *hing* turns slightly brown, add spinach and the next 6 ingredients including chilies. Cook until the spinach is soft, about 7 minutes, stirring occasionally.

Add carrots, mix well, and cook for 3 more minutes. Serve hot.
Serves 3–4.

## Collard Greens with Onions—collard *saag*

In this simple recipe, collard greens are highlighted by the hearty flavor of cumin. The greens should be cooked quickly on high heat to enable them to absorb the flavor from the spices and onions. They should wilt and soften but not get soggy. Serve with breads made with either rice flour (p. 432) or corn flour (p. 437).

| | |
|---|---|
| 2 tablespoons | oil |
| 1 teaspoon | cumin seeds |
| 1 medium | onion, chopped |
| ½ teaspoon | chili powder |
| ¼ teaspoon | turmeric |
| 1 teaspoon | salt, or to taste |
| 1 cup | water |
| 1 bunch | collard greens, chopped, washed |

Heat oil in a medium saucepan over high heat and add cumin. When cumin starts to sizzle, add onions and cook stirring well until onions are slightly golden, about 7 minutes. Add ingredients through collard greens and cook for 15 minutes or until greens are cooked but not overly soft.

Serve hot.

Serves 2–3.

## Collard Green with Split Bengal Grams—collard *patalbhaji*

This Maharashtian recipe is usually made with either taro or spinach leaves. I have varied the traditional recipe with the use of collard greens. Serve with any Indian bread.

| | |
|---|---|
| 1 cup | split chickpeas (*chana dal*), soaked four hours |
| 6 cups | water |
| 2 (10-ounce) packets | frozen, chopped collard greens |
| ½ cup | coarsely ground, raw peanuts |
| ¼ cup | chickpea flour, mixed with little water |
| 2 ½ teaspoons | salt, or to taste |
| 1 teaspoon | chili powder |
| ½ teaspoon | turmeric |
| 2 teaspoons | *garam masala*-2 (p. 22) |
| 1 tablespoon | sesame seeds |
| 2–inch piece | fresh ginger, peeled, ground |
| 3 | serrano or jalapeño chilies, ground |
| 1 tablespoon | brown sugar, or to taste |
| 2 teaspoons | tamarind concentrate |
| 2 tablespoons | oil |
| 2 teaspoons | black mustard seeds |
| ½ teaspoon | *hing* (asafoetida) |
| 2 | dried, whole red chili peppers (optional) |

Pick over, wash (see note, p. 336) and soak *chana dal* for four hours.

In a medium stainless steel saucepan over high heat, bring water to a full boil. Drain split chickpeas and add to boiling water, cooking on high heat until almost done but not completely soft, about 7 minutes.

Add collard greens and cook on high heat until the greens have defrosted and mixed with the *dal*. Collard greens may alternatively be defrosted in a microwave before adding to split chickpeas.

Add peanuts and the next 10 ingredients including tamarind concentrate. Stir well and lower the heat to medium.

In a small frying pan over medium heat, heat oil and add mustard, when mustard starts to crackle, add *hing* and red chili peppers, cook for few seconds and add to collard mixture. Cook, stirring well for 5 more minutes, or until the *dal* and collard greens are cooked to taste. Serve hot. Serves 6–8.

## Amaranth Greens with Cumin—*cholai*

During the winter months in most Gujarati homes, this dish is a staple. It is light and extremely tasty and is usually served with *rotla* (p. 434) and a bowl of hot milk. Of the varieties of amaranth available in produce markets; I prefer that with red stems, which tends to be more flavorful. Can also be served with hot *chapati* (p. 404).

| | |
|---|---|
| 1 tablespoon | oil |
| 1 teaspoon | cumin seeds |
| ½ teaspoon | *hing* (asafoetida) |
| 8 cups | chopped amaranth greens, washed |
| 1 cup | water or as desired |
| 1 teaspoon | salt, or to taste |
| ½ teaspoon | chili powder |
| ¼ teaspoon | turmeric |

Heat oil in a small saucepan over medium heat and add cumin. When cumin starts to sizzle, add *hing*. As soon as *hing* turns brown add greens and all remaining ingredients including turmeric.

Cook on high heat until greens are soft, to desired texture. Indians normally prefer to cook the greens until very soft. Serve hot.
Serves 4.

## Amaranth Greens with Onions—*kandane cholai*

Taking not much longer than 15 minutes to prepare, this aromatic recipe is a healthy item for any menu. Serve with any flat Indian bread.

| | |
|---|---|
| 2 tablespoons | oil |
| 1 teaspoon | black mustard seeds |
| 1 teaspoon | cumin seeds |
| ½ teaspoon | fenugreek seeds |
| ½ teaspoon | *hing* (asafoetida) |
| 1 three–inch stick | cinnamon |
| 2 tablespoons | chopped onions |
| 3 bunches | amaranth greens, trimmed, chopped, washed |
| 2 ½ cups | water or as desired |
| 2 teaspoons | salt, or to taste |
| ½ cup | chickpea flour |
| 1 teaspoon | chili powder |
| 1 tablespoon | ground coriander seeds |
| ½ teaspoon | turmeric |

Heat oil in a medium saucepan over medium heat and add mustard, cumin and fenugreek. When mustard starts to crackle, cumin sizzles and fenugreek turns brown, add *hing*. After a few seconds, when *hing* turns brown, add cinnamon and onions. Cook the mixture for 3 minutes. Add amaranth, 2 cups water and salt. Stir well and cook for 5 minutes. Meanwhile, combine chickpea flour with ½ cup water.

Add flour/water mixture, and remaining 3 ingredients including turmeric and mix well. Lower the heat and cook for 10 more minutes. Serve hot.

Serves 6.

# Okra

## Stuffed Okra—*bhindi masala*

This is a wonderful recipe that even my son—who normally tends to avoid okra—loves. Look for small tender okra for this recipe. Serve with any Indian bread.

**Stuffing:**

| | |
|---|---|
| 2 medium | potatoes, boiled, peeled, mashed |
| 1 small | onion, finely chopped |
| 2–inch piece | fresh ginger, peeled, ground |
| 3 cloves | garlic, peeled, ground |
| 3 | serrano chilies, ground with seeds |
| 1 ½ teaspoons | ground cumin seeds |
| 2 tablespoons | ground coriander seeds |
| 2 tablespoons | unsweetened, finely grated, coconut (optional) |
| ¼ teaspoon | turmeric |
| 2 teaspoons | sugar, or to taste |
| 1 teaspoon | salt, or to taste |
| ¼ cup | chopped cilantro |

**Okra:**

| | |
|---|---|
| 1 ½ pounds | okra, wiped clean, trimmed |
| 3 tablespoons | oil |
| 1 teaspoon | fenugreek seeds |
| 1 tablespoon | lemon juice |

**Stuffing:**

Combine mashed potato with ingredients through cilantro.

**Okra:**

Wipe okras with wet towels. Trim and discard the ends. Place a cut, lengthwise along each okra, taking care not to cut the okra in half. Set aside. Opening the cuts on the okra, stuff each okra with as much stuffing as can be held by the vegetable. Make sure to save adequate stuffing for all of the okra. Set aside.

Heat oil in a large frying pan over medium heat and add fenugreek seeds. Add okra when fenugreek turns slightly brown, keeping stuffed side of the okra up. Reduce heat to low and cook okra for about 10 minutes. Carefully turn and cook for 10 more minutes. A little mixture may drop out while turning. Maintain the heat on low. If any stuffing remains unused, add it to the okra at this point. Cook until okras are slightly golden. Sprinkle lemon juice on top before serving.

Serves 4–5.

# Okra with Onions—*Punjabi bhindi*

Serve this North Indian recipe with any flat Indian bread.

| | |
|---|---|
| 2 pounds | tender okra, wiped clean, trimmed |
| 3 tablespoons | oil |
| ½ teaspoon | fenugreek seeds |
| 1 teaspoon | cumin seeds |
| ½ teaspoon | *hing* (asafoetida) |
| 2 cups | finely sliced onions |
| 1 teaspoon | salt, or to taste |
| ¼ teaspoon | turmeric |
| 1 teaspoon | chili powder |
| 2 tablespoons | ground coriander seeds |
| 2 teaspoons | ground cumin seeds |
| 2 tablespoons | chopped cilantro, for garnish |

Wipe okras with wet towels. Trim and discard the ends. (The okra will be added whole to the recipe.)

Heat oil in a medium frying pan over high heat and add fenugreek and cumin seeds. When fenugreek turns slightly brown and cumin sizzles, add *hing*. Add onions when *hing* turns slightly brown.

Lower the heat and cook onions, stirring well, for about 7 minutes or until they are slightly golden. Add okra and salt, mix well and cook stirring occasionally, for 15 minutes or until the okra is cooked and slightly golden.

Add next 4 ingredients including ground cumin, mix well and cook for 4 more minutes.

Serve garnished with cilantro.

Serves 3–5.

## Vegetarian "Gumbo"—*bhinda, kandane paneer* (dairy)

Here is an Indian vegetarian version of "gumbo." If you do not have time to make *paneer*, buy it from an Indian store or, for a non-dairy recipe, use extra-firm tofu. Whereas the other okra recipes in this chapter are dry, this gumbo is cooked with added water, making it necessary to dry the okra prior to cooking, thereby improving its texture. Serve with any bread.

| | |
|---|---|
| 1 ½ ounds | okra, wiped clean, trimmed, quartered |
| 4 tablespoons | oil |
| 1 cup | *paneer* cubes (p. 60) |
| 1 ½ cups | chopped onions |
| 3 | serrano or jalapeño chilies, sliced thin |
| 3 cloves | garlic, peeled chopped |
| 3 | vegetable bouillon cubes, finely crushed |
| 4 cups | water |
| 2 tablespoons | white unbleached flour |
| ¼ cup | chopped cilantro |

Wipe okras with wet towels. Trim and discard the ends, cut lengthwise into halves, and cut halves again to make quarters. Spread okra pieces on paper towels, and allow to dry for about two hours.

Heat 2 tablespoons oil in a large, nonstick frying pan over medium heat and add *paneer*. Fry *paneer* turning gently until the edges are golden, about 3 minutes. Using a slotted spoon, remove *paneer* to a bowl.

In the same frying pan, heat 1 more tablespoon oil and add okra. Fry stirring well until they are golden, about 12 minutes. Remove with *paneer*.

In the same pan add remaining 1 tablespoon oil, add onions and fry, stirring well, until almost brown, about 15 minutes. Add the next 4 ingredients including water. Cook on high heat for 5 minutes.

Combine flour with ¼ cup water and add to boiling liquid, mix well. Boil for 1 minute. Add *paneer* and okra, stir and heat through.

Garnish with cilantro and serve hot.
Serves 6–8.

# Mixed Vegetables

## Vegetable Casserole—*dum shak*

Gujarati cooks are known for their vegetable casserole, called *Undhiyu*. As opposed to the more traditional recipe in my first book, the version here is prepared with ingredients that are easily available. If preferred, substitute any dried bean or vegetable, in the same proportions. Serve with any meal.

| | |
|---|---|
| 1 cup | dried yellow peas, soaked four hours |
| 6 cups | water |
| 4 teaspoons | salt |
| 2 cups | unsweetened, finely grated coconut |
| 8 | serrano or jalapeño chilies, ground |
| 3–inch piece | fresh ginger, peeled, ground |
| 8 cloves | garlic, peeled, ground |
| 3 cups | chopped cilantro |
| 2 teaspoons | sugar |
| 2 medium | eggplants, trimmed, cubed |
| 4 cups | peeled, cubed sweet potatoes |
| 3 medium | potatoes, peeled, cubed |
| 2 tablespoons | oil |
| 1 tablespoon | cumin seeds |
| ½ teaspoon | *hing* (asafoetida) |

Pick over, wash (see note, p. 336), and soak peas for four hours. Preheat oven to 400 °F.

Drain yellow peas, discarding water. In a medium saucepan over high heat, boil 4 cups water (saving 2 cups), add 1 teaspoon salt and drained peas. Cook for 10 minutes, or until the peas are almost done. Drain peas and discard water. Place peas in a large, ovenproof saucepan or baking dish. In a separate bowl, combine remaining 3 teaspoons salt, coconut, and the next 5 ingredients including sugar. Add 4 tablespoons of mixture to the peas and mix well.

Combine remaining mixture with eggplant, sweet potatoes and potatoes, mixing well. Spread the eggplant-potato mixture over the peas.

Heat oil in a small frying pan over medium heat and add cumin. Add *hing* when cumin starts to sizzle. As soon as *hing* turns brown pour oil mixture over the vegetables, add remaining 2 cups water and cover the saucepan.

Bake at 400 °F for 40 minutes or until the peas and potatoes are cooked. Mix well and serve hot. Can be garnished with chopped cilantro. Serves 8–10.

# Fruits as Vegetables

## Stuffed Bananas with Fresh Spices—*bharela kela*

Though the ripe, yellow varieties are normally served as fruit, I have here used them in an unusual recipe that requires cooking. This extremely simple recipe was extremely popular at *The Ganges*—in fact, I regard it as one of my signature dishes. The dish goes very well with any flat Indian bread or even with tortillas. Note that only the ends are trimmed from the bananas, and that they remain unpeeled until eaten.

| | |
|---|---|
| 2 | ripe bananas, trimmed, cut into 2 ½–inch rounds |
| ¼ cup | unsweetened, finely grated coconut |
| ¼ teaspoon | salt, or to taste |
| 1 tablespoon | lemon juice |
| 2–3 | serrano or jalapeño chilies, ground |
| 2–inch piece | fresh ginger, peeled, ground |
| ¾ cup | chopped cilantro |
| 2 teaspoons | oil |

Wash and trim the ends off of both bananas, making sure not to remove any additional peel. Cut each banana crosswise, into 3–4 pieces. On one flat side of each piece, place two cuts, making a "plus sign" (illus. p. 259). The cuts should extend half way into the piece.

Combine coconut with ingredients including cilantro and gently stuff the bananas in the cuts. Heat oil in a frying pan over medium heat and place the bananas sideways into the pan, such that the fruit part does not touch the surface of the pan. Gently turn the bananas when the underside is dark, about 3 minutes. Cook for 2 more minutes or until the other side is dark.

Alternatively, preheat oven to 375 °F, place bananas in a lightly oiled oven tray. Place the tray in the oven and bake for about 10 minutes, turning the bananas once or twice, until the skin of the banana darkens.

If microwave cooking is preferred, bake all banana pieces together, without oil, for 3 minutes on high, or until the skin darkens. Though microwaves will vary, baking each (3–4 pieces) should take about 1 ½ minutes to cook.

Serves 2.

## Stuffed Bananas with Chickpea Flour and Spices
### —*kelana ravaiya*

This is my mother's unique version of the Stuffed Banana recipe. Serve with plain Indian bread.

| | |
|---|---|
| ½ cup | chickpea flour |
| ¼ teaspoon | salt, or to taste |
| ¼ teaspoon | chili powder |
| ¼ cup | chopped cilantro |
| 2 tablespoons | ground coriander seeds |
| 2 teaspoons | ground cumin seeds |
| 1 tablespoon | water |
| 2 | ripe bananas |
| 1 tablespoon | oil |

To make the stuffing, combine ingredients through water. If the stuffing remains very dry add one more tablespoon of water. The stuffing should not assume a dough-like consistency, nor should it be completely dry.

Wash and trim the ends off of both bananas, making sure not to remove any additional peel. Cut each banana crosswise, into 3–4 pieces. On one flat side of each piece, place two cuts, making a "plus sign" (illus. p. 259). The cuts should extend half way into the piece. Gently stuff the bananas in the cuts.

Heat oil in a frying pan over medium heat, rotating the pan so that the oil spreads over the cooking surface. Gently place the stuffed bananas sideways in the frying pan. Turn after about 5 minutes or when the underside is dark. Cook for 5 more minutes.

Alternatively, preheat oven to 375 °F, place bananas in a lightly oiled oven tray, place the tray in the oven and bake for about 10 minutes turning the bananas once or twice, until the bananas are cooked on all sides. The skin will turn dark and the stuffing will be deep yellow when cooked. Serve hot. Leftovers can be reheated.
Serves 2.

## Honeydew Melon with Green Peas
### —*khadbucha vatana* (no oil)

Steamed dumplings (p. 194) may be added to the original version of this recipe, which I invented in *The Ganges* kitchen. Cooked honeydew melon, while it may not sound appetizing, is surprisingly delicious. Note that there is no added oil in this recipe.

| | |
|---|---|
| 2 cups | green peas, frozen |
| 2 teaspoons | toasted, coarsely ground cumin seeds |
| 4 | serrano or jalapeño chilies, ground |
| 2–inch piece | fresh ginger, peeled, ground |
| 1 ½ teaspoons | salt, or to taste |
| 1 medium | honeydew melon, peeled, cubed in to ½–inch pieces |
| ¼ cup | chopped cilantro, for garnish |

In a medium saucepan over high heat, cook peas, adding ground cumin and next 3 ingredients including salt. Cook peas, stirring well until warmed through and still bright green. Remove and let cool.

Peel and cut melon into halves, remove all the seeds. Cut melon into slices and then into ½–inch cubes. Combine melon with the peas and refrigerate until ready to serve. Prior to eating, warm the melon and peas mixture in a microwave (cooking on a stove will result in the honeydew melon losing its texture). You may add dumplings (p. 194) just prior to warming.

Serve garnished with cilantro.
Serves 6–8.

## Mango Vegetable—*kerinu shak*

In some Gujarati homes this intensely flavored dish would be offered either as a pickle or relish, or served as an entrée along with another vegetable, *dal* and Indian bread—*chapati* (p. 404) or *parotha* (p. 411).

| | |
|---|---|
| 3 | unripe mangoes, peeled, cubed small, about 2 cups |
| 4 cups | water |
| 2 tablespoons | oil |
| ¼ teaspoon | fenugreek seeds |
| ¼ teaspoon | black mustard seeds |
| ½ teaspoon | *hing* (asafoetida) |
| 3 | dried, whole red chili peppers |
| 1 teaspoon | salt, or to taste |
| ½ cup | jaggery or to taste |

Place cubed mangoes and water in a small, stainless steel saucepan, over high heat. Bring to a boil, and cook mangoes for 4 minutes. Strain mangoes and discard water.

Heat oil in the same saucepan, over medium heat. Add fenugreek and mustard. Add *hing* when fenugreek turns slightly golden and mustard starts to crackle. Cook for few seconds and add red chili peppers. Cook until peppers change color, about 10 seconds.

Add mangoes and ingredients including jaggery. Lower the heat and cook, stirring well until jaggery melts. Cook for 1 more minute and remove. Serve as desired. Refrigerate until finished.

Yield: Approximately 3 cups.

## Persimmon with Cumin—*jeera* persimmon

Sometime back, my daughter's neighbor gave us two large bags of both Fuyu and Hachiya persimmons. Using the firm, Fuyu variety, I experimented with the fruit. The results were delicious.

| | |
|---|---|
| 1 tablespoon | oil |
| 1 three–inch stick | cinnamon, broken |
| 5 | cloves |
| ½ teaspoon | cumin seeds |
| ½ teaspoon | *hing* (asafoetida) (optional) |
| 4–5 | Fuyu persimmons, stems trimmed, cubed (about 4 cups) |
| 1 teaspoon | salt, or to taste |
| ½ teaspoon | chili powder |
| ½ teaspoon | turmeric |
| 2 tablespoons | ground coriander seeds |
| 1 tablespoon | brown sugar |
| 1 tablespoon | lemon juice |
| 2 tablespoons | chopped cilantro |

Heat oil in a small stainless steel saucepan over high heat. Add cinnamon, cloves and cumin. When cumin sizzles, add *hing*. Immediately add persimmon and the next 4 ingredients including coriander. Lower the heat and cook stirring well for 3 minutes. Add brown sugar and lemon juice and mix well. Cook for 1 more minute and remove. Serve hot garnished with cilantro.

Serves 4.

**Note:** For a thicker consistency, mix 2 tablespoons chickpea flour with ¼ cup water; add together with spices. Adding flour to this recipe will give a nice consistency.

# Rice, Bulgur and Other Grains

*Basmati* Rice—*bhat*

Precooked Rice with Bell Peppers and Yogurt—*vagharelo bhat* (dairy)

Saffron Rice—*kesarwalo bhat*

Eggplant Rice—*vangi bhat*

Coconut Rice—*koprano bhat*

Lucknowi Rice with Vegetables—*tahri*

Tamarind Rice with Nuts and *Dal*—*pulihara*

South Indian Sweet Rice—*pongal* (dairy)

Brown Rice with *Toor Dal*—*karadni khichadi*

Lentil Pilaf—*masoorno pulav*

Vegetable Pilaf—*shakno pulav*

Tricolor Pilaf—*trirangi pulav*

Dry Peas Pilaf—*suka vatanano pulav*

Split Lima Bean *Khichadi*—*valdalni khichadi*

Unhulled Split Mung *Khichadi*—*kathiawadi khichadi*

Cashew and Saffron *Khichadi*—*kesarwali khichadi*

Cumin and Pepper *Khichadi*—*masalawali khichadi* (dairy)

Sorghum *Khichadi*—*juwarni khichadi* (dairy)

Three Grain Savory Porridge—*bajri*, mung, *chokhanu bhadku*

Bulgur with Spices—*khati lapsi* (dairy)

Bulgur with Split Mung Beans and Onions—*masala bhadku*

Bulgur with Vegetables—*lapsi pilaf*

Vegetable *Biryani*—*shakni biryani* (dairy)

Quinoa—*kodri*

Wild Rice Pilaf—*jungli pulav*

# Rice, Bulgur and Other Grains

Unhulled rice is called *askshat* in Sanskrit, meaning that which is without defect. A symbol of fertility and prosperity, rice occupies an important role in Hindu religious rituals. During marriage ceremonies, for example, a few grains are placed on the foreheads of both bride and groom as a beacon of hope that the couple may be blessed with children and good fortune.

Rice accrues similarly important value in the domain of the kitchen as the temple. A staple food for the majority of the Indian population, rice is both the most versatile and the most important cultivated grain on the subcontinent. It is easy and relatively inexpensive to grow and, especially when combined with beans, its nutritious value enhances vegetables and dairy products.

Indians prefer to eat rice with the main meal of the day, accompanied by *dal*, vegetables or yogurt. Its preparation can vary from plain rice served with *dal*, to savory dishes featuring the diverse flavors of onions, potatoes, vegetables, *dals*, fruit and nuts. Rice is also widely used in dessert preparations like *payas*, a creamy milk pudding made from cooked rice, cardamom, raisins and nuts.

For most of my recipes I use *basmati* rice. Grown on the mountain foothills of both India and Pakistan, *basmati* rice has been cultivated on the South Asian continent for centuries. The name "*basmati*" is Hindi for "fragrant," referring to the aroma and nutlike flavor of this small, long-grained rice. Traditionally minimally processed between harvesting and packaging, *basmati* rice exudes a wonderful perfume, and a visit to an Indian store or a specialty/imported food shop is worth the trip, if only to enjoy the concentrated scent of *basmati* in open bins. Comparatively few Indians use brown rice, though I have seen brown *basmati* sold in stores.

The longer *basmati* rice has been aged, the better it cooks, and the less water it requires. However, the popularity of *basmati* is such that to meet the demand, it is usually exported soon after harvesting, when the rice is young and unseasoned. Unless you know the dealer, it is difficult to determine whether rice is older or recently harvested. While cooking, it is better to start with less water than called for until you know how the particular stock responds to water. When using something other than white *basmati*, some experimentation with the quantity of water used may be necessary. I recommend purchasing rice from sacks or bins. If you purchase in packages, always start with less water than the package recommends.

Recipes using bulgur, sorghum, quinoa, etc. instead of rice are included in this section. When cooking recipes in this chapter, you may substitute any grain of your choice: brown rice, quinoa, wild rice, bulgur etc. In *khichadi* recipes that mix rice with *dal*, you may also substitute coarsely ground millet for the rice. Note that you may have to experiment with the quantity of water needed in the recipe to cook these different grains.

## *Basmati* Rice—*bhat*

This is the most basic of the variety of rice dishes cooked in Indian kitchens. As a child learning the art of cooking I was taught that each grain of rice should be properly cooked to be fluffy and not sticky.

Even the simple act of cooking rice brings back old memories. When I was hardly fourteen years old, my grandmother received a proposal from a local family asking for my hand in marriage to their son. Much to my dismay, my grandmother proceeded with arranging the engagement. Girls in strict Gujarati families had no say! My only recourse for rebellion was to convince the young man's parents that I was a less than ideal match, thereby inciting them to break the engagement. I was asked to visit the family's home and, according to tradition, to cook rice for the family. With a straight face, yet secretly determined to disqualify myself, I purposely added extra water to the cooking rice, creating a sticky and soggy mess. So strong was my desire to be released from this engagement, that I would have happily let the rice burn. After several more incidents like this in which I ruined dishes I had been asked to cook, and three years later, the engagement was broken and I was free!

For best results, when first preparing a new stock of rice, start with less water than called for in the recipe. Remember that the first cup of rice generally requires more water than the second cup i.e. 2 cups water to 1 cup uncooked rice for the first cup, thereafter 1 cup liquid for each 1 cup rice.

| | |
|---|---|
| 3 cups | water |
| 2 cups | *basmati* rice, washed |
| 1 teaspoon | salt, or to taste |
| 2 teaspoons | oil (optional) |

In a small saucepan, bring water to a full boil and then add rice and salt. Add oil now, if using, as it helps separate each grain. Alternatively you may add a few drops of lemon juice.

Lower the heat to medium, cover the saucepan partially, and cook until the rice is soft, about 15 minutes. If the rice is still not done and looks dry, add just a little more water—2 tablespoons or more, depending on how dry the rice is—and cook for a few additional minutes.
Serves 4–6.

## Precooked Rice with Bell Peppers and Yogurt
### —*vagharelo bhat* (dairy)

With or without the yogurt called for in the instructions, this recipe trans-forms leftover rice into an interesting, savory entrée infused with bell pep-pers. Note that since the cooked *basmati* rice is already salted (as in my recipe), no added salt is required. Serve with any meal.

| | |
|---|---|
| 2 tablespoons | oil |
| 2 teaspoons | black mustard seeds |
| ¼ cup | chopped onions |
| 6 cups | cooked *basmati* rice |
| ½ teaspoon | turmeric (optional) |
| ¼ cup | chopped red and green bell peppers |
| ½ cup | yogurt |
| 3 tablespoons | chopped cilantro, for garnish |

Heat oil in a medium frying pan over medium heat and add mustard seeds. When the mustard seeds start to crackle, add onions and cook, stir-ring well for 3 minutes. Add rice and the next 3 ingredients including yogurt. Mix well, reduce heat to low and cook for 7 minutes, or until the yogurt is absorbed, stirring gently two or three times in between. Serve garnished with cilantro.
Serves 6–8.

# Saffron Rice—*kesarwalo bhat*

Indians frequently add saffron to dishes, on special occasions when added color and flavor are called for. Nuts and fresh fruit make a special addition to this delicately flavored rice, which can be served alongside vegetables and either *raita* (p. 99) or *kadhi* (p. 293).

| | |
|---|---|
| 4 tablespoons | oil |
| 1 three–inch stick | cinnamon |
| 5 pods large | cardamom (*elcha*) (p. 11) |
| 2 tablespoons | golden raisins |
| ¼ cup | almonds, blanched |
| ¼ cup | cashew nuts, unsalted |
| 3 cups | *basmati* rice, washed |
| 4 ½ cups | water |
| 2 teaspoons | salt, or to taste |
| ½ teaspoon | saffron, crushed, mixed with 2 tablespoons warm water |
| 1 | red apple, peeled, sliced thin, brushed with lemon juice |
| 1 | pear, sliced |
| ½ cup | green seedless grapes, for garnish |

Heat oil in a large saucepan, over high heat. Add cinnamon and cardamom pods. When cinnamon starts to swell and cardamom darkens in color, add the next 3 ingredients including cashews, and stir well for 1 minute. Add rice, water and salt. Mix well and cook the rice on high heat. When the rice is almost cooked, about 12 minutes, lower the heat and partially cover the saucepan. Cook until the rice is done, about 7 more minutes.

Add crushed saffron-water mixture, but do not stir. The rice will color unevenly, thereby adding visual appeal. Gently combine fruit with rice and cook for 2 or 3 minutes. Garnish with grapes before serving. Serve hot. Serves 6–8.

## Eggplant Rice—*vangi bhat*

This Maharashtrian specialty looks both attractive and appetizing when served garnished with cilantro. Serve with either yogurt or *kadhi* (p. 293).

| | |
|---|---|
| 3 tablespoons | oil |
| 2 teaspoons | black mustard seeds |
| ½ teaspoon | fenugreek seeds |
| ½ teaspoon | *hing* (asafoetida) |
| 8 | *curry* leaves (optional) |
| 10 | cashew nuts, unsalted |
| 2 tablespoons | peanuts |
| 2 cups | *basmati* rice, washed |
| ½ medium | eggplant, quartered, cut into wedges |
| 2 ½ cups | water |
| 1 tablespoon | *garam masala*-2 (p. 22) |
| 2 teaspoons | salt, or to taste |
| ¼ cup | unsweetened, grated coconut |
| 2 tablespoons | chopped cilantro, for garnish |

Heat oil in a medium saucepan over medium-high heat, and add mustard and fenugreek seeds. Add *hing* and *curry* leaves when mustard starts to crackle. Immediately add cashews and peanuts, and fry, stirring well until nuts are golden brown.

Add rice and next 5 ingredients, including coconut. Mix well and cook on high heat for 10 minutes. Lower the heat, cover and cook until the rice is done, about 10 more minutes.

Serve hot, garnished with chopped cilantro.
Serves 6.

## Coconut Rice—*koprano bhat*

This simple, very flavorful version of rice cooked with coconut milk is popular throughout South India, where coconut grows in abundance. Green chilies contribute an additional bite. Serve with yogurt based recipes.

| | |
|---|---|
| 1 tablespoon | oil |
| 1 three–inch stick | cinnamon |
| 3 | serrano or jalapeño chilies, sliced lengthwise |
| 2 cups | *basmati* rice, washed |
| 2 teaspoons | salt, or to taste |
| 1 cup | fresh or frozen green peas |
| 3 (15-ounce) cans | coconut milk (p. 14) |
| ½ cup | water |
| ½ cup | chopped cilantro, for garnish |

In a medium saucepan over high heat, heat oil and add cinnamon. When cinnamon starts to swell, add chilies, and cook the mixture for few seconds.

Add rice and salt as well as green peas now, if using fresh. Add coconut milk and water, stir well and cook on high heat until the mixture comes to a full boil. Cover, lower the heat and cook until the rice is done, about 15 minutes.

If using frozen peas, add when the rice is almost done, mix gently and cook for few more minutes until the rice is ready, and peas are heated through.

Serve hot garnished with cilantro.

Serves 4–6.

## Lucknowi Rice with Vegetables—*tahri*

My niece Rati gave me this wonderful recipe. The combination of green peas, cumin and *garam masala* results in a flavorful, aromatic dish that is typical of the style of cooking originating in Lucknow. Serve with yogurt and sliced carrots.

| | |
|---|---|
| 3 tablespoons | oil |
| 1 teaspoon | cumin seeds |
| 1 | bay leaf |
| 1 medium | onion, finely sliced |
| 2 | dried, whole red chili peppers |
| 1 medium | potato, peeled, sliced |
| 1 small | tomato, cut |
| 1 teaspoon | ground coriander seeds |
| ½ teaspoon | coarsely ground cumin seeds |
| ¼ teaspoon | turmeric |
| ½ teaspoon | *garam masala*-1 (p. 21) |
| 2 cups | water |
| 1 cup | *basmati* rice, washed |
| 1 teaspoo | salt or to taste |
| ½ cup | frozen green peas |
| 2 tablespoons | chopped cilantro, for garnish |

Heat oil in a small saucepan over medium heat, and add cumin. When cumin starts to sizzle, add bay leaf. After 10 seconds, add onions and sauté for 3 minutes or until the onions are translucent.

Add peppers and potato, mix well and cook for 7 minutes stirring frequently. Add the next 6 ingredients including water and bring the mixture to a full boil.

Add rice, mix well and lower the heat to medium. Cook covered until the rice is done, about 15 minutes. Gently mix green peas with rice and cook for 2 more minutes, until the rice is heated through. Serve hot, garnished with cilantro.

Serves 3–4.

## Tamarind Rice with Nuts and *Dal*—*pulihara*

This recipe is from the city of Hyderabad, where Arun's sister, Chandra, lived for several years. Though the ingredients are numerous, the recipe is actually fairly easy. The combination of fresh, dry, sweet and spicy ingredients such as ginger, coriander, raisins and peppers yields a flavorful dish. Serve with either cucumber *raita* (p. 99) or plain yogurt.

| | |
|---|---|
| 2 tablespoons | split chickpeas (*chana dal*), soaked three hours |
| 2 tablespoons | split black beans (*urid dal*), soaked three hours |
| 2 ½ cups | water |
| 2 cups | *basmati* rice, washed |
| 1 teaspoon | salt, or to taste |
| ¼ teaspoon | turmeric |
| 2–inch square | tamarind slab **or** |
| 1 teaspoon | tamarind concentrate |
| 2 | serrano or jalapeño chilies, chopped |
| 2–inch piece | fresh ginger, peeled, finely chopped |
| 3 tablespoons | oil |
| 1 teaspoon | coriander seeds |
| 1 tablespoon | raisins |
| 1 teaspoon | black mustard seeds |
| 2 tablespoons | sesame seeds |
| 2 | dried, whole red chili peppers, chopped, seeded |
| 15 | cashew nuts |
| 2 tablespoons | peanuts, unsalted, raw |
| 2 | serrano or jalapeño chilies, chopped |
| 2 tablespoons | chopped cilantro, for garnish |

Pick over, wash (see note, p. 336) and soak both the *dals* together for three hours. Drain both the *dals* and lay on paper towels to dry for about 10 minutes.

In a medium saucepan, over high heat, bring water to a full boil and add rice, salt and turmeric. Cover, lower the heat to medium and cook until the rice is done, about 20 minutes. Set aside the cooked rice. If using tamarind slab, soak it in ½ cup hot water for about 30 minutes. Using your fingers squeeze the tamarind pulp in the water. Strain and save the liquid, discarding skin and seeds, if any.

Spread chopped chilies and ginger in a large baking tray or a platter. Gently layer cooked rice over chilies and ginger and cover the platter with aluminum foil or a large lid. Set aside—the chilies and ginger will infuse the rice with flavor.

Heat 1 tablespoon oil in a medium frying pan over high heat and add coriander seeds. Fry until coriander seeds become brown in color and emit a strong aroma. Remove with a slotted spoon onto paper towels. In the same oil, fry raisins until they swell. Using a slotted spoon remove raisins to a small bowl. Set aside.

Add the remaining oil to the frying pan; when hot, add mustard seeds. As soon as the mustard starts to crackle, add sesame seeds and peppers. Fry for few seconds, stirring well. Add cashew and peanuts and fry until nuts are golden in color. Add either tamarind water or concentrate and *dals* to the mixture. If using concentrate add ½ cup more water.

Stir well, lower the heat and cook for 5 minutes, or until the mixture attains the consistency of thick soup.

Uncover the rice, and evenly spread the mixture over it. Add coriander seeds and mix gently. Remove the rice to a saucepan and heat through, covered, before serving.

Serve garnished with raisins, and chopped cilantro.
Serves 4–6.

## South Indian Sweet Rice—*pongal* (dairy)

This festive South Indian rice is usually made on special occasions, and is very similar to a dish from Gujarat and Maharashtra (*karadni khichadi*), the recipe for which follows after this one.

Both dishes are extremely aromatic and flavorful, especially when made with brown rice. If using brown rice, use split pigeon peas (*toor dal*) instead of split mung beans (mung *dal*), as *toor dal* and brown rice have comparable cooking times. Additionally, note that brown rice also requires more water for cooking.

While this dish traditionally calls for butter or ghee, I have used margarine instead. Use a sugar substitute, if desired. Serve with any pickle.

| | |
|---|---|
| 2 cups | *basmati* rice, washed, drained, dried |
| 2 cups | split mung beans (mung *dal),* washed, drained, dried |
| 3 tablespoons | unsalted margarine |
| ½ cup | cashew nuts unsalted |
| ¼ cup | golden raisins |
| 4 cups | water or as required |
| 2 cups | milk |
| 2 teaspoons | coarsely ground black pepper |
| 2 teaspoons | salt, or to taste |
| 2–inch piece | fresh ginger, peeled, ground |
| 1 cup | sugar, or to taste |
| 1 teaspoon | coarsely ground cardamom |

Wash rice and drain well. Pick over and wash *dal.* (see note, p. 336), drain well. Spread rice and *dal* on paper towels to dry for at least 10 minutes.

Add rice and *dal* to a medium saucepan, and dry-cook, stirring well until the ingredients change color—about 10 minutes. Remove from heat and set aside.

In a small frying pan, heat 1 ½ tablespoons margarine and fry cashews. When golden, remove with a slotted spoon onto paper towels. Fry raisins in the same margarine; when plump, remove and set aside with cashews. Discard leftover margarine.

In a medium saucepan, bring water and milk to a full boil. Add rice, *dal*, black pepper, salt and ginger. Cook until the rice and *dal* are soft, about 15 minutes. If not cooked at this point, add a little more water and cook for few minutes longer. Gently fold in sugar, cardamom and the remaining margarine. Serve hot garnished with cashews and raisins. Serves 8–10.

## Brown Rice with *Toor Dal*—*karadni khichadi*

In both Maharashtra and Gujarat, this dish is made on the particular religious day when the cobra is worshipped. Hindu mythology holds that the cobra carries the world on its head. On the day of *nagpanchami*, the female head of the family performs a *puja* (religious ceremony) for the cobra, in order that family lineage be preserved and that health, happiness and longevity are granted. The whole family consumes this rice dish on the holy day.

Fresh turmeric, *leeli haldar* accents the nutty flavors of the rice and *dal*. In Gujarat, we serve this with a special pickle called *bafanu,* made with ripe, juicy mangoes. It is equally delicious served with yogurt or any hot pickle, available at Indian grocery stores.

| | |
|---|---|
| 1 cup | split pigeon peas (*toor dal*), washed |
| 6 cups | water or as needed |
| 1 ½ cups | brown rice, washed |
| 2 teaspoons | salt, or to taste |
| ½ teaspoon | turmeric |
| 3–inch piece | fresh ginger, peeled, chopped |
| 1 tablespoon | sliced fresh turmeric (p. 32) (optional) |
| Sugar | as needed |
| Margarine | as needed |

Pick over and wash *toor dal* with hot water at least 3 times (see note, p. 336). In a medium saucepan bring water to a full boil over high heat. Add *dal* and rice to boiling water. Add salt, turmeric, ginger and fresh turmeric, if available. Lower the heat to medium and cook until the rice and *dal* are done and slightly soft, about 30 minutes. Add more water and cook longer, if needed, as this *khichadi* must be soft.

While serving, allow each dinner guest to add sugar and margarine to taste, and mix well. Traditionally, it is served with sugar and clarified butter. Serves 6–8.

## Lentil Pilaf—*masoorno pulav*

This simple, delicious and colorful recipe is particularly wonderful when served with yogurt-based dishes, such as *kadhi*(p. 293). Alternatively, serve with any meal or with plain yogurt.

| | |
|---|---|
| 1 cup | brown lentils, washed |
| 2 tablespoons | oil |
| 2 three–inch sticks | cinnamon |
| 10 | cloves |
| 2 | bay leaves |
| 4 cups | water |
| 2 teaspoons | salt, or to taste |
| 1 ½ cups | *basmati* rice, washed |
| 2 cups | chopped green and red bell peppers, for garnish |

Pick over and wash brown lentils (see note, p. 336). Set aside. In a medium saucepan over high heat, heat oil and add cinnamon and cloves. When cloves start to swell, add bay leaves and cook for a few seconds. Add water, and let the mixture come to a full boil.

Add lentils and salt, and cook for about 5 minutes. While lentils are cooking, wash rice. Add rice and bring the mixture to a full boil. Lower the heat, partially cover the saucepan, and cook until the lentils and rice are soft, about 20 minutes. If all of the liquid evaporates, and the rice and lentils are still underdone, add just a little more water, cover the pan and cook for a few more minutes. Serve garnished with bell peppers.
Serves 4–6.

## Vegetable Pilaf—*shakno pulav*

Though slightly more complicated than other recipes in this chapter, this recipe is well worth the effort. Fresh and dry spices combine to add texture and intense flavor to this very savory dish, which combines the lighter flavors of ingredients such as lemon with the deeper aroma of a variety of spices including cardamom and ginger. You may prepare the spice mixtures one day ahead of time, or even prepare the dish the previous day, and refrigerate when cool. Warm the dish in an oven or a microwave before serving. Prepared with vegetables, this is an ideal recipe for large parties as it cuts down on the need for many extra dishes.

You may reduce the spiciness of the recipe by cutting the number of chilies added into the spice mixtures. Serve with any *dal*, any yogurt-based recipe, or with plain yogurt alone.

**Green Spice Mixture:**

| | |
|---|---|
| ½ cup | unsweetened, grated coconut |
| 3–inch piece | fresh ginger, peeled, chopped |
| 6 | jalapeño or serrano chilies, chopped |
| 1 ½ cups | chopped cilantro |
| 2 teaspoons | lemon juice |
| 1 teaspoon | salt, or to taste |

Using a food processor, fitted with a metal blade, grind above ingredients into a coarse paste. Set aside.

**Dry Spice Mixture:**

| | |
|---|---|
| 2 three–inch sticks | cinnamon, broken |
| 7 | cloves |
| ¼ teaspoon | cardamom seeds |
| ½ teaspoon | black peppercorns |
| ¼ teaspoon | anise seeds |
| 1 teaspoon | cumin seeds |

| 2 | dried, whole red chili peppers |
|---|---|

In a medium frying pan over low heat, toast, stirring well, cinnamon together with all ingredients, including red chili peppers, until they change color, about 10 minutes. Let cool and finely grind in a coffee grinder. Set aside.

**Rice and Vegetables:**

| 6 tablespoons | oil |
|---|---|
| ½ cup | cashews, unsalted |
| 2 teaspoons | black mustard seeds |
| 3 three–inch sticks | cinnamon |
| 10 | cloves |
| 10 | *curry* leaves **or** |
| 5 | bay leaves |
| 1 cup | finely sliced onions |
| 2 cups | peas, fresh or frozen |
| 1 small head | cauliflower, cut into florets |
| 2 medium | potatoes, peeled, halved, cut into ½–inch slices |
| 5 cups | water, or as needed |
| 3 cups | *basmati* rice, washed |
| 1 tablespoon | salt, or to taste |
| ½ cup | chopped tomatoes, preferably roma, for garnish |

Heat the oil in a medium saucepan over medium heat. Add cashew, lower the heat and fry stirring well until golden. Using a slotted spoon, remove the cashews to a bowl lined with paper towels.

To the same oil, add the mustard seeds. Add cinnamon and cloves when the mustard seeds start to crackle. When cinnamon and cloves start to swell, add *curry* leaves or bay leaves. Cook for a few seconds and add the onions. Cook the mixture, stirring well, for about 7 minutes or until the onions are slightly golden.

Add the peas now if using fresh, followed by the cauliflower and pota-toes. Fry, stirring well, for a few seconds. Add water and allow the mixture to come to a full boil. Add the rice and salt. Add half of each of the two spice mixtures, reserving the remainder for garnishing. Mix well, and cook on high heat, covered partially, until the pilaf is almost done, about 15 minutes.

If using frozen peas, add them now and stir gently. Cover the saucepan, reduce heat to medium, and cook for 5 more minutes. If the rice is not soft enough, add a little more water and cook for few more minutes until done.

Serve hot, garnished with the remaining spice mixtures, tomatoes and cashews.

Serves 10–12.

## Tricolor Pilaf—*trirangi pulav*

The striking color combination presented by this pilaf is attributable not to any artificial colorings, but to the careful use of complementary ingredients that lend the dish vibrant flavor and color. In this three-layered dish, green peas, cilantro and mint provide spicy accent with vivid green hues, and tomatoes and carrots offer soothing reds matched by subtle flavors. I like to make this recipe in a clear glass, ovenproof bowl, showcasing the appearance of this dish, which is comprised of three layers of differently colored rice. Serve with yogurt-based dishes or with any meal.

**Mixture-1:**

| | |
|---|---|
| 1 teaspoon | salt, or to taste |
| 2 cups | green peas, cooked |
| 2 cups | chopped cilantro |
| 6 | serrano or jalapeño chilies, ground |
| 2 teaspoons | lemon juice |
| 1 tablespoon | mint leaves, chopped |

**Mixture-2:**

| | |
|---|---|
| 2 | ripe tomatoes, chopped, cooked without water, strained |
| 2 medium | carrots, chopped, boiled |
| ½ teaspoon | chili powder |
| 2 teaspoons | sugar, or to taste (optional) |

**Mixture-3:**

| | |
|---|---|
| 1 teaspoon | salt, or to taste |
| 2 medium | potatoes, boiled, peeled, sliced |
| ½ cup | unsweetened, grated coconut |
| 3–inch piece | fresh ginger, peeled, grated |
| ¼ teaspoon | turmeric |

**Rice:**

| | |
|---|---|
| 5 cups | water |
| 4 cups | *basmati* rice, washed |

| 1 teaspoon | salt |
| 1 tablespoon | oil |
| | |
| 4 tablespoons | oil |
| 3 three–inch sticks | cinnamon |
| 8 | cloves |
| 2 teaspoons | cumin seeds |
| 2 tablespoons | unsweetened, finely grated coconut, for garnish |
| ½ cup | chopped cilantro, for garnish |

Combine Mixture-1 ingredients. Set aside.

For Mixture-2, chop tomatoes and cook over medium heat in a small saucepan until the tomatoes are soft. Strain the cooked tomatoes by pushing through a sieve: save the liquid and discard all skin and seeds. Combine strained liquid with the 3 remaining ingredients—carrots, chili and sugar. Set aside.

Combine Mixture-3 ingredients including turmeric. Set aside.

In a medium saucepan, over high heat, bring water to a full boil and add rice, salt and oil. Cook, partially covered, until the rice is dry, about 10 minutes. The rice will remain slightly undercooked.

Remove the rice from heat and divide into 3 separate bowls.

Combine each Mixture with a separate portion of rice.

Preheat oven to 375 °F. Heat the oil in an ovenproof medium saucepan over high heat. Add the cinnamon, cloves and cumin seeds. When the cinnamon and cloves start to swell and cumin is slightly golden, remove the saucepan from heat and add Mixture-1 rice. Gently press the rice mixture with the back of a spoon. Spread Mixture-2 rice on top, and press to set. Repeat with Mixture-3, gently pressing over the second layer.

Cover the top layer of rice with foil, cover the saucepan with a lid, and place it in the oven preheated to 400 °F. Cook until the rice is soft, about 30 minutes. Alternatively, prepare oil mixture in a frying pan, and then pour it into an ovenproof bowl. Arrange layers as directed above, cover the rice with a foil. Cover the bowl and cook it in the oven until the rice is soft.

Prior to serving, combine coconut with 3 tablespoons water and set aside for few minutes. As it absorbs the water, the coconut will look freshly grated. Garnish rice with coconut and cilantro before serving.
Serves 10–12.

# Dry Peas Pilaf—*suka vatanano pulav*

Yellow peas, green onions and mint combine with rice in this recipe to yield a subtly flavored dish that is versatile insofar as it pairs well with almost any vegetable entrée. Wild rice may be used for this recipe in place of *basmati*, though more water will be needed to cook the recipe.

| | |
|---|---|
| 1 cup | whole yellow peas, soaked four hours |
| 2 tablespoons | oil |
| 10 | cloves |
| 1 three–inch stick | cinnamon |
| 2 cups | green onions, chopped |
| 2 tablespoons | mint leaves, chopped |
| 2 cups | *basmati* rice, washed |
| 1 medium | potato, peeled, cubed |
| 3 ½ cups | water |
| 2 teaspoons | salt, or to taste |
| ¼ cup | chopped cilantro, for garnish |

Pick over, wash (see note, p. 336) and soak peas for four hours.

Heat oil in a medium saucepan over high heat and add cloves and cinnamon. When the cinnamon and cloves start to swell, add onions and mint. Cook for 2 minutes, drain and add yellow peas and cook stirring well for 7 minutes.

Add rice, potato, water and salt. Bring the mixture to a full boil. Lower the heat to medium and cook until the rice and peas are soft, about 20 minutes. Serve garnished with cilantro.

Serves 6–8.

## Split Lima Bean *Khichadi*—*valdalni khichadi*

Though I prefer to make this dish with sprouted lima beans (p. 343), it may also be prepared with split lima beans, available in Indian stores. Serve with *kadhi* (p. 293).

| | |
|---|---|
| 1 ½ cups | split lima beans (*valni dal*), soaked four hours **or** |
| 1 cup | lima beans, sprouted |
| 3 tablespoons | oil |
| 8 | cloves |
| 1 three–inch stick | cinnamon |
| 8 cloves | garlic, peeled, chopped |
| 2 | serrano or jalapeño chilies, chopped |
| 2–inch piece | fresh ginger, peeled, finely chopped |
| 2 cups | *basmati* rice, washed |
| 2 teaspoons | salt, or to taste |
| 3 cups | water |
| 2 tablespoon | golden raisins |
| ¼ cup | chopped cilantro, for garnish |

If using split lima beans, pick over, wash (see note, p. 336) and soak for at least four hours. Drain and set aside. For sprouted lima beans, follow instructions on page 343.

Heat 2 tablespoons oil (save 1 tablespoon) in a medium saucepan over high heat and add cloves and cinnamon. When cloves and cinnamon start to swell, add garlic and fry the mixture until garlic is golden.

Add chilies, ginger and lima beans (either split or sprouted). Cook, stirring well, for 2 minutes. Add rice, salt and water and cook on high heat for 10 minutes. Lower the heat to medium, cover the saucepan, and cook until the rice and *dal* are soft about 10 more minutes. If the rice and *dal* are not soft, add a little more water and cook for few more minutes longer until done.

In a small frying pan, heat the remaining 1 tablespoon oil and fry raisins until plump. Using a slotted spoon remove raisins from oil and drain on paper towels. Discard oil.

Garnish *khichadi* with cilantro and raisins and serve hot.

Serves 6.

## Unhulled Split Mung *Khichadi*—*kathiawadi khichadi*

This is a simple, popular dish from Kathiawad, in West Gujarat. This very soft *khichadi* is usually served with *kadhi* (p. 293) or yogurt. It also tastes wonderful topped with a little butter.

| | |
|---|---|
| 1 cup | unhulled split mung beans (mung *dal*), washed |
| 2 cups | *basmati* rice, washed |
| 6 ½ cups | water |
| 2 teaspoons | salt, or to taste |
| ½ teaspoon | turmeric |
| 2–inch piece | fresh ginger, peeled, ground |

Pick over and wash *dal* (see note, p. 336).

In a medium saucepan, combine rice, *dal* and the next 4 ingredients including ginger. Bring the mixture to a full boil over high heat. Cook for 10 minutes and lower the heat to medium. Cover the saucepan, and cook until the rice and *dal* are soft, about 20 minutes. Rice and *dal* will partially dissolve together in this particular recipe but the result will be delicious. Serve as desired.

Serves 4–6.

## Cashew and Saffron *Khichadi*—*kesarwali khichadi*

This unusual recipe came from our late, dear friend, Dr. A.T. Ganesan. Any variety of rice can be used for this recipe, though I always prefer *basmati*. Serve with plain yogurt or onion *raita* (p. 105).

| | |
|---|---|
| ½ cup | split mung beans (mung *dal*), washed |
| 4 tablespoons | margarine or butter |
| ¼ cup | finely chopped onions |
| 6 cloves | garlic, peeled, chopped |
| 8 | cloves |
| 8 | cardamom pods |
| 4 one–inch sticks | cinnamon |
| ½ teaspoon | allspice, whole |
| 2–inch | fresh ginger, peeled, finely chopped |
| 2 cups | *basmati* rice, washed |
| 3 ¼ cups | water |
| ¼ teaspoon | turmeric |
| 1 ¼ teaspoons | salt, or to taste |
| 1 tablespoon | oil |
| ¼ cup | cashew nuts, unsalted |
| ¼ teaspoon | loosely packed saffron, crushed |
| ¼ cup | chopped cilantro, for garnish |

Pick over and wash *dal* (see note, p. 336).

Heat margarine or butter in a saucepan over medium heat and add onions and the next 6 ingredients including ginger. Fry the mixture for 10 minutes, stirring well and taking care not to allow the onions to brown.

Add rice and *dal* to onion mixture. Mix well and reduce the heat to very low.

In a separate saucepan, boil water. Add the boiling water to the rice and *dal* mixture. Add turmeric and salt, and mix well. Raise the heat and return the mixture to a full boil. After 2 minutes lower the heat to medium-low, cover and cook until the *dal* and rice are soft, about 20 minutes.

In a small frying pan heat oil, and fry the cashew until slightly golden. Remove with a slotted spoon, and drain on paper towels. Discard oil.

Just before serving, gently mix saffron with *khichadi*.

Serve garnished with cashew and cilantro.

Serves 4–6.

## Cumin and Pepper *Khichadi*—*masalawali khichadi* (dairy)

Two varieties of cumin lend wonderful flavor to this slightly spicy *khichadi*. Either bulgur or quinoa may substitute for the rice in this recipe. Serve with any meal.

| | |
|---|---|
| 2 teaspons | black pepper |
| 1 tablespoon | coriander seeds |
| 2 teaspoons | black cumin seeds (p. 15) |
| 1 teaspoon | cumin seeds |
| ½ teaspoon | cardamom seeds |
| 10 | cloves |
| 3 | dried, whole red chili peppers |
| 1 cup | split mung beans (mung *dal*), washed |
| 3 tablespoons | oil or butter |
| 4 cups | water |
| 2 cups | *basmati* rice, washed |
| 2 teaspoons | salt, or to taste |
| ½ teaspoon | turmeric |
| 1 cup | plain yogurt |
| ¼ cup | chopped cilantro, for garnish |

In a small frying pan over medium heat, toast—stirring well—black pepper together with the next 6 ingredients including red peppers, until they change color to light brown, about 5 minutes. Allow to cool. Using a coffee grinder or a mill, grind toasted spices and set aside.

Pick over and wash *dal* (see note, p. 336). Set aside.

In a medium saucepan, heat the oil over medium heat and add the ground spices. Cook for 2 minutes, stirring well. Add water and bring it to a full boil over high heat. Add rice, *dal*, salt and turmeric. Cook until all the water is absorbed, about 10 minutes. Gently fold in yogurt, cover and cook on very low heat for about 10 more minutes or until rice and *dal* are soft.

Serve hot, garnished with cilantro.

Serves 6–8.

## Sorghum *Khichadi—juwarni khichadi* (dairy)

In the *Kathiawad* area, the Gujarati region from where this recipe originates, it is believed that sorghum provides "warmth" to the body. This recipe is hence seen as being good to eat during cold, winter months. In the U.S., sorghum is available in most natural food stores—I use a coffee grinder to coarsely grind it. Bulgur may be substituted if sorghum is difficult to find. Expect a dish with the consistency of a thick porridge. I sometimes add ¼ cup frozen green peas or 1 cup frozen chopped spinach to this *khichadi* during the last 5 minutes of cooking, and serve it as a nutritious, simple one-dish meal.

| | |
|---|---|
| 4 ½ cups | water |
| 1 cup | split pigeon peas (*toor dal*), washed |
| 2 cups | sorghum, coarsely ground |
| 2 cups | yogurt |
| 3–inch piece | fresh ginger, peeled, chopped |
| 4 | serrano or jalapeño chilies, chopped |
| ½ teaspoon | turmeric |
| 1 tablespoon | salt, or to taste |
| 3 tablespoons | oil or butter |
| 2 teaspoons | black mustard seeds |
| ½ teaspoon | *hing* (asafoetida) |

In a medium saucepan, over high heat, bring water to a full boil. Meanwhile, pick over and wash *dal* (see note, p. 336) and add it to boiling water. When the *dal* is just about half cooked, about 12 minutes, add sorghum and cook the mixture for another 10 minutes, stirring intermittently. Add yogurt and the next 4 ingredients including salt, and mix well. Lower the heat, cover and allow to simmer for about 3 minutes.

In a frying pan, heat the oil and add mustard seeds. Add *hing* when mustard starts to crackle. Cook for a few seconds and add the mixture to the *khichadi*. Mix well and cook for 2 more minute. Serve hot. Serves 6–8.

## Three Grain Savory Porridge—*bajri,* mung, *chokhanu bhadku*

Whole millet is available in some Indian stores, however, if unavailable, substitute with other whole grains such as wheat or sorghum. This is a very light and satisfying dish that, along with yogurt, may be served as a one-dish meal.

| | |
|---|---|
| ½ cup | millet |
| ½ cup | mung beans, picked over |
| ½ cup | *basmati* rice |
| 6 cups | water |
| 2 teaspoons | oil |
| 1 teaspoon | *ajwain* (p. 9) |
| 2 teaspoons | salt, or to taste |

In a coffee grinder, separately grind millet, mung beans and rice until coarse. Remove together to a bowl, add 3 cups water, mix well, and set aside for about 30 minutes.

Heat oil in a medium saucepan over medium heat, and add *ajwain*. When *ajwain* turns slightly brown, add soaked grains with water. Add remaining 3 cups water and salt. Lower the heat and cook, stirring well for about 10 minutes or until mixture attains thick porridge-like consistency. Serve hot.

Serves 4–6.

## Bulgur with Spices—*khati lapsi* (dairy)

This light and exceedingly simple dish does not require many ingredients, and can be served in place of rice. With the addition of some vegetables (of your choice), this dish can suffice as an easy one-dish meal.

Provided that the grain has not excessively aged, bulgur is quick to cook. In general, I recommend purchasing bulgur from those places where it sells well—such as Indian markets or health food stores—to ensure a constant, new supply.

| | |
|---|---|
| 1 cup | bulgur |
| 3 cups | water |
| 2 teaspoons | salt, or to taste |
| ½ cup | yogurt |
| ¼ teaspoon | turmeric |
| 2 | serrano or jalapeño chilies, ground |
| 2–inch piece | fresh ginger, peeled, ground |
| ½ cup | chopped cilantro, for garnish |

In a medium saucepan, combine bulgur with the next 6 ingredients including ginger. Cook on medium-low heat, until bulgur is soft, about 30 minutes. Serve hot, garnished with cilantro.
Serves 3–4.

# Bulgur with Split Mung Beans and Onions—*masala bhadku*

This Doshi family favorite, is a savory, filling and nutritious dish that goes well with yogurt or *kadhi*, a yogurt-based sauce (p. 293). If the *dal* used in this dish is soaked ahead of time, it takes about 20 minutes to cook this dish.

| | |
|---|---|
| ½ cup | split mung beans (mung *dal)*, soaked four hours |
| 1 tablespoon | oil |
| 1 three–inch stick | cinnamon |
| 5 | cloves |
| 1 medium | onion, chopped |
| 2 | dried, whole red chili peppers |
| ½ cup | bulgur |
| 1 ½ teaspoons | salt, or to taste |
| 3 cups | water |
| 3 | serrano or jalapeño chilies, chopped |
| 2–inch piece | fresh ginger, peeled, grated |
| 4 cloves | garlic, peeled, chopped |
| ½ cup | chopped fresh or frozen spinach |
| ¼ teaspoon | turmeric |
| ¼ cup | chopped cilantro |

Pick over, wash and soak *dal* for four hours (see note, p. 336).

Heat oil in a medium saucepan over high heat and add cinnamon and cloves. When cloves start to swell, add onions and peppers. Cook over medium heat, stirring well, until the onions turn slightly golden—about 5 minutes.

Drain and add soaked mung *dal* and bulgur to onion mixture. Add the next 7 ingredients including turmeric and mix well. Lower the heat to medium, cover and cook until bulgur and *dal* are soft, about 20 minutes. Add cilantro and mix well. Serve hot.

Serves 2–4.

## Bulgur with Vegetables—*lapsi pilaf*

Any number of your favorite vegetables can be added to this dish; simply add them in with the eggplant. Serve with plain yogurt.

| | |
|---|---|
| 2 tablespoons | oil |
| 2 three–inch sticks | cinnamon, broken |
| 10 | cloves |
| 10 | *curry* leaves (optional) |
| 2 medium | potatoes, peeled, cut into 1–inch cubes |
| 2 cups | bulgur |
| 3 | serrano or jalapeño chilies, chopped |
| 2–inch piece | fresh ginger, peeled, chopped |
| 1 ½ teaspoons | salt, or to taste |
| ½ teaspoon | turmeric |
| 1 small | Japanese eggplant, sliced |
| 4 cups | water |
| 1 cup | frozen peas |
| 1 small | tomato, chopped |
| ½ cup | chopped cilantro, for garnish |

Heat oil in a medium saucepan over high heat and add cinnamon and cloves. Add *curry* leaves as soon as cinnamon and cloves start to swell. Add potatoes, bulgur and next 5 ingredients including sliced eggplant. Cook stirring well, for 3 minutes. Lower the heat to medium, add water and mix well. Cover and cook until the potatoes and bulgur are almost done, about 20 minutes.

Add peas and tomato, mix gently, cover and cook for 3 more minutes or until heated through. Serve garnished with cilantro.
Serves 6–8.

## Vegetable *Biryani*—*shakni biryani* (dairy)

Though this recipe may appear daunting, it is in fact not that complicated. Saffron, ginger, mint and the *garam masala* infuse the rice and vegetables with intoxicating flavor and aroma. When I have prepared this at home, I have had neighbors and even the postman stop and ask me what smells so good! The most time-consuming procedure in this recipe is browning the onions. To break up preparation of cooking time, brown the onions days in advance. Refrigerate fried onions in a paper bag (the bag will absorb most oil from the onions) within a sealable plastic bag until ready to use.

Serve with salad and plain yogurt.

**Rice:**

| | |
|---|---|
| 4 cups | *basmati* rice, washed |
| 4 cups | water |
| 2 teaspoons | salt, or to taste |

**Onion Mixture:**

| | |
|---|---|
| 4 medium (8 cups) | onions, finely sliced |
| 1 ½ cups | oil for frying, |
| 4 tablespoons | butter or oil |
| 2 teaspoons | cumin seeds |
| 2 cups | green peas, fresh or frozen |
| 1 cup | cilantro, chopped |
| 2 large | potatoes, red, peeled, quartered |
| 2 tablespoons | chopped mint leaves |
| 3 | serrano or jalapeño chilies, ground |
| 4–inch piece | fresh ginger, peeled, ground |
| 10 cloves | garlic, peeled, chopped |
| 2 teaspoons | salt, or to taste |
| 2 teaspoons | *garam masala*-1 (p. 21) |
| 2 medium | tomatoes, chopped |

| ½ teaspoon | turmeric |
| 3 tablespoons | ground coriander seeds |
| 2 teaspoons | ground cumin seeds |
| 2 cups | yogurt |
| ½ teaspoon | saffron, crushed |
| 3 tablespoons | milk |
| ¼ cup | chopped cilantro, for garnish |

Add rice, 4 cups water and 2 teaspoons salt to a medium saucepan and cook over high heat until the water is absorbed. Take care not to let the rice burn. The rice will remain slightly undercooked.

While the rice is cooking, heat oil and fry half of the onions until crisp and brown. Remove with a slotted spoon and drain on paper towels. Repeat with remaining onions, frying in the same oil. Remove to paper towels, with first batch of onions, when crisp and brown. When cool, crush onions using back of a large spoon. Onions may be fried several days in advance and can be refrigerated as noted above.

Preheat oven to 450 °F. Prepare the vegetable mixture while frying the onions, and as the rice continues to cook. Heat butter or oil in a medium saucepan and add cumin seeds. When cumin begins to sizzle, add peas and the next 12 ingredients including ground cumin. Cook on high heat for at least 5 minutes, stirring well. Remove mixture from heat. Allow to cool, for 5 minutes. Add yogurt, mix well and set aside.

In a heavy-bottomed saucepan, layer fried onions, layer vegetable mixture, then rice in that order over the onions. Depending on the size of your saucepan, you may need to repeat layers several times finishing with rice.

Crush saffron threads and add to milk. Heat milk for 30 seconds in microwave or gently on stovetop until warm so that the saffron melts. Drizzle the saffron mixture over the layered rice with a spoon. Cover the rice with aluminum foil secured around the edges and cover the pan with a lid.

Place the saucepan in the middle of the preheated oven. Cook for 30 minutes, then lower oven to 350 °F and cook for another 30 minutes, or until rice is done.

Serve hot, spreading the rice on a large platter with the vegetable mixture on top. Garnish with chopped cilantro.

Serves: 8–10.

## Quinoa—*kodri*

This dish is very popular in my home state of Gujarat. High in B-vitamins and a complete protein, quinoa is a nutritious grain that Indians have consumed for centuries. Some toasted and coarsely ground cumin may be added to this recipe for added flavor. Serve in place of rice with any meal.

| | |
|---|---|
| 1 cup | quinoa |
| 2 cups | water |
| ¼ teaspoon | salt, or to taste |

Rinse quinoa with cold water two or three times. In a saucepan combine quinoa, water and salt and cook on medium heat, until fluffy, about 12 minutes.

Serves 2–3.

**Note**: Variety of raw vegetables can be cooked with quinoa. Substitute quinoa in any recipe in this chapter. Quinoa can also be made adding ¼ cup yogurt together with water.

## Wild Rice Pilaf—*jungli pulav*

In the early sixties, while working for the Consulate in New York, I was assigned to work for the late Dr. H. J. Bhabha, Chairman of the Atomic Energy Commission of India. Dr. Bhabha, prior to his return to India, gave me flowers and a pack of wild rice. Before this I had never cooked wild rice. This dish was a favorite of my husband, Arun. Any recipe in this section may be made using this variety of rice. Also try a mixture of brown and wild rice together for varied texture.

The mixture of black wild rice and green peas looks very attractive and elegant. Serve garnished with cilantro and sliced carrots. Any *raita* preparation will go well with this.

| | |
|---|---|
| 2 tablespoons | oil |
| 1 three–inch stick | cinnamon |
| 2 | bay leaves |
| 1 cup | wild rice |
| 2 cups | water or as required |
| 1 teaspoon | salt, or to taste |
| 1 | serrano or jalapeño chili, chopped |
| 1 cup | frozen green peas |

Heat oil in a small saucepan over high heat and add cinnamon and bay leaves. When cinnamon starts to swell, add rice, water, salt and chili. Cook the mixture on high heat for 5 minutes, lower the heat to medium and cover partially. Cook until the rice is almost done, about 20 minutes.

Add peas and cook for 3 more minutes or until the peas are heated through, stir gently. Garnish with chopped cilantro if desired. Serves 3–4.

# *DALS*: BEANS, PEAS AND LENTILS

Spiced Black-Eyed Peas—*chola*

Spiced Aduki Beans (Red Black-Eyed Peas)—*lal choli*

Garbanzo Beans with Mint—*fudinawala chana*

Garbanzo Beans in Basic "Curry" Sauce—*chhole*

Bengal Grams with Onions and Lemon—*kala chana*

Split Chickpeas with Cinnamon and Green Chili—*chana dal*

Pigeon Peas Consommé—*dalnu osaman*

Whole Pigeon Peas with Yogurt and Spices—*toor kadhi* (dairy)

Split Pigeon Peas and Tomatoes with Bulbous Root—*suranwali dal*

Split Pigeon Peas with Mung Beans—*tuver mugni dal*

Indian Pasta with Split Pigeon Peas—*dal dhokli*

Green Mung Beans with Ginger—*mug*

Sweet, Sour and Hot Mung Beans—*mugno ragdo*

Split Mung Beans—*mugni dal*

Split Mung Beans with Zucchini—zucchini *mugni dal*

Split Indian Black Beans—*urid dal*

Kidney Beans with Potatoes—*kashmiri rajma*

Sprouted Mung Beans with Garlic—*sangavela mug*

Variation 1: Sprouted Brown Mung Beans—*sangavela muth*

Variation 2: Sprouted Brown Mung Beans with Dumplings—*muth dhokli*

Split Indian Lima Beans—*valni dal*

Yellow Split Peas with Garlic and Cloves—*vatanani dal*

South Indian *Sambar*—*sambar*

Onion *Sambar*—onion *sambar*

Split and Whole Indian Black Beans—*moglai dal* (dairy)

Lima Beans with Tamarind—*sabut val*

Indian Black Beans with *Dals* and Spices—*Punjabi dal*
Five *Dals*—*panch dal*
Green Peas with Cilantro-Coconut Sauce—*leela vatana*
Yellow Peas in Onion-Yogurt Sauce—*dopiaza matar* (dairy)
Black-Eyed Peas *Kofta* in Onion Sauce—*kofta* "curry"
Yogurt-Chili Sauce—*kadhi* (dairy)
Tamarind Sauce—*panoo*

# *Dals*: Beans, Peas and Lentils

*Dals*, the many distinct varieties of beans, peas and lentils, all belong to the legume family of plants. Complementing vegetables in satisfying ways, they fulfill the Indian vegetarian's diet with protein. The majority of recipes are actually quite simple, requiring neither special ingredients nor specific equipment. As I have mentioned in other chapters in this book, it is my hope that the guidelines presented here will furnish readers with sufficient knowledge that they may try inventing their own *dal* recipes by substituting ingredients.

A note on the term "*dal*": Strictly speaking, "*dal*" refers to split beans. Through usage, though, "*dal*" has now come to refer to any cooked, split or whole bean, pea or lentil dish. In this book, I similarly use "*dal*" to refer to any cooked legume dish. However, when I use "*dal*" in the context of a proper name, such as "*chana dal*" or "*toor dal*," I am referring to the split variety and not to whole beans, peas or lentils.

## Fat-free Recipes

At *The Ganges*, I frequently received requests for fat-free *dals*. In fact, a wide variety of Indian recipes may be made without the addition of oil or any other fat (p. 48). For fat-free *dals*, spices that are normally cooked in oil, such as black mustard, cumin or fenugreek seeds, can instead be dry toasted prior to addition into the *dal*. *Hing* may likewise be dry-toasted before adding to a recipe. If you are dry toasting black mustard seeds, be sure to cover the frying pan with a lid to prevent losing the seeds, as they will "pop" when heated. Note that onions and garlic may also be browned in a nonstick frying pan before being added to the *dal*.

### A Note on Cleaning, Washing and Rinsing *Dals*

To pick over *dals*, spread a handful of *dal* over a large, flat surface. You may use a clean platter, flat baking sheet or even a tabletop. Look closely, remove and discard stems, tiny rocks, spoiled grains and other foreign objects.

Remove *dal* from surface and continue with another handful. All *dals*, either prepackaged or loose, should be picked over carefully prior to use.

Note that *dals* that are toasted prior to being used in a recipe are generally not washed prior to use, though they do need to be picked over. If washing is required, the dals will need to be completely dry prior to toasting.

Washing *dals* involves placing the *dal* into a bowl much larger than the amount of *dal* needing to be washed. Add water into the bowl such that the *dal* is completely immersed. Using your hands, gently stir, using your fingers to agitate the *dal* in the water to clean the grains. Empty the water from the bowl, holding your hand at the mouth of the bowl, or using a strainer, so that no *dal* is lost as you pour out the water. You should repeat washing *dals* until the water runs clear. Note that *toor dal* must be washed with hot water in order to remove the oil coating that is applied to the *dal* as a preservative.

Alternatively, place *dal* into a colander (making sure that the holes in the colander are not larger than the *dal*). Hold colander under running water, and gently run hands through *dal*/beans, making sure that all are rinsed.

## Buying And Storing Dals

Though *dals* sold in stores are, for the most part, clean, I nevertheless recommend that you carefully inspect all *dal* before purchase. If buying loose from bins, pick up a handful, and check for spoiled, shriveled grains, tiny rocks, stems or other foreign objects. If too many grains appear bad, or if there is an abundance of foreign objects, I would caution against purchase. Store *dals* in airtight containers in a cool place. For those who do not plan to make *dal* on a regular basis, I recommend buying the legumes in small quantities, as they do eventually spoil.

## Varieties of Beans, Peas and Lentils:

**Aduki Beans or Red Black-Eyed Peas (*choli*):** Available in either Indian or health-food stores, these red beans are smaller and have a slightly different taste than regular black-eyed peas. They add variety to the repertoire of commonly prepared *dals*. It is advisable to buy them in small quantities and pick over before use. Aduki beans can be cooked without soaking.

**Bengal Grams (*kala chana*):** See Chickpeas.

**Black-Eyed Peas (*chola* or *lobya*):** Less commonly known as cowpeas, black-eyed peas can be cooked alone or mixed with other *dals* and vegetables. Dried black-eyed peas should be distinguished from the fresh frozen type available in grocery stores. Whereas the texture of the dried peas is more suitable for making *dals,* that of the fresh-frozen is better for vegetable dishes. Split and hulled black-eyed peas are called *chola-ni-dal* and can be difficult to find in this country. When shopping for either the whole or split varieties, buy in small quantities and pick over before use. Can be soaked before cooking.

**Chickpeas:**
    **Garbanzo Beans (*chana*):** Two varieties are available in Indian stores. *Kabuli chana* are the English garbanzo beans, common to most North American markets. *Kala chana* or Bengal grams are darker in color, have a nuttier flavor and are mostly available only in Indian food stores. Prior to cooking either variety, soak beans for eight hours and pick over, removing and discarding the beans that don't soak—those that remain hard. The canned variety of garbanzo may be substituted for the dry beans.

    One cup of dry garbanzo beans yields about 2 ½ cup soaked or about 1 ½ cups ground. Ground garbanzo may be substituted for chickpea flour in some recipes.

    **Split chickpeas (*chana dal*):** Slightly rough on the surface, *chana dal* should not be confused with yellow split peas, or *vatanani dal,* which have a smooth surface and a different flavor. *Chana dal* spoils easily, and extra caution should be taken prior to purchase, that no pests are in the lot. Pick over and heat through at low heat in either an oven or a microwave before storing.

*Chana dal* can be cooked alone or mixed with other *dals* or vegetables. It is also used in snacks and in chutneys. Not to be confused with garbanzo bean flour, flour made from *chana dal* is called chickpea flour, gram flour or *besan,* and is added to both vegetables and certain breads and desserts. Though the flour does not stale easily, I recommend buying in small quantities if using only occasionally. *Chana dal* can be cooked with or without soaking (soak for four hours).

### Black Beans

**Indian black beans (*urid*):** Most commonly used in North India, cooked whole *urid* is high in protein. Soaking these beans will not accelerate cooking time, and I do not recommend it. Allow extra cooking time when preparing recipes that list these beans as an ingredient. Dry beans store well, and keep for a long time.

**Split black beans (*urid dal*):** Available hulled or unhulled, *urid dal* flour is often used to make *papadum,* though mung bean flour is also sometimes used. I particularly enjoy cooked split *urid* mixed with yogurt. *Urid dal* may be soaked (four hours) before cooking, though this is not absolutely necessary.

**Kidney beans (*rajma*):** While not commonly used in Gujarat, I like adding these to recipes or cooking them with onions. Since cooking the dry beans can be very time consuming, I recommend soaking for at least eight hours beforehand. For convenience, the canned variety may be used. These beans are easily available in many supermarkets. Buy in small quantities.

### Lentils

**Lentils (*masoor*):** Versatile, inexpensive and quick to cook, *masoor* is one of the staples of the Indian pantry. I like to combine whole lentils with the red variety, to yield exquisite *dal* recipes that are smooth in texture and striking in appearance. Lentils need not be soaked prior to cooking.

**Red lentils (*masoor dal*):** Of the two available sizes, the smaller tends to be sweeter. At *The Ganges*, however, I preferred the larger variety since picking over large quantities of the smaller type can be very time-consuming. This reddish-orange *dal* softens to a pleasing yellow when cooked. Red lentils may be cooked without soaking.

## Lima Beans

**Lima beans (*val*):** Gujarati cooks use whole, split or sprouted lima beans in a number of different dishes. Both large and small, Indian lima beans are now commonly available in both Indian groceries and produce markets, in fresh or dry forms.

When cooking with fresh Indian lima beans, use either size for recipes in this book. Trim the pods and peel open, saving the beans inside. Discard the tough pods of the large-bean variety, but save those of the tiny variety (as the tiny beans and pods will cook together). Discard beans and pods with holes in them.

When buying dry lima beans, purchase in small quantities if infrequently used. Of the two varieties, the large or the small, the smaller is more intensely flavored and cooks faster. When soaked and then picked over, fewer beans of this small variety remain hard. All dry lima beans should be soaked for at least 12 hours and picked over before cooking; the beans that do not soften should be removed and discarded.

**Split lima beans (*valni dal*):** Cooked alone, lightly seasoned with cinnamon, clove, fenugreek and red chili, this *dal* is a treat, when served alongside *parotha* (p. 411). Available in Indian stores, this *dal* may be cooked with or without prior soaking

**Mung Beans**

**Mung beans (*mug* and *muth*)—Green, Brown and Black:**

The three varieties of mung beans can be cooked separately or mixed with other *dals*.

1. Green mung beans or *leela mug*: These are further subdivided by size. Available in some Asian stores, the regular, large-grained variety is more common than other mung beans in Indian cooking. The smaller size grain, called *mugdi* by some Gujaratis, is sometimes seen in Indian stores. Whereas the larger variety is paler in color, the smaller variety is greener and tastes somewhat sweeter. Generally, one only needs to soak green mung beans for sprouting.

2. Brown or red mung beans, known as *muth*: Very popular in Gujarat, these beans are cooked either whole or sprouted. Flour made from split, hulled *muth* is used to make the Gujarati snack, "*mathiya*," a traditional favorite around the Festival of Lights or *Diwali*. Prior to cooking, *muth* should be soaked for at least eight hours in warm water and picked over—the beans that do not soften when soaked should be discarded.

3. Black mung beans or *kala mug*: Not to be confused with whole *urid* or Indian black beans, *kala mug* appear almost black, but look dark green when cooked. I have yet to see these flavorful beans in this country. They should be soaked only if they are to be sprouted.

**Split Mung Beans (*mugni dal*):** Hulled or unhulled, mung *dal* is available in two sizes, the smaller variety being more flavorful. These split beans may be soaked for at least four hours before cooking, though this is not absolutely necessary. Note that when soaked, the grains of the unhulled variety may shed their skins.

**Peas:**

**Peas (*vatana*):** Both green and yellow varieties are available—I sometimes use both in the same dish. They should be soaked for at least four hours before cooking. Buy in small quantities.

**Split peas** (*vatanani dal*): Of the two varieties—yellow and green—be careful not to confuse the yellow with split chickpeas (*chana dal*). Split peas may be mixed with other grains and *dals* to yield interesting color combinations and delicious dishes. Soaking (four hours minimum) is optional.

**Pigeon Peas:**

**Pigeon peas** (*tuver*): Recipes in this book call for both dry and fresh pigeon peas. Fresh pigeon peas are available at farmer's markets or frozen in Indian stores. Since whole dry pigeon peas do not store for long periods of time, some Gujaratis use boric power as a preservative. Personally, I would advise simply buying this type of pea in small quantities. Dry peas should be soaked for at least eight hours and picked over before cooking.

When I lived in Kenya, I remember visiting our family friend Fitz DeSouza at his beach house in Mombasa, and picking the fresh pigeon peas that grew in his backyard. Cooking them with fresh coconut milk extracted from coconuts that grew along the beach, I prepared a magnificent pilaf, the recipe for which is in my Kenya cookbook.

**Split pigeon peas** (*tuverni dal* or *arar dal*): Split pigeon peas are available either coated with castor oil or uncoated (the oil acts as a preservative). Though all peas, beans or lentils should be washed prior to use, oil-coated split pigeon peas should be washed three times with hot water to remove the oil. This *dal* should be cooked without prior soaking.

**Soybeans:** Though not commonly consumed in Gujarat, soybeans may be added to *dals* if preferred. They may in fact replace garbanzo beans in many of the recipes in this chapter. In terms of vegetables, soybeans are an excellent pairing for eggplant. Soybeans should be soaked before use.

**Sprouted beans:** Though Gujarati cooks most frequently sprout green and brown mung beans, any variety may be sprouted following the directions below.

Pick over and wash beans. Soak beans in fresh, cold water for at least 12 hours. Drain and pick over, discarding any hard or unsoaked beans. Tie beans in a cheesecloth. Place the bundle in a covered saucepan, and store saucepan in an area free of draft. After 12 hours, when the beans have begun to sprout, untie, remove cloth store beans for another 12 hours, in the covered saucepan. Pick over again, discarding unsoaked beans that may have not been seen earlier.

Note: A Gujarati superstition maintains that beans do not soak well if the cook talks while washing and immersing the beans in water!

## Spiced Black-Eyed Peas—*chola*

Clove and red chili pepper accent the flavor of black-eyed peas in this simple recipe. While cooking, I like to sew the red chilies together prior to adding them to the peas, as this simplifies the task of removing the peppers when the dish is done. As I remove the chain of chilies, I use the back of a spoon to squeeze the spicy juice of the chili into the *dal*.

Serve with rice and any yogurt-based dish.

| | |
|---|---|
| 2 cups | black-eyed peas, soaked four hours |
| 5 cups | water |
| 2 teaspoons | salt, or to taste |
| 1 tablespoon | oil |
| 1 teaspoon | cumin seeds |
| 10 | cloves |
| ½ teaspoon | *hing* (asafoetida) |
| 5 | dried, whole red chili peppers |
| ¼ teaspoon | turmeric |
| ¼ teaspoon | chili powder (optional) |
| 2 tablespoons | chopped cilantro, for garnish |

Pick over and rinse peas (see note, p. 336). Soak peas for four hours. (If soaked longer than four hours, the peas may lose some of their skin.)

In a medium saucepan over high heat, bring water to full boil. Drain and add black-eyed peas. Add salt, and cook peas until soft, but not soggy—about 12 minutes. Remove and discard any scum that rises from the boiling peas. When the beans are done, reduce heat to very low and let simmer.

Heat oil in a small frying pan over medium heat. Add cumin seeds and cloves. When cumin starts to sizzle and cloves swell, add *hing* and red chili peppers. Cook for a few seconds and add the mixture to the peas, mixing well.

Stir in turmeric and chili powder, if desired, and simmer for 3 more minutes. Remove from heat. Serve garnished with cilantro.

Serves: 4.

**Note:** 1 bunch fresh or 1 packet frozen, chopped spinach may be added with the black-eyed peas to the recipe.

## Spiced Aduki Beans (Red Black-Eyed Peas)—*lal choli*

Aduki beans may be cooked alone or mixed with other beans, following the recipe below. I prefer to combine 2/3 cup each (unsoaked), aduki beans, yellow split peas and green mung beans.

Serve with rice and *kadhi* (p. 293).

| | |
|---|---|
| 8 cups | water |
| 2 cups | aduki beans (*choli*) |
| 2 teaspoons | salt, or to taste |
| 4 | serrano or jalapeño chilies, ground |
| 3–inch piece | fresh ginger, peeled, ground |
| ½ teaspoon | turmeric |
| 3 tablespoons | oil |
| 8 cloves | garlic, peeled, chopped |
| ½ teaspoon | *hing* (asafoetida) |
| 2 tablespoons | chopped mixed green and red bell peppers, for garnish |
| 2 tablespoons | chopped cilantro, for garnish |

Pick over and wash aduki beans (see note, p. 336). In a medium saucepan, bring water to a full boil. Add beans and salt. Cook on high heat for 10 minutes. Reduce heat to medium and cook until the beans are soft but still hold their shape—about 10 more minutes.

Add chilies, ginger and turmeric, mix well, and adjust heat to maintain a low simmer.

Heat oil in a small frying pan over medium heat and add garlic. Fry garlic until slightly golden, add *hing* and cook the mixture for a few seconds. Add oil mixture to beans, raise heat slightly and cook for 2 more minutes. Serve garnished with bell peppers and cilantro.

Serves 6–8.

**Note:** For a creamy consistency, add ½ cup yogurt mixed with 2 tablespoons chickpea flour to the beans, just before the addition of seasoned oil.

## Garbanzo Beans with Mint—*fudinawala chana*

To save time the following recipe may be made using canned garbanzo beans: use three 15-ounce cans for the recipe.

Serve with *bhatura* (p. 419) or any Indian bread.

| | |
|---|---|
| 1 cup | garbanzo beans, soaked eight hours **or** |
| 3 (15-ounce) cans | garbanzo beans |
| 8 cups | water |
| 2 teaspoons | salt, or to taste |
| ½ teaspoon | baking soda |
| 3 tablespoons | oil |
| 2 cups | finely sliced onions |
| 6 cloves | garlic, peeled, chopped |
| 6 | serrano or jalapeño chilies, ground |
| 3–inch piece | fresh ginger, peeled, ground |
| 4 tablespoons | ground coriander seeds, |
| 1 tablespoon | ground cumin seeds, |
| 2 teaspoons | *aamchoor* (p. 27) **or** |
| 2 tablespoons | lemon juice |
| 3 tablespoons | chopped mint leaves |
| 2 tablespoons | chopped cilantro, for garnish |

Pick over and wash garbanzo beans (see note, p. 336). Soak beans for at least eight hours.

If using dry beans: In a medium stainless steel saucepan over high heat bring 8 cups water to a full boil. Drain and add garbanzo beans, salt and baking soda. Cook the beans over high heat until almost done, about 30 minutes.

If using canned beans: Bring 3 cups water to a boil in a medium saucepan. Drain and add canned beans to boiling water. Heat for 5 minutes.

Adjust heat to maintain a low simmer.

Heat oil in a small frying pan over high heat and add onions. Cook onions stirring well for 5 minutes. Add garlic and cook the mixture for 2 more minutes. Add the mixture to beans. Raise the heat to medium and add the next 6 ingredients including mint. Cook for 5 minutes

Serve hot, garnished with cilantro.

Serves 4–5.

# Garbanzo Beans in Basic "Curry" Sauce—*chhole*

Commonly featured on the menus of Indian restaurants, this dish has many variations. At *The Ganges*, I frequently added sour cream and mushrooms to this version of the basic curry recipe.

| | |
|---|---|
| 1 recipe | basic sauce (p. 195) |
| 3 (15-ounce) cans | garbanzo beans, drained |
| 1 ½ cups | water |
| ½ teaspoon | ground anise (optional) |
| 2 teaspoons | *garam masala*-1 (p. 21) |
| 2 tablespoons | chopped mint leaves |
| 2 tablespoons | finely grated, unsweetened coconut |
| ½ cup | chopped cilantro |

In a large stainless steel saucepan over medium heat, mix basic sauce with garbanzo beans and the next 3 ingredients including *garam masala*. Stir well to prevent the mixture from sticking to the bottom. Cook for 2 minutes and then reduce heat to low, letting the mixture simmer.

In a food processor, fitted with a metal blade, grind together mint, coconut and cilantro and add to garbanzo beans. Mix well and cook for 7 more minutes. Serve hot.

Serves 6–8.

**Note:** You may add 2 cups chopped mushrooms and ½ cup sour cream to the above recipe, during the last 2 minutes of cooking.

## Bengal Grams with Onions and Lemon—*kala chana*

In both Hindi and Gujarati, "*kala*" means "black." The name *kala chana* therefore alludes to the dark hue that the beans assume when cooked. The addition of lemon juice adds a refreshing twist to the flavor of this semi-dry dish. Serve with rice and *kadhi* (p. 293) or any yogurt-based dish.

| | |
|---|---|
| 1 cup | Bengal grams (*kala chana*), soaked eight hours |
| 6 cups | water |
| 2 teaspoons | salt, or to taste |
| ½ teaspoon | baking soda |
| 2 tablespoons | oil |
| 1 medium | onion, finely chopped |
| 1 teaspoon | chili powder |
| 2 tablespoons | ground coriander seeds |
| 2 teaspoons | ground cumin seeds |
| ¼ teaspoon | turmeric |
| 1 tablespoon | lemon juice |
| 1 small | sliced carrot, for garnish |
| 2 tablespoons | chopped cilantro, for garnish |

Pick over and wash Bengal grams (see note, p. 336). Soak grams for at least eight hours.

In a medium saucepan over high heat, bring water to a full boil and add salt and baking soda. Drain and add Bengal grams and cook until the grams are soft, about 20 minutes. Remove from heat, drain and discard water. Pick over again, discarding uncooked grams.

In the same saucepan, heat oil over high heat, and add onions. Cook the onions, stirring well, until they are slightly golden, about 7 minutes. Add the next 4 ingredients including turmeric, mix well, lower the heat, and cook for 1 minute. Add cooked grams and lemon juice. Mix well and cook for 2 minutes. Serve hot garnished with carrot and cilantro.
Serves 4.

# Split Chickpeas with Cinnamon and Green Chili—*chana dal*

Redolent of chilies, ginger and cinnamon, this dish is both flavorful and warming; I like to serve it on cold evenings. As a variation, 2 cups of chopped cabbage may be added with the turmeric, at the end of cooking. Serve with rice, *kadhi* (p. 293) and any eggplant-based dish.

| | |
|---|---|
| 2 cups | split chickpeas (*chana dal*), soaked four hours |
| 8 cups | water |
| 2 teaspoons | salt, or to taste |
| 4 | serrano or jalapeño chilies, ground |
| 3–inch piece | fresh ginger, peeled, ground |
| 3 tablespoons | oil |
| 1 three–inch stick | cinnamon, broken |
| 5 | cloves |
| 5 cloves | garlic, peeled, chopped |
| ½ teaspoon | *hing* (asafoetida) |
| ¼ teaspoon | turmeric |
| ¼ cup | chopped cilantro, for garnish |
| ¼ cup | chopped red and green bell peppers, for garnish |

Pick over and wash *chana dal* (see note, p. 336). Soak *dal* for four hours.

In a medium saucepan, over high heat, bring water to a full boil. Drain and add *dal* and salt. Cook until the *dal* is soft, about 15 minutes. Add chilies and ginger mix well. Lower the heat to medium and let simmer.

Heat oil in a small frying pan, over medium heat, and add cinnamon and cloves. Add garlic when the cloves start to swell. When the garlic turns slightly golden, add *hing*. Cook the mixture for about 10 seconds and add it to boiling *dal*.

Add turmeric and cook for 2 more minutes. For a thick consistency, mash a little *dal* with the back of a spoon and mix well. Serve hot garnished with cilantro and bell peppers.

Serves 6–8.

## Pigeon Peas Consommé—*dalnu osaman*

Gujarati *osaman* is similar in consistency to the South Indian dish called *rasam*; though the seasonings vary, both recipes involve separating a thin, flavored soup (*osaman*) from the thicker *dal*. Both the thin and thick portions are then served separately. Nutritious and light, *osaman* is served alongside vegetables, rice and bread, though some Indians prefer to drink it at the end of a meal. Some Gujaratis regard this recipe as the western world would regard chicken soup, i.e.: as the cure for the common cold.

| | |
|---|---|
| 16 cups | water |
| 1 cup | split pigeon peas (*toor dal*) |
| ½ teaspoon | baking soda |
| 1 teaspoon | salt, or to taste |
| ¼ teaspoon | turmeric |
| 1 tablespoon | brown sugar (optional) |
| 1 tablespoon | oil |
| 1 teaspoon | black mustard seeds |
| 1 teaspoon | cumin seeds |
| ½ teaspoon | *hing* (asafoetida) |
| 2 tablespoons | chopped cilantro, for garnish |
| 2 tablespoon | finely grated, unsweetened coconut, for garnish |
| 2 teaspoons | butter (optional) |

In a large saucepan over high heat, bring water to a full boil. Pick over and thoroughly wash *toor dal* (see note, p. 336). Add *dal* and baking soda to boiling water. Maintaining high heat, cook *dal* until done, about 30 minutes. Add salt and turmeric and boil for 5 more minutes. Remove and let cool. The thick *dal* will settle to the bottom leaving thinner broth at the top. Carefully pour the thin *dal* into another saucepan. Set aside the saucepan with thick *dal*.

If desired, the thick *dal* may be reheated and served with the addition of 1 teaspoon butter and a pinch uncooked, raw *hing*.

Add brown sugar to the thin *dal*, and bring to a boil over medium heat. While *dal* is boiling, in a small frying pan, heat the oil over medium heat, and add mustard and cumin seeds. When mustard starts to crackle and cumin sizzles, add the *hing*. When *hing* turns brown, add oil mixture to the thin *dal*. Boil for 1 minute. Remove from heat and serve garnished with cilantro and coconut.

Serve with any meal—the thick *dal* is often served with the same meal. Serves 3–4.

# Whole Pigeon Peas with Yogurt and Spices
## —*toor kadhi* (dairy)

For a non-dairy version of this recipe, substitute 2 tablespoons chopped tomato for the yogurt. Either way, the recipe is delicious: the tanginess of tomatoes or yogurt complements the earthiness of the pigeon peas. Serve with rice and any bread.

| | |
|---|---|
| 1 cup | dried whole pigeon peas, soaked eight hours in hot water |
| 4 cups | water |
| 1 ½ teaspoons | salt, or to taste |
| 4 | serrano or jalapeño chilies, ground |
| 2–inch piece | fresh ginger, peeled, ground |
| 2 tablespoons | oil |
| ½ teaspoon | *hing* (asafoetida) |
| ¼ cup | chickpea flour |
| ½ cup | plain yogurt **or** |
| 2 tablespoons | finely chopped tomatoes |
| 2 tablespoons | chopped cilantro, for garnish |

Pick over and wash pigeon peas (see note, p. 336) and soak in hot water for eight hours.

In a medium stainless steel saucepan, bring 4 cups water to a full boil and add salt. Drain and add pigeon peas and cook over high heat. When the pigeon peas are almost done (about 20 minutes), add chilies and ginger. Reduce heat to low.

While beans simmer, heat oil in a small frying pan over medium heat and add *hing*. When *hing* turns brown, add mixture to the pigeon peas and cook until peas are soft, about 5 more minutes.

If using yogurt: Using a whisk, combine flour and yogurt, taking care that the mixture is smooth and not lumpy. Add the mixture to peas and mix well. Simmer until the sauce thickens, about 3 minutes.

If using chopped tomato: Add tomato to peas. Mix flour with ½ cup water, making sure that the mixture is smooth. Stir the flour mixture into the peas and simmer until the sauce thickens, about 5 minutes.

Serve hot, garnished with cilantro.

Serves 4–6.

## Split Pigeon Peas and Tomatoes with Bulbous Root
### —*suranwali dal*

Though it may not sound appetizing, bulbous root is in fact delicious. In taste and in texture, it is perhaps closest to white yams. I have yet to see this root sold fresh in the United States, though it is commonly sold in cans in Indian grocery stores. If preferred, substitute potatoes or any other root for the bulbous root, using the same proportions. Serve with plain rice and any *raita*.

| | |
|---|---|
| 10 cups | water |
| 1 cup | split pigeon peas (*toor dal*) |
| 2 teaspoons | salt, or to taste |
| 4 | serrano or jalapeño chilies, ground |
| 3–inch piece | fresh ginger, peeled, ground |
| ¼ teaspoon | turmeric |
| 4 tablespoons | ground coriander seeds |
| 1 tablespoon | ground cumin seeds |
| 2 | tomatoes, chopped |
| 3 tablespoons | brown sugar, or to taste |
| 1 cup | cubed bulbous root (optional) |
| 3 tablespoons | oil |
| 1 teaspoon | black mustard seeds |
| ½ teaspoon | fenugreek seeds |
| ½ teaspoon | *hing* (asafoetida) |
| ¼ cup | chopped cilantro, for garnish |

In a medium stainless steel saucepan over high heat, bring water to a full boil. Pick over, wash *dal* (see note, p. 336) and add it to boiling water. Add salt and cook on high heat, until the *dal* is soft, about 30 minutes. Add the next 8 ingredients including the bulbous root (or substitution of your choice), lower the heat to medium and let simmer.

Heat oil in a small frying pan, over medium heat, and add mustard and fenugreek. When mustard starts to crackle and fenugreek turns slightly golden, immediately add *hing*. When *hing* turns brown, add the mixture to *dal* and simmer for 10 more minutes.

Serve garnished with cilantro.

Serves 4–6.

## Split Pigeon Peas with Mung Beans—*tuver mugni dal*

Cooked with peanuts, tomatoes, green chilies and spices, this *dal* combines hot, slightly sour and slightly sweet flavors. It is a family favorite, especially liked by my daughter Bella and my son-in-law Jong. Serve with plain rice and an eggplant-based dish.

| | |
|---|---|
| 10 cups | water |
| 1 cup | split pigeon peas (*toor dal*) |
| 1 cup | mung beans |
| 1 tablespoon | salt, or to taste |
| ½ cup | peanuts, raw, unsalted |
| 2 medium | tomatoes, chopped |
| ¼ teaspoon | turmeric |
| 4–inch piece | fresh ginger, peeled, ground |
| 5 | serrano or jalapeño chilies, ground |
| 4 tablespoons | ground coriander seeds |
| 1 tablespoon | ground cumin seeds |
| 2 tablespoons | brown sugar, or to taste |
| 1 tablespoon | lemon juice |
| 2 tablespoons | oil |
| 2 teaspoons | black mustard seeds |
| 1 teaspoon | fenugreek seeds |
| ½ teaspoon | *hing* (asafoetida) |
| 2 tablespoons | chopped cilantro, for garnish |
| 2 tablespoons | unsweetened, grated coconut, for garnish (optional) |

In a medium stainless steel saucepan over high heat, bring water to a full boil.

While the water is heating, pick over and wash *toor dal* and mung beans together (see note, p. 336). Add *dal* and mung beans to the boiling water.

Add salt and peanuts and cook on high heat until *toor dal* is soft enough that it falls apart, about 30 minutes. Note that the mung beans will remain almost whole.

Add the next 6 ingredients including ground cumin, mix well, and let the mixture boil for about 7 minutes. Add brown sugar and lemon juice and continue boiling for 3 more minutes. Reduce heat to low and let simmer.

If you desire a thinner consistency, add additional water, as desired, at this point.

Heat the oil over medium heat, in a small frying pan. Add mustard and fenugreek seeds. As soon as mustard starts to crackle and fenugreek turns slightly brown, add *hing*. Immediately add oil mixture to the *dal*. Raise heat to medium and cook for 5 more minutes. Serve garnished with cilantro and coconut.

Serves: 6–8.

## Indian Pasta with Split Pigeon Peas—*dal dhokli*

In this recipe, seasoned pigeon peas are cooked with rolled, spiced *chapati* dough which, when prepared in the manner described below, assumes a delicious, pasta-like texture. Though the directions may appear difficult, *dal dhokli* is in fact not hard to make at all—the most time-consuming step being the rolling of the dough for the *dhokli*. Note that a pasta maker may be used in lieu of rolling the dough by hand. Serve this one-dish meal with both *papadum* (p. 152) and onion *raita* (p. 105).

### *Dal*:

| | |
|---|---|
| 16 cups | water |
| 1 cup | split pigeon peas (*toor dal*) |
| 1 tablespoon | salt, or to taste |
| 6–8 | serrano or jalapeño chilies, ground |
| 4–inch piece | fresh ginger, peeled, ground |
| 2 small | tomatoes, chopped |
| 2 teaspoons | tamarind concentrate **or** |
| 3 tablespoons | lemon juice |
| ½ teaspoon | turmeric |
| 4 tablespoons | ground coriander seeds |
| 2 teaspoons | ground cumin seeds |
| 3 tablespoons | brown sugar, or to taste |

### *Dhokli*:

| | |
|---|---|
| 1 ½ cups | *chapati* flour |
| ½ teaspoon | salt, or to taste |
| 1 tablespoon | oil |
| 2 teaspoons | ground coriander seeds |
| 1 teaspoon | ground cumin seeds |
| ¼ teaspoon | turmeric |
| ½ teaspoon | chili powder |
| 7 tablespoons | water |
| Flour | any variety, for dusting |

**Seasoned oil:**

| | |
|---|---|
| 3 tablespoons | oil |
| 2 three–inch sticks | cinnamon, broken |
| 1 ½ teaspoons | black mustard seeds |
| ½ teaspoon | fenugreek seeds |
| 8 | cloves |
| 10 cloves | garlic, peeled, chopped |
| ½ teaspoon | hing (asafoetida) |

**Garnish:**

| | |
|---|---|
| ½ cup | chopped cilantro, for garnish |
| 2 tablespoons | unsweetened, grated coconut, for garnish (optional) |

In a medium stainless steel saucepan over high heat, bring 8 cups water to a full boil. Meanwhile, pick over and wash *toor dal* (see note, p. 336). Add both the *dal* and the salt to the boiling water and cook until soft and fully cooked, about 30 minutes. As the *dal* cooks, begin preparing the dough for the *dhokli*.

In a mixing bowl, combine flour, salt and oil. Add the next 4 ingredients including chili powder and mix well. Gradually add water and prepare a smooth, yet slightly stiff, dough. Apply little oil to your palms and knead the dough for about 1 minute. If using a pasta maker, cover dough and set aside, otherwise, divide the dough into 10 portions and shape each into a smooth patty. Cover patties, set aside and check *dal*.

When *dal* is ready, the grains will become tender, and the mixture of water and *dal* will assume a soup-like consistency. Add remaining 8 cups water, chilies and the next 8 *dal* ingredients including brown sugar. Lower the heat to medium and simmer. As you return to the preparation of the *dhokli*, occasionally stir the *dal,* adding ½ cup water if the *dal* becomes thick.

If using a pasta maker, feed the dough through, at a medium thickness setting. Cut the sheet of rolled dough into 1 ½–inch squares.

If using a rolling pin, lightly dust each patty with flour and roll into a circle approximately 8–inches in diameter. Stack the circles, sprinkling each with little flour to prevent sticking. When all the patties have been rolled, place one circle on a cutting board and using a knife, cut the circle vertically and horizontally, into approximately 1 ½–inch pieces. Set pieces aside and continue, quickly until all the circles are cut.

Drop all of the squares in the boiling *dal*, one at a time, to prevent them from sticking. Raise the heat to high and when the mixture comes to a full boil, lower the heat to medium and prepare the seasoned oil.

For seasoned oil, heat oil in a frying pan over high heat, and add the next 4 ingredients including cloves. Add garlic when mustard seeds start to crackle. Cook the mixture until garlic is slightly golden. Add *hing* and cook the mixture for 5 seconds. Add the oil mixture to boiling *dal dhokli*.

Garnish with cilantro and coconut and serve hot. Note that the *dal dhokli* should be served immediately, as it will thicken if it sits. (Leftovers will be thick, but still delicious!)

Serves 6–8.

# Green Mung Beans with Ginger—*mug*

This *dal* was a favorite of my patrons at *The Ganges*. A variation of this recipe may be made by substituting 1 cup of the mung beans with 1 cup of any other split *dal*. Serve with any meal or with *parotha* (p. 411) and mango pickle (p. 117).

| | |
|---|---|
| 8 cups | water |
| 2 cups | mung beans |
| 2 teaspoons | salt, or to taste |
| 4 | serrano or jalapeño chilies, ground |
| 3–inch piece | fresh ginger, peeled, ground |
| ¼ teaspoon | turmeric |
| 2 tablespoons | oil |
| ½ teaspoon | fenugreek seeds |
| 6 cloves | garlic, peeled, chopped |
| ½ teaspoon | *hing* (asafoetida) |
| ¼ cup | chopped cilantro, for garnish |
| ¼ cup | chopped red and green bell peppers, for garnish |

In a medium saucepan, bring water to a full boil over high heat. While water is heating, pick over and wash mung beans (see note, p. 336). Add to boiling water. Add salt, lower the heat to medium, and cook until the beans are soft, about 30 minutes. Add an additional ½ cup water if the beans appear dry, or if there appears to be very little water remaining in the saucepan. Add chilies, ginger and turmeric, and let simmer.

Heat oil in a small frying pan over medium heat, and add fenugreek. When fenugreek turns brown, add garlic and *hing*. When garlic turns slightly golden, add the mixture to mung beans and stir gently. Serve, garnished with cilantro and peppers.

Serves 6–8.

## Sweet, Sour and Hot Mung Beans—*mugno ragdo*

Typical Gujarati *dals* frequently include some sort of sweetener as an ingredient, intended to balance spicy and sour flavors. In this mung bean dish, jaggery combines with chilies, garlic and either tart tamarind or lemon juice to yield a spiced, aromatic *dal.* Serve with any Indian bread or rice.

| | |
|---|---|
| 1–inch square | tamarind slab **or** |
| 2 tablespoons | lemon juice |
| 6 cups | water |
| 1 cup | green mung beans |
| 1 teaspoon | salt, or to taste |
| 2 small | onions, chopped |
| 1 tablespoon | chopped mint |
| 1 teaspoon | *garam masala*-1 (p. 21) |
| ¼ teaspoon | turmeric |
| 2 tablespoons | chopped cilantro |
| 1 tablespoon | ground coriander seeds |
| ½ teaspoon | ground cumin seeds |
| 3 tablespoons | oil |
| 5 | cloves |
| 5 cloves | garlic, peeled, chopped |
| 2–inch piece | fresh ginger, peeled, ground |
| 2 | serrano or jalapeño chilies, ground |
| 1 tablespoon | jaggery or brown sugar, or to taste |

If using tamarind, soak tamarind slab in ½ cup water for about 30 minutes. Using your hands, squeeze the tamarind in water, straining and discarding skin and seeds, if any. Set aside.

In a medium saucepan over high heat, bring water to a full boil. While water is heating, pick over and wash mung beans (see note, p. 336). Add beans to water. Add salt, half of the onions, and stir gently. Reduce heat to medium-low, cover and cook until beans are half-cooked, about 15 minutes.

Add mint and next 5 ingredients including cumin. Cover and cook until the beans are soft, about 10 more minutes. Reduce heat to low, cover again and let simmer.

In a small frying pan over medium heat, heat oil over high heat, and add the remaining onions, cloves and garlic. Brown lightly, for 5 minutes, add ginger and chilies and cook for 10 seconds. Add mixture to the beans, stir well and continue to simmer.

Add tamarind juice to mung beans. (As indicated in the ingredients list, you may substitute lemon juice for the tamarind.) Add jaggery, stir well and simmer uncovered for 5 more minutes. Serve hot.

Serves 4–6.

## Split Mung Beans—*mugni dal*

I have observed that Indian restaurants in America rarely serve dry *dals* such as this. In India and particularly Gujarat, however, this recipe is common fare, and is often served at banquets or festive occasions. If the beans are soaked ahead of time, this recipe will not take much longer than 20 minutes to prepare. Serve with plain Indian bread and hot pickle.

| | |
|---|---|
| 1 ½ cups | split mung beans (mung *dal*), washed, soaked four hours |
| 1 ½ cups | water, or as needed |
| 1 teaspoon | salt, or to taste |
| ½ teaspoon | turmeric |
| ½ teaspoon | baking soda |
| 1 tablespoon | oil |
| 6 cloves | garlic, peeled, chopped |
| ½ teaspoon | *hing* (asafoetida) |
| ½ teaspoon | chili powder |
| 2 tablespoons | chopped cilantro, for garnish |

Pick over and wash mung *dal* (see note, p. 336). Soak *dal* for four hours.

In a medium saucepan, drain and add *dal*, water, salt and turmeric. Mix well and bring to a boil over high heat. Do not stir while cooking, as the *dal* should stay whole and not become soupy. Add baking soda, lower the heat to medium and simmer.

Heat oil in a small frying pan over medium heat, and add garlic. When garlic turns golden, add *hing*. Add chili powder when *hing* turns brown, and immediately add oil mixture to the *dal*. Gently stir, lower the heat and cook until the *dal* is soft but not mushy, drizzling 2 tablespoons water over the *dal* if it becomes too dry while cooking.

Serve garnished with cilantro.

Serves 4.

# Split Mung Beans with Zucchini—zucchini *mugni dal*

In this recipe, adding zucchini just prior to serving ensures that it maintains its crunchy texture, thereby offering a pleasing contrast to mung *dal* which is cooked until soft. Serve with rice, *kadhi* (p. 293) and any vegetable.

| | |
|---|---|
| 7 cups | water, or as needed |
| 2 cups | split mung beans (mung *dal*) |
| 2 teaspoons | salt, or to taste |
| 2 tablespoons | oil |
| 8–10 cloves | garlic, peeled, chopped |
| ½ teaspoon | chili powder |
| ½ teaspoon | *hing* (asafoetida) |
| ¼ teaspoon | turmeric |
| 2 teaspoons | flour *masala* (p. 25) (optional) |
| 2 small | zucchini, cubed small |
| ¼ cup | chopped cilantro, for garnish |

In a medium saucepan over high heat, bring water to a full boil. While water is heating, pick over and wash *dal* (see note, p. 336). Add *dal* and salt to boiling water. Lower the heat to medium when the mixture comes to a full boil. Cook until the *dal* is creamy, about 20 minutes.

Once the *dal* is cooked, reduce heat to low and let simmer. In a small frying pan, heat oil over medium heat, and add garlic. When the garlic turns golden, add chili powder and *hing*. Cook for a few seconds and add oil mixture to *dal*. Add turmeric and flour *masala* (if using), mix well and simmer for 2 more minutes. Add zucchini and mix well. Remove from heat and serve, garnished with cilantro.

Serves 6.

## Split Indian Black Beans—*urid dal*

*Urid dal* is a staple in many Indian cuisines. In the South, for instance, it is used in recipes such as *idlee* (p. 159) and *dosa* (p. 426). In Gujarat, especially in Kathiawar, split *urid dal* is often served with millet (p. 434) or sorghum breads (p. 435). Serve with Indian bread and yogurt-based recipes.

| | |
|---|---|
| 1 ½ cups | split Indian black beans (*urid dal*), soaked four hours |
| 8 cups | water |
| 2 teaspoons | salt, or to taste |
| ½ teaspoon | chili powder |
| ¼ teaspoon | turmeric |
| 1 teaspoon | *garam masala*-1 (p. 21) |
| 2 | serrano or jalapeño chilies, ground |
| 2–inch piece | fresh ginger, peeled, ground |
| 1 tablespoon | oil |
| ½ teaspoon | *hing* (asafoetida) |
| 2 | dried, whole red chili peppers |
| 10 | *curry* leaves (optional) |
| 2 tablespoons | chopped cilantro, for garnish |

Pick over and wash *dal* (see note, p. 336). Soak *dal* for four hours.

In a medium saucepan, bring water to a full boil. Drain and add *dal*. Add salt, lower the heat to medium and cook the *dal* until soft, about 20 minutes. Add next 5 ingredients including ginger and mix well.

In a small frying pan over medium heat, heat the oil and add *hing*. Add peppers and *curry* leaves, if available. Cook the mixture for 10 seconds and add to simmering *dal*. Cook for 2 more minutes. Remove and serve garnished with cilantro.

Serves 4–6.

## Kidney Beans with Potatoes—*kashmiri rajma*

My Kashmiri friend Sayed Mujtaba gave me this delicious recipe. Pomegranate seeds and black cumin seeds, both optional ingredients, can be found at Indian groceries. Black cumin in particular, is an important ingredient in Kashmiri cooking. Its mellow flavor and sweet aroma distinguish it from the normal, white cumin that is commonly used in Indian cooking.

| | |
|---|---|
| 1 cup | kidney beans, soaked eight hours |
| ¼ cup | unsweetened, grated coconut |
| 2–inch piece | fresh ginger, peeled |
| 4 | serrano or jalapeño chilies |
| 8 cloves | garlic, peeled |
| 1 cup | chopped cilantro |
| 2 teaspoons | pomegranate seeds (optional) |
| 8 cups | water |
| 2 ½ teaspoons | salt, or to taste |
| ½ teaspoon | baking soda |
| 1 large | potato, peeled, cubed |
| 2 medium | tomatoes, chopped |
| 1 tablespoon. | ground coriander seeds |
| 2 teaspoons | ground cumin seeds |
| ½ teaspoon | turmeric |
| 2 tablespoons | oil |
| 1 three–inch stick | cinnamon, broken |
| 5 | cloves |
| 1 teaspoon | black cumin seeds (optional) |
| ½ teaspoon | *hing* (asafoetida) |
| ½ teaspoon | mace |
| ¼ cup | chopped cilantro, for garnish |

Pick over and wash kidney beans (see note, p. 336). Soak beans for eight hours.

In a liquidizer or a blender, grind until smooth, coconut together with the next 5 ingredients including pomegranate seeds (if using), adding 1 cup water for grinding. Set aside.

In a medium stainless steel saucepan over high heat, bring remaining 7 cups water to a full boil. Drain and add kidney beans. Add salt and baking soda. Reduce heat to medium, cover and cook until the beans are soft, about 35 minutes. During cooking, if the water begins to boil away, add an additional 1 to 2 cups water so that the beans are barely covered.

Add potatoes, tomatoes and ground mixture to cooked kidney beans. Add coriander, cumin and turmeric. Lower the heat to medium. In a small frying pan over medium heat, heat oil, and add cinnamon, cloves and black cumin, if any. When cinnamon and cloves start to swell, add *hing* and cook until the *hing* turns brown—just a few seconds. Add oil mixture to kidney beans. Add mace and simmer for 2 minutes. Serve garnished with cilantro.

Serves 4–6.

## Sprouted Mung Beans with Garlic—*sangavela mug*

In this recipe, sprouted mung beans assume a mild, slightly sweet flavor that is accented by garlic. Note that Indians generally do not sprout beans beyond the point that the tails from the beans are much longer than ¼–inch. Serve with rice and *kadhi* (p. 293), or as a side dish with any meal.

| | |
|---|---|
| 2 cups | green mung beans, picked over, washed, sprouted (p. 343) |
| 2 tablespoons | oil |
| 6 cloves | garlic, peeled, chopped |
| ½ teaspoon | *hing* (asafoetida) |
| ½ teaspoon | baking soda |
| ½ teaspoon | chili powder, or to taste |
| 1 ½ teaspoons | salt, or to taste |
| ¼ teaspoon | turmeric |
| 2 tablespoons | chopped cilantro, for garnish |

Pick over and wash mung beans (see note, p. 336).

Following directions on page (343), sprout mung beans. Pick over and discard any unsoaked, hard beans.

Heat oil in a wok or a medium saucepan over medium heat and add garlic. When garlic turns slightly golden, add *hing*. Fry for 5 seconds and add baking soda, chili powder, salt and mung beans. Reduce heat to low and cook the beans, stirring frequently, for about 10 minutes.

Add turmeric, mix well and cook for 3 more minutes or until the beans are soft. If the recipe is excessively dry, and if a moister dish is preferred, drizzle 1–2 tablespoons of water over the beans and cook for 2 more minutes. Serve garnished with cilantro.

Serves 4–6.

## Variation 1: Sprouted Brown Mung Beans—*sangavela muth*

Many Gujaratis prefer sprouted brown beans to the green variety. Though similarly sweet, brown beans have a slightly earthier taste. For ingredients and procedure, follow the preceding recipe, substituting brown beans for the green.

## Variation 2: Sprouted Brown Mung Beans with Dumplings—*muth dhokli*

Combine cooked dumplings (p. 192)—in desired proportions—with cooked beans, following the preceding recipe. Heat through and serve garnished with cilantro.

## Split Indian Lima Beans—*valni dal*

Denser in texture and more intense in flavor than the American variety, Indian lima beans became very popular among the regulars who frequented *The Ganges*. In fact, I received many advance requests for this dish. Serve with any bread, rice and either *kadhi* (p. 293) or any yogurt-based dish.

| | |
|---|---|
| 2 cups | split lima beans (*valni dal*), soaked four hours |
| 3 tablespoons | oil |
| 1 three–inch stick | cinnamon, broken |
| 8 | cloves |
| 1 teaspoon | black mustard seeds |
| ½ teaspoon | fenugreek seeds |
| 3 | dried, whole red chili peppers |
| 5 cloves | garlic, peeled, chopped |
| ½ teaspoon | *hing* (asafoetida) |
| ½ teaspoon | baking soda |
| 1 ½ teaspoons | salt, or to taste |
| ½ teaspoon | turmeric |
| 2 ½ cups | water, or as needed |
| 2 teaspoons | sugar, or to taste |
| 2–inch piece | fresh ginger, peeled, ground |
| 2 tablespoons | chopped cilantro, for garnish |

Pick over, wash (see note, p. 336), and soak *dal* for four hours. Drain the soaked *dal* and set aside. Though this *dal* can be cooked without soaking, I recommend soaking, as the cooked, unsoaked *dal* will not have a smooth texture.

Heat oil in a medium saucepan over high heat, and add cinnamon and cloves. When cloves start to swell, add mustard and fenugreek seeds. Add the peppers when mustard starts to crackle. Add garlic when peppers change color. Fry the mixture, stirring well for about 2 minutes. Add *hing*, and after 3 seconds add the drained *dal*, baking soda and salt. Mix well.

Stir in turmeric and the next 3 ingredients including ginger. Lower the heat and simmer *dal* until it is cooked through, but not overly soft, about 12 minutes. If the dish dries before *dal* is completely done, drizzle 3 table-spoons water over the dish and continue to cook. Serve garnished with cilantro.

Serves 4–6.

# Yellow Split Peas with Garlic and Cloves—*vatanani dal*

Dried, yellow split peas—not to be confused with *chana dal* (split garbanzo)—are generally available in any grocery store. Though *hing* adds flavor to the dish, it is optional if unavailable. When serving this *dal*, I sometimes add a few grains of cooked, black-eyed peas to each serving for variation. (Since cooking the black-eyed peas with the *dal* would darken the color of the dish, I cook them separately and add them at the end.)

| | |
|---|---|
| 6 cups | water |
| 1 cup | yellow split peas |
| 1 teaspoon | salt, or to taste |
| ½ teaspoon | turmeric |
| 2 tablespoons | oil |
| 8 | cloves |
| 4 cloves | garlic, peeled, chopped |
| ½ teaspoon | *hing* (asafoetida) |
| 2 tablespoons | chopped red and green bell peppers |
| 2 tablespoons | chopped cilantro, for garnish |

In a medium saucepan over high heat bring water to a full boil. While water is heating, pick over and wash split peas (see note, p. 336). Add split peas to boiling water. Add salt and turmeric, and cook until the *dal* is soft and completely cooked—about 20 minutes. Reduce heat to medium and let simmer.

Heat oil in a small frying pan over medium heat, and add cloves. When cloves start to swell add garlic and cook until garlic turns golden. Add *hing* and immediately add oil mixture to the *dal*. Stir well, cook for 1 additional minute and remove from heat. Mix in bell peppers. Serve hot garnished with cilantro.

Serves 4–6.

## South Indian *Sambar—sambar*

This popular South Indian dish is commonly served alongside *idlee* (p. 159) or *dosa* (p. 426). Though pre-packaged *sambar* spice is available in Indian grocery stores, I prefer to grind my own (recipe below), using my own proportions of spices. Also, this recipe yields a slightly thicker *sambar* than the packaged mixes.

Note that the dry spice mixture can be ground ahead of time and stored. Though the recipe is traditionally made with split pigeon peas, red lentils may be substituted.

*Sambar* **spice:**

| | |
|---|---|
| 4 tablespoons | coriander seeds |
| 2 teaspoons | cumin seeds |
| 1 teaspoon | fenugreek seeds |
| 2 teaspoons | black peppers |
| 6 | cloves |
| 3 | dried, whole red chili peppers |
| 2 three–inch sticks | cinnamon |
| ¼ cup | coconut powder |

*Sambar*:

| | |
|---|---|
| 10 cups | water, or as needed |
| 1 ½ cups | red lentil **or** |
| 1 ½ cups | split pigeon peas (*toor dal*) |
| 2 teaspoons | salt, or to taste |
| ½ teaspoon | turmeric |
| 2 tablespoons | lemon juice |
| 2 medium | tomatoes, chopped |
| ½ cup | cubed eggplant |
| 5 | serrano or jalapeño chilies, ground |
| 3–inch piece | fresh ginger, peeled, ground |
| 3 tablespoons | oil |

| 2 teaspoons | black mustard seeds |
| ½ teaspoon | *hing* (asafoetida) |
| ½ cup | chopped onions |
| ½ cup | chopped cilantro, for garnish |

***Sambar* spice:**

In a medium frying pan over low heat, toast coriander together with the next 6 ingredients including cinnamon, stirring well, until they change color, about 10 minutes. Remove, let cool. Using a coffee grinder, grind toasted spices to a fine powder and set aside.

In the same frying pan, toast coconut until slightly golden, remove with the ground spices and mix well.

***Sambar*:**

In a medium stainless steel saucepan over high heat, bring water to a full boil. While the water is heating, wash red lentils or *toor dal* (see note, p. 336). Add to boiling water. Add salt and cook until the *dal* is soft and completely cooked, about 30 minutes. Add turmeric, and the next 5 ingredients including ginger. Lower the heat to medium.

Add ground *sambar* spice and stir well.

Heat oil in a frying pan over medium heat, and add mustard seeds. When mustard crackles, add *hing*. When *hing* turns brown, add onions and cook for about 2 minutes, stirring well. Add onion mixture to the *sambar* and boil for 5 more minutes. If *sambar* is too thick or if a thinner *sambar* is preferred, add more water and balance salt. Serve, garnished with cilantro.

Serves: 6–8.

## Onion *Sambar*—onion *sambar*

My old friend, the late Professor A. T. Ganesan passed this recipe on to me. A wonderful cook, dear "Gan" touted this recipe as one of his favorites. Serve with either *idlee* (p. 159) or rice.

| | |
|---|---|
| 2 tablespoons | *Sambar* powder (preceding recipe) |
| 8 ½ cups | water |
| 1 cup | yellow split peas or split pigeon peas (*toor dal*) |
| 2–inch square | tamarind slab |
| 2 tablespoons | oil or butter |
| 10–15 | shallot onions, cut |
| 4 cloves | garlic, peeled, chopped |
| 1 medium | potato, peeled cubed small |
| 2 teaspoons | salt, or to taste |
| 1 teaspoon | black mustard seeds |
| ¼ teaspoon | fenugreek seeds |
| 1 teaspoon | split Indian black beans (*urid dal*) |
| ¼ cup | chopped cilantro, for garnish |

Prepare *sambar* powder as in preceding recipe, set aside.

In a medium saucepan over high heat, bring 6 cups water to a boil (saving 2 ½ cups). When the water is heating, pick over and wash *dal* (see note, p. 336) and add it to the boiling water. Cook until the *dal* is soft, about 30 minutes.

While *dal* is cooking, soak tamarind in the remaining water. Set aside for about 30 minutes. Using your hands squeeze tamarind in water, strain and discard skin and seeds, if any. Save the liquid.

In a small saucepan, over medium heat, heat 1 tablespoon oil or butter, add shallots and garlic and fry for 10 seconds. Add tamarind juice and potato and cook the mixture for about 10 minutes. Add salt and *sambar* powder. Mix and simmer for 1 minute. Add mixture to the *dal* and lower the heat to medium.

In a small frying pan, heat the remaining oil over medium heat and add mustard and fenugreek seeds. When mustard starts to crackle and fenugreek turns slightly golden, add *urid dal*. *Urid* will turn golden in a few seconds. Add this mixture to the *sambar*, mix well and simmer for 5 more minutes. Serve garnished with cilantro.

Serves 4–6.

## Split and Whole Indian Black Beans—*moglai dal* (dairy)

The addition of cream into this *dal* identifies it as a North Indian dish, inspired by Moghul cuisine. Note that the recipe calls for both whole *urid* as well as the split variety. When making this *dal* for my son, who particularly loves it, I use light cream in order to limit the fat content. Serve with either rice or *naan* (p. 422).

| | |
|---|---|
| 1 cup | Indian black beans (whole *urid*) |
| ¼ cup | kidney beans |
| 7 cups | water |
| 1 ½ teaspoons | salt, or to taste |
| ¼ cup | split Indian black beans (*urid dal*) |
| 2 | bay leaves |
| ¼ teaspoon | turmeric |
| 3 | serrano or jalapeño chilies, seeded, cut |
| 3 tablespoons | oil or margarine |
| ½ teaspoon | chili powder |
| ½ cup | cream, (light cream if preferred) |
| ¼ cup | yogurt |
| 2 tablespoons | chopped cilantro, for garnish |

Pick over and wash whole *urid* and kidney beans (see note, p. 336). Set aside.

In a medium stainless steel saucepan over high heat, bring water to a full boil, adding salt. Add whole *urid* and kidney beans and cook for about 15 minutes.

Meanwhile, pick over, wash (see note, p. 336) and add *urid dal* to boiling whole *urid* and kidney beans. Add bay leaves, turmeric and chilies. Mix well. Reduce heat to medium and cook until beans are soft, about 30 minutes. Using the back of a spoon, mash about 3 tablespoons cooked beans, making the consistency of the *dal* creamy. Lower the heat to medium.

In a small frying pan over medium heat, heat the oil and add chili powder. Cook for few seconds and add mixture to the *dal*. Simmer for 5 minutes, add cream and yogurt and mix well. Simmer for 3 more minutes. Serve garnished with cilantro.

Serves 4–6.

## Lima Beans with Tamarind—*sabut val*

This is a recipe that my mother passed on to me. In this dish, *ajwain*, which closely resembles the flavor of Italian oregano, combines with brown sugar and tamarind to produce a subtly sweet and sour *dal*. The addition of chickpea flour adds texture and a nutty highlight to this delicious recipe. Serve with either rice and *kadhi* (p. 293) or any Indian bread.

| | |
|---|---|
| 1 ½ cups | Indian lima beans (*val*), soaked overnight |
| 8 cups | water, or as needed |
| 2 teaspoons | salt, or to taste |
| ½ teaspoon | baking soda |
| 2–inch square | tamarind slab |
| 4 | serrano or jalapeño chilies, chopped |
| 3–inch piece | fresh ginger, peeled, grated |
| ½ teaspoon | turmeric |
| 2 tablespoons | brown sugar, or to taste |
| ¼ cup | chickpea flour |
| 3 tablespoons | oil |
| 6 cloves | garlic, peeled, chopped |
| 2 | dried, whole red chili peppers |
| 1 teaspoon | *ajwain* (p. 9) |
| ½ teaspoon | *hing* (asafoetida) |
| 2 tablespoons | chopped cilantro, for garnish |

Pick over and wash lima beans (see note, p. 336). Soak beans overnight.

In a medium stainless steel saucepan over high heat, bring 7 cups water to a full boil. While heating water, drain lima beans and pick over again, removing and discarding unsoaked, hard beans, if any. Add beans to the boiling water and add salt and baking soda. Cook on high heat for 5 minutes, lower the heat to medium, cover and cook until the beans are soft, about 30 minutes.

While beans are cooking, soak tamarind in ½ cup water for at least 30 minutes. Using your hand, squeeze tamarind in water. Strain and discard skin and seeds, if any.

Once beans are soft, uncover saucepan. Add tamarind juice and the next 4 ingredients including brown sugar to beans. Combine chickpea flour with remaining ½ cup water and add to beans. Reduce heat to low and stir well.

While the *dal* simmers, heat oil in a small frying pan over medium heat. Add garlic and red peppers. Add *ajwain* and *hing*, when the peppers turn deep, dark red in color. Cook for 10 seconds and add the mixture to the beans. Mix well, cover and simmer for 5 more minutes. Serve hot, garnished with cilantro.

Serves: 6–8.

## Indian Black Beans with *Dals* and Spices—*Punjabi dal*

This is my version of a North Indian recipe that was a favorite of my husband Arun. It is a simple dish, whose complex flavor results from the combination of 2 whole beans and 2 varieties of split bean. Serve with Indian rice and bread.

| | |
|---|---|
| 1 cup | Indian black beans (*urid*) |
| ¼ cup | kidney beans |
| ¼ cup | split Indian black beans (*urid dal*) |
| ¼ cup | split chickpeas (*chana dal*) |
| 10 cups | water |
| 3 | serrano or jalapeño chilies, cut |
| 2–inch piece | fresh ginger, peeled, chopped |
| 2 | bay leaves |
| 1 tablespoon | salt, or to taste |
| ½ teaspoon | turmeric |
| 2 medium | tomatoes, chopped |
| 3 tablespoons | oil |
| 1 medium | onion, sliced finely |
| 1 teaspoon | chili powder |
| ¼ cup | chopped cilantro, for garnish |

Pick over and wash together beans and *dals* (see note, p. 336). In a medium stainless steel saucepan over high heat, bring water to a full boil and add the beans and the *dals*. Add chilies and next 3 ingredients including salt and return the mixture to a full boil. Lower the heat to medium, cover and cook until the whole beans are soft, about 35 minutes. Split *dals* will be soft and velvety by this time. Uncover the *dal* and with the back of a spoon, mash some beans to give the mixture a creamier consistency.

Add turmeric and tomatoes, reduce heat to low and continue to cook. Stir frequently to ensure that the *dal* does not stick to the bottom of the saucepan.

In a small frying pan over medium heat, heat oil and add onions. Fry onions until they are golden, about 7 minutes. Add chili powder and cook for few more seconds. Add the mixture to the *dal*, mix well and cook for 1 minute. Remove from heat and serve, garnished with cilantro.

Serves 6–8.

## Five *Dals*—*panch dal*

In both Hindi and Gujarati, *panch* means 5. The name of this dish therefore refers to the 5 varieties of *dals* combined in this recipe. You may, however, mix any number of *dals* or beans into the recipe, using proportions that amount to 1 ¼ cups. (Once, I actually mixed 18 varieties of whole and split *dals* for my customers at *The Ganges*.) If you are planning to use whole beans, it is better to soak them for at least eight hours before cooking with split *dals*. Also note that if cooking with whole beans, an additional 2 cups water should be added to the 8 cups specified below. Serve with rice or *chapati* (p. 404) or with any meal.

| | |
|---|---|
| ¼ cup | red lentil (*masoor dal*) |
| ¼ cup | split chickpeas (*chana dal*) |
| ¼ cup | split Indian black beans (*urid dal*) |
| ¼ cup | split mung beans (mung *dal*) |
| ¼ cup | split pigeon peas (*toor dal*) |
| 8 cups | water |
| 1 ¾ teaspoons | salt, or to taste |
| 1 medium | tomato, chopped |
| 4 tablespoons | oil |
| 1 large | onion, sliced finely |
| 3 | serrano or jalapeño chilies, cut |
| 2–inch piece | fresh ginger, peeled, chopped |
| 6 cloves | garlic, peeled, chopped |
| 1 teaspoon | ground black pepper |
| 1 teaspoon | *garam masala*-1 (p. 21) |
| 1 tablespoon | ground coriander seeds |
| 1 teaspoon | ground cumin seeds |
| 2 | dried, whole red chili peppers |
| ¼ cup | chopped cilantro, for garnish |

Pick over, combine and then wash (see note, p. 336) all of the *dals*. In a medium stainless steel saucepan over high heat, bring water to a full boil. Add *dals* to boiling water. Add salt and cook *dals* until soft and completely cooked, about 30 minutes. Add tomato, stir well, and lower heat to medium-low and let simmer.

Heat oil in a small frying pan over medium heat, and add onions. Cook until the onions are brown, about 10 minutes. Add chilies, ginger and garlic and fry the mixture for about 15 seconds. Add the next 5 ingredients including chili peppers and fry the mixture for about 20 seconds. Add 2 tablespoons water and cook for 1 minute. Add the mixture to boiling *dal*. Simmer, stirring well for 5 minutes. Serve garnished with cilantro.

Serves 6.

## Green Peas with Cilantro-Coconut Sauce—*leela vatana*

Ground onions, chilies, cilantro and coconut form the base for the sauce of this simple to prepare, spicy dish. Serve with rice and any yogurt-based dish.

| | |
|---|---|
| 1 cup | dry green peas, soaked four hours |
| 6 cups | water |
| ½ teaspoon | baking soda |
| 1 ½ teaspoons | salt, or to taste |
| 1 medium | onion |
| 2 | serrano or jalapeño chilies |
| 1–inch piece | fresh ginger, peeled |
| ½ cup | chopped cilantro |
| ¼ cup | grated, unsweetened coconut |
| 2 tablespoons | oil |
| 1 teaspoon | black mustard seeds |
| ½ teaspoon | *hing* (asafoetida) |
| 3 | bay leaves |
| 2 tablespoons | chopped onions |
| 2 tablespoons | chopped cilantro, for garnish |

Pick over, wash peas (see note, p. 336), and soak for four hours.

In a medium saucepan over high heat, bring water to a full boil. Drain and add peas, baking soda and salt. Cook the peas until they are soft but still hold their shape, about 20 minutes. As the peas cook, in a liquidizer or a blender, grind until smooth onion together with the next 4 ingredients including coconut. Set aside. Once the peas are cooked, reduce heat to low and bring to a simmer.

Heat oil in a small frying pan over medium heat, and add mustard seeds. Add *hing* and bay leaves, when mustard starts to crackle. Add chopped onions after 5 seconds. Cook the mixture for 1 minute and add to peas. Add ground onion mixture set aside earlier, stir well and simmer for 10 more minutes.

Serve garnished with cilantro.

Serves 4–6.

# Yellow Peas in Onion-Yogurt Sauce—*dopiaza matar* (dairy)

Both fried and raw onions are added to this recipe, the combination of which adds distinct texture and flavor that is dominated by the slight sweetness of fried onions. Serve with rice or any meal.

| | |
|---|---|
| 1 cup | whole yellow peas, soaked four hours |
| 6 cups | water |
| 1 teaspoon | salt, or to taste |
| 1 | bay leaf |
| 1 | dried, whole red chili pepper |
| 2 | serrano or jalapeño chilies, chopped |
| 2 cups | finely sliced onions |
| ½ cup | yogurt |
| 1–inch piece | fresh ginger, peeled, grated |
| 3 tablespoons | oil |
| ½ teaspoon | chili powder |
| ¼ cup | chopped cilantro, for garnish |

Pick over and wash peas (see note, p. 336). Soak peas for four hours.

In a medium saucepan over high heat, bring water to a full boil. Drain and add peas. Add salt, bay leaf, red pepper, chilies and 1 ½ cups of sliced onions. Cook until the peas are soft but still hold their shape, about 20 minutes. Reduce heat to low, maintaining a simmer. Using a large spoon, mash about 2 tablespoons of cooked peas to add texture to the recipe.

Add yogurt and ginger. Mix well and maintain simmer.

In a frying pan, heat oil over high heat, and add remaining onions. Fry until the onions are golden, about 7 minutes. Add chili powder and let the mixture cook for few seconds. Add mixture to peas and cook for about 5 minutes.

Add ½ the cilantro and cook for 3 more minutes, stirring well a couple of times. For more sauce add ½ cup water, mix well and simmer for 1 minute. Serve hot, garnished with remaining cilantro.

Serves 4.

**Note**: As a variation, you may add 1 cup very finely cubed zucchini to this recipe before serving.

# Black-Eyed Peas *Kofta* in Onion Sauce—*kofta* "curry"

Made from black-eyed peas, the vegetarian *kofta* in this recipe are sim-
mered in an aromatic onion gravy, yielding a delightful dish that San
Francisco restaurant critics have raved about. Serve with rice, any yogurt-
based recipe and *chapati* (p. 404) or *parotha* (p. 411).

**Kofta:**

| | |
|---|---|
| 2 cups | black-eyed peas, soaked overnight |
| 6 | serrano or jalapeño chilies, chopped |
| 1 cup | chopped cilantro |
| 8 cloves | garlic, peeled |
| 2 teaspoons | salt, or to taste |
| 1 cup | dried onion granules or flakes (p. 38) |
| 2 teaspoons | toasted, coarsely ground cumin |
| ½ teaspoon | baking soda |
| 2 teaspoons | *garam masala*-1 (p. 21) |
| Oil | for frying |

**Sauce:**

| | |
|---|---|
| 4 cups | basic sauce (p. 195) |
| 2 teaspoons | *garam masala*-1 (p. 21) |
| 3 tablespoon | ground coriander seeds |
| 2 teaspoons | ground cumin seeds |
| 8 cups | water |
| ½ cup | chopped cilantro, for garnish |

*Kofta:*

Pick over, wash (see note, p. 336) and soak black-eyed peas overnight.

The next day: Using a food processor fitted with a metal blade, grind
chilies with cilantro and garlic for about 10 seconds, or until coarse. Drain
and add black-eyed peas and grind until the mixture is slightly coarse but

not smooth. Remove to a mixing bowl; add ingredients including *garam masala* and mix well.

Heat about 3–inches of oil in a *karai* or a wok and lower the temperature to 375 °F.

Using your hands, shape 2 tablespoons ground mixture into a round ball, and slide into the hot oil. Gently drop several at a time and fry until they are medium brown all around. Remove and drain on paper towels. You will have about 60 *kofta*.

**Sauce:**

Add 4 cups basic sauce to a medium stainless steel saucepan. Add ingredients including water and bring the mixture to a full boil. Add *kofta*, lower the heat to medium and cook until *kofta* absorb sauce and soften. For more sauce, you may add more basic sauce and water. Serve garnished with cilantro.

Yield: 60 *kofta*.

## Yogurt-Chili Sauce—*kadhi* (dairy)

The following is a simple *kadhi* recipe. Many Gujaratis keep ground and frozen *kadhi masala* ready as they make this almost every day. The spice mixture they make includes fresh pigeon peas, *curry* leaves, cilantro, fresh turmeric, mango turmeric, green chilies, ginger and cumin. Instead of sugar they add mashed banana to *kadhi*.

To vary this recipe, add 2 tablespoons chopped mint leaves with the yogurt. Serve with any rice, bulgur or quinoa dish.

| | |
|---|---|
| 1 ½ cups | yogurt |
| ¼ cup | chickpea flour |
| 1 ¼ teaspoons | salt, or to taste |
| 6 cups | water |
| 2–inch piece | fresh ginger, peeled, ground |
| 4 | serrano or jalapeño chilies, ground |
| 2 tablespoons | brown sugar, or to taste |
| 1 tablespoon | oil |
| 1 teaspoon | black mustard seeds |
| 1 teaspoon | cumin seeds |
| ½ teaspoon | *hing* (asafoetida) |
| 2 tablespoons | chopped cilantro, for garnish |

In a bowl, combine yogurt with next 6 ingredients including brown sugar. Set aside.

In a stainless steel saucepan over medium heat, heat the oil and add mustard and cumin. When mustard starts to crackle and cumin sizzle, add *hing* and immediately add the yogurt mixture into the saucepan. Cook stirring well, until the sauce thickens, about 7 minutes. Serve garnished with cilantro.

Serves 4–6.

**Note:** 2 medium-sized, mashed bananas may substitute for brown sugar in this recipe.

## Tamarind Sauce—*panoo*

Before my family kept a cow, as we traveled from place to place, my family often lived in areas where milk for making yogurt and *kadhi* was in short supply. My mother therefore frequently made *panoo*, the wonderful recipe for which is passed on here. Serve with rice or *khichadi* recipes (p. 318-324).

| | |
|---|---|
| 2–inch square | tamarind slab |
| 6 cups | water |
| 3 tablespoons | brown sugar, or to taste |
| ¼ cup | chickpea flour |
| 1 ½ teaspoon | salt, or to taste |
| 1 | serrano or jalapeño chili, ground |
| 2–inch piece | fresh ginger, peeled, ground |
| 2 tablespoons | ground coriander seeds |
| ¼ teaspoon | turmeric |
| ¼ teaspoon | chili powder |
| 1 tablespoon | oil |
| 1 teaspoon | black mustard seeds |
| 1 teaspoon | cumin seeds |
| ½ teaspoon | *hing* (asafoetida) |
| 6 | *curry* leaves (optional) |
| 2 tablespoons | chopped cilantro, for garnish |

Soak tamarind in water for at least 30 minutes. Using your hands squeeze tamarind in water. Strain the liquid; discard skin and seeds, if any. In a stainless steel saucepan, combine tamarind juice with water. Add next 8 ingredients including chili powder and mix well with a whisk. Place the saucepan over high heat and bring the mixture to a full boil. Reduce heat to low and simmer for 7 more minutes.

While *panoo* simmers, heat oil in a small frying pan over medium heat, and add mustard and cumin. When mustard starts to crackle and cumin sizzle, add *hing* and *curry* leaves (if any). Cook for 5 seconds and add mixture to *panoo*. Simmer for a few more seconds. Serve garnished with cilantro. Serves 6–8.

# Indian Breads

Paper-Thin Gujarati Bread—*fulka*
Eggplant Bread—*baigan roti*
Thick Gujarati Bread—*bhakhari*
Variation 1: *Bhakhari* with *Ajwain* and Turmeric—*ajma mithani bhakhari*
Variation 2: *Bhakhari* with Squash and Spices—*doodhini bhakhari*
Banana *Bhakhari*—*kelani bhakhari* (dairy)
Layered Indian Bread—*parotha*
Potato-Stuffed *Parotha*—*aaloo parotha*
Cabbage-Stuffed *Parotha*—*kobijna parotha*
*Paneer*-Stuffed *Parotha*—*paneer parotha* (dairy)
Wheat and Millet Bread—*dhebra* or *thepla* (dairy)
Deep-Fried Puffed Bread with Yogurt—*bhatura* (dairy)
Deep-Fried Indian Bread—*puri*
Festive *Puri*—*Surti puri*
Leavened Indian Bread—*naan* (dairy)
Variation 1: Leavened Bread with Raisins—raisin *naan*
Variation 2: Spicy *Naan*—*masala naan*
Variation 3: Leavened Indian Bread with Onions—*kulcha*
South Indian Crepes—*sada dosa*
South Indian Crepes with Stuffing—*masala dosa*
Mixed Flour Savory Pancakes—*handvana lotna puda* (dairy)
Vegetarian Omelettes—*puda*

## Fat-Free Breads

Rice Flour Bread—*chokhani roti*
Millet Flour Bread—*bajrina rotla*

**Variation 1: Sorghum Flour Bread**—*juwarna rotla*
**Variation 2: Spiced Bread**—*masalana rotla*
**Cornmeal Bread**—*makaini roti* or *makkeki roti*
**Amaranth Flour Bread**—*rajagarani bhakhari*

.

# Indian Breads

Freshly prepared Indian breads accompany vegetables, *dal* and Indian pickles. In the traditional manner, food is eaten without silverware, with pieces of Indian flat bread used to scoop vegetables. In my home, the aroma of fresh bread cooking signals that the meal is about to be served.

The following pages outline the techniques involved in making Indian bread. I have indicated how alterations in these basic steps produce differences in both taste and texture.

## Ingredients in Indian Breads

Different flours and seasonings, with variations in mixing, kneading and cooking technique, result in a wide selection of nutritious breads that are economical to make at home.

Of the many varieties of flours used to make Indian breads, Indian whole-wheat and *chapati* flours are by far the most common. More finely ground than American whole-wheat flour, Indian flours yield bread dough that is soft, easy to handle and light. Whereas American wheat flour, with its large fragments of bran flakes, yields dense breads, Indian flours are ideal for making delicate, paper-thin *fulka*; layered, flaky *parotha*; puffed *puri* and the other varieties of breads that distinguish Indian cooking.

Though *chapati* flour is readily available in Indian stores, you may substitute a combination of equal portions all-purpose and whole-wheat flour. Another option is to use whole-wheat pastry flour in place of *chapati* flour. Note that, of the two alternatives, I find that whole-wheat pastry flour provides a lighter texture for breads and requires less oil in preparation.

In addition to the commonly used *chapati* flour, other grain and legume flours play important roles in creating the noted array of Indian breads. For instance: flour made from millet or sorghum (a relative of millet native to India's drier climates) is used for the dense wholesome flat bread, *rotla*, (p. 434), and chickpea flour, mixed with several other flours, greatly enhances the flavor of common one-flour flat breads.

Further variations are also created by adding spices (turmeric, chilies, cumin, *ajwain* and salt), vegetables (zucchini, bottle gourd, cabbage, potatoes, white radish), and even greens (spinach, fenugreek leaves, green garlic, green onions, cilantro) to Indian bread dough.

Lastly, note that any variety of oil may be used in the recipes here. I prefer either canola or corn oil for the taste that they impart to the breads.

## Mixing, Kneading and Variations

As you read recipes and begin to assemble bread ingredients, notice the proportion of oil and water called for in the dough. Understanding how the addition of oil and water affects the consistency of bread dough is an important, first step in making beautiful Indian breads. The below notes present a comparative discussion of just a few breads, though the best way to learn is, of course, practice.

*Chapati* (p. 404) require very soft, pliable dough, which is achieved by the addition of water and a little oil while kneading. In contrast, *parotha* (p. 411), a layered, slightly thicker bread, calls for a soft dough as well, but a higher proportion oil to water is needed to prepare a dough that is less malleable than *chapati* dough. Where less water creates stiffer dough, added oil imparts flakiness and soft texture to the *parotha*.

To this, compare the thicker bread *bhakhari* (p. 408), which requires harder dough. The use of oil equals the amount in *parotha*, but even less water is needed. At the other end of the spectrum, *Rotla* (p. 434), the millet or sorghum flour breads and rice flour *chapati* are made with only flour and water. Some *rotla* recipes will call for seasonings as well.

As you compare ingredients and preparation techniques of each version, and as you experiment with the recipes themselves, you will acquire a feel for the different consistencies of dough.

## Mixing

The basic mixing technique is relatively simple.

In a large, shallow bowl or tray, measure out the flour and spices (if any) called for in the recipe. Spices and herbs should be combined with the flour before adding oil and water.

Then add the oil in the amount indicated. Using both hands, mix the oil with the flour and spices. After the oil has been added, if the recipe calls for chopped or grated vegetables, these ingredients should be included at this point. The water content of the vegetables will determine how much additional water is added to the dough to make it pliable enough to knead.

After the oil has been worked in with the flour, start adding a small stream of water with one hand. With the other hand, mix flour and water in a circular motion, moving slowly from the center to the periphery of the mixing vessel. Add water slowly since it is easier to add additional water later, than adding too much too soon and having to rectify it with additional flour. Whether the dough is hard or soft, it should form a large ball which has lost it stickiness and with which you can scrape bits of dough left on the sides of the tray.

## Kneading the Dough

You can knead the dough in the same tray or bowl in which the ingredients are mixed. Or if it is more convenient, move the ball of dough to a flat, unfloured surface for kneading. Commence by making a fist in the dough, and pushing the dough away from you with the knuckles of both hands, pressing downward while pushing. Fold the dough towards you two or three times before repeating this two-step action (illus. p. 433).

Another method is to use the heels and palms of both hands to push the dough away while pressing downwards. The second folding step remains the same. Either way, continue the action for about 2 minutes or until the dough acquires a shine and becomes very malleable.

*Rotla* dough requires a different kneading technique. Use only the heel of one palm on this oil-less millet or sorghum flour dough. Starting on one side of the mass, push down on the dough, twisting your hand as you do so. The thin layer that spreads out on the surface beneath your hand is shifted in a different direction.

Secondly, fold the dough towards yourself (the unkneaded side over to the side being kneaded) and repeat the first step of pushing down on the dough mass, twisting your hand as you push. Continue this process about 2 minutes. It is very important to knead *rotla* dough thoroughly until is has a very soft consistency, since it contains no oil. This will make the cooked bread soft and only slightly chewy.

You may use a food processor to prepare bread dough. However, using your hands in adding oil and water permits you to feel the progress of the bread, as well as effectively monitor the moisture content of the dough. I recommend that you knead the dough first until you are familiar with the consistencies that make for a good bread of each type.

If time is a problem, you can prepare dough a day in advance and store it in the refrigerator, wrapped tightly with plastic wrap. There will be a slight darkening of color, but the cooked results are perfect. However, note that dough prepared with fresh vegetables requires same-day cooking. The grated vegetables tend to lose water when refrigerated, altering the water balance in the dough, making the dough softer.

The practice of mixing, kneading and rolling bread becomes less time-consuming with practice, such that it is possible and in fact easy to prepare breads each evening. My children vehemently agree that nothing compares to fresh hot bread with a meal.

## Resting the Dough

Before rolling out the dough (dough that includes vegetables or greens as an added ingredient is an exception), cover it with an inverted bowl, a damp towel, or plastic wrap to prevent drying. To let the dough soften so that it is easily rolled, let it rest for 10 to 30 minutes in a warm place or any area free of draft. Dough left longer than 30 minutes tends to soften further and may become more difficult to roll. If left longer than three hours, the dough starts to sour. If your schedule does not permit rolling the dough and cooking the bread in 30 minutes, refrigerate it, and when ready, let it sit at room temperature for 30 minutes before rolling and cooking.

## Rolling, Cooking and Variations

Differences in preparation involve bread thickness, the sizes of individually rolled pieces and the manner in which they are rolled.

*Chapati* are thin, evenly shaped circles about 5 or 6–inches in diameter. *Fulka* are *chapati* rolled paper-thin, and *bhakhari* are a thicker version of *chapati.*

*Parotha* are rolled once into flat circles, basted with a small amount of oil, sprinkled with little flour, folded into half circles, basted again with oil and sprinkled with little flour and then folded into quarters. The quarters are rolled until about 5–inches in diameter, and slightly triangular in shape.

To prepare *parotha* for stuffing, first roll the dough into a circle. Then place a tablespoon of the stuffing in the center. Gather the edges of the circle and pinch together so they will not open while cooking. Gently press the gathered circle into a patty and lightly roll (illus. p. 425). A second method of making stuffed *parotha*—which I prefer—requires using more stuffing. Taking two pieces of dough, roll two circles, each about 5–inches in diameter. Spread stuffing mixture on one circle, cover with the second circle and pinch the edges of both circles shut. Lightly roll the *parotha* and then cook.

The daily breads, such as *chapati* and *fulka,* are toasted on a griddle or *tava* without oil or butter. When the bread is partially cooked, the griddle is removed from the fire, and the bread is held with tongs over a flame until it puffs with air.

Thicker versions of *chapati*—such as *parotha, bhakhari,* spiced *dhebra* or *thepla* and their variations, require oil for cooking. Oil that is both added into the dough and used in cooking and basting contributes to a flaky bread texture. Denser than the griddle-roasted breads, these breads do not puff so much during the cooking process.

*Puri* are small and generally not more than 3–inches in diameter, though some cooks prefer them bigger. Deep-fried breads, *puri* and its many variations (Surti *puri* is an exception) puff and acquire a deep-golden color as they cook.

Thick types of *puri*, *bhatura* are impressive in size and a crowd-pleaser when they arrive large and puffed, fresh from the stove.

A teardrop-shaped, leavened bread, *Naan* is traditionally prepared in a *tandoor* oven, which lends the bread a light, smoky flavor. Though it loses some of its aroma when prepared in the standard gas or electric oven, it is nevertheless soft and flavorful.

## Tools and Utensils for Making Indian Breads

For all types of Indian breads, the Indian rolling pin, which is much narrower than the western rolling pin is the ideal tool for effective Indian bread making. Available in most Indian stores, its size, shape and weight allow for a high degree of control, enabling you to roll evenly shaped and correctly sized circles.

Other utensils required for bread making include: a plate or tray for dusting, a pastry board, a griddle or frying pan for cooking, a wok or *karai* for frying, a slotted spoon, a spatula, a plate or basket for finished bread, tongs and a pastry brush if you wish to brush cooked breads with a little *ghee*.

## Paper-Thin Gujarati Bread—*Fulka or Chapati*

In traditional Gujarati families, this bread serves as a definitive test of a young woman's cooking abilities. In such families, all young girls must be able to make and roll perfect *fulka*. Though the recipe appears simple, the process is somewhat more challenging: first, the dough needs to be rather soft so that it can be rolled evenly and thinly. Secondly, the cooked bread should be delicate, without the appearance of brown specks marring its even beige surface.

My grandfather Thakordas taught me how to make *fulka* when I was nine. He guided me through every step, from mixing and kneading the ingredients, to rolling the dough until evenly-sized, soft, flat and perfectly circular in shape, then finally cooking the bread on the griddle and briefly over an open flame, where the *fulka* puffed into steam-filled balloons without acquiring the slightest black singe from the heat.

For your first attempt at *fulka*, your aim should be manageable dough, so add a little less water. Though the delicate texture may be somewhat compromised, the dough will be easier to handle. With more experience, you will be able to make dough with the correct consistency and to roll the authentic bread.

| | |
|---|---|
| 2 cups | *chapati* flour (p. 41) |
| ¼ teaspoon | salt |
| 2 tablespoons | oil |
| 10 tablespoons | water, or as required |
| Flour | any variety, for dusting |

In a medium-sized mixing bowl, combine flour, salt and 1 ½ tablespoons oil. Add water gradually, mixing well with one hand while pouring with the other, and prepare smooth, soft dough. If the dough remains hard, add a little more water (no more than 1 tablespoon at a time) and work it into the dough. The dough should not adhere to the sides of the bowl.

Add the remaining oil and, using both hands, knead the dough well for about 1 minute either in the bowl used for mixing or on a clean surface. The dough surface should be shiny and the dough itself very soft and malleable.

Cover the dough to prevent drying, and set aside.

After 30 minutes uncover the dough and knead it again for few seconds. Divide dough into 20 portions, keeping portions separate. When working with the dough, keep unrolled pieces covered (using a bowl or plastic wrap).

Heat the griddle or a frying pan on medium-high heat, and then reduce heat to low. For an electric stove, use a moderately low setting.

Shape each portion of dough into a smooth ball and cover. To roll, slightly flatten one portion with your hands, and dip it into the dusting flour, making sure both sides are coated. Roll into a thin, flat circle about 5–inches in diameter.

A little additional flour may be necessary to dust the dough and to prevent sticking while rolling. Hold rolling pin lightly, moving it forward and backward over the flattened section as lightly as possible. As you become more experienced in rolling with a light pressure, the bread will rotate on its own as the rolling pin moves backward and forward. Until you achieve this stage of expertise, rotate the bread manually to make all sides even.

Place the bread on the griddle gently so it lies flat without wrinkles. If wrinkles appear, let the bread cook slightly and become firmer before attempting to smooth out.

Tiny bubbles will appear on the bread as it starts to cook. Turn over immediately as these bubbles appear.

There will be light golden specks on the facing side. More bubbles will appear as the second side cooks. When these bubbles appear, remove the griddle from the stove and increase the heat. Lifting the bread by the edges with tongs, turn once and hold directly over the heat to puff. Within seconds, the *fulka* will fill with steam and puff.

Remove the *fulka* from the heat and place it on the plate. You may brush with a bit of clarified butter, Indian fashion, but it is just as delicious plain. Repeat with the remaining portions of dough. Serve hot. Yield: 20.

## Eggplant Bread—*baigan roti*

Made with baked or roasted eggplant, this bread is soft and flavorful. I use a small amount of oil to provide added texture and softness, though you may omit it for a fat-free version. The bread will keep in the refrigerator for several days.

| | |
|---|---|
| 1 medium | eggplant, baked or roasted, peeled |
| 2 cups | *chapati* flour |
| 2 tablespoons | oil |
| 1 teaspoon | salt, or to taste |
| 1 teaspoon | chili powder, or to taste |
| 1 teaspoon | toasted, coarsely ground cumin (optional) |
| ¼ teaspoon | turmeric |
| 4 cloves | garlic, peeled, chopped finely |
| Flour | any variety, for dusting |

Wash and wipe eggplant. Stand eggplant with stem side up, on gas stove over a low flame. Cook until the bottom of the eggplant is well charred, about 5 minutes. Using a pair of tongs, lay eggplant on its side over the flame and roast all around, turning every few minutes until the eggplant is soft and blistered, about 15 minutes.

Alternatively, wrap the eggplant loosely in aluminum foil and bake in an oven preheated to 500 °F for 20 minutes, or until soft. Let the roasted or baked eggplant cool for few minutes, remove skin and mash vegetable meat with a fork. You will have about 1 cup mashed eggplant. Set aside.

In a bowl, combine flour with the next 6 ingredients, including garlic. Add eggplant and mix well. Once a soft dough has formed, knead it for about a minute until it achieves a smooth texture. Divide the dough into 8 portions and shape each into a smooth round patty. Set aside.

Heat a griddle or a frying pan over medium-low heat. Dust the first patty with a little flour and roll it into a circle, about 5–inches in diameter.

Place it in the frying pan and cook until the underside shows golden spots. Turn it over and cook until the second side also develops spots. Turn again, and gently press the surface with a spatula, and cook it a little longer, about 10 seconds. Remove to a platter lined with paper towels. Repeat with the remaining portions of dough.

You can make eggplant *parotha* (p. 411) using the same dough, rolling and folding the dough as in the plain, *parotha* recipe. I have also received rave reviews for eggplant *puri* cooked following the *puri* recipe on (p. 420). Yield: 8.

## Thick Gujarati Bread—*bhakhari*

Though I included this recipe in my first cookbook, I reprint it here, as this is one of the more common daily breads of Western India. It is very easy to make, and will keep in or out of the refrigerator for 2 or 3 days. Even cold, leftover *bhakhari* with tea the next morning is delicious. Serve with any vegetable or with any meal.

| | |
|---|---|
| 2 cups | *chapati* flour |
| ¼ teaspoon | salt, or to taste |
| 4 tablespoons | oil |
| ½ cup | warm water |
| Vegetable shortening | for frying |

In a bowl, combine flour and salt. Add oil and mix well. Gradually add water, and prepare a stiff dough. You may not need all the water called for in the recipe, so start with less and add more as needed. Knead well for a few minutes, or until the dough achieves a smooth consistency. Divide into 8 portions. Make a smooth round patty from each portion and set aside.

Heat a frying pan over medium-low heat. Roll a patty into a circle about 5–inches in diameter, and gently place it directly into the frying pan. Roll another patty into a circle while the first one is cooking.

When the underside turns light golden in color with brown spots, meaning that it is cooked, turn the *bhakhari* over. Turn again when the second side is cooked. Apply a little shortening (about ¼ teaspoon) on the side facing you, turn again, press gently with the spatula. Apply a little shortening on the second side facing you, turn again and press. Both sides will have golden brown spots. Remove to a platter lined with paper towels. Repeat until all are ready. When cold, store covered, until ready to serve. Yield: 8.

## Variation 1: *Bhakhari* with *Ajwain* and Turmeric
### —ajma mithani bhakhari

Add 1 teaspoon *ajwain* and ¼ teaspoon turmeric to the above recipe. Add the ingredients with salt, mix well and follow the preceding recipe. You may fry this *bhakhari* with oil instead of shortening.

## Variation 2: *Bhakhari* with Squash and Spices
### —doodhini bhakhari

*Bhakhari* may also be made using grated squash instead of water, as indicated below. The squash adds both moisture and flavor.

| | |
|---|---|
| ¼ teaspoon | chili powder |
| ¼ teaspoon | turmeric |
| 1 teaspoon | toasted, coarsely ground cumin seeds |
| ½ cup | peeled, grated squash of any variety |

Add dry ingredients to above recipe, combining with salt, flour and oil, then mix well. Add squash instead of water and prepare dough as in *bhakhari* recipe. You will need dusting flour to roll these *bhakhari*, as the moisture in the squash will make the dough sticky. Follow above recipe for directions. Use oil for frying instead of shortening.

## Banana *Bhakhari*—*kelani bhakhari* (dairy)

When left with ripe bananas, my mother would make *bhakhari* using a delightful combination of mashed banana, yogurt and chilies in the dough. This was one of our favorite snacks as children. Serve with any hot chutney or pickle.

| | |
|---|---|
| 2 cups | *chapati* flour |
| ¾ teaspoon | salt, or to taste |
| 3 tablespoons | oil |
| 3 tablespoons | plain yogurt |
| 1 | very ripe banana, peeled, mashed |
| 3 | serrano or jalapeño chilies, ground |
| Oil | for frying |

In a mixing bowl, combine flour with salt and oil. In a small bowl combine yogurt with mashed banana and chilies and add the mixture to the flour. Mix well and lightly knead for about a minute to prepare a stiff dough. Divide the dough into 8 portions, make a smooth round patty from each portion and set aside.

Heat a frying pan over medium-low heat. Roll a patty into a circle about 5-inches in diameter, and gently place it directly into the frying pan. Roll another patty into a circle while the first one is cooking.

When the underside turns light golden in color with brown spots, meaning that it is cooked, turn the *bhakhari* over. Turn again when the second side is cooked. Apply a little oil (about ¼ teaspoon) on the side facing you, turn again, press gently with the spatula. Apply a little oil on the second side facing you, turn again and press. Both sides will have golden brown spots. Remove to a platter lined with paper towels. Repeat until all are ready. Serve hot or at room temperature.
Yield: 8.

# Layered Indian Bread—*parotha*

The dough for this Indian bread is folded as it is rolled, creating light, flaky layers during cooking. Though *parotha* taste better hot, they are equally good if served at room temperature. As the process of folding and frying over low heat can be time consuming, I recommend that cooks set aside ample time to prepare this bread. Some cooks fry these on high heat to save time but the resulting texture is not as delicate. Serve with any Indian meal, tea, or chutneys/pickles.

| | |
|---|---|
| 2 cups | *chapati* flour |
| ½ teaspoon | salt, or to taste |
| 6 tablespoons | oil |
| ¾ cup | warm water |
| Flour | any variety, for dusting |
| Oil or vegetable shortening | for frying |

In a mixing bowl, combine flour and salt. Add 4 tablespoons oil (saving 2 tablespoons for brushing) and mix well. Gradually add water and using your hands prepare dough. At this point, the dough should be smooth and clumped into a large ball. Apply a little oil on your palms and knead the dough for a minute. The dough should be smooth and will be medium-soft in consistency. Cover and set aside for about 30 minutes.

Knead the dough again for about a minute, and divide it into 8 equal portions. Shape each into a smooth, round patty. To prepare the folded bread, dust it with flour, and roll it into a round circle, about 5–inches in diameter. Brush a little oil on the circle, sprinkle flour over the oil, and fold into a semicircle. As before, brush oil over and sprinkle flour onto the semicircle. Fold the dough once more into a quarter circle or a triangle and set aside. In the same manner, prepare all the dough portions into triangles. Gently flatten each triangle with your palm, and roll it into a triangular *parotha*, about 5–inches on each side.

Heat a griddle or a frying pan over medium-high heat. Reduce heat to low and place one *parotha* on the griddle. Turn the *parotha* over when it puffs a little. Drizzle about one-half teaspoon of oil or shortening on the surface, and around the edges of the *parotha*. When golden spots appear on the lower side, turn it over to cook the second side. Turn again and press the *parotha* gently, so that it becomes slightly crisp. Remove to a platter lined with paper towels. Repeat until all are cooked. Serve hot.

*Parotha* can be reheated on low heat if necessary; heating at higher temperature will result in a soggy bread.

Yield: 8.

## Potato-Stuffed *Parotha*—*aaloo parotha*

*Aaloo parotha* can make a very satisfying meal or snack. Many Indians enjoy cucumber *raita* (p. 99) with this bread. Note that the dough for stuffed *parotha* is not folded as it is rolled.

| | |
|---|---|
| 1 recipe | *parotha* dough (p. 411) |
| **Stuffing:** | |
| 4 medium | potatoes, boiled, peeled, mashed |
| 6 | serrano or jalapeño chilies, ground |
| 1 ¼ teaspoons | salt, or to taste |
| 1 tablespoon | lemon juice |
| ¼ cup | chopped cilantro |
| Flour | any variety, for dusting |
| Oil | for frying |

Prepare *parotha* dough as in preceding recipe.

Combine mashed potatoes with the next 4 stuffing ingredients including cilantro and set aside.

Divide the dough into 16 portions. Shape each into a smooth round patty. Using a little flour for dusting, roll two patties separately into circles about 5–inches in diameter. Spread ⅛ of the stuffing mixture on one circle and position the second circle on top of the potato mixture. Gently press the edges shut. Roll lightly into a thinner *parotha*, about 6–inches in diameter.

You may roll all the circles first and then proceed with stuffing and further rolling of each *parotha*. Heat the griddle or a frying pan, over medium heat, and using a little oil instead shortening, fry both sides, as directed in the recipe for plain *parotha* (p. 411). Repeat until all the *parotha* are ready. Can be reheated on low heat.

Yield: 8.

## Cabbage-Stuffed *Parotha*—*kobijna parotha*

Stuffed with lightly cooked, crunchy, spiced cabbage, these *parotha* make for either a tasty snack or wonderful accompaniment to a meal. Though it can be served with any *raita*, I find that this stuffed *parotha* pairs well with fruit *raita* (p. 109).

| | |
|---|---|
| 1 recipe | *parotha* dough (p. 411) |
| **Stuffing:** | |
| 1 medium head | cabbage, very finely cut |
| 1 teaspoon | salt, or to taste |
| 2 teaspoons | oil |
| 1 teaspoon | black mustard seeds |
| 4 | serrano or jalapeño chilies, finely chopped |
| 2 teaspoons | sugar, or to taste |
| 2 teaspoons | lemon juice |
| 2 tablespoons | chopped cilantro |
| Flour | any variety, for dusting |
| Oil | for frying |

Prepare dough as in *parotha* recipe (p. 411), set aside covered.

In a bowl, combine cabbage and salt and set aside for about 10 minutes. Mix well again, and squeeze cabbage, between your hands, removing as much water as possible. Set aside; discard water.

Heat oil in a small saucepan, over medium heat, and add mustard seeds. When mustard starts to crackle, lower the heat. Add cabbage and the remaining 4 ingredients for stuffing including cilantro. Mix well and cook just for few seconds. Set aside to cool.

Divide the dough into 16 portions. Shape each portion of dough into a smooth round patty. Using a little flour for dusting, roll two patties separately into circles about 5–inches in diameter. Spread ⅛ of the stuffing mixture on one circle and position the second circle on top of the cabbage mixture. Gently press the edges shut. Roll lightly into a thinner *parotha*, about 6–inches in diameter.

You may roll all the circles first and then proceed with stuffing and further rolling of each *parotha*. Heat the griddle or a frying pan, over medium heat, and using a little oil instead shortening, fry both sides, as directed in the recipe for plain *parotha* (p. 411). Repeat until all the *parotha* are ready. Can be reheated on low heat.

Yield: 8.

**Variation**: Substitute one green unripe papaya instead of cabbage in above recipe. Peel and cut papaya into halves, discard seeds and finely grate the firm green fruit. Prepare stuffing as in preceding cabbage *parotha* recipe. Note that you do not need to squeeze water from papaya.

## *Paneer*-Stuffed *Parotha*—*paneer parotha* (dairy)

These *parotha* are delicate and tasty. Allow extra time to prepare *paneer*. Serve with any *raita*.

| | |
|---|---|
| 1 recipe | *parotha* dough (p. 411) |
| **Stuffing:** | |
| 1 cup | *paneer*, crumbled (p. 60) |
| ¼ teaspoon | salt, or to taste |
| ¼ cup | finely chopped onions |
| 2 teaspoons | coarsely ground toasted cumin seeds |
| 2 tablespoons | finely chopped cilantro |
| 1 | serrano or jalapeño chili, chopped with seeds |

Prepare dough as directed in *parotha* recipe (p. 411); cover and set aside. Combine ingredients for stuffing.

Divide the dough into 16 portions. Shape each portion of dough into a smooth round patty. Using a little flour for dusting, roll two patties separately into circles about 5–inches in diameter. Spread ⅛ of the stuffing mixture on one circle and position the second circle on top of the *paneer* mixture. Gently press the edges shut. Roll lightly into a thinner *parotha*, about 6–inches in diameter.

You may roll all the circles first and then proceed with stuffing and further rolling of each *parotha*. Heat the griddle or a frying pan, over medium heat, and using a little oil instead shortening, fry both sides, as directed in the recipe for plain *parotha* (p. 411). Repeat until all the *parotha* are ready. Can be reheated on low heat.

Yield: 8.

## Wheat and Millet Bread—*dhebra* or *thepla* (dairy)

In this recipe, wheat flour combines with millet and yogurt to yield an unusually soft, savory bread that is accented by spices, chilies and sesame. Paired with a sweet chutney or a fruit *raita*, this nutritious, flavorful Indian bread may be served as either a light one-dish meal or an afternoon snack.

| | |
|---|---|
| 1 cup | *chapati* flour |
| 1 cup | *bajri* (millet) flour (p. 43) |
| 1 tablespoon | oil |
| 1 ½ teaspoons | salt, or to taste |
| 1 teaspoon | chili powder |
| ½ teaspoon | turmeric |
| 1 teaspoon | fenugreek seeds, toasted, coarsely ground |
| 2 tablespoons | sesame seeds, lightly crushed |
| ¾ cup | yogurt |
| 8 cloves | garlic, peeled, chopped |
| 3–inch piece | fresh ginger, peeled, ground |
| 6 | serrano or jalapeño chilies, ground |
| Flour | any variety, for dusting |
| Oil | for frying |

In a large mixing bowl, combine both flours and oil. Add salt and the next 4 ingredients including sesame seeds, and mix well.

In a small bowl, combine yogurt with garlic, ginger, and chilies. Add the yogurt mixture to the flour mixture. Mix well and prepare dough using your hands. Knead until smooth, about 2 minutes. Divide the dough into 15 portions. Shape each into a round patty. Heat the griddle or a frying pan on medium-low heat.

Dip both sides of the patty in the flour to coat well. Using a rolling pin, roll the patty into a circle, about 5–inches in diameter, and place it on the griddle. Turn over when the underside has tiny golden spots. When second side has tiny spots, apply a small amount of oil (one-quarter tea-spoon) on the top and turn. Press the surface gently with a spatula until the spots become large and golden. Apply little oil on the side facing you and turn and fry again pressing the surface gently. When both sides have golden spots, remove *dhebra* to a platter lined with paper towels. Repeat until all are ready.

Serve hot or at room temperature. Leftovers can be kept at room temperature.

Yield: 15.

**Note:** If you do not have millet flour, substitute with the same amount of *chapati* flour, adding an additional 2 tablespoons of oil to the recipe.

## Deep-Fried Puffed Bread with Yogurt—*bhatura* (dairy)

Made with yogurt, this delicate and light North Indian puffed bread is popular all over India. *Bhatura* are slightly tart in flavor, and are wonderful served with *chhole* (p. 349).

| | |
|---|---|
| 1 cup | all-purpose flour |
| 1 cup | self-rising flour |
| 2 tablespoons | oil |
| ½ cup | yogurt |
| ¼ cup | water, warm |
| Flour | any variety, for dusting |
| Oil | for frying |

In a mixing bowl, combine both flours and mix in oil. Add yogurt and mix well. Gradually add warm water and, using your hands, prepare soft dough. Apply a few drops of oil to your palms and knead the dough for about 2 minutes. Cover and set aside for two hours to rise.

Divide dough into 15 portions and shape each into a ball. Dip each ball into flour to coat. Beginning with the first, press and flatten slightly and with a rolling pin, roll into a circle, about 3 or 4–inches in diameter. Repeat until all portions are ready, placing each rolled circle separately on a lightly floured surface, to prevent them from sticking.

Heat about 3–inches of oil in a *karai* or a wok over medium-high heat. Lower the heat to about 375 °F. (I lower the heat to medium once I notice the oil starting to slightly smoke). Fry *bhatura*, one or two at a time, turning once to cook both sides. They should puff as they cook. Fry until slightly golden. Remove with a slotted spoon and drain on paper towels. Repeat until all are ready. Serve hot or at room temperature.
Yield: 15.

## Deep-Fried Indian Bread—*puri*

When younger, my children loved fresh, hot *puri* served with vegetables and pureed mangoes. Rather than oil, which imparts a greasy texture to the bread, I use vegetable shortening for frying.

| | |
|---|---|
| 2 cups | *chapati* flour |
| 2 tablespoons | oil |
| ¼ teaspoon | salt, or to taste |
| 8 tablespoons | water, or as required |
| Vegetable shortening | for frying |

In a mixing bowl, combine flour, oil and salt. Gradually add water and prepare dough. The dough should be soft, smooth and pliable in your hands. If the dough is too stiff, add little more water, and knead for about 1 minute, or until the necessary texture is achieved. Set aside, covered, for about 15 minutes. Knead again for a minute, and then divide into 40 portions. Shape each portion into a smooth round patty.

Heat about 3–inches of vegetable shortening in a *karai* or a wok and lower the heat to 375 °F. Roll several patties into circles about 3–inches in diameter and set aside. When you have rolled about 8 or 10, gently slide 4 or 5 *puri* into the shortening. Raise the heat for a few seconds to encourage puffing of the *puri* and then lower it again to 375 °F. Turn the *puri* and using a slotted spoon, gently press the surface of each *puri*, making sure not to press them too firmly, down into the shortening. This should also cause the *puri* to puff. Turn them once more, and cook until the bottom surface becomes slightly golden. Remove to a platter lined with paper towels. Repeat until all are ready. Serve hot.
Yield: 40.

## Festive *Puri*—*Surti puri*

This crisp, flaky bread is usually served on festive occasions in Gujarat. Available in Indian stores, the farina or thin *sooji* called for in this recipe is a smaller grain variety of the commonly available "Cream of Wheat." Plan to make the recipe ahead of time, as it must be served at room temperature. To add a spicy twist, you may add one teaspoon of both coarsely ground cumin and coarsely ground black pepper to the flour, before preparing the dough. Serve with any meal.

| | |
|---|---|
| 1 ½ cups | all-purpose flour |
| 1 ½ cup | thin *sooji* |
| 8 tablespoons | unsalted margarine, softened |
| 1 teaspoon | salt, or to taste |
| ½ cup | water, or as needed |
| Vegetable shortening | for frying |

In a mixing bowl, combine flour and *sooji*. Add margarine and salt and mix well using your hands. Gradually add water and prepare a smooth, yet stiff dough. This particular dough need not "rest." Knead the dough for about a minute. Divide it into 24 portions, and shape each portion into smooth round patty. Roll each patty into about 4–inch circle. Using a fork, prick each *puri* in 4 or 5 spots to prevent puffing, and to create a crisp flat bread. Repeat until several circles are ready.

Heat about 3–inches of shortening in a *karai* or a wok. When the temperature reaches about 375 °F, reduce the heat to low. Drop 2 or 3 *puri* in the shortening. Fry on both the sides, turning gently only twice, until very slightly golden on both the sides. Using a slotted spoon, remove *puri* to a platter lined with paper towels. Repeat until all are ready. Let cool to room temperature before serving. Leftover will keep for several days at room temperature in an airtight container.

Yield: 24.

## Leavened Indian Bread—*naan* (dairy)

*Naan* may perhaps be the most well known Indian bread, given the proliferation of north Indian restaurants out of India. Traditionally cooked in a *tandoor* or clay oven, which imparts a wonderfully smoky flavor and soft texture to the bread, *naan* can also be made in a conventional oven or on stovetop, though the results will be slightly different.

This is a favorite mealtime accompaniment of my son. While he was in graduate school, I would send him monthly parcels of about 30–40 *naan,* which he would freeze, and then pop into the toaster to serve with meals.

| | |
|---|---|
| 2 cups | all-purpose flour |
| ¼ teaspoon | salt |
| ¼ ounce | active, dry yeast |
| ½ teaspoon | sugar |
| 4 tablespoons | lowfat milk |
| 2 tablespoons | butter |
| 9 tablespoons | yogurt |
| ½ teaspoon | baking soda |
| ½ teaspoon | baking powder |
| Flour | any variety, for dusting |

In a mixing bowl, combine flour, salt, yeast and sugar. In a small saucepan over low heat, heat milk and butter. As soon as the butter melts, stand the pan in a large saucepan containing water, double-boiler fashion, over high heat. Add next 3 ingredients including baking powder. Mix well, and remove the pan from the heat when the mixture becomes frothy.

Gradually add heated milk mixture to flour, and prepare a smooth, soft dough, as you work the mixture through the flour with your hands. If the dough sticks to your hands, use a little dusting flour and mix well. Knead the dough (as directed in chapter introduction) for about 3 minutes.

Cover and set aside to rise in a warm place for at least three hours, or until the dough has doubled in volume.

Knead again and divide dough into 10 portions. Shape each into smooth patty, and set aside, covered well, for at least 30 minutes. Portions will rise again.

Heat a griddle or a frying pan and lower the heat to medium-low. Roll one patty into a circle, using dusting flour as needed to prevent sticking, about 5–inches diameter, and gently place it on the griddle. As soon as you see some bubbles forming on the surface of the *naan*, turn it over with a flat spatula and let the second side cook on low heat. The *naan* will start to puff. Turn it over again and press the surface against you gently, with the spatula, for a few seconds, so that it will puff further. Cook until both sides have golden spots. Remove onto a wire rack. Repeat until all *naan* are ready.

Serve hot, or when cool, cover tightly in foil and refrigerate or freeze. Reheat in a toaster, or in an oven loosely covered with foil. Cooked *naan* will keep well in the freezer (just ask my son!).
Yield: 10.

## Variation 1: Leavened Bread with Raisins—raisin *naan*

Add 1 or 2 tablespoon raisins to the dough for *naan* and follow the preceding recipe.

## Variation 2: Spicy *Naan*—*masala naan*

To prepare a spicy version of *naan*, add any combination of the following spices to the dough: 1 teaspoon toasted cumin, 2 serrano green chilies, chopped finely, ½ teaspoon chili powder, 1 teaspoon *ajwain* or ¼ teaspoon turmeric.

## Variation 3: Leavened Indian Bread with Onions—*kulcha*

Once you know how to make basic *naan*, the varieties will be very simple to make. Prepare onion mixture as follows and divide the mixture into 10 portions. Stuff each portion of *naan* dough (p. 422) with one portion of mixture as directed below.

**Stuffing:**

| | |
|---|---|
| 1 cup | chopped onions |
| 6 | serrano or jalapeño chilies, ground |
| ¼ cup | chopped cilantro |

In a frying pan, cook onions for about 15 seconds without any oil. Add chilies and cilantro, mix well and remove from heat. When cold, divide the mixture into 10 portions.

Roll one portion of the *naan* dough into a circle and then place one portion of the stuffing in the center. Gather the edges of the circle (illus. p. 425) and press together. Press circle gently to make a large patty, and roll lightly before cooking as directed in *naan* recipe (p. 422).

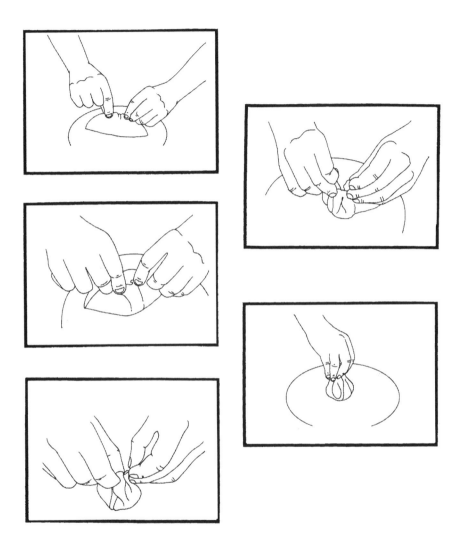

*Method for Stuffing Kachori—Single Layer Method for Stuffing Parotha and Kulcha*

## South Indian Crepes—*sada dosa*

These crispy, savory crepes, normally served with coconut chutney (p. 71), are a wonderful snack and a popular "fast food" item. Placing a scoop of onion and potato stuffing in the center and folding the crepe over yields *masala dosa*, the recipe for which follows. Though I have used an Indian flat griddle, called a *tava*, a nonstick frying pan works equally well.

Please note that this recipe does call for some advance preparation in that the rice and *dal* must be soaked in water in advance. Additionally, the batter must sit for about 8–12 hours prior to cooking.

| | |
|---|---|
| 2 cups | long grain rice, any variety, washed, soaked overnight |
| ½ cup | split Indian black beans (*urid dal*), soaked overnight |
| 1 teaspoon | fenugreek seeds |
| 1 teaspoon | salt, or to taste |
| Oil | for frying |

Separately pick over and wash both rice and *dal* (see note, p. 336). Add fenugreek seeds to the *dal*, and soak rice and *dal* separately for 8 to 12 hours or overnight. After soaking, drain and grind rice and *dal* separately in a blender or liquidizer, adding a small amount of water to make both the batters smooth. The consistency should be that of a thick pancake batter (I find that a food processor does not produce the required, fine texture).

In a stainless steel bowl, combine ground rice and *dal*, add salt and mix well. Cover and set aside for about eight hours, or until the batter rises slightly.

Heat a griddle or a large frying pan over medium-high heat. Add about 1 teaspoon oil. When hot, spread the oil evenly over the pan with a wet paper towel wiping off excess droplets. Pour about ½ cup batter into the pan and, with the back of a spoon, spread the batter thinly and evenly, making a circle about 10–inches in diameter or larger, if your pan allows for it. As the batter cooks, it will soon start showing tiny holes. When the top appears cooked—when it is covered with tiny holes, spread little oil around the edges of the *dosa*. Using a spatula, remove *dosa* from the pan—it is not necessary to fry both sides. Wipe the pan again with a wet paper towel before proceeding to spread the second *dosa*. (This step of wiping is important so that the *tava* or frying pan cools slightly and that it is clean for the next *dosa*.) Continue, the same way, until all the batter is used up. Serve hot with chutney. Each *dosa* must be served immediately to preserve its crisp outer texture.

Serves 4–6.

## South Indian Crepes with Stuffing—*masala dosa*

The most efficient way to serve *masala dosa* is to prepare the stuffing just prior to cooking *dosa*. As you remove each *dosa* from the pan, spread a scoop of stuffing along the center of the unfried side of the *dosa*(the side that is face-up during cooking). Fold the edges of the crepe up over the stuffing. Serve with a dollop of Coconut and Split Chickpea Chutney (p. 71) alongside.

**Crepes:** See preceding recipe.

**Stuffing:**

| | |
|---|---|
| 2 tablespoons | oil |
| 1 teaspoon | split Indian black beans (*urid dal)* |
| pinch | *hing* (asafoetida) |
| 4 medium | potatoes, boiled, peeled, cut into ½–inch cubes |
| 1 small | onion, chopped |
| 1 teaspoon | salt, or to taste |
| ¼ teaspoon | turmeric |
| 3 | serrano or jalapeño chilies, ground |

In a small saucepan, heat oil over medium heat, and add *urid dal* and *hing.* Within a few seconds the *dal* will turn golden and the *hing* will turn brown. Immediately add remaining ingredients, stir to mix and lower the heat. Cook mixing well for about 5 minutes. Remove from heat.

Prepare *dosa* following the directions in preceding recipe. Spread about ¼ cup stuffing in the center of *dosa* and fold both edges of the *dosa* over the stuffing to cover. Serve each *dosa* immediately as it comes off of the griddle.

Serves 4–6.

## Mixed Flour Savory Pancakes—*handvana lotna puda* (dairy)

This recipe is also known as *dangeru* around Gujarat. Unlike *dosa*, *puda* can be made ahead of time and reheated prior to serving. If *handva* flour is unavailable, use a mixture of rice and split chickpeas (*chana dal*) (p. 42). Soak rice and *dal* for several hours before grinding. Serve with sweet pickle or chutneys. Traditionally, *puda* is served with *galvanu* (p. 443), with bite-size pieces of *puda* dipped into the sweet, milk-based sauce. The combination of sweet and spicy is unusual and appetizing.

| | |
|---|---|
| 1 ½ cups | *handva* flour (p. 42) |
| 1 cup | buttermilk |
| 1 cup | water |
| 1 ½ teaspoons | salt, or to taste |
| 1 teaspoon | *ajwain* (p. 9) |
| ½ teaspoon | turmeric |
| 4 | serrano or jalapeño chilies, ground **or** |
| ½ teaspoon | chili powder |
| 2–inch piece | fresh ginger, peeled, ground (optional) |
| 4 cloves | garlic, peeled, chopped finely |
| 2 tablespoons | chopped cilantro (optional) |
| 2 tablespoons | oil |
| Oil | for frying |

In a mixing bowl, combine flour, buttermilk and water and set aside for at least eight hours. The mixture will assume the consistency of very thick pancake batter. If after the soaking period, the batter is thicker, add more water, if necessary to thin to the appropriate consistency. Add all the remaining ingredients including 2 tablespoons oil, and mix well.

Add 2 teaspoons oil to a nonstick frying pan, and heat well over medium heat. Lower the heat, and pour in about 4 tablespoons batter. Using the back of a spoon, spread the batter into a circle about 4–inches in diameter. Cover and cook until the top surface changes color to pale yellow, about 5 minutes. The underside will also turn a golden color. Gently flip over the *puda*. Drizzle a little oil around the edges, and fry until the underside has golden spots, about 2 more minutes. You may turn and check for spots. Repeat until the batter is used up. Serve hot.

Yield: 6–8.

**Note:** For variety, add ½ cup of your choice of vegetables, such as grated zucchini (or any other grated squash), fresh chopped spinach, crushed peas or grated onions to the batter.

## Vegetarian Omelettes—*puda*

These *puda* can be made with the flour combination below or with 2 ½ cups of *pakora* flour (p. 133). Serve with *galvanu* (p. 443).

For additional variety, add partially sautéed, chopped spinach, coarsely ground peas, or other finely grated vegetables to the batter.

| | |
|---|---|
| 1 ½ cups | chickpea flour |
| 1 cup | *chapati* flour |
| 1 teaspoon | salt or to taste |
| 1 ½ cups | water |
| 2 teaspoons | oil |
| ¼ cup | finely chopped onions |
| 2 | serrano or jalapeño chilies, chopped |
| ¼ teaspoon | baking soda |
| 2 tablespoons | chopped cilantro |
| Oil | for frying |

In a mixing bowl, combine both flours, salt and water. Set aside for 5 minutes.

Heat 2 teaspoons oil in a griddle or a frying pan over medium heat. Reduce heat to low, add onions and chilies. Sauté for about 2 minutes, and stir into the batter. Mix in chopped cilantro.

In the same griddle or frying pan, heat another 2 teaspoons oil over medium-low heat, and pour in about ¼ cup batter. With the back of a spoon, spread the batter evenly, into a circle, about 5–inches in diameter.

When the side facing you changes color to deep yellow and gold spots appear on the underside, turn gently. Drizzle a little oil around the edges, and cook for one minute or until the second side develops golden spots. Remove and set aside on paper towels. Serve hot. You may cook all the *puda* before serving, keeping them warm on a plate placed in an oven on low heat.
Yield: Approximately 12.

# Fat-Free Breads

## Rice Flour Bread—*chokhani rotli*

This bread is very simple and light, a perfect accompaniment to vegetables for those watching their dietary fat intake.

| | |
|---|---|
| 1 cup | water |
| 1 cup | rice flour |
| ¼ teaspoon | salt |
| Rice Flour | for dusting |

In a saucepan over high heat, bring water to a full boil. Add flour and salt, and mix well. Lower the heat to medium-low, cover the pan, and cook further for about 20 seconds or until the mixture forms a soft dough. Remove the dough to any flat surface or a cutting board, and knead for about twenty seconds or until smooth.

Heat a griddle or frying pan over medium heat. Divide the dough into 8 portions. Using rice flour for dusting, to prevent sticking, lightly roll one portion into a 6–inch circle. Reduce heat to low and gently place one circle into the frying pan or griddle. Cook each side for 1 minute, turning once. With a spatula, lightly press the top surface of the bread to make it puff. If it doesn't puff, place it directly over the flame for a few seconds. When the bread fills with steam, remove from heat. Cover with a paper towel, while rolling and preparing the remaining portions.
Yield: 8.

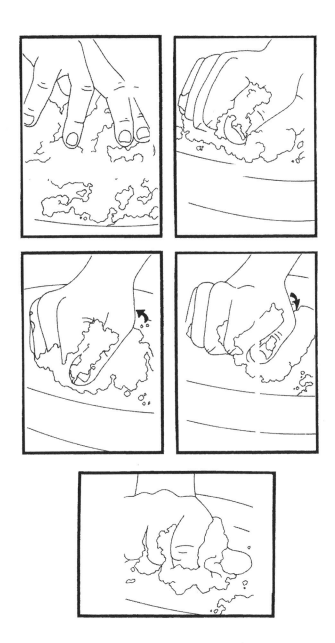

*Method for Kneading Dough*

## Millet Flour Bread—*bajrina rotla*

This hearty, rustic bread pairs well with mung bean or cabbage recipes. The challenge in preparing this bread is that the dough must be made and kneaded in small portions. Available in most Indian stores, millet flour stales easily and should be stored with a few cloves added as a preservative. Sift before use to remove cloves. Refrigerate if storing flour for long periods of time.

| | |
|---|---|
| 2 ½ cups | millet (*bajri*) flour |
| ½ teaspoon | salt, or to taste |
| ¾ to 1 cup | warm water |

For dusting and rolling, set aside about ¼ cup of the flour called for in the recipe. In a platter, combine the remaining 2 ¼ cups flour and salt. As mentioned above, the dough for this recipe must be prepared in small portions: separate one-fifth part of the flour, add 3 or 4 tablespoons of water, and mix well to prepare a stiff but malleable dough. To knead, press the dough with the heel of your hand and slide away from you. Gather the dough again and repeat about 10 times. Shape it into a large patty.

Dust a flat surface or a cutting board with flour. With your hands, shape the patty into a round *rotla,* by pressing and turning the dough in a circular motion with your fingers (illus. p. 436), just a few degrees at a time, until it is about 5 or 6–inches in diameter. You can use your fingers and palms to make it even larger, if thinner bread is preferred.

Heat a griddle or a frying pan on medium-high heat. Lower the heat and carefully slide *rotla* off the work surface onto the palm of your hand. Gently turn it over on to the griddle so that the floured underside is on top. Drizzle little water on the side facing you, and spread with your fingers, to prevent the bread from cracking. When the water dries out, carefully turn the *rotla* and let the second side cook until it has light brown spots. Lift the *rotla* gently with a pair of tongs, and place it on the direct flame with spotted side facing you. The *rotla* will puff slightly, remove from flame and serve hot.

While the first *rotla* is cooking, prepare and knead the dough for the second. Repeat in the same manner until all 5 *rotla* are cooked.

This bread may be prepared ahead of time, and reheated on a low open flame; alternatively, serve at room temperature.
Yield: 5.

## Variation 1: Sorghum Flour Bread—*juwarna rotla*

This light colored flour creates less-dense bread than millet flour. Follow the preceding recipe substituting sorghum flour for millet flour.

## Variation 2: Spiced Millet Bread—*masalana rotla*

1 tablespoon finely chopped green garlic, 1 teaspoon *ajwain*, ¼ teaspoon turmeric and ½ teaspoon chili powder can be added to the flour in either of the about recipes to make *rotla* flavorful.

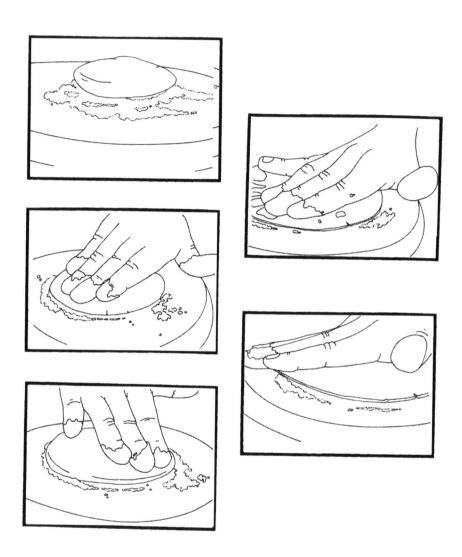

*Method for Shaping Rotla with Hands*

## Cornmeal Bread—*makaini rotli* or *makkeki roti*

Popular in Gujarat and in North India, this bread is suitable for those who are allergic to wheat products. In North India it is mostly served with *sarsoka saag* (vegetable made with mustard greens). Corn flour, available in Indian stores, may be substituted for cornmeal. Serve with any vegetable made with greens.

| | |
|---|---|
| 2 cups | cornmeal, white or yellow |
| 2 ½ cups | water |
| ½ teaspoon | salt, or to taste |
| Flour | any variety, for dusting |

Measure cornmeal into a mixing bowl. In a small saucepan, boil water, adding salt. Immediately add water to cornmeal and mix well. All the water will be absorbed in just a few minutes. Knead well when slightly cold to yield dough that is smooth and slightly sticky.

Divide the dough into 10 portions. Make a smooth patty from each portion and, dusting with flour as necessary, roll into a circle about 5–inches in diameter.

Heat a griddle or a frying pan and gently place *rotli* on it. Lower the heat to medium and turn the bread when tiny bubbles appear on top. Toast until golden spots appear on both the sides. Serve hot.

Yield: 10.

## Amaranth Flour Bread—*rajagarani bhakhari*

On the religious day of *Ekadesi*, two varieties of meals were made in my parents' home: a special religious menu (including this bread) for worshipping members, and regular meals for the rest. In the morning I would inform my mom that I too would participate, since most of all, I wanted to eat this bread.

Serve with Sweet Potatoes and Potatoes with Peanuts (p. 208) or with any Indian meal.

| | |
|---|---|
| 1 cup | amaranth flour |
| ¼ cup | water or as required |
| Amaranth flour | for dusting |

In a mixing bowl, combine flour and water to make smooth yet slightly stiff dough. If the dough is flaky use a little more water. Divide into 4 portions and shape each portion into a small patty. Using little flour for dusting, roll each patty into a circle about 5–inches in diameter.

Heat the griddle or a frying pan and lower the heat to medium-low. Gently place the *bhakhari* on it. When light brown spots appear on the bottom side, turn and cook the other side. When the underside has spots, turn again and press gently to puff the *bhakhari*, or you can place it directly on open flame. Keep the flame low and gently press the edges. Remove and serve hot. Keeps in the refrigerator for 2 days; can be reheated before serving.

Yield: 4.

# DESSERTS AND SWEETMEATS

Cream of Wheat Pudding—*sooji kheer* or *galvanu*
Rice Pudding with Raisins—*payas*
Ground Rice with Nuts—*shahi firnee*
Chickpea Flour with Cardamom—*besan laadu*
Indian Ice Cream with Saffron—*kesar kulfi*
Milk Powder and Flour Balls in Rose Flavored Syrup—*gulab jaman*
Sweetened Yogurt Dessert—*shreekhand*
Sweet Yogurt Dessert with Black Pepper—*matho*
Almond Fudge—*badam barfi*
Bulgur with Milk and Nuts—*fadano doodhpaak*
Rice and Split Pigeon Peas with Saffron—*beeranj*
*Paneer* Patty in Sweet, Cream Sauce—*ras malai*
Walnut Pudding—*akhrotni basudi*
Amaranth Pudding—*rajagarani kheer*
Carrot *Halwa*—*gajar halwa*
Stuffed, Half-Moon-Shaped Pastry—*ghughra*
Stuffed Round Pastry—*ghari*

## Non-Dairy Desserts

Unripe Mango Dessert—*khandkeri*
Cream of Wheat with Cardamom and Saffron—*kesari sheera*
Buckwheat *Halwa*—*fafar sheera*
Rice Pudding with Coconut—*kopra doodhpaak*
Cashew Diamonds—*kaju katni*
Date Rolls—*khajur pilla*

**Bulgur Dessert**—*lapsi*

## Fruits As Dessert

**Cantaloupe**—*sakkarteti*
**Papaya**—papaya with cumin
**Watermelon**—*tarbuch*
**Thick Mango Juice**—*kerino ras*

# Desserts and Sweetmeats

In India, desserts are traditionally served only on festive occasions such as birthdays, *Diwali*, *Holi,* weddings, etc. Custom also holds that desserts be served alongside entrees. Following Western customs, however, it is now more common for sweets to be served following a meal.

Two common ingredients in both Indian desserts and many sweetmeats are *khoya* (also called *mavo)*, a solidified-milk preparation, and *paneer,* a milk product that some refer to as the Indian version of cheese. The preparation of either ingredient involves boiling milk—in fact, milk for *khoya* is boiled for an especially long period of time. Traditionally made with whole milk (or sometimes with buffalo milk) *khoya* can be a caloric, high-fat content food. My own, time saving, healthy shortcut is to use part-skim ricotta cheese to yield lighter desserts. As with many activities, however, extra labor yields extra-special results. There is no true substitute for *khoya* or *paneer* prepared in the authentic, painstaking manner.

Besides being used in prepared desserts, fruit—especially mango, cantaloupe or banana—is also often consumed with or following a meal. The Indian mango comes into season just before the monsoons, during the summer months in India. Wonderfully juicy and sweet, the Indian mango is either juiced or peeled and cut, and served alongside meals. There is nothing quite comparable to the combination of hot, fresh and flaky Indian *parotha* bread, a spicy vegetable dish, and cool, sweet Indian mango. Mango juice is commonly added to milkshakes, *kulfi*, and *lassi*, and even *papadum*. In this chapter, I have indicated some of the ways in which Indians season their fruit.

# A Note on Vegetarianism, Sweeteners and Restricted Diets

Many vegetarians object to consuming table sugar, as processed sugarcane syrup is often filtered through charcoal or chemical resin filters that are made from animal by-products, trees, or artificial substances that are harmful to the environment. Since natural sugar products are not available in all areas, I have used table sugar in this book. Feel free to substitute, though proportions may need to be altered, depending on the intensity of the flavor of the sweetener that is used.

For those on restricted diets, sugarless desserts may be prepared with the use of fresh or dried fruits pureed with either milk or water (I often received requests for such desserts at *The Ganges*). I have also included several non-dairy recipes in this chapter.

# Cream of Wheat Pudding—*sooji kheer* or *galvanu*

This simple recipe does not require many ingredients and can be made quickly. Though many Gujaratis prefer to eat this dish warm, served alongside meals, it can also be served chilled. Note that the pudding will thicken as it cools.

| | |
|---|---|
| 1 tablespoon | butter |
| ½ cup | thin *sooji* (p. 42) **or** |
| ½ cup | Cream of Wheat |
| 4 cups | milk |
| 3 tablespoons | sugar, or to taste |
| 2 teaspoons | coarsely ground cardamom seeds |
| 2 tablespoons | chopped unsalted pistachios |
| 2 tablespoons | slivered almonds |

Heat butter in a small saucepan over medium heat, and add the *sooji* or Cream of Wheat. Lower the heat and cook the mixture, stirring well until the *sooji* or Cream of Wheat turns golden-yellow, about 10 minutes.

Add the milk and sugar. Stirring well, cook until the mixture thickens, about 10 more minutes. Add cardamom and mix again. Remove and serve garnished with pistachio, and almonds.

Serves 4.

## Rice Pudding with Raisins—*payas*

At *The Ganges*, we called this pudding by its Bengali name, *payas*. In South India, where the dish is more commonly known as *payasam*, split chickpeas (*chana dal*) are usually substituted for rice.

Made with lowfat milk and served chilled, *payas* is light and refreshing. The cardamom infuses the dish with a fragrant aroma that accents the sweetness of the raisins. Though nuts are traditionally an essential component of the Gujarati version of this dessert, known as *doodhpaak*, I have omitted the ingredient here, as I did at *The Ganges*, out of consideration of the dietary restrictions of many of my regular customers. Though Gujaratis tend to prefer their rice pudding warm and as an accompaniment to their meal, I like it chilled and served after spicy meals. Note that any long-grain rice variety may be used in place of *basmati*.

| | |
|---|---|
| ½ gallon | lowfat milk |
| ¾ cup | *basmati* or long-grain rice, washed |
| 1 cup | sugar, or to taste |
| 2 teaspoons | cardamom seeds, ground |
| ¼ cup | raisins, black and seedless |

In a medium saucepan, bring milk to a full boil over high heat, stirring well. Take care to prevent milk from sticking to the bottom of the pan.

Add rice to the boiling milk, and immediately continue stirring to prevent the rice from sticking to the bottom. Lower the heat to medium-low and cook the pudding, stirring occasionally.

After about 30 minutes, check to see if the rice is nearly cooked. Remove and squeeze one grain of rice between your fingers; there should be no hard particles left in the grain. Add sugar and continue cooking until the rice is quite soft, about 10 minutes. Add cardamom, mix well, and remove from heat.

As the pudding cools, stir occasionally to prevent a thick layer of cream from forming on the top (partially cover the pudding, if desired). The mixture will cool to room temperature in about two hours. If in a hurry, place the saucepan in a tray filled with cold water.

Rinse raisins and add to the pudding. Mix well and chill before serving. Can be garnished with extra raisins.

Serves 8–10.

**Note:** For a Gujarati version of the above recipe, omit raisins and instead add 2 tablespoons each of blanched, slivered almonds and chopped, unsalted, pistachio nuts. Add ¼ teaspoon crushed saffron and mix well.

## Ground Rice with Nuts—*shahi firnee*

In Hindi, *Shahi* means royal: the title of the dish therefore refers to the richness of the dessert. Although ground nuts and rice give the dessert a thick texture, this dish is actually not very heavy. Vanilla, rose, or even almond essence may be substituted for the screwpine essence (p. 46).

| | |
|---|---|
| 1 cup | long grain rice, washed, soaked overnight |
| 5 cups | milk, preferably low fat |
| 1 ½ cups | sugar, or to taste |
| 2 teaspoons | cardamom seeds, coarsely ground |
| 2 tablespoons | almonds, coarsely ground |
| ¼ cup | broken cashews |
| ¼ teaspoon | screwpine essence (*kewra*) |
| ¼ teaspoon | saffron, crushed |
| 2 tablespoons | slivered almonds, for garnish |

Drain rice and grind in a liquidizer or a blender, adding 1 cup of milk. When smooth, set aside.

In a medium saucepan, over high heat, bring the remaining 4 cups of milk to a full boil. Lower the heat and add the ground rice. Stirring immediately and continuously, add sugar and cook the mixture for about 7 minutes. Add cardamom, and the next 4 ingredients, including the saffron. Mix well and cook for a few seconds.

Remove pudding to a bowl and refrigerate when cool. Serve chilled, garnished with slivered almonds.

Serves 4-6.

## Chickpea Flour with Cardamom—*besan laadu*

A regular item on *The Ganges* menu, *laadu* was a favorite of many customers. Note that no liquid is added to this recipe, giving the dessert a dense texture and also contributing to the long shelf-life of the preparation.

| | |
|---|---|
| ¾ pound | unsalted butter |
| 4 cups | chickpea flour |
| 2 ¼ cups | powdered sugar, or to taste |
| 1 tablespoon | ground cardamom seeds |

Melt butter in a medium saucepan over medium-high heat. As the butter starts to melt, add flour and mix well. Reduce heat to low and cook, stirring frequently, while the flour turns golden and exudes a nutty aroma. Keep stirring every few minutes, until the mixture becomes very soft (about one hour); take care not to let the flour burn.

Remove saucepan from heat and let the mixture cool for about one hour. Add sugar and cardamom, mix well, and allow it to cool for another hour. When cool, mix well again with your hands. Using your hands, shape about ¼ cup mixture into a smooth, round ball. Set aside in a container with a lid, repeating until all the *laadu* are ready. Cover the container. Serve as desired. You may garnish each *laadu* with sliced almonds prior to serving.

Yield: Approximately 14.

## Indian Ice Cream with Saffron—*kesar kulfi*

A frozen dessert, *kulfi* is commonly marketed and labeled in Indian restaurants as "Indian ice cream." In India *kulfi* is made by simmering milk over low heat until it thickens. Sugar, nuts and saffron are added, and the mixture is poured into conical *kulfi* molds, which are then frozen.

Below, I have provided a shortcut to this time-consuming recipe. I recommend freezing *kulfi* in individual-sized serving cups. At the restaurant, we would use 4-ounce soufflé cups. Freezing may take a day. When serving, remove the *kulfi* into individual serving bowls. Garnish with nuts or a sprig of mint, if desired, and serve as a cooling, delicious dessert.

| | |
|---|---|
| 1 (15-ounce) container | part-skim ricotta cheese |
| 4 cups | milk |
| ¾ cup | sugar, or to taste |
| 2 tablespoons | ground almonds |
| 1 tablespoon | ground unsalted pistachio nuts |
| 1 teaspoon | ground cardamom seeds |
| ¼ teaspoon | loosely packed saffron, crushed |

In a small saucepan, cook ricotta over low heat, stirring well. Ricotta will initially soften and liquify, but will then start to solidify within minutes. Remove from heat when ricotta is almost dry, after approximately 30 minutes.

In another saucepan, bring milk to a boil, stirring well. Lower the heat after it comes to a boil. Add sugar and simmer for 20 minutes, stirring continuously.

Using a blender or a liquidizer, blend the ricotta and milk mixture together. Pour this mixture into a bowl and add nuts, cardamom and saffron. Mix well, and pour the final mixture into an ice tray, "kulfi" molds, or 4-ounce soufflé cups. As you pour the mixture into individual containers or molds, stir the mixture frequently so that the spices and nuts are distributed evenly into the molds.

Cover with lids or plastic wrap, and freeze for at least a day. Remove into individual serving bowls prior to serving. If frozen in "kulfi" molds, gently remove with a knife into bowls or plates, and cut into several small horizontal pieces before serving.

Serves 6–8.

## Milk Powder and Flour Balls in Rose Flavored Syrup
### *—gulab jaman*

Traditionally, *gulab jaman* are made from *khoya*, which is boiled-down or solidified milk. Some cooks in India also add in a small amount of mashed potatoes to the *khoya* for additional texture. Nonfat milk powder and flour yields equally good results. These sweet balls may be served warm or chilled, after any meal. Refrigerated, leftovers will keep for several days.

| | |
|---|---|
| 2 cups | nonfat milk powder |
| 1 cup | all purpose flour |
| ¼ teaspoon | baking soda |
| 6–8 ounces | milk or water |
| 40 | cardamom seeds |
| Vegetable shortening | for frying |
| **Rose Syrup:** | |
| 3 cups | sugar |
| 6 cups | water |
| ½ teaspoon | rose essence |
| ¼ teaspoon | saffron, crushed (optional) |

Combine the milk powder, flour, and baking soda in a bowl. Gradually add milk or water, and mix well using your hands, to prepare a soft, smooth dough. Use only as much liquid as necessary to prepare the dough. If the dough remains lumpy after adding all 8 ounces of milk, apply a little shortening to your hands, and knead well. If the mixture gets too soft, such that it doesn't hold its shape, set it aside for few minutes to allow it to become firmer.

In a medium saucepan over high heat, combine water and sugar, and bring the liquid to a full boil. Boil the syrup until the sugar dissolves. Lower the heat and let the syrup simmer for a minimum of 7 more minutes. Continue to simmer the syrup over low heat, until you are ready to immerse the first batch of *jaman*, at which point you should remove the saucepan from the heat. The syrup must be hot, but not boiling when the *jaman* are immersed.

Heat about 3–inches of vegetable shortening in a *karai* or a wok to about 375 °F. Lower the heat to bring the temperature of the shortening to 355 °F. Taking about 1 teaspoon of the dough, place a single cardamom seed in the center, and shape it into a smooth round ball. Prepare several balls at a time and gently slide them into the hot vegetable shortening. (The recipe should make about 40 balls, each approximately 1–inch in diameter.)

Gently stir the balls as they fry in the shortening; they should double in size. Fry until evenly golden-brown. Remove with a slotted spoon, and drain on paper towels. Roll them gently on paper towels to absorb the shortening.

Place *jaman* balls gently into the hot syrup. The balls will swell further in the hot liquid. Gently stir in the rose essence and saffron. Remove the *jaman* to a bowl when they are soft. Serve hot or chilled.

Yield: 40.

## Sweetened Yogurt Dessert—*shreekhand*

This unique and popular Indian dessert is often served with *puri* (p. 420) in Gujarat. Though most Gujaratis prefer to use thickened yogurt as the base for this dessert, some Indian cooks in the United States use sour cream.

Small yogurt drainers are available in cookware stores. However, for a large quantity, draining can be achieved quickly in the following manner: In a clear, cool area away from direct sunlight, spread two layers of cheesecloth over several layers of paper towels or newspaper. Thinly spread the yogurt over the cheesecloth—moisture from the yogurt will seep through the cheesecloth, leaving a thick, rich curd. Allow to drain for one hour. Collect the thickened yogurt and proceed as indicated below.

Serve with any Indian meal or as desired.

| | |
|---|---|
| 8 cups | yogurt |
| 1 cup | sugar, or to taste |
| 2 teaspoons | coarsely ground cardamom seeds |
| ½ teaspoon | crushed saffron (optional) |
| 1 tablespoon | slivered unsalted pistachio |
| 1 tablespoon | slivered almonds |

Drain the yogurt following the instructions above. (Also see relevant section in dairy basics, (p. 53). Remove thickened yogurt to a sieve with a fine mesh. Add sugar, mix well in the sieve, and push the mixture through the sieve gently with the back of a spoon, into a bowl. When all the *shreekhand* has passed through the sieve, add cardamom and saffron, and mix well.

Remove to a serving bowl and garnish with pistachio and almonds.

Chill and serve.

Serves 4–6.

**Note:** You may fold in a variety of chopped fresh fruit to make *fruit shreekhand*. My family particularly loves finely chopped fresh mango pieces. Importantly, also note that combining sugar and thickened yogurt without the use of a net or a mesh does not produce similarly good results.

## Sweet Yogurt Dessert with Black Pepper—*matho*

This yogurt dessert does not need much effort. Its simplicity and lightness complements many heavy Indian dishes. Serve *matho* as a light dessert with any meal.

| | |
|---|---|
| 6 cups | yogurt |
| 4 tablespoons | sugar, or to taste |
| ¼ teaspoon | salt, or to taste |
| ¼ teaspoon | coarsely ground black pepper |

Drain the yogurt following instructions on page (58). In a glass bowl, combine thickened yogurt with sugar, salt and black pepper. Chill and serve.

Serves 3–4.

## Almond Fudge—*badam barfi*

Once the almonds have been blanched, this delicate almond and saffron-flavored fudge takes about half an hour to prepare. Bearing resemblance to famous Bombay *badampuri*—thin, round almond "cakes" flavored with saffron and pistachio—this dessert makes an excellent gift any time of the year, and will keep for several days at room temperature.

| | |
|---|---|
| 3 cups | almonds, blanched |
| 1 ½ cups | sugar, or to taste |
| 1 ½ cups | water |
| 1 cup | milk |
| 1 teaspoon | saffron, crushed |
| 1 tablespoon | coarsely ground cardamom seeds |
| ½ teaspoon | nutmeg |
| 1 cup | nonfat milk powder |
| 2 tablespoons | clarified butter (*ghee*) (p. 59) |
| 2 tablespoons | finely slivered, unsalted pistachio |
| 2 tablespoons | slivered almonds **or** |
| 3 | silver leaves (p. 30), optional |

**Blanching Almonds:**

Place almonds in a saucepan with just enough water to cover the nuts. Place the saucepan over high heat, bring to a boil, and lower heat slightly. Allow the almonds to boil for 10 seconds. Remove from heat and set aside for 5 minutes.

Drain and discard water from the almonds. Holding each almond between the thumb and forefinger, squeeze gently. The nut should slide out of its skin. Allow peeled almonds to cool completely. Grind almonds in a food processor fitted with a metal blade until they achieve a fine texture, similar to fine farina or "Cream of Wheat."

**Dessert:**

In a large saucepan, combine sugar and water. Place the saucepan over high heat. As soon as the sugar melts, start stirring the mixture. Continue to cook for 15 minutes, stirring frequently. Add milk and saffron, and bring the mixture to a boil. Adjust heat to prevent overboiling; stir well, and cook for about 7 minutes.

Add ground almonds, and continue to cook while constantly stirring. The mixture will harden in about 7 minutes. Add clarified butter, mix well and cook for 3 more minutes. Pick up a little of the mixture with a spoon and shape it into a tiny ball. If it holds, the fudge is ready. If not, cook a little longer until firm, about 3 more minutes.

Add cardamom, nutmeg and milk powder, mix well and remove the mixture onto a cutting board covered with wax paper. Spread the mixture with the back of a spoon into a layer about ½–inch thick, keeping the shape square. Garnish with pistachio and almonds, or gently spread silver leaves over the dessert. Cut into about 1 ¼–inch squares. Allow to cool. Gently lift the squares to separate, and store them in a tightly covered container, in the refrigerator.

Yield: Approximately 40 pieces.

## Bulgur with Milk and Nuts—*fadano doodhpaak*

Indian stores sell bulgur in three grades: small, medium and large. Medium-grade bulgur is best used for this recipe as it cooks quickly while retaining a chewy texture. This light and nutty-flavored pudding may be served after any spicy meal.

| | |
|---|---|
| 2 teaspoons | unsalted margarine or butter |
| ½ cup | bulgur |
| 4 cups | milk |
| 5 tablespoons | sugar, or to taste |
| 15 | unsalted pistachio, slivered |
| 2 tablespoons | slivered almonds |
| 1 teaspoon | coarsely ground cardamom seeds |

In a medium saucepan, heat the margarine, over low heat. Add the bulgur and stir well. Cook until the bulgur changes color to off-white, approximately 3 minutes. Note that the bulgur may not evenly change color.

Add milk and raise the heat to high. Cook, stirring well, for about 15 minutes or until the bulgur is soft. Add sugar, and cook for another minute. Remove from heat and let cool. Add pistachios, almonds and cardamom; mix well and chill before serving. Dessert will thicken as it cools. Serves 4–6.

## Rice and Split Pigeon Peas with Saffron—*beeranj*

This recipe is usually made using either split pigeon peas (*toor dal*) or split chickpeas (*chana dal*), though common yellow split peas may also be used. *Beeranj* may be cooked on the stovetop, in an oven, or in a rice cooker.

This dry dessert is an excellent accompaniment to meals in which rice is not served as a main course. For a lower fat, non-dairy version, substitute non-dairy margarine for the butter.

| | |
|---|---|
| 1 cup | split pigeon peas (*toor dal*), washed |
| 2 cups | *basmati* rice, washed |
| 2 tablespoons | unsalted butter or margarine |
| 15 | cloves |
| 6 one–inch sticks | cinnamon |
| 4 cups | water |
| ½ teaspoon | saffron, crumbled |
| 2 ½ cups | sugar, or to taste |
| 1 tablespoon | coarsely ground cardamom seeds |
| 2 tablespoons | blanched almonds, for garnish |

Pick over and wash (see note, p. 336) *dal*. Set aside. Over medium heat, heat butter in a saucepan; add cloves and cinnamon. When cloves start to swell, stir in *dal*. Add water and saffron and raise the heat. When the mixture comes to a boil, add rice, mix well, and cook on high heat, for about 15 minutes. Lower the heat to medium.

When the *beeranj* is just about cooked, add sugar and cardamom and mix gently. Cover and cook on low heat, until almost dry, about 7 minutes. Check to see if the *dal* is cooked through. If not, cover and cook a little longer.

Remove to a platter and serve hot, garnished with blanched almonds. Serves 8–10.

## *Paneer* Patty in Sweet, Cream Sauce—*ras malai*

Popular all over India, this recipe has many variations, calling for different amounts of spices, nuts, or saffron. The recipe below is authentic, and results in an exquisite and impressive dessert. Note that I have substituted half and half for the traditional Buffalo milk used in India!

*Paneer*:

| | |
|---|---|
| ½ gallon | whole milk |
| 4 tablespoons | lemon juice |
| 3 tablespoons | sugar |

**Cream Sauce:**

| | |
|---|---|
| ½ gallon | half and half |
| 5 tablespoons | sugar, or to taste |
| 1 cup | milk |

**Sugar Syrup:**

| | |
|---|---|
| 1-¾ cups | sugar |
| 8 cups | water |
| 1 tablespoon | all purpose flour |

**Garnish:**

| | |
|---|---|
| 2 teaspoons | coarsely ground cardamom seeds |
| 2 tablespoons | unsalted pistachio, sliced |

*Paneer:*

In a medium stainless-steel saucepan, bring milk to a full boil. Once boiling, lower the heat and gradually add the lemon juice. Within a few minutes, the milk will separate into milk solids and whey (p. 60). Turn off the heat and cover the saucepan. Allow to cool for 10 minutes. Line a mesh strainer with a double layer of cheesecloth and pour the milk solids (*paneer*) and whey through. Remove the whey. (The whey may be used later in lieu of water for cooking rice or other dishes). Gather the four ends of the cheesecloth, forming a bundle. Squeeze out as much of the whey as possible from the bundle, using your hands.

Place the bundle on several layers of paper towels. Place a heavy weight on top of the bundle to squeeze the remaining whey from the *paneer*. (I use a large saucepan filled with water). Set aside for about 30 minutes. In the meantime, prepare the sauce and sugar syrup.

After 30 minutes, remove the *paneer* to a platter or a cutting board and knead for about 5 minutes until smooth. The *paneer* should be free of any grain. You may alternatively use a food processor fitted with a metal blade for kneading; process for about 1 ½ minutes or until a smooth consistency is achieved. Divide the *paneer* into 15 portions. Shape each portion into a patty in your palms. Make a deep dimple in the center, and fill with ¼ teaspoon of sugar. Pinch the ends shut and shape into a smooth patty, enclosing sugar in the center. Set aside. Repeat until all are ready.

**Cream Sauce:**

Bring half-and-half to a full boil, in a large non-stick saucepan, over high heat. Lower the heat to medium when the half-and-half comes to a boil, and cook, stirring every few minutes, until the liquid is reduced down to half the quantity, about 30 minutes. Scrape the milk residue on the sides of pan, and stir it into the sauce, for texture. Add sugar, and simmer until the sugar has dissolved. Remove from heat and set aside.

Note: To cut down the fat content in this recipe, you may use a quarter gallon each of half-and-half and whole milk instead of exclusively half-and-half. In this case, it will take longer, approximately 45 minutes to boil down the mixture.

**Sugar Syrup:**

In a large saucepan, over high heat, bring sugar and water to a full boil. Lower the heat to medium when the water comes to a boil. Mix flour with about 3 tablespoons of water, and add to the syrup. (The addition of flour will prevent the *paneer* patties from sticking to each other). Bring syrup to a full boil again, and add the *paneer* patties, one at a time. When the syrup comes to a full boil after adding the patties, lower the heat to medium-low, and cover the pot. Boil until the patties double in size, about 20 minutes.

Pour one cup of milk into a serving platter. Remove the sweetened *paneer* patties from the syrup with a slotted spoon and gently arrange them on the platter over the milk, leaving a little space between each patty. (The milk will prevent the patties from sticking to the bottom). Let the patties rest for 5 minutes in the platter. Spoon the cream sauce over the patties.

Garnish with cardamom and pistachios. Chill *ras malai* for at least six hours before serving.

Yield: 15.

# Variation 1: Shortened Method

This fantastic shortcut to *ras malai* is much less time-consuming, taking an average 30–45 minutes to prepare.

**Patties:**

| | |
|---|---|
| 1 (15-ounce) container | part-skim ricotta cheese |
| ½ cup | sugar, or to taste |
| 1 teaspoon | ground cardamom seeds |
| ½ cup | nonfat milk powder |

**Cream Sauce:**

| | |
|---|---|
| 1 (15-ounce) container | part-skim ricotta cheese |
| 2 (12-ounce) cans | evaporated milk |
| 1 (14-ounce) can | sweetened condensed milk |

**Garnish:**

| | |
|---|---|
| 2 tablespoons | slivered almonds |
| 2 tablespoons | sliced pistachio nuts |
| 1 teaspoon | ground cardamom seeds |

**Patties:**

In a small saucepan, cook one container of ricotta over low heat, stirring every few minutes. Ricotta will initially soften and become watery, but after about 20 minutes it will start to solidify. As soon as it solidifies, add sugar, and cook for just a few seconds, or until the sugar has dissolved. Remove the saucepan from heat, and set aside to cool. Add cardamom and milk powder, mixing well. Divide the mixture into 10 portions, and shape each portion into a smooth round patty. Set aside.

**Cream Sauce:**

In another small saucepan, cook another container of ricotta, as above until dry, about 20 minutes. Remove to a food processor fitted with a metal blade. Add one can of evaporated milk and one can of condensed milk, and blend the mixture until smooth; remove to a bowl. Add the second can of evaporated milk and mix well.

Spread a couple of serving spoons of the sauce in a flat serving dish, then arrange the patties about a ¼–inch apart. Top with the remaining milk and ricotta sauce. Garnish with nuts and cardamom. Chill and serve. Yield: 10.

**Note:** If you do not wish to use ricotta for making the thickened milk, you may follow the directions for the latter in the preceding recipe and serve ricotta patties with the authentic cream sauce.

# Walnut Pudding—*akhrotni basudi*

This pudding is both extremely delicious and simple to prepare. I made this every few weeks at *The Ganges*. Although I recommend using pure orange extract, you may substitute an extract or flavoring of your choice. Serve chilled, after any meal.

| | |
|---|---|
| 2 pounds | part-skim ricotta cheese |
| 1 pound | walnuts, coarsely chopped |
| 1 (14-ounce) can | sweetened condensed milk |
| 2 (12-ounce) cans | evaporated milk |
| 2 teaspoons | coarsely ground cardamom seeds |
| 1 teaspoon | orange extract |

In a small saucepan, heat ricotta over medium heat, stirring well. Cook for about 20 minutes until most of the fluids evaporate. Alternatively, cook ricotta in a covered container in the microwave, on high heat, for about 18 minutes, stopping to stir every 5 or 6 minutes.

In a food processor fitted with a metal blade, coarsely chop the walnuts (just a few rotations will do the job). Remove to a bowl. In the same processor, combine the cooked ricotta, condensed milk and one can of evaporated milk. Blend until smooth. Fold this mixture into the walnuts, add one more can of evaporated milk, cardamom, and orange extract, and mix well. Chill and serve.

Serves 6–8.

## Amaranth Pudding—*rajagarani kheer*

Amaranth is available in most health food stores. The nutty flavor of this dessert is enhanced by the addition of cardamom and nutmeg. For variation, you may substitute vanilla extract for cardamom and nutmeg.

| | |
|---|---|
| 4 cups | milk, (preferably lowfat) |
| 1 cup | amaranth grains |
| 3 tablespoons | sugar, or to taste |
| 1 teaspoon | ground cardamom seeds |
| ¼ teaspoon | nutmeg |
| 1 tablespoon (each) | ground almonds and unsalted pistachio (optional) |
| 1 tablespoon | ground cashews (optional) |

In a medium saucepan, bring milk to a full boil, over high heat, and add the amaranth grains. As soon as the milk comes to a boil, lower the heat to medium, and continue cooking the amaranth, stirring well every few minutes. Cook until the grain becomes translucent, like tapioca, about 30 minutes.

Add sugar and continue cooking for about 10 more minutes. Add the cardamom, nutmeg and nuts, mix well, and remove from heat. The pudding will thicken as it cools—if desired, add additional milk and mix well. Chill and serve. Garnish with slivered or sliced almonds before serving, if desired.

Serves 4–6.

## Carrot *Halwa*—gajar halwa

Using nonfat milk powder instead of either traditional *khoya* (solidified whole milk), or ricotta cheese (as I did in my first book), this is an easy to prepare, extremely delicious recipe. Caramelizing the sugar adds flavor and a deep, reddish color to this dish. In India, this dessert is often garnished with microthin leaves of silver.

| | |
|---|---|
| 4 ½ cups (about 6) | coarsely grated carrots |
| 1 tablespoon | unsalted butter |
| ¾ cup | sugar or to taste |
| 10 tablespoons | water |
| ¾ cup | nonfat milk powder |
| 1 teaspoon | coarsely ground cardamom seeds |
| 2 tablespoons | slivered almonds or pistachios |

Trim and discard stems from, lightly peel and coarsely grate carrots. Set aside.

In a medium saucepan over medium heat, melt butter and add carrots. Stir well, and reduce heat to low.

While the carrots are cooking, place sugar in a small saucepan over high heat and continually stir with a wooden spoon. The sugar will start turning into lumps. Continue cooking and stirring until the sugar turns into a golden syrup, about 6 minutes. Remove the pan from the heat and immediately begin to add about 4 tablespoons of water, a little at a time, while constantly stirring. Return the pan to high heat, add the remaining water and continue to cook. Remove from heat when the mixture comes to a boil, set aside.

Add cardamom to carrots and raise the heat to medium. Stir well and cook carrots for 3 minutes. Add sugar syrup, mixing well, and continue to cook for 3 more minutes. Add milk powder, mix well and cook until the syrup is absorbed, approximately 4 minutes. Garnish with slivered almonds or pistachios before serving. Serve either warm or chilled. Serves 3–4.

## Stuffed, Half-Moon Shaped Pastry—*ghughra*

I have received several requests from my clients at *The Ganges* to include this recipe in my book. Surprise your Indian friends by making this around the time of *Diwali*—the Indian festival of lights, when *ghughra* with either *sooji* or coconut are traditionally made.

**Stuffing:**

| | |
|---|---|
| 6 tablespoons | clarified butter (*ghee*) (p. 59) |
| 1 cup | thin *sooji* (p. 42) |
| 1 tablespoon | milk |
| ½ cup | powdered sugar, or to taste |
| 1 teaspoon | coarsely ground cardamom seeds |
| ¼ teaspoon | ground nutmeg |

**Casing:**

| | |
|---|---|
| ¾ cup | unbleached all purpose flour |
| 2 tablespoons | clarified butter (*ghee*) |
| 5 ½ tablespoons | warm milk, or as needed |
| 24 | cloves |
| vegetable shortening | for frying |

**Stuffing:**

In a small saucepan, heat 6 tablespoons of clarified butter, over medium heat. Lower the heat and add the *sooji*. Cook stirring well, until the *sooji* is golden-brown, about 5 minutes. Quickly add one tablespoon milk, mix well, and cook for 2 minutes, continuing to stir. Remove the pan from the heat and allow to cool completely. Add the sugar, cardamom and nutmeg, and mix well. Taste, and adjust the sugar to taste.

**Casing:**

In a mixing bowl, combine the flour and 2 tablespoons of clarified butter. Gradually add the milk to create a soft, smooth dough; add more milk as needed. Knead for about 2 minutes. Divide the dough into 24 portions.

Shape each portion into a smooth patty. Repeat until all the patties are ready. Flatten and roll each patty into an approximately 3–inch circle. Lift the circle and place it in your open, cupped hand. Gently fold the circle, taking care not to flatten it, and join the edges partially—no more than mid-way along the edges of the circle—to create an open pocket into which the stuffing may be added (illus. p. 468). Place about 1 tablespoon of stuffing in the center. Tightly pinch the edges shut. Flute the edges of the *ghughra* using your thumb and index finger, or use a fork or a tailor's marker to trim the edge. Stick a single clove into the center of the turnover, such that the head of the clove protrudes. Set each pastry aside and cover them with a damp cloth until ready to fry.

In a wok or a *karai*, heat about 3–inches of vegetable shortening. Lower the temperature of the shortening to 365 °F, and gently slide a few *ghughra* in the heated oil. Keep the heat low to prevent the *ghughra* from browning too quickly. Fry the pastries, turning once or twice in the process, until they are golden on both sides. Remove to a platter lined with paper towels. Repeat until all the *ghughra* are done. Store in a container when cool. Yield: 24.

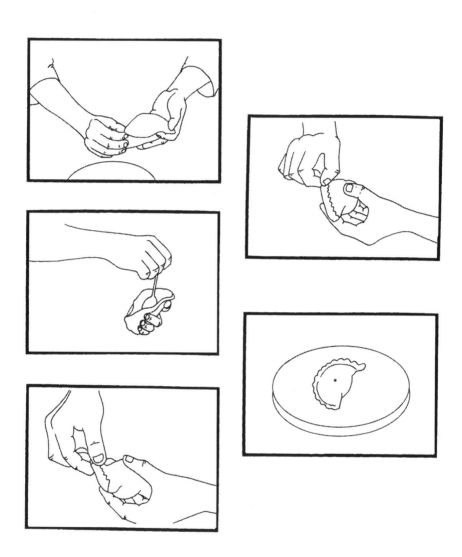

*Method for Preparing Ghughra*

# Stuffed Round Pastry—*ghari*

Two types of *ghari* are traditionally served in Indian cuisine; I have included only one recipe in this book, since the second type is complicated and especially time consuming. Both varieties are equally popular around *Diwali* time.

The type of *ghari* described below is stuffed with a mixture that somewhat resembles *laadu* (p. 447). My son loves this recipe.

**Stuffing:**

| | |
|---|---|
| 4 tablespoons | clarified butter (*ghee*) (p. 59) |
| 1 cup | chickpea flour |
| 3 tablespoons | powdered sugar |
| 1 teaspoon | coarsely ground cardamom seeds (optional) |

**Casing:**

As in *ghughra* recipe (p. 466)

| | |
|---|---|
| 12 | cloves |

**Stuffing:**

Heat the clarified butter in a small saucepan over medium heat. Stir in chickpea flour. Lower the heat and cook, stirring well, until the flour deepens in color to dark gold, about 7 minutes. Keep stirring and cooking until the mixture is very soft, about 20 minutes. Remove from the heat and allow to cool completely. Add the sugar and cardamom. Mix well, and divide into 12 portions. Shape each portion into a smooth, round patty and set aside.

**Casing:**

Prepare the casing dough as in the preceding recipe (p. 466). Divide into 24 portions, shape each into a smooth, round patty, and repeat until all the portions are ready. Roll each patty into a round circle about 2–inches in diameter; repeat until all the patties are rolled. Cover and set aside.

Place a single chickpea flour patty in the center of a *puri*. Sandwich another rolled *puri* over the stuffing and pinch the edges tightly to encase the chickpea flour patty. Flute the *ghari* using your thumb and index finger, or use a fork or tailor's marker to trim the edges. Insert one clove in the center. Set the pastries aside and cover with a damp cloth, until all are ready to fry.

In a wok or a *karai*, heat about 3–inches of vegetable shortening. Lower the temperature of the shortening to 365 °F, and gently slide a few *ghari* in the heated oil. Keep the heat low to prevent the *ghari* from browning too quickly. Fry the pastries, turning once or twice in the process, until they are golden on both sides. Remove to a platter lined with paper towels. Repeat until all the *ghari* are done. Store in a container when cool. Yield: 12.

# Non-Dairy Desserts

## Unripe Mango Dessert—*khandkeri*

This very typical Gujarati desert is almost prepared every day during mango season. It may be eaten while still warm, accompanying the main meal or chilled and served as dessert at the end of the meal. With the main meal, it is usually served with *chapati* (p. 404) or *puri* (p. 420). When chilled, it will become thick in consistency.

| | |
|---|---|
| 1 medium | unripe mango, peeled, sliced, steamed |
| 1 tablespoon | unsalted margarine |
| 2 tablespoons | wheat flour or farina (Cream of Wheat) |
| 3 | cloves, coarsely ground |
| 3 cups | water |
| 3 tablespoons | sugar, or to taste |
| 1 teaspoon | coarsely ground cardamom seeds |

Prepare the steamer (p. 50). Wash, peel and slice the mango into about ¼–inch thick slices. Discard the stone, if any. Steam the slices for about 5 minutes. Remove and set aside.

In a medium stainless-steel saucepan, heat the margarine, over medium heat, and add the flour or Cream of Wheat. Lower the heat and cook the flour, stirring well, until slightly golden, about 5 minutes. Add cloves, water, and sugar and bring the mixture to a boil, over high heat, stirring well, to ensure that the mixture does not become lumpy. Lower the heat again when boiling, and simmer for 5 minutes.

Add the sliced, steamed mangoes and simmer for about 5 more minutes. Remove from the heat, add cardamom and mix well. Serve hot or chilled.

Serves 4.

# Farina (Cream of Wheat) with Cardamom and Saffron
## —*kesari sheera*

This dessert is always offered to deities at the *Satyanarayana puja*, a prayer ritual during which Vishnu and his consort Lakshmi are worshipped. As previously mentioned, *Vaishnavas* make sweet offerings to the deity made with milk and clarified butter, but never with water or oil. In the following recipe, however, I have substituted margarine and water in order to make this dessert light and nondairy. While Indian deities do not have to worry about either their weight or their heart-health, we unfortunately do!

| | |
|---|---|
| 1 cup | farina (Cream of Wheat) |
| 4 tablespoons | unsalted margarine |
| 2 cups | water |
| 1 cup | sugar, or to taste |
| ½ teaspoon | ground nutmeg |
| ¼ teaspoon | crushed saffron |
| 2 teaspoons | ground cardamom seeds |

In a small saucepan, over low heat, melt the margarine. Add farina and cook, stirring frequently for about 10 minutes, or until the farina turns a golden color.

While the farina cooks, boil the water and sugar together in a separate saucepan. When the sugar has completely dissolved, add the mixture to the farina. Add nutmeg, saffron and half the cardamom and raise the heat. Cook, stirring constantly, until the mixture becomes thick, with a porridge-like consistency. Remove from heat. The pudding will thicken further as it cools.

*Sheera* can be served hot or chilled. Garnish with the remaining cardamom, and if desired, with sliced almonds or pistachios.

*Sheera* will keep 4 days refrigerated. It can also be frozen, and reheated before serving.

Serves: 4-6.

## Buckwheat *Halwa*—*fafar sheera*

While I was searching for chestnut flour in a health-food store, I was advised to try using buckwheat flour as a substitute. To my surprise, the texture and taste of the following dessert made with buckwheat is exactly that of the authentic version made with chestnut flour! Though the dessert may appear glutinous while cooking, it acquires a much drier and more appealing texture when cool. Serve reheated, if desired.

| | |
|---|---|
| 4 tablespoons | unsalted margarine |
| 1 cup | buckwheat flour |
| 2 cups | water |
| ¾ cup | sugar, or to taste |
| 2 teaspoons | orange extract |
| 2 teaspoons | cardamom seeds, coarsely ground |
| 2 tablespoons | slivered almonds, for garnish |

Heat margarine in a small saucepan and add the buckwheat flour. Cook on medium heat, stirring well until the flour changes color to dark gold, about 7 minutes.

In another saucepan, combine sugar and water and bring the mixture to a boil. Add the mixture to the buckwheat flour, and mix well. Add orange extract and cardamom, and cook, stirring well, until the *halwa* thickens like porridge (about 7 minutes). Remove and set aside to cool. Serve garnished with almonds.

Serves 4–6.

## Rice Pudding with Coconut—*kopra doodhpaak*

At *The Ganges,* whenever I received same-day requests for a non-dairy dessert, I would quickly prepare this recipe. It tastes better when chilled (to hasten cooling, spread the pudding on a flat platter, chill over ice, and then refrigerate). The grated coconut becomes pleasantly crunchy when cooked, and the brown rice adds a dense, chewy texture to the pudding. This dessert keeps in the refrigerator for about 5 days.

| | |
|---|---|
| ½ cup | brown rice, washed |
| 6 cups | water, or as required |
| 1 teaspoon | coarsely ground cardamom seeds |
| 4 tablespoons | sugar, or to taste |
| 1 (13 ½-ounce) can | coconut milk |
| ½ teaspoon | saffron, crushed |
| 2 tablespoons | unsweetened, coarsely grated coconut |

In a medium saucepan, over high heat, cook rice with water until soft, about 30 minutes. Lower the heat and add the cardamom, sugar and coconut milk. Stir well and simmer for 10 more minutes, or until the rice is soft.

Crush saffron and add it to the pudding. Add the grated coconut and cook for 1 more minute. Remove from heat and set aside to cool; pudding will thicken as it cools. Chill prior to serving.

Serves 6–8.

**Note:** The above recipe can be made without processed sugar with the substitution of dry fruit; I like to use unsweetened, dry papaya pieces.

## Cashew Diamonds—*kaju katni*

This simple, yet unique, dessert or sweetmeat can be offered as a gift, or served after any meal. It will keep at room temperature for a few days, and longer, up to 3 weeks, when refrigerated.

| | |
|---|---|
| ¼ cup | water |
| ½ cup | sugar |
| 2 cups | finely ground cashew nuts |
| 1 teaspoon | ground cardamom seeds |
| 2 | silver leaves (optional) |

Heat water in a small saucepan and add sugar. Stir well and boil on high heat for about 7 minutes, until the syrup thickens. To taste for appropriate thickness, place a drop of syrup on a plate, cover with your index finger. A tiny thread should form between the plate and your index finger as you separate them slowly.

Add ground cashews and cardamom, and mix well. Remove the mixture onto a cutting board covered with wax paper. Flatten the mixture, cover again with another piece of wax paper, and using a rolling pin, roll it into a thin slab, about ¼–inch thick. Remove wax paper and spread silver leaves over it and cut into squares or diamond shapes. Remove gently with a spatula, and store in a covered container. If you do not have access to silver leaves, press some chopped pistachios over the surface of *kaju katni* before cutting. Serve as desired.

Makes: Approximately 20 pieces.

## Date Rolls—*khajur pilla*

This recipe is simple to prepare and will keep for weeks. It makes a good gift as well. Dates available in this country are usually very soft, therefore eliminating the need for much added fat.

| | |
|---|---|
| 1 tablespoon | unsalted margarine |
| 2 pounds | pitted dates, chopped coarsely |
| ¼ cup | coarsely ground almonds |
| 2 tablespoons | coarsely ground unsalted pistachio |
| 2 tablespoons | coarsely ground cashew nuts |
| 2 teaspoons | ground cardamom seeds |
| 1 tablespoon | slivered or blanched almonds, for garnish |

Heat margarine in a medium saucepan over medium-low heat, and add dates. Lower the heat, and cook for 5 minutes or until the dates are soft. Add the next 4 ingredients, including cardamom; mix well, and cook for another minute.

Remove the mixture to a cutting board and allow to cool. Shape the mass into a roll or a cylinder about 1 ½–inches in diameter. If it is still too soft, let cool for a few minutes longer before shaping. Cover with foil, and refrigerate. After about six hours, remove from refrigerator, unwrap, and cut the roll into about ½–inch thick rounds. Press one blanched almond on one side to decorate each roll.

Makes: Approximately 20 rounds.

## Bulgur Dessert—*lapsi*

*Lapsi* is made on many special occasions in Gujarat and is usually served along with the meal, rather than at the end. I prepared it often at *The Ganges*, and my customers loved the chewy texture of bulgur flavored with cardamom, cinnamon and cloves. This dessert may be made in large quantities and then refrigerated for several days; it can also be frozen and reheated before serving.

| | |
|---|---|
| 2 tablespoons | unsalted margarine |
| 1 ½ cups | bulgur |
| 3 cups | water |
| 1 cup | sugar, or to taste |
| 2 teaspoons | coarsely ground cardamom seeds |
| 1 ½ teaspoons | ground cinnamon |
| ¾ teaspoon | ground cloves |
| 2 tablespoons | slivered almonds, for garnish |

Heat margarine in a medium saucepan over medium heat, and add the bulgur. Cook, stirring frequently, until bulgur changes color, about 5 minutes. Lower the heat, add water and sugar, and cook for about 15 minutes, until the bulgur is soft and the most of the water has been absorbed. Add cardamom, cinnamon and cloves; mix well, and cook for 2 more minutes. Remove from heat, and serve garnished with almonds.
Serves 6–8.
**Note:** This dessert may also be prepared without margarine. Simply-toast the bulgur until it changes color and proceed.

# Fruits as Dessert

## Cantaloupe—*sakkarteti*

In India, cantaloupe, when in season, is served alongside the main meal of the day. The cool fruit is a refreshing addition to spicy food.

| | |
|---|---|
| 1 medium | cantaloupe |
| 2 teaspoons | sugar, or to taste |
| ½ teaspoon | ground cardamom seeds |

Peel the cantaloupe, cut it into halves, remove the seeds, and cut the fruit into about ½-inch cubes. Add sugar and cardamom and mix well. Chill and serve.
Serves 4.

## Papaya—papaya with cumin

Papaya is, of course, wonderful when eaten alone. Sprinkling very small amounts of salt and cumin on the fruit adds a distinctive taste to the sweet fruit.

| | |
|---|---|
| 1 medium | ripe papaya |
| ½ teaspoon | salt, or to taste |
| 1 teaspoon | toasted, coarsely ground cumin seeds |

Peel papaya, cut into halves and remove the seeds. Cut the fruit into about ½-inch cubes. Add salt and cumin and mix well. Serve chilled.
Serves 4.

## Watermelon—*tarbuch*

I often sprinkle rose syrup onto cubed watermelon prior to serving as a dessert.

| | |
|---|---|
| 1 medium | seedless watermelon |
| 1 tablespoon | rose syrup (p. 496) |

Cut watermelon into bite-sized pieces and sprinkle rose syrup over the fruit. Chill before serving.

Serves 6–8.

## Thick Mango Juice—*kerino ras*

The variety of mangoes available in India is enormous. I have only recently noticed different varieties of mangoes becoming available in the United States. In India, especially in Gujarat, mango juice is very popular during mango season, and is usually served with either *puri* (p. 420) or *chapati* (p. 404.) Cooling and very light, the juice is both refreshing and delicious. My children used to make a meal out of hot *puri* dipped in mango juice.

In India, two major categories of mangoes are available: one for extracting juice and one for cutting and eating. Since the juice-variety of mango is very fibrous, the juice is traditionally extracted by hand and strained through a sieve to remove the fibers. In the U.S., I simply peel and chop up any variety of ripe mango, and liquidize in a blender. The fruit's fibers blend into the juice, making it very thick. Some Indians add milk or water to thin the juice. Some Gujaratis also add ginger powder and a dash of *ghee* to the juice before serving, as they believe that the addition of these ingredients enhances the juice's digestibility.

| | |
|---|---|
| 4 medium-large | fully ripe mangoes |
| 1 cup | milk or water (optional) |

Wash and trim the mangoes. Peel and remove the pulp to a bowl. Discard the stones. In a liquidizer or a blender, liquidize the pulp, adding milk or water, if desired. Juice without milk or water will be quite thick. Remove to a bowl or jug. Chill before serving.
Serves 4–6.

# BEVERAGES

Indian Tea—*chai*
Indian Spiced Tea—*masala chai*
Tea with Mint and Cardamom—*fudinani chai*
Tea without Tea Leaves—*ukalo*
Flour with Jaggery and Water—*raab*
Buttermilk—*chhash* or plain *lassi*
Buttermilk with Cumin and Mustard—*vaghareli chhash*
Buttermilk with Mango—*aam lassi*
Buttermilk with Papaya—*papaya lassi*
Buttermilk with Strawberries—strawberry *lassi*
Buttermilk with Saffron—*kesar lassi* or *piyush*
Rose *Lassi*—*gulab lassi*
Yogurt with Milk—*golvo*
*Mahashivratri* Drink—*thandai*
Rose Syrup—*gulabnu* syrup
Rose *Sherbat*—*gulabnu sherbat*
Rose Milk—*gulabnu doodh*
Milk with Saffron and Nuts—*kesar mevanu doodh*
Lemonade, Indian Style—*limbunu sherbat*
Watermelon Juice—*tarbuchno ras*
Milk with Rose, Tapioca and Vermicelli—*falooda*
Tamarind Aperitif—*jaljeera* or *jeerapani*

# Beverages

Western meals are a celebration of food *and* drink. The selection of beverages, from *apéritif*, wines complementing the different courses of a fine meal, to *digestif*, or after-dinner drink, requires a sense of how individual flavors combine with various foods. To balance the already complex interplay of spices in dishes composing an Indian meal, beverages served with Indian food tend to be simple. Most Indians prefer to drink only water, milk or *lassi*, a cool, frothy yogurt drink, with or after their meals. Called *Chhash* in Gujarati, *lassi* is regarded as a digestive aid, to be consumed after a meal. *Lassi* is commonly referred to as "buttermilk" in English; however, it must be distinguished from the supermarket variety, as *lassi* is in fact, a whipped yogurt drink.

Beer has, of late, become more commonplace in restaurants in India: but for the most part beverages remain non-alcoholic in many Indian homes. One exception to this is a drink similar to wine (although with a lower alcohol per volume ratio) produced in India and used in ayurvedic medicine for the treatment of gastric problems. The drink is called *drakshasava*, from the Hindi word for grapes, *draksh*. I remember feigning stomach aches as a teenager so that I could have a small amount of this delicious potion!

From sidewalk tea stands, where it is served steaming hot in tiny clay cups, to the most elegant of settings, tea is perhaps the most popular beverage through most of India. Redolent with cardamom and cinnamon, tinged with black pepper, and fragrant with thick chunks of ginger, mint leaves or lemon grass, sweet *chai* is served with milk in the morning, afternoon and evening. Coffee is the hot beverage of choice in South India, prepared by boiling powdered coffee with water, milk and sugar. Coffee is often served with ground cardamom in other parts of India, including Gujarat.

Many Indian beverages, in fact, contain either milk or yogurt. To these, fruits, nuts, herbs, and a few aromatic spices (mostly cinnamon, cardamom, saffron or cumin), are sometimes added. Bottled milk drinks flavored with saffron and pistachio, mango and cardamom, or essence of rose, are available all over India, and are popular with both adults and children. I prefer to make my own drinks, though, using freshly ground spices and fruits. *Kesar meva nu doodh* (p. 497), milk heated with cardamom and saffron, and then sweetened and sprinkled with ground pistachios and almonds, has always been a favorite with my children. Rose *sherbat* (p. 496), sweet syrup made with rose essence, is divine in milk chilled with a few ice cubes. When homemade cornstarch noodles are added to this beverage, it is called *falooda* (p. 499), a delicious combination that also makes a light finale to an elaborate meal.

Fresh-squeezed juices are also very popular throughout the year. Juice stands on streets offer tempting selections such as fresh sugarcane, pomegranate, and watermelon juices, as well as blends of every fruit imaginable. Late-night trips to these stands during summer months are not uncommon. Also quite popular, though perhaps more so in the South, is *neera*, which is the sweet sap of the coconut tree. Interestingly, if *neera* is not consumed within 12 hours of tapping, it ferments into a drink called *toddy*. When my husband and I traveled to the Seychelles, I actually tried a little *toddy* and found it to be quite sour.

Coconut water is also popular around many of the beaches of India. The vendor slashes off the top of a fresh green coconut with a sharp knife and hands the coconut base over to the customer with a straw. The fruit's water is very cooling and sweet; the vendor will scrape out the *malai,* the cool, creamy coconut pulp for you, after you have consumed the water. My mother believed that coconut water is very good for various kidney ailments.

Rose *sherbat* mixed with milk and shaved ice is also very popular in India. Many families either make this syrup themselves or buy it ready-made to serve to unexpected guests during the summer months. I occasionally made this beverage at *The Ganges* to surprise my guests. Many beverages like *mangola* (made from mango juice) and *falsa* (made from the berry-like fruit) are also popular in India and are actually sold readymade in bottles. Even Ganges water is sold in bottles! As a matter of fact, one of my customers, John Gilmore, touched me deeply by bringing me such a bottle from Hardwar.

Ganges water is mainly used in *pooja* rituals. The Ganges river is supposed to be quite clear and unpolluted at the point where it drops from the mountains. The bottled water is quite clean and is probably collected from somewhere around Gangotri. By the time it reaches, Varanasi, the famous holy city, however, the water in the Ganges is highly polluted. Nevertheless, devout Hindus flock to Varanasi to bathe in the holy water, believing that a dip in the river absolves one of all sins. My daughter, Bella, had a dip in the river, on a trip to Varanasi after college, and before medical school. After going to medical school she couldn't believe she did that.

# Indian Tea—*chai*

This tea is sold at every train station or every bus stop , and street-side corner in India. Kept perpetually boiling, the roadside version of *chai* can be quite strong. In some large hotels, however, tea is still served British style, without the familiar boiling ritual.

| | |
|---|---|
| 3 cups | water |
| 1 ½ cups | milk, preferably lowfat |
| 6 teaspoons | sugar, or to taste |
| 4 teaspoons | loose black tea leaves |

In a small saucepan, combine water, milk and sugar, and bring the liquid to a full boil. When the mixture comes to a boil, add tea leaves. Remove the saucepan immediately from the heat and cover for 2 minutes. Strain and serve.

Yield: Approximately 4 cups.

## Indian Spiced Tea—*masala chai*

Hot *Chai*, as it was called at *The Ganges,* is a cup of hot tea with spices. I made the tea very mild, and sweetened with honey instead of sugar.

The recipe below is the one my family makes at home, using the same spices that most Gujarati households employ in their morning tea.

| | |
|---|---|
| 3 cups | water |
| 1 cup | milk, preferably lowfat |
| 6 teaspoons | sugar, or to taste |
| ¼ teaspoon | ground cardamom seeds |
| ¼ teaspoon | ground black pepper |
| ½ teaspoon | ground cinnamon |
| 1–inch piece | fresh ginger, grated with the skin |
| 4 teaspoons | loose black tea leaves |

In a medium saucepan, bring water, milk, sugar and spices, including the ginger, to a full boil. Lower the heat and let the mixture simmer for about 30 seconds. Raise the heat and bring the mixture to a full boil again. At this point add tea leaves, and remove the saucepan from heat immediately. Cover and allow the tea leaves to steep for 2 minutes.

Strain and serve.

Yield: 4 cups

## Tea with Mint and Cardamom—*fudinani chai*

Flavored with fresh mint and sugar, this tea is very comforting on a cold morning.

| | |
|---|---|
| 2 cups | water |
| 1 cup | milk, preferably lowfat |
| 3 teaspoons | sugar, or to taste |
| 6–8 | mint leaves |
| 1–inch piece | fresh ginger, grated with skin |
| ¼ teaspoon | ground cardamom seeds |
| 3 teaspoons | loose black tea leaves |

In a small saucepan over high heat, combine water and milk. Add sugar, mint, ginger and cardamom; bring to a full boil. Add the tea leaves when the mixture comes to a boil, and remove the saucepan immediately from the heat. Cover, and allow the tea to steep for 2 minutes. Strain and serve.

Yield: 3 cups.

## Tea without Tea Leaves—*ukalo*

My son-in-law, Jong, loves this drink, essentially a spiced milk beverage, reminiscent of *masala chai*, but without the caffeine.

| | |
|---|---|
| 2 cups | water |
| 2 cups | milk, preferably low fat |
| 1–inch piece | fresh ginger, grated with skin |
| 4 teaspoons | sugar, or to taste |
| 2 tablespoons | chopped lemon grass (optional) |
| 8 | mint leaves |
| ¼ teaspoon | ground cardamom |

Combine water and milk in a small saucepan over high heat. Add ginger, sugar, lemon grass, mint and cardamom, and bring the mixture to a full boil. Lower the heat and simmer for about 20 seconds.

Strain and serve.

Serves 4.

## Flour with Jaggery and Water—*raab*

I did not consider including this drink in the book until Bella visited Mexico and tasted a beverage called "atole", a thick breakfast drink made with masa harina, milk, uriaman and spices. She described the drink to me and it reminded me of a similar hot beverage, called *raab*, that I drank as a child in India. Whereas in Mexico, different flavors like vanilla or chocolate, may be added to the mix, Indians add jaggery, ginger powder, coconut, and sometimes, slivered almonds and white poppy seeds to *raab*.

| | |
|---|---|
| 1 tablespoon | unsalted butter or margarine |
| ¼ cup | wheat flour |
| 2 tablespoons | unsweetened, grated coconut |
| 1 tablespoon | slivered almonds (optional) |
| 1 teaspoon | white poppy seeds (optional) |
| 2 cups | water |
| ¼ cup | jaggery or brown sugar, or to taste |
| ½ to 1 teaspoon | ginger powder |

In a small saucepan, melt the butter over medium heat. Add the wheat flour and coconut. Cook, stirring well, until the flour turns golden, about 3 minutes. If using almonds and/or white poppy seeds, add them now and cook the mixture, stirring well, for an additional 15 seconds. Add water, jaggery or brown sugar and ginger powder, and mix well, making sure to break any lumps. Bring the mixture to a full boil, lower the heat, and simmer until the flour is cooked and the mixture thickens.

Remove and serve hot.

Serves: 2–3.

## Buttermilk—*chhash* or plain *lassi*

As mentioned in the introduction, *lassi* is a yogurt drink which, though it is commonly called buttermilk in English, is to be distinguished from the supermarket variety. Plain *lassi* is usually served after lunch in most *Kathiawari* homes. Since I married into such a family, I, too, adopted the habit. It is quite cooling, sweet, and light.

| 1 cup | yogurt (p. 56) |
| 2 cups | water or as desired |

Using a whisk or an eggbeater, mix the yogurt and water until frothy and blended. Chill and serve.
Yield: 3 cups.

## Buttermilk with Cumin and Mustard—*vaghareli chhash*

In my parents' home, *lassi* was always seasoned with mustard and cumin. This beverage is light and flavorful.

| | |
|---|---|
| 1 cup | yogurt |
| 3 cups | water |
| ¾ teaspoon | salt, or to taste |
| 2 teaspoons | oil |
| ¼ teaspoon | black mustard seeds |
| ¼ teaspoon | cumin seeds |

In a large pitcher, whisk together the yogurt and water until frothy. Add the salt, and set aside. In a small frying pan, over medium-low heat, heat the oil. Add the mustard and cumin. As soon as the mustard starts to crackle and the cumin sizzles, add this mixture to the buttermilk. Mix well, chill, and serve.

Yield: 4 cups.

## Buttermilk with Mango—*aam lassi*

*Lassi* can be made using any fruit of your choice. However, at *The Ganges*, we served mango *lassi* most of the time. In the winter months, when fresh mango is not readily available, mango *lassi* may be made with canned mango pulp, which is sold in most Indian stores.

| | |
|---|---|
| 1 cup | yogurt |
| 2 cups | water |
| ½ cup | mango juice (p. 480) or canned mango pulp |
| 1 tablespoon | sugar, or to taste |

Combine all of the above ingredients in a blender and blend for 1 minute, or until the sugar has dissolved. Remove to a pitcher, chill, and serve. Yield: 3 ½ cups.

## Buttermilk with Papaya—*papaya lassi*

This *lassi* is a wonderful finale to a light afternoon meal.

| | |
|---|---|
| 1 small | ripe papaya, peeled, cut |
| 1 cup | plain yogurt |
| 3 cups | water |
| 2 tablespoons | honey, or as desired |
| 1 teaspoon | toasted, coarsely ground cumin seeds |

Peel and cut the papaya into halves, remove the seeds, and slice the halves into large pieces. Using a liquidizer or a blender, blend, all ingredients together until smooth. Remove to a pitcher; chill, and serve. Yield: 5 cups.

## Buttermilk with Strawberries—strawberry *lassi*

This is a more modern take on the traditional fruit *lassi*. Frozen strawberries work best for this recipe.

| | |
|---|---|
| 2 cups | yogurt |
| 3 cups | water |
| 1 can (small) | frozen strawberries |
| 3 tablespoons | sugar, or as needed |
| ¼ teaspoon | ground cardamom seeds |

Using a blender or a liquidizer, blend the yogurt with the rest of the ingredients until smooth. Remove to a pitcher; chill, and serve.
Yield: 6 cups.

## Buttermilk with Saffron—*kesar lassi* or *piyush*

| | |
|---|---|
| 1 cup | yogurt |
| 3 cups | water |
| 2 tablespoons | sugar, or to taste |
| ½ teaspoon | saffron, ground |
| ¼ teaspoon | ground cardamom seeds |

In a large pitcher, using a hand mixer or a whisk, blend the yogurt with the rest of the ingredients until the sugar has dissolved. Chill and serve.
Yield: 4 cups.

## Rose Lassi—*gulab lassi*

Rose flavoring is as commonly used in Indian cooking as vanilla is used in the West. Rose *lassi* is an unusual, cooling and refreshing summer drink.

| | |
|---|---|
| 1 cup | plain yogurt |
| 2 cups | water |
| 2 tablespoons | rose syrup or to taste (p. 496) |

In a wide-mouthed pitcher, blend the yogurt and water, with a whisk or hand mixer. Add rose syrup and mix again. Chill, and serve.
Yields: 3 cups.

## Yogurt with Milk—*golvo*

*Golvo* drink has been a popular beverage since Vedic times. Milk tames the tartness of yogurt; the quantity of milk used can be adjusted to your taste.

| | |
|---|---|
| 1 cup | yogurt |
| 1 ½ cups | milk, preferably lowfat |
| 2 teaspoons | sugar, or to taste **or** |
| 2 teaspoons | rose syrup, or to taste (p. 496) |

In a small mixing bowl, blend together all the ingredients with a hand mixer or a whisk. Chill and serve.
Yield: 2 ½ cups.

# *Mahashivratri* Drink—*thandai*

On the religious day of *Mahashivratri*, worshipping Indians consume only milk, nuts and fruits. On this special day, *thandai* is made in most homes.

| | |
|---|---|
| 4 cups | milk, preferably lowfat |
| 4 teaspoons | sugar, or to taste |
| 1 teaspoon | white poppy seeds, ground |
| 2 tablespoons | almonds, blanched, ground fine |
| ½ teaspoon | anise or fennel seeds, ground |
| 5 | black peppercorns, ground |
| 1 teaspoon | cardamom seeds, ground |
| 1 cup | water |

In a medium saucepan, bring milk to a full boil; add sugar, and mix well. Remove from heat, and set aside to cool.

On a cutting board, using a rolling pin, grind the poppy seeds, adding just a few drops of water to hold the seeds together. Remove with a spatula and set aside.

In a liquidizer or blender, grind the almonds, anise, black peppers and cardamom, adding 1 cup of water to make a fine paste. Add in the ground poppy seeds and blend the mixture for few more seconds. Remove and stir into the boiled milk. Mix well. Chill and serve.

Yield: 5 cups.

**Note:** In some Indian homes, the ground mixture is made even finer by straining it through cheesecloth before adding it to the milk.

## Rose Syrup—*gulabnu* syrup

The quantity of sugar called for in this recipe may seem high, but the syrup is in fact a concentrate that will be diluted into a variety of recipes provided in this book. Rose essence is available in most Indian groceries.

| | |
|---|---|
| 3 cups | water |
| 4 cups | sugar |
| ¾ teaspoon | red food coloring |
| 2 teaspoons | rose essence |

In a medium saucepan, combine the water and sugar and bring the mixture to a full boil, over high heat, stirring well. Lower the heat to medium-high, and continue boiling for about 8 minutes. Remove and set aside to cool.

When cool, add in the red food coloring and rose essence, and stir well. Store in a jar with a tight lid. Use as called for in recipes.
Yield: 4 cups.

## Rose *Sherbat*—*gulabnu sherbat*

*Sherbat* refers to a cool drink made with concentrated, flavored syrup. It may be made with either milk or with water, and is a distant relative of Italian sodas.

| | |
|---|---|
| 2 cups | water |
| 2 tablespoons | rose syrup or to taste |
| Few | ice cubes |

In a pitcher, combine the water and rose syrup. Place ice cubes into glasses and add the rose drink.
Yield: 2 ¼ cups.
**Note:** For a delicious variation, immerse several large cubes of watermelon in each glass, prior to serving.

## Rose Milk—*gulabnu doodh*

| | |
|---|---|
| 2 cups | milk |
| 1 tablespoon | rose syrup, or to taste (p. 496) |

In a small saucepan, bring milk to a full boil. Remove and set aside to cool. When cool, add the rose syrup and stir well. Chill and serve.
Yield: 2 cups.

## Milk with Saffron and Nuts—*kesar mevanu doodh*

Ready-made preparations for this popular beverage are commonly available in Indian stores. Preparing your own mixture, however, allows you to adjust the ingredients to your taste.

| | |
|---|---|
| 4 cups | milk |
| 4 teaspoons | sugar, or to taste |
| 1 tablespoon | ground almonds |
| 1 tablespoon | ground pistachios |
| 1 teaspoon | ground cardamom seeds |
| ½ teaspoon | saffron, crushed |

In a medium saucepan, bring milk to a full boil. Add all the ingredients, including the saffron, and simmer for 1 minute. Remove and serve hot or chilled.
Yield: 4 cups.

## Lemonade, Indian Style—*limbunu sherbat*

Indians frequently make this quick drink during the lengthy hot season.

| | |
|---|---|
| 4 fresh | lemons, juiced, strained |
| 3 cups | cold water |
| 2 tablespoons | sugar, or to taste |
| ½ teaspoon | salt, or to taste |
| ½ teaspoon | ground black pepper (optional) |
| ½ cup | crushed ice |

In a stainless-steel saucepan, combine the lemon juice with water and the next 3 ingredients and stir until the sugar has dissolved. Remove to a pitcher, add ice, and serve.

Yield: 3 ½ cups.

## Watermelon Juice—*tarbuchno ras*

To make the preparation of this refreshing drink easier, I recommend using seedless watermelon.

| | |
|---|---|
| 1 medium | watermelon, seedless |
| 2 tablespoons | rose syrup, or to taste (p. 496) |

Cut watermelon into chunks and remove the seeds if any. In a blender or a liquidizer, blend the watermelon until pureed. Remove to a pitcher, mix in the rose syrup, and chill before serving. Crushed ice may be added to the drink before serving.

Yield: 4–6 cups.

# Milk with Rose, Tapioca and Vermicelli—*falooda*

I have fond childhood memories of drinking this sweet beverage as a treat on sweltering, summer afternoons. Consisting of soft vermicelli steeped in an intoxicating, sweet, rose syrup flavored milk, *falooda* is a delicious, albeit filling, treat that may be served as either a dessert or a beverage.

Note that a noodle press—*sev no sancho*—(illus. p. 175) is required to make the cornstarch vermicelli. Dried *falooda* noodles are available in Indian stores, but nothing beats the homemade variety.

| | |
|---|---|
| ¾ cup | cornstarch |
| 3 ½ cups | water |
| 8 ½ cups | milk, preferably lowfat |
| 4 tablespoons | rose syrup, or to taste (p. 496) |
| 2 tablespoons | sego or tapioca |
| 2 teaspoons | ground cardamom seeds |
| 2 teaspoons | *tulsi* seeds (p. 31) (optional) |

**Vermicelli or noodles:**

In a medium saucepan, use a whisk or hand mixer to combine the cornstarch with 1 cup water. When the mixture is smooth, add 2 more cups of water and mix well. Bring the mixture to a full boil over high heat, stirring well, to prevent sticking and the formation of lumps.

Lower the heat when the mixture comes to a full boil, and continue stirring. Within about 20 minutes, the mixture will start to thicken. (The thickened mixture will be less likely to stick to the bottom of the pan.) While cooking, note that the cornstarch mixture will first thicken and then turn translucent. Lower the heat, and keep stirring and cooking until the thickened, translucent mixture pulls away from the sides of the pan, about 30 minutes.

Fill the Indian noodle press, *sevno sancho* (p. 175), fitted with a tiny-holed disc, with only a small amount of the cooked cornstarch dough.

Screw the lid on tightly and squeeze the press by turning the handle, dropping the vermicelli size noodles directly into a large bowl filled with cold water. Lift some of the vermicelli out of the water; if it holds together well, the dough is ready. If the noodles break apart, the dough will need to be cooked a little more.

When the dough is ready, drop all the freshly pressed vermicelli into the water and refrigerate

**Milk Base:**

In a large pitcher, combine 7 ½ cups milk (save 1 cup milk) with rose syrup and refrigerate.

**Tapioca:**

Wash the tapioca and drain out all the water. Set aside for 15 minutes—the tapioca balls will swell. In a small saucepan, combine the tapioca with ½ cup of water and bring to a full boil over high heat. Lower the heat to medium-low when the mixture comes to a boil, and cook, stirring well, for 2 minutes. The tapioca will start to turn translucent. Cook for a few more seconds, and add the remaining 1 cup milk. Cook on low heat, stirring well, until tapioca is almost completely translucent, about 7 minutes. Add cardamom, mix well. Set aside to cool and refrigerate.

If using *tulsi* seeds in this recipe, soak them in 2 tablespoons water for about 30 minutes before using.

To serve the drink, spoon some vermicelli noodles into a large glass. Add about 2 tablespoons of the tapioca milk mixture. Add a few *tulsi* seeds, if using. Fill the glass with rose milk. Provide a spoon with the glass. For an even richer dessert, top with a scoop of either rose or vanilla ice cream.

Serves 8.

## Tamarind Aperitif—*jaljeera* or *jeerapani*

In some restaurants, this slightly sweet and savory drink is served in small glasses before the soup or appetizer.

| | |
|---|---|
| 2–inch square | tamarind slab |
| 8 cups | water |
| 2 teaspoons | toasted, coarsely ground cumin seeds |
| 2 teaspoons | salt, or to taste |
| 2 teaspoons | paprika |
| 1 tablespoon | sugar, or to taste |
| 1 tablespoon | finely chopped mint leaves |
| 2 teaspoons | lemon juice |
| ½ cup | *bundi* (p. 106) (optional) |

Soak tamarind in 1 cup water for at least 30 minutes. Squeeze the water from the tamarind and strain the liquid into a stainless-steel saucepan. Discard the fiber and seeds, if any.

Add remaining water and the next 6 ingredients including lemon juice. Stir well and chill for a few hours. Stir again before serving.

Pour *jaljeera* in individual cups, add a few *bundi* to each, and serve. Serves 12–15.

# GLOSSARY

| | |
|---|---|
| *Adhtyamik* | The state of spiritual perfection |
| *Ahimsa* | Love or non-violence |
| *Aloona* | Religious salt-free meals |
| *Atta* | flour |
| *Ayurveda* | The ancient Indian system of medicine |
| *Bhagavad Gita* | The Hindu religious scripture |
| *Bhelwala* | A vendor of a specialty called *bhel* meaning mixture |
| *Dharma* | Hindu code of conduct or religion |
| *Diwali* | Festival of lights |
| *Drakshasava* | Ayurvedic medicine made with grapes |
| *Ekadesi* | The bi-monthly religious day falling on the eleventh day of the waxing and waning moon |
| *Farsan* | Appetizers |
| *Ghee* | Clarified butter |
| *Holi* | First day of harvest celebrated with colors |
| *Mahashivratri* | Religious day observed once per year, when many Indians worship Shiva and refrain from sleep for 24 hours |
| *Makhan* | butter |
| *Malai* | The cream that collects on the milk surface after boiling |
| *Masala* | spices |
| *Mithai* | sweetmeats |
| *Mistan* | The Indian word for desserts |
| *Padma Purana* | The Hindu scripture |
| *Panchamrat* | Five nectars, milk, yogurt, honey, ghee and sugar |
| *Parijat* | Coral Jasmine |

| | |
|---|---|
| *Peni* or *karai* | Indian deep frying pan or Indian wok |
| *Prasadam* | Offering blessed by the Gods |
| *Puja* | Rituals or worship |
| *Rajasik food* | Rich food, or that which stimulates |
| *Sattvic* | pure food |
| *Satyanarayan puja* | Ritual on the day of the full moon, during which offerings are presented to Vishnu and his consort Lakshmi |
| *Sevno sancho* | Noodle making machine or press |
| *Tamasik* | Dark, spoiled or forbidden |
| *Tava* | Indian griddle |
| *Tandoor* | A clay oven |
| *Thali* | A large round stainless steel plate with a vertical rim about 2–inches high |
| *Vaishnav* | A devotee of Vishnu |

# About the Author

Born in Surat, Gujarat, Malvi Doshi grew up traveling through India. After living in both New York and Nairobi, Kenya she settled with her family in San Francisco, where she began to write about Indian cooking. Following the publication of her first cookbook, *A Surti Touch* (Strawberry Hill Press), Chef Doshi and her husband opened the Ganges Restaurant in 1986. Her unique, magnificent vegetarian cooking quickly established her reputation as a premier Indian chef. Now retired, Malvi Doshi resides in Berkeley, California from where she writes and teaches Indian cooking.

# INDEX

Note: Page numbers in **bold type** refer to ingredient descriptions and handling instructions. Page numbers in *italic type* refer to illustrations.

## A

*aadu* (ginger, fresh), **26**

*aaloo gobi* (cauliflower with potatoes), 212

*aaloo parotha* (potato-stuffed *parotha*), 413

*aam* (mango). *See* mango

*aamli/imli* (tamarind), **31**

*adadno lot* (split black bean (*urid dal*) flour), **45**

*adhyatmik jivan,* 2

*adrak/aadu* (ginger, fresh), **26**

aduki beans (*choli*), **337–38**

    spiced aduki beans (*lal choli*), 346

*ahimsa* and vegetarianism, 2

*ajma mithani bhakhari* (*bhakhari* with *ajwain* and tumeric), 409

*ajwain,* **9**

    ajwain dumplings (*ajmani vadi*), 194

    *bhakhari* with *ajwain* and tumeric (*ajma mithani bhakhari*), 409

*akhrot* (walnuts), **37**

*akhrotni basudi* (walnut pudding), 463

almonds (*badam*), **36**

    almond fudge (*badam barfi*), 454–55

    toasted almonds (*shekeli badam*), 184

*Aloona Vrat,* 49

amaranth (*rajagaro*), **40**
   amaranth pudding (*rajagarani kheer*), 464
amaranth flour (*rajagarano lot*), **40**
   amaranth flour bread (*rajagarani bhakhari*), 438
amaranth greens
   with cumin (*cholai*), 281
   with onions (*kandane cholai*), 282
*amba haldar* (mango turmeric), **32**
*amchoor* (mango powder), **27**
*Amlika* (tamarind), **31**
*Amra. See* mango
*ananas* (pineapple), **35**
*ananasno chhundo* (pineapple relish with cumin), 96
*anardana/darukhatta* (pomegranate seeds), **29**
anise (*chhoti saunf*), **9–10**
   stuffed bitter gourd with anise (*saunfwale karele*), 264–65
*anjeer* (fig), **34**
appetizers, 130
   *See also* fried appetizers; non-fried appetizers
apple (*safarjan*), **33**
apricot (*jardalu*), **33**
   apricot chutney (*jardaluni chutney*), 77
*arar dal* (split pigeon peas), **342**
arrow root flour (*tapkir no lot*), **40**
asafoetida (*hing*), **10**
*askshat,* 296
asparagus
   with potatoes (asparagus *bateta*), 209
   in yogurt sauce (*dahiwala* asparagus), 210
*athanano masalo* (basic pickling spice), 115–16
*Ayurveda,* 8

# B

*badam* (almonds), **36**

*badam barfi* (almond fudge), 454–55

*badi. See* dumplings (*vadi*)

*badi elaichi/elcha,* **12**

*badi saunf* (fennel seeds), **19**

*badiyan* (star anise), **9**

*badshahi baigan* (eggplant with nuts and yogurt), 238–39

*baigan roti* (eggplant bread), 406–07

*bajri* (millet), **43**

*bajri,* mung, *chokhanu bhadku* (three grain savory porridge), 325

*bajrino lot* (millet flour), **43**

    *bajrina rotla* (millet flour bread), 434–35

baked savory cake (*handvo/ bhakhar*), 163–64

banana (*kela*), **33**

    banana *bhakhari* (*kelani bhakhari*), 410

    banana *raita* (*kelanu raitu*), 108

    mashed banana *pakora* (*kela methi pakora*), 138

    stuffed banana with fresh spices (*bharela kela*), 289–90

    stuffed bananas with chickpea flour and spices (*kelana ravaiya*), 291

basil (*tulsi/ tulasi*), **10–11**

basil seeds (*tukmaria*), **31**

*basmati* rice, **43**

    about, 296–97

    preparation of (*bhat*), 298–99

    rice and split pigeon peas with saffron (*beeranj*), 457

*bateta. See* potatoes

*bateta vada* (spicy mashed potato rounds), 151

*batetane shing* (potatoes with peanuts), 199

*batetani chutney* (potato chutney), 72

*batetanu raitu* (potato *raita*), 113

battered vegetables (*pakora/bhajia*), 134–35

bay leaves (*tejpatta*), **11**

bean and spinach cake (*chola chanano handvo*), 165

bean patties. *See* patties

beans. *See dals*

beans, green. *See* green beans and long beans

beer, 482

*beeranj* (rice and split pigeon peas with saffron), 457

beets, **38**

bell peppers

    precooked rice with bell peppers and yogurt (*vagharelo bhat*), 300

    *See also* red peppers

Bengal grams (*kala chana*). *See* chickpeas

ber/berries, **34**

*besan* (chickpea flour), **41**

*besan laadu* (chickpea flour with cardamom), 447

beverages

    about, 482–84

    buttermilk (*chhash*/plain *lassi*), 490

    buttermilk with cumin and mustard (*vaghareli chhash*), 491

    buttermilk with mango (*aam lassi*), 492

    buttermilk with papaya (*papaya lassi*), 492

    buttermilk with saffron (*kesar lassi/piyush*), 493

    buttermilk with strawberries (strawberry *lassi*), 493

    flour with jaggery and water (*raab*), 489

    Indian spiced tea (*masala chai*), 486

    Indian tea (*chai*), 485

    lemonade (*limbunu sherbat*), 498

    Mahashivratri drink (*thandai*), 495

    milk with rose, tapioca and vermicelli (*falooda*), 499–500

    milk with saffron and nuts (*kesar mevanu doodh*), 497

    rose *lassi* (*gulab lassi*), 494

beverages (*continued*)
  rose milk (*gulabnu doodh*), 497
  rose *sherbat* (*gulabnu sherbat*), 496
  tamarind aperitif (*jaljeera/jeerapani*), 501
  tea with mint and cardamom (*fudinani chai*), 487
  tea without tea leaves (*ukalo*), 488
  watermelon juice (*tarbuchno ras*), 498
  yogurt with milk (*golvo*), 494
*Bhagavata Gita*, food categories in, 2
*bhaji koprama bateta* (stuffed potatoes in spinach and coconut sauce), 205–06
*bhaji ragad* (spiced spinach with sesame), 275
*bhajia* (fried, battered vegetables), 134–35
*bhajinu raitu* (spinach *raitu*), 102
*bhakhar* (baked savory cake), 163–64
*bhakhari*, 408–10
  with *ajwain* and tumeric (*ajma mithani bhakhari*), 409
  amaranth flour bread (*rajagarani bhakhari*), 438
  banana *bhakhari* (*kelani bhakhari*), 410
  described, 399
  with squash and spices (*doodhini bhakhari*), 409
  thick Gujarati bread, 408
*bharela kela* (stuffed banana with fresh spices), 289–90
*bhareli* zucchini (stuffed zucchini), 257–58
*bharta*
  roasted eggplant with onions (*bharta*), 235
  roasted eggplant with yogurt (*bharta*), 236
*bhat. See basmati* rice
*bhatura* (deep-fried puffed bread with yogurt), 419
*bhelpuri* (Bombay snack mix), 178–79
*bhinda, kandane paneer* (vegetarian "gumbo"), 286
*bhindi masala* (stuffed okra), 283–84

*bhoyphali* (peanuts), **37**

*biryani,* vegetable *biryani* (*shakni biryani*), 329–31

Bishop's Weed. *See ajwain*

bitter gourd and tinde (ivy gourd)

    ivy gourd with potatoes (*tindora bateta*), 268

    ivy gourd with spicy potatoes and onions (*tindora, bateta, kanda*), 269

    stuffed bitter gourd with anise (*saunfwale karele*), 264–65

    sweet and sour bitter gourd with onions and potatoes (*karela, kandane bateta*), 266–67

    *See also* squash

bitter melons. *See* bitter gourd and tinde (ivy gourd)

black bean and rice cake with cracked pepper (*idada*), 160

black beans

    Indian black beans (*urid*), **339**

    Indian black beans with *dals* and spices (*Punjabi dal*), 384–85

    split and whole Indian black beans (*moglai dal*), 380–81

    split black beans (*urid dal*), **339**, 368

black cumin seeds (*kala jeera/shah jeera*), **15**

black-eyed peas (*chola*), 344–45

    black-eyed peas *kofta* in onion sauce (*kofta* "curry"), 391–92

black mung beans. *See* mung beans

black pepper. *See* pepper

black salt. *See* salt

Bombay snack mix (*bhelpuri*), 178–79

*bor,* **34**

    *See also* cherry

bottle gourd and ridge gourd

    bottle gourd *kofta* in onion sauce (*doodhina kofta*), 252–53

    bottle gourd with potatoes (*doodhi bateta*), 249

    bottle gourd with split chickpeas (*doodhi chana*), 250–51

    ridge gourd with cucumber and yam (*turia kakdi*), 255

    ridge gourd with mustard and lemon (*turia*), 254

    *See also* squash

breads
  about, 397–403
  deep-fried Indian bread (*puri*), 420–21
  deep-fried puffed bread with yogurt (*bhatura*), 419
  eggplant bread (*baigan roti*), 406–07
  fat-free breads, 432–38
  flours, 397
  ingredients in, 397–98
  kneading techniques, 400–401, *433*
  layered Indian bread (*parotha*), 411–16
  leavened Indian bread (*naan*), 422–24
  mixed flour savory pancakes (*handvana lotna puda*), 429–30
  mixing technique, 399–400
  paper-thin Gujarati bread (*fulka/chapati*), 404–05
  resting the dough, 201
  rolling, cooking and variations, 402–03
  South Indian crepes (*sada dosa*), 426–27
  South Indian crepes with stuffing (*masala dosa*), 428
  stuffing methods illustrated, *425*
  thick Gujarati bread (*bhakhari*), 408–10
  utensils and tools, 403
  vegetarian omelettes (*puda*), 421
  wheat and millet bread (*dhebra/thepla*), 417–18
brown mung beans. *See* mung beans
brown rice with *toor dal* (*karadni khichadi*), 309
brown sugar. *See* jaggery
buckwheat flour (*fafar atta*), **41**
  buckwheat *halwa* (*fafar sheera*), 473
bulbous root (*suran*), **38**
bulgur. *See* rice, bulgur and other grains
*bundi raita* (dumpling *raita*), 106
butter biscuits (*Surti khari biscuit*), 182
buttermilk *lassi*. *See* lassi

# C

cabbage
   cabbage relish (*kobijnu kachumber*), 97
   cabbage-stuffed *parotha* (*kobijna parotha*), 414–15
   cabbage with chickpea flour (*kobij khalva*), 241
   cabbage with potatoes and *garam masala* (*kobi bateta*), 240
   savory cabbage cake (*kobijno bhakhar*), 167–68
   spicy cabbage, stir-cooked with mustard seeds (*vaghareli kobij*), 242
camphor (*kapoor*/*karpoor*), **11**
canola oil, 398
cantaloupe (*sakkarteti*), 478
carambola or star fruit (*kamrakh*), **34**
   carambola chutney (*kamrukhni chutney*), 85
caraway seeds (*gunyan*), **11**
cardamom (*elchi*/*elaichi*/*elcha*), **11–12**
   cardamom cookies (*nankhatai*), 183
carrots (*gajar*), **38**
   carrot chutney (*gajarni chutney*), 81
   carrot *halwa* (*gajar halwa*), 465
   carrot *raita* (*gajarnu raitu*), 100
   carrot relish (*gajarno chhundo*), 95
   fresh carrot and cucumber pickle (*gajar kakdinu athanu*), 124
   spinach with carrots (*sai bhaji*), 277
   sweet and hot carrot pickle (*gajarnu athanu*), 119
cashews (*kaju*), **36**
   cashew and saffron *khichadi* (*kesarwali khichadi*), 321–22
   cashew diamonds (*kaju katni*), 475
   Cream of Wheat with yogurt and cashew nuts (*upama*), 180–81
cauliflower
   cauliflower in coconut sauce (*koprana doodhma gobi*), 211
   cauliflower *raita* (*flowernu raitu*), 101
   cauliflower with potatoes (*aaloo gobi*), 212
   cauliflower with spicy yogurt sauce (*gobi korma*), 214
   creamy cauliflower with potatoes and peas (*moglai gobi*), 213

*chai*
about, 482
Indian spiced tea (*masala chai*), 486
Indian tea, 485
tea with mint and cardamom (*fudinani chai*), 487
*chakri* (rice flour curls), 172–73
*chana* (garbanzo beans), **338**
*chana dal* (split chickpeas), **338–39**
with cinnamon and green chili, 351
*See also* chickpeas
*chana dal chutney* (toasted split chickpea chutney), 83
*chana dal vada* (split chickpea patties), 150
*chanano lot* (chickpea or gram flour), **41**
*chanano lot* (garbanzo flour), **42**
*chania bor,* **34**
*chapati*
described, 399
paper-thin Gujarati bread (*fulkal chapati*), 404–05
*chapati* flour, about, 397
*charoli* (chironjia), **36**
cheese (*chenna/paneer*), 60–61
cheese with spices, 61
"curried" spinach with *paneer* (*palak paneer*), 274
in desserts, 441
*paneer* patty in sweet, cream sauce (*ras malai*), 458–60, 461–62
*paneer*-stuffed *parotha* (*paneer parotha*), 416
peas and *paneer* in raisin sauce (*drakshawala matar paneer*), 247
ricotta cheese (part-skim) as substitute, 441
vegetarian "gumbo" (*bhinda, kandane paneer*), 286
*chenna. See* cheese
*cherinu athanu* (unripe cherry pickle), 123
cherry, **34**
unripe cherry pickle (*cherinu athanu*), 123

*chhash*
buttermilk/plain *lassi,* 490
buttermilk with cumin and mustard (*vaghareli chhash*), 491
*See also lassi*
*chhoti saunf* (anise), **9–10**
*chhowk,* 51
*chhundo* (mango relish with cumin), 93
*chickoo,* **34**
chickpea flour (*besan*), **41**
cabbage with chickpea flour (*kobij khalva*), 241
chickpea flour noodles (*sev*), 174
chickpea flour rolls (*khandvi/pilla patodi*), 161–62
chickpea flour with cardamom (*besan laadu*), 447
sliced eggplants with onions and chickpea flour (*khalva*), 237
stuffed bananas with chickpea flour and spices (*kelana ravaiya*), 291
chickpeas, **338–39**
Bengal grams (*kala chana*), **338**
Bengal grams with onions and lemon (*kala chana*), 350
bottle gourd with split chickpeas (*doodhi chana*), 250–51
coconut and split chickpea chutney (*koprune chana dal chutney*), 71
collard green with split Bengal grams (collard *patalbhaji*), 279–80
spinach with split chickpeas (*palak moglai*), 276
split chickpea patties (*chana dal vada*), 150
split chickpeas with cinnamon and green chili (*chana dal*), 351
toasted split chickpea chutney (*chana dal chutney*), 83
toasted split chickpeas (*dalia*), **29**
chili *pakora* (*mirch pakora*), 136
chili powder (*lal mirch*), **12–13**
chilies, green (*hari mirch*), **12**
chilies, red (*sabut lal mirch*), **12**
Chinese parsley. *See* cilantro
chironjia (*charoli*), **36**

*chokha* (rice). *See* rice, bulgur and other grains
*chokhani rotli* (rice flour bread), 432
*chokhano lot* (rice flour), **43**
*chola* (spiced black-eyed peas), 344–45
*chola chanano handvo* (bean and spinach cake), 165
*cholai* (amaranth greens with cumin), 281
*choli*. *See* aduki beans (*choli*)
*choli vengan* (long beans with eggplant), 218
chutneys and relishes
    about, 65–66, 67
    apricot chutney (*jardaluni chutney*), 77
    cabbage relish (*kobijnu kachumber*), 97
    carambola or star fruit chutney (*kamrukhni chutney*), 85
    carrot chutney (*gajarni chutney*), 81
    carrot relish (*gajarno chhundo*), 95
    cilantro chutney (*kothmirni chutney*), 70
    coconut and red pepper chutney (*koprune lal marchani chutney*), 73
    coconut and split chickpea chutney (*koprune chana dal chutney*), 71
    cranberry chutney, 78
    cucumber relish (*kakdini kachumber*), 87
    daikon relish (*muli kachumber*), 91
    garlic and red chili chutney (*lasanni thikhi chutney*), 75
    green garlic chutney (*leela lasanni chutney*), 82
    green papaya relish (*kacha papayani kachumber*), 89
    lemon peel chutney (*limbuni chutney*), 84
    mango and onion relish (*keri kandani kachumber*), 88
    mango chutney (*kerini chutney*), 79–80
    mango relish with cardamom (*murrabbo*), 94
    mango relish with cumin (*chhundo*), 93
    pairing with other foods, 68
    *papadum* relish (*papadni kachumber*), 92
    persimmon chutney, 76

chutneys and relishes (*continued*)

    pineapple relish with cumin (*ananasno chhundo*), 96

    potato chutney (*batetani chutney*), 72

    raisin and tamarind chutney (*draksh aamlini chutney*), 69

    spicy green papaya relish (*papayani chhin*), 90

    storage, 67

    toasted split chickpea chutney (*chana dal chutney*), 83

    tomato and onion relish (*tametane kandani kachumber*), 86

    tomato chutney (*tametani chutney*), 74

cilantro (*hara dhania*), **13**

    cilantro chutney (*kothmirni chutney*), 70

    cilantro-coconut sauce, 388

    cilantro *raita* (*kothmirnu raitu*), 103

    stuffed eggplants in cilantro sauce (*kothnirma ravaiya*), 231–32

cinnamon (*dalchini/taj*), **13**

    split chickpeas with cinnamon and green chili (*chana dal*), 351

citric acid (*nimbuka sat/limbuna phool*), **13**

Citronella, 27

clarified butter. *See ghee*

cloves (*laung/lavang*), **14**

    yellow split peas with garlic and cloves (*vatanani dal*), 375

cluster beans

    with coriander and cumin (*guwarnu shak*), 225

    with yogurt (*dahiwali guwar*), 226

cocktail *idlee* maker, 160

coconut (*nariyel*), **14**

    cilantro-coconut sauce, 388

    coconut and red pepper chutney (*koprune lal marchani chutney*), 73

    coconut and split chickpea chutney (*koprune chana dal chutney*), 71

    coconut-onion sauce, 203–04

    coconut rice (*koprano bhat*), 303

    rice pudding with coconut (*kopra doodhpaak*), 474

    sauce for cauliflower, 211

    spinach and coconut sauce, 205–06

coconut sap (*neera*), 483

coffee, 483

collard greens

    with onions (collard *saag*), 278

    with split Bengal grams (collard *patalbhaji*), 279–80

cookies, cardamom cookies (*nankhatai*), 183

cooking recommendations and hints, 51–52

cooking utensils, 47

coriander seeds (*dhania*), **15**

    coriander and cumin mix (*dhania jeera*), 26

corn (*makkai*), **41**

corn flour (*makkaino lot*), **41**

corn oil, 47, 398

cornmeal bread (*makaini rotli/makkeki roti*), 437

cow, reverence of, 54

cranberry chutney, 78

Cream of Wheat (*sooji*), **42**

    Cream of Wheat pudding (*sooji kheer/galvanu*), 443

    Cream of Wheat with cardamom and saffron (*kesari sheera*), 472

    with yogurt and cashew nuts (*upama*), 180–81

cream sauce, 459, 461–62

creamy cauliflower with potatoes and peas (*moglai gobi*), 213

crepes (*dosa*), 426–28

cucumbers

    cucumber *raita* with green chilies (*kakdinu raitu*), 99

    cucumber relish (*kakdini kachumber*), 87

    cucumber savory cake (*kakdina dhokla*), 157–58

    fresh carrot and cucumber pickle (*gajar kakdinu athanu*), 124

    ridge gourd with cucumber and yam (*turia kakdi*), 255

cumin seeds (*jeera/safed jeera*), **15**

    amaranth greens with cumin (*cholai*), 281

    coriander and cumin mix (*dhania jeera*), 26

    cumin and pepper *khichadi* (*masalawali khichadi*), 323

    persimmon with cumin (*jeera* persimmon), 294

"curried" spinach with *paneer* (*palak paneer*), 274
curry leaves (*limdo*/*limdana paan*), **16**

# D

*dahi* (yogurt), 56–57
*dahivada* (mixed bean patties with yogurt), 146–47
*dahiwala* asparagus (asparagus in yogurt sauce), 210
*dahiwali guwar* (cluster beans with yogurt), 226
daikon relish (*muli kachumber*), 91
dairy basics, 54–62
   cheese (*chenna*/*paneer*), 60–61
   *ghee*, 59
   non-dairy desserts, 471–77
   solidified milk (*khoya*/*mavo*), 62
   yogurt (*dahi*/*maska*), 56–58
*dal dhokli* (Indian pasta with split pigeon peas), 360–62
*dalchini*/*taj* (cinnamon), **13**
*dalia* (toasted split chickpeas), **29**
*dalnu osaman* (pigeon peas consommé), 352–53
*dals*
   about, 336
   buying and storing, 337
   cleaning of, 336–37
   described and listed, **337–43**
   fat-free recipes, 336
   five *dals* (*panch dal*), 386–87
   storage of, 337
   *See also specific names of dals*
*dangeru*, mixed flour savory pancakes (*handvana lotna puda*), 429–30
*darukhatta* (pomegranate seeds), **29**
dates (*khajur*), **16**
   date rolls (*khajur pilla*), 476

deep-fried Indian bread (*puri*), 420–21
deep-fried puffed bread with yogurt (*bhatura*), 419
desserts and sweetmeats
    about, 441
    almond fudge (*badam barfi*), 454–55
    amaranth pudding (*rajagarani kheer*), 464
    buckwheat *halwa* (*fafar sheera*), 473
    bulgur dessert (*lapsi*), 477
    bulgur with milk and nuts (*fadano doodhpaak*), 456
    cantaloupe (*sakkarteti*), 478
    carrot *halwa* (*gajar halwa*), 465
    cashew diamonds (*kaju katni*), 475
    chickpea flour with cardamom (*besan laadu*), 447
    Cream of Wheat pudding (*sooji kheer/galvanu*), 443
    Cream of Wheat with cardamom and saffron (*kesari sheera*), 472
    date rolls (*khajur pilla*), 476
    fruits as desserts, 478–80
    ground rice with nuts (*shahi firnee*), 446
    Indian ice cream with saffron (*kesar kulfi*), 448–49
    milk powder and flour balls in rose flavored syrup (*gulab jaman*), 450–51
    non-dairy desserts, 471–77
    *paneer* patty in sweet, cream sauce (*ras malai*), 458–60
    papaya with cumin, 478
    rice and split pigeon peas with saffron (*beeranj*), 457
    rice pudding with coconut (*kopra doodhpaak*), 474
    rice pudding with raisins (*payas*), 444–45
    stuffed, half-moon shaped pastry (*ghughra*), 466–67, *468*
    stuffed round pastry (*ghari*), 469–70
    sweetened yogurt dessert (*shreekhand*), 452
    sweetened yogurt dessert with black pepper (*matho*), 453
    sweeteners and restricted diets, 441–42

desserts and sweetmeats (*continued*)
    thick mango juice (*kerino ras*), 480
    unripe mango dessert (*khandkeri*), 471
    walnut pudding (*akhrotni basudi*), 463
    watermelon (*tarbuch*), 479
*dhania* (coriander seeds), **15**
*dhania jeera* (coriander and cumin mix), 26
*dharma,* 1
*dhebra* (wheat and millet bread), 417–18
*dhokaliyu* (steamer), 50
*dhokla* (steamed savory cake), 155–56
*dhokla* flour (*dhoklano lot*), **41–42**
*dhoklano lot* (*dhokla* flour), **41–42**
*doodhi bateta* (bottle gourd with potatoes), 249
*doodhi chana* (bottle gourd with split chickpeas), 250–51
*doodhina kofta* (bottle gourd *kofta* in onion sauce), 252–53
*doodhini bhakhari* (*bhakhari* with squash and spices), 409
*dopiaza matar* (yellow peas in onion-yogurt sauce), 389–90
*dosa* (crepes), 426–28
*dosa* flour (*dosano lot*), **42**
*dosano lot* (*dosa* flour), **42**
*draksh aamlini chutney* (raisin and tamarind chutney), 69
*drakshasava,* 482
*drakshawala matar paneer* (peas and *paneer* in raisin sauce), 247
*drakshnu athanu* (raisin pickle), 127
dry fruit pickle (*suka mevanu athanu*), 122
dry fruit *raita* (*suka mevanu raitu*), 107
dry peas pilaf (*suka vatanano pulav*), 317
*dum bateta* (stuffed potatoes in onion and yogurt sauce), 200–201
*dum shak* (vegetable casserole), 287–88

dumplings (*vadi*), **16–17**, 192–94
    ajwain dumplings (*ajmani vadi*), 194
    green beans with dumplings (*fansi dhokli*), 216–17
    lima beans with dumplings (*papdi dhokli*), 220–21
    mock potatoes (*labaad aaloo*), 192
    mung *dal vadi,* 18
    *raita* (*bundi raita*), 106
    spaghetti squash with dumplings (spaghetti squash *ne vadi*), 262–63
    spinach dumplings (*palak vadi*), 193
    sprouted brown mung beans with dumplings (*muth dhokli*), 372
*durbari raita* (fresh fruit and nut *raita*), 109


**E**

eggplant
    eggplant bread (*baigan roti*), 406–07
    eggplant rice (*vangi bhat*), 302
    eggplant with nuts and yogurt (*badshahi baigan*), 238–39
    eggplant with peas (*vengan vatana*), 227
    eggplant with split Indian lima beans (*vengan valni dal*), 228
    lima beans with eggplant (*papdi vengan*), 224
    long beans with eggplant (*choli vengan*), 218
    roasted eggplant with onions (*bharta*), 235
    roasted eggplant with yogurt (*bharta*), 236
    sliced eggplants with onions and chickpea flour (*khalva*), 237
    stuffed eggplants in cilantro sauce (*kothnirma ravaiya*), 231–32
    stuffed eggplants in spicy sauce (*ravaiya vengan*), 229–30
    stuffed eggplants with peas (*vatana bharela vengan*), 233–34
*elchi/elaichi/elcha* (cardamom), **11–12**
elephant's foot (*suran*), **38**
essences, **46**

# F

*fadano doodhpaak* (bulgur with milk and nuts), 456
*fafar atta* (buckwheat flour), **41**
*fafar sheera* (buckwheat *halwa*), 473
*falooda* (milk with rose, tapioca and vermicelli), 499–500
*fansi bateta* (green beans with potatoes), 215
*fansi dhokli* (green beans with dumplings), 216–17
farina. *See* Cream of Wheat (*sooji*)
fat-free cooking. *See* low fat cooking
fats and oils, 47
    cooking without oil, 48
    fat-free breads, 432–38
    fat-free *dals,* 336
    oils for breads, 398
    *See also* low fat cooking
fennel (*saunf*), **9**
fennel seeds (*varialil badi saunf*), **19**
fenugreek (*methini bhajil methi*), **19**
festive *puri* (*Surti puri*), 421
fig (*anjeer*), **34**
five *dals* (*panch dal*), 386–87
flour *masala* (*lotwalo masalo*), 25
flour tortillas, *samosa* preparation with, *139*
flour with jaggery and water (*raab*), 489
flours and grains, described and listed, **40–45**
*flowernu raitu* (cauliflower *raita*), 101
food categories in the *Bhagavata Gita*, 2
fresh carrot and cucumber pickle (*gajar kakdinu athanu*), 124
fresh fruit and nut *raita* (*durbari raita*), 109
freshness of ingredients, 5

fried appetizers
    about, 130–32
    battered vegetables (*pakora/bhajia*), 134–35
    chili *pakora* (*mirch pakora*), 136–37
    for large groups, 131–32
    lentil kebabs (*masoorna muthia*), 148–49
    lentil wafers (*papadum/papad*), 152
    mashed banana *pakora* (*kela methi pakora*), 138
    mixed bean patties with yogurt (*dahivada*), 146–47
    pairing with other foods, 131
    *pakora* flour mix (*pakora atta*), 133
    rice wafers (*papdi*), 153–54
    *samosa,* 140–43
    spicy mashed potato rounds (*bateta vada*), 151
    split chickpea patties (*chana dal vada*), 150
    split mung patties (*mung dal kachori*), 144–45
    storage of, 130
fruits
    described and listed, **33–35**
    as desserts, 478–80
    stuffing method illustrated, *259*
    as vegetables, 289–94
frying pans, 47
*fudinani chai* (tea with mint and cardamom), 487
*fudinanu raitu* (mint *raita*), 104
*fudinawala chana* (garbanzo beans with mint), 347–48
*fudino/pudino* (mint), **27**
*fulka/chapati*
    described, 402
    paper-thin Gujarati bread, 404–05

# G

*gajar* (carrots), **38**

*gajar halwa* (carrot *halwa*), 465

*gajar kakdinu athanu* (fresh carrot and cucumber pickle), 124

*gajarni chutney* (carrot chutney), 81

*gajarno chhundo* (carrot relish), 95

*gajarnu athanu* (sweet and hot carrot pickle), 119

*gajarnu raitu* (carrot *raita*), 100

*galvanu* (Cream of Wheat pudding), 443

Gandhi, Mahatma, on cows, 54

*The Ganges* restaurant, 4–5

Ganges water, 483–84

*garam masala*

   described, **20**

   recipes, 21–22

garbanzo beans (*chana*), **338**

   garbanzo beans with mint (*fudinawala chana*), 347–48

garbanzo flour (*chanano lot*), **42**

   caution about confusing with chickpea flour, 41

garlic (*lasun/lasan*), **19**

   healing properties of, 2

   peeling tip, 19

   as *rajasic* food, 2

   sprouted mung beans with garlic (*sangavela mug*), 371

   yellow split peas with garlic and cloves (*vatanani dal*), 375

garlic, green (*hara lasun/lilu lasan*), **20**

   green garlic chutney (*leela lasanni chutney*), 82

garlic and red chili chutney (*lasanni thikhi chutney*), 75

*ghari* (stuffed round pastry), 469–70

*ghaun* (wheat), 44

*ghaunno lot* (wheat flour), 44

*ghavno kakario lot* (wheat flour, coarsely ground), **45**

*ghee*, 47
  described, 55
  recipe, 59

*ghughra* (stuffed, half-moon shaped pastry), 466–67, *468*

ginger, fresh (*adrak/aadu*), **26**
  green mung beans with ginger (*mug*), 363

ginger, powdered (*sonth*), **26**

*gobi korma* (cauliflower with spicy yogurt sauce), 214

gold or silver leaves (*varak/vark*), **30**

*golvo* (yogurt with milk), 494

*gor/good* (jaggery), **26–27**

gourds. *See* bitter gourd and tinde (ivy gourd); bottle gourd and ridge gourd

grains. *See* rice, bulgur and other grains

grains and spice *raita* (*methkoot*), 110–11

gram flour (*chanano lot*), **41**

green beans and long beans
  green beans with dumplings (*fansi dhokli*), 216–17
  green beans with potatoes (*fansi bateta*), 215
  long beans with eggplant (*choli vengan*), 218

green garlic (*hara lasun/lilu lasan*), **20**
  green garlic chutney (*leela lasanni chutney*), 82

green mung beans. *See* mung beans

green onions
  mushroom with green onions (*pyazwali gucchi*), 270
  *See also* onions

green papaya relish (*kacha papayani kachumber*), 89

green papaya relish, spicy (*papayani chhin*), 90

green peas. *See* peas

griddle, 47

ground rice with nuts (*shahi firnee*), 446

*gucchi palak* (*masala* mushrooms with spinach), 271
Gujarati cooking influence, 3
*gulab jaman* (milk powder and flour balls in rose flavored syrup), 450–51
*gulab lassi* (rose *lassi*), 494
*gulabnu doodh* (rose milk), 497
*gulabnu sherbat* (rose *sherbat*), 496
*gulabnu* syrup (rose syrup), 496
*gunyan* (caraway seeds), **11**
*guwarnu shak* (cluster beans with coriander and cumin), 225

# H

*haldi/haldar* (turmeric), **31–32**
*halwa*
    buckwheat *halwa* (*fafar sheera*), 473
    carrot *halwa* (*gajar halwa*), 465
*handva* flour (*handvano lot*), **42**
*handvana lotna puda* (mixed flour savory pancakes), 429–30
*handvano lot* (*handva* flour), **42**
*handvol bhakhar* (baked savory cake), 163–64
*hara dhania* (cilantro), **13**
*hara lasun/lilu lasan* (green garlic), **20**
*hari mirch* (green chilies), **12**
herbs. *See* spices and herbs
Hinduism
    reverence of cows, 54
    vegetarianism and, 1–3
*hing* (asafoetida), **10**
honeydew melon with green peas (*khadbucha vatana*), 292
hot and sweet chili pickle (*marchanu tikhune galu athanu*), 126
hot chili pickle (*marchanu athanu*), 125

# I

ice cream with saffron (*kesar kulfi*), 448–49
*idada* (black bean and rice cake with cracked pepper), 160
*idlee* (steamed savory rounds), 159–60
*idlee* flour (*idleeno lot*), **42–43**
*idlee* maker, 47, 160
*idleeno lot* (*idlee* flour), **42–43**
*imli* (tamarind), **31**
Indian black beans. *See* black beans
Indian black beans with *dals* and spices (*Punjabi dal*), 384–85
Indian ice cream with saffron (*kesar kulfi*), 448–49
Indian lima beans. *See* lima beans
Indian pasta with split pigeon peas (*dal dhokli*), 360–62
Indian plum, **34**
Indian spiced tea (*masala chai*), 486
Indian tea (*chai*), 485
ivy gourd. *See* bitter gourd and tinde (ivy gourd)

# J

jaggery (*gor/good*), **26–27**
*jaiphal* (nutmeg), **28**
*jaljeera/jeerapani* (tamarind aperitif), 501
*jaman* balls, 450–51
*jardalu* (apricot), **33**
*jardaluni chutney* (apricot chutney), 77
*javitri/javantri* (mace), **27**
*jayfull/jaiphal* (nutmeg), **28**
*jeera* persimmon (persimmon with cumin), 294
*jeera/safed jeera* (cumin seeds), **15**
*jeerapani* (tamarind aperitif), 501
juices. *See* beverages

jujube tree (*bor*), **34**

*jungli pulav* (wild rice pilaf), 333

*juwar* (sorghum), **43**

*juwarna rotla* (sorghum flour bread), 435

*juwarni khichadi* (sorghum *khichadi*), 324

*juwarno lot* (sorghum flour), **44**

## K

*Kabuli chana*, **338**

*kacha papayani kachumber* (green papaya relish), 89

*kacha tameta khalva* (sweet and spicy green tomatoes), 245

*kachori*, stuffing method, *425*

*kadhi* (yogurt-chili sauce), 393

*kaju* (cashews), **36**

*kaju katni* (cashew diamonds), 475

*kakdina dhokla* (cucumber savory cake), 157–58

*kakdini kachumber* (cucumber relish), 87

*kakdinu raitu* (cucumber *raita* with green chilies), 99

*kala chana* Bengal grams, **338**, 350

*kala jeera/shah jeera* (black cumin seeds), **15**

*kala mari*, **28–29**

*kala mug* (black mung beans), **341**

*kala namak* (black salt), **30**

*kala tal* (black sesame seeds), **30**

*kamrakh* (star fruit), **34**

*kamrukhni chutney* (carambola or star fruit chutney), 85

*kanda bateta* (onions with potatoes), 196

*kanda/pyaz. See* onions

*kandana rasama bharela bateta* (stuffed potatoes in coconut-onion sauce), 203–04

*kandane cholai* (amaranth greens with onions), 282

*kandanu raitu* (onion *raita*), 105

*kapoor/karpoor* (camphor), **11**

*karadni khichadi* (brown rice with *toor dal*), 309

*karai*, 47

*karela, kandane bateta* (sweet and sour bitter gourd with onions and potatoes), 266–67

*kashmiri rajma* (kidney beans with potatoes), 369–70

*kathiawadi khichadi* (unhulled split mung *khichadi*), 320

kebabs

    lentil kebabs (*masoorna muthia*), 148–49

    lima beans with spinach kebabs (*papdi muthia*), 222–23

    spinach kebabs (*palakna muthia*), 169–70

*kela* (banana), **33**

*kela methi pakora* (mashed banana *pakora*), 138

*kelana ravaiya* (stuffed bananas with chickpea flour and spices), 291

*kelani bhakhari* (banana *bhakhari*), 410

*kelanu raitu* (banana *raita*), 108

*keri kandani kachumber* (mango and onion relish), 88

*kerini chutney* (mango chutney), 79–80

*kerino ras* (thick mango juice), 480

*kerinu athanu/methia keri* (mango pickle), 117

*kerinu galune tikhu athanu* (sweet and hot mango pickle), 118

*kerinu shak* (mango vegetable), 293

*kesar* (saffron), **29**

*kesar kulfi* (Indian ice cream with saffron), 448–49

*kesar lassi/piyush* (buttermilk with saffron), 493

*kesar mevanu doodh* (milk with saffron and nuts), 497

*kesari sheera* (Cream of Wheat with cardamom and saffron), 472

*kesarwali khichadi* (cashew and saffron *khichadi*), 321–22

*kesarwalo bhat* (saffron rice), 301

*kewra* essence (screw pine), **46**

*Khada hing*, **10**

*khadbucha vatana* (honeydew melon with green peas), 292
*khajur* (dates), **16**
*khajur pilla* (date rolls), 476
*khalva* (sliced eggplants with onions and chickpea flour), 237
*khaman* flour, **41**
*khand* (sugar), **30–31**
   cooking without, 49
*khandkeri* (unripe mango dessert), 471
*khandvi/pilla patodi* (chickpea flour rolls), 161–62
*khati lapsi* (bulgur with spices), 326
*khichadi*
   cashew and saffron *khichadi* (*kesarwali khichadi*), 321–22
   cumin and pepper *khichadi* (*masalawali khichadi*), 323
   sorghum *khichadi* (*juwarni khichadi*), 324
   split lima bean *khichadi* (*valdalni khichadi*), 318–19
   unhulled split mung *khichadi* (*kathiawadi khichadi*), 320
*khoya* (solidified milk), 62
   in desserts, 441
*khus khus* (poppy seeds), **29**
kidney beans (*rajma*), **339**
   with potatoes (*kashmiri rajma*), 369–70
*kobi bateta* (cabbage with potatoes and *garam masala*), 240
*kobij khalva* (cabbage with chickpea flour), 241
*kobijna parotha* (cabbage-stuffed *parotha*), 414–15
*kobijno bhakhar* (savory cabbage cake), 167–68
*kobijnu kachumber* (cabbage relish), 97
*kodri* (quinoa), **44**
   preparation of, 332
*kofta* "curry" (black-eyed peas *kofta* in onion sauce), 391–92
*kohlu, valdalne palak* (pumpkin with split lima beans and spinach), 261
*kohlu vatana* (pumpkin with peas and tamarind), 260
*kopra doodhpaak* (rice pudding with coconut), 474

*koprana doodhma gobi* (cauliflower in coconut sauce), 211
*koprano bhat* (coconut rice), 303
*koprune chana dal chutney* (coconut and split chickpea chutney), 71
*koprune lal marchani chutney* (coconut and red pepper chutney), 73
*kothmirma ravaiya* (stuffed eggplants in cilantro sauce), 231–32
*kothmirni chutney* (cilantro chutney), 70
*kothmirnu raitu* (cilantro *raita*), 103
*Krishna tulsi* (basil), **10–11**
*kulcha* (leavened bread with onions), 424
    stuffing method, *425*
*kulfi,* 448–49

## L

*laadu,* 447
*labaad aaloo* (mock potatoes), 192
*lal choli* (spiced aduki beans), 346
*lal mirch* (chili powder), **12–13**
*lapsi* (bulgur), **40**
*lapsi* (bulgur dessert), 477
*lapsi pilaf* (bulgur with vegetables), 328
*lassi*
    about, 482
    buttermilk with cumin and mustard (*vaghareli chhash*), 491
    buttermilk with mango (*aam lassi*), 492
    buttermilk with papaya (*papaya lassi*), 492
    buttermilk with saffron (*kesar lassi/piyush*), 493
    plain *lassi,* 490
    rose *lassi* (*gulab lassi*), 494
    strawberry *lassi,* 493
*lasun/lasan. See* garlic
*laung/lavang* (cloves), **14**

layered Indian bread (*parotha*), 411–16
leavened Indian bread (*naan*), 422–24
*leela lasanni chutney* (green garlic chutney), 82
*leela mari*, **28–29**
*leela mug* (green mung beans), **341**
*leela vatana* (green peas with cilantro-coconut sauce), 388
*leeli chai* (lemon grass), 27
*leeli haldar* (fresh turmeric), **32**
*leeli tuver* (fresh pigeon peas), 248
legumes. *See dals*
lemon (*limbu*), **35**
    lemon peel chutney (*limbuni chutney*), 84
    sweet and hot lemon pickle (*limbunu galu athanu*), 120–21
lemon grass (*leeli chai*), **27**
lemonade (*limbunu sherbat*), 498
lentils (*masoor*), **339–40**
    lentil kebabs (*masoorna muthia*), 148–49
    lentil pilaf (*masoorno pulav*), 310
    lentil wafers (*papadum/papad*), 152
    red lentils (*masoor dal*), **340**
    *See also dals*
*lilu lasan* (green garlic), **20**
lima beans (*val*), **340**
    eggplant with split Indian lima beans (*vengan valni dal*), 228
    lima beans with dumplings (*papdi dhokli*), 220–21
    lima beans with eggplant (*papdi vengan*), 224
    lima beans with fresh spices (*papdinu shak*), 219
    lima beans with spinach kebabs (*papdi muthia*), 222–23
    lima beans with tamarind (*sabut val*), 382–83
    pumpkin with split lima beans and spinach (*kohlu, valdalne palak*), 261
    split lima bean *khichadi* (*valdalni khichadi*), 318–19
    split lima beans (*valni dal*), **340**, 373–74

*limbu* (lemon), **35**
*limbuna phool* (citric acid), **13**
*limbuni chutney* (lemon peel chutney), 84
*limbunu galu athanu* (sweet and hot lemon pickle), 121
*limbunu sherbat* (lemonade), 498
*limdo/limdana paan* (curry leaves), **16**
long beans. *See* green beans and long beans
*lotwalo masalo* (flour *masala*), 25
low fat cooking
    cooking without oil, 48
    fat-free breads, 432–38
    fat-free *dals,* 336
    low fat milk, 55
    of vegetables, 190
    *See also* non-fried appetizers
Lucknowi rice with vegetables (*tahri*), 304

**M**

mace (*javitri/javantri*), **27**
Mahashivratri drink (*thandai*), 495
*makaini rotli/makkeki roti* (cornmeal bread), 437
*makkai* (corn), **41**
mango (*aam*), **35**
    buttermilk with mango (*aam lassi*), 492
    mango and onion relish (*keri kandani kachumber*), 88
    mango chutney (*kerini chutney*), 79–80
    mango pickle (*kerinu athanu/methia keri*), 117
    mango relish with cardamom (*murrabbo*), 94
    mango relish with cumin (*chhundo*), 93
    mango vegetable (*kerinu shak*), 293
    sweet and hot mango pickle (*kerinu galune tikhu athanu*), 118
    thick mango juice (*kerino ras*), 480
    unripe mango dessert (*khandkeri*), 471

mango essence, **46**
mango powder (*amchoor*), **27**
*marchanu athanu* (hot chili pickle), 125
*marchanu tikhune galu athanu* (hot and sweet chili pickle), 126
mari (pepper), **28–29**
*masala bhadku* (bulgur with split mung beans and onions), 327
*masala chai* (Indian spiced tea), 486
*masala dosa* (South Indian crepes with stuffing), 428
*masala* mushrooms with spinach (*gucchi palak*), 271
*masala naan* (spicy *naan*), 423
*masalana rotla* (spiced millet bread), 435
*masalas*
   flour *masala* (*lotwalo masalo*), 25
   *garam masalas,* 21–22
   vegetable *masala* (*shakno masalo*), 23–24
*masalawali khichadi* (cumin and pepper *khichadi*), 323
*maska* (thickened yogurt), 58
*masoor. See* lentils
*masoor dal* (red lentils), **340**
*masoorna muthia* (lentil kebabs), 148–49
*masoorno pulav* (lentil pilaf), 310
*mathdi* (stuffed crispy rounds), 176–77
*matho* (sweetened yogurt dessert with black pepper), 453
*mavo. See* solidified milk
medicinal properties of spices and herbs, 8
*methi* (fenugreek), **19**
*methi na kuria,* **19**
*methia keri* (mango pickle), 117
*methini bhaji/methi* (fenugreek), **19**
*methkoot* (grains and spice *raita*), 98, 110–11
milk
   low fat milk use, 55
   as the most perfect *sattvic* food, 54

milk (*continued*)

    with rose, tapioca and vermicelli (*falooda*), 499–500

    with saffron and nuts (*kesar mevanu doodh*), 497

    solidified milk (*khoya/mavo*), 62

milk powder and flour balls in rose flavored syrup (*gulab jaman*), 450–51

millet (*bajri*), **43**

    three grain savory porridge (*bajri*, mung, *chokhanu bhadku*), 325

millet flour (*bajrino lot*), **43**

    millet flour bread (*bajrina rotla*), 434–35

    spiced millet bread (*masalana rotla*), 435

    wheat and millet bread (*dhebra/thepla*), 417–18

mint (*fudino/pudino*), **27**

    garbanzo beans with mint (*fudinawala chana*), 347–48

    mint *raita* (*fudinanu raitu*), 104

    tea with mint and cardamom (*fudinani chai*), 487

*mirch pakora* (chili *pakora*), 136–37

mixed bean patties with yogurt (*dahivada*), 146–47

mock potatoes (*labaad aaloo*), 192

*moglai dal* (split and whole Indian black beans), 380–81

*moglai gobi* (creamy cauliflower with potatoes and peas), 213

*moongphali* (toasted peanuts), 184

*moongphali/bhoyphali* (peanuts), **37**

mortar and pestle, *28*

*mug* (green mung beans with ginger), 363

*mugni dal* (split mung beans), **341**, 366

*mula* (white radish), **39**

*muli kachumber* (daikon relish), 91

mung beans

    black mung beans (*kala mug*), **341**

    brown or red mung beans (*muth*), **341**

    bulgur with split mung beans and onions (*masala bhadku*), 327

    green mung beans (*leela mug*), **341**

mung beans (*continued*)
    green mung beans with ginger (*mug*), 363
    *mung dal kachori* (split mung patties), 144–45
    mung *dal vadi*, 18
    split mung beans (*mugni dal*), **341**, 366
    split mung beans with zucchini (zucchini *mugni dal*), 367
    split pigeon peas with mung beans (*tuver mugni dal*), 358–59
    sprouted beans, **343**
    sprouted brown mung beans (*sangavela muth*), 372
    sprouted brown mung beans with dumplings (*muth dhokli*), 372
    sprouted mung beans with garlic (*sangavela mug*), 371
    sweet, sour and hot mung beans (*mugno ragdo*), 364–65
    unhulled split mung *khichadi* (*kathiawadi khichadi*), 320
*mungo ragdo* (sweet, sour and hot mung beans), 364–65
*murrabbo* (mango relish with cardamom), 94
mushrooms
    *masala* mushrooms with spinach (*gucchi palak*), 271
    mushroom with green onions (*pyazwali gucchi*), 270
    zucchini with mushrooms (zucchini *gucchi*), 272
mustard oil, 47
mustard seeds (*rai*), **27–28**
    spicy cabbage, stir-cooked with mustard seeds (*vaghareli kobij*), 242
*muth* (brown or red mung beans), **341**
*muth dhokli* (sprouted brown mung beans with dumplings), 372

## N

*naan*
    leavened Indian bread, 422–23
    with onions (*kulcha*), 424
    with raisins, 423
    spicy *naan* (*masala naan*), 423

*namak* (salt), **30**
   cooking without, 48
*nankhatai* (cardamom cookies), 183
*Narikela* (coconut), **14**
*nariyel* (coconut), **14**
*neera* (coconut sap), 483
*nimbuka satl limbuna phool* (citric acid), **13**
non-dairy desserts, 471–77
non-fried appetizers
   about, 130–32
   baked savory cake (*handvol bhakhar*), 163–64
   bean and spinach cake (*chola chanano handvo*), 165
   black bean and rice cake with cracked pepper (*idada*), 160
   chickpea flour rolls (*khandvil pilla patodi*), 161–62
   cucumber savory cake (*kakdina dhokla*), 157–58
   for large groups, 131–32
   pairing with other foods, 131
   savory cabbage cake (*kobijno bhakhar*), 167–68
   spicy spinach squares (*bhajina dhokla*), 166
   spinach kebabs (*palakna muthia*), 169–70
   steamed savory cake (*dhokla*), 155–56
   steamed savory rounds (*idlee*), 159–60
   steamed spinach and peas rounds (*palak vatanana muthia*), 171
   storage of, 130
noodle press (*sevno sancho*), 47, *175*
nutmeg (*jayfull jaiphal*), **28**
nuts
   almond fudge (*badam barfi*), 454–55
   described and listed, **36–37**
   eggplant with nuts and yogurt (*badshahi baigan*), 238–39
   ground rice with nuts (*shahi firnee*), 446
   tamarind rice with nuts and *dal* (*pulihara*), 305–06

# O

oils. *See* fats and oils

okra

   okra with onions (*Punjabi bhindi*), 285

   stuffed okra (*bhindi masala*), 283–84

   vegetarian "gumbo" (*bhinda, kandane paneer*), 286

olive oil, 47

one-dish meals. *See* fried appetizers; non-fried appetizers; snacks

onions (*kanda/pyaz*)

   amaranth greens with onions (*kandane cholai*), 282

   black-eyed peas *kofta* in onion sauce (*kofta* "curry"), 391–92

   bottle gourd *kofta* in onion sauce (*doodhina kofta*), 252–53

   bread with onions (*kulcha*), 424

   browning of, 38–39

   coconut-onion sauce, 203

   collard greens with onions (collard *saag*), 278

   described, **38–39**

   healing properties of, 2, 38

   ivy gourd with spicy potatoes and onions (*tindora, bateta, kanda*), 269

   mango and onion relish (*keri kandani kachumber*), 88

   okra with onions (*Punjabi bhindi*), 285

   onion and yogurt sauce, 200

   onion *raita* (*kandanu raitu*), 105

   onion *sambar,* 378–79

   onion-yogurt sauce, 389–90

   onions with chickpea flour and yogurt (*pitla*), 197

   onions with potatoes (*kanda bateta*), 196

   onions with tomatoes and spices (basic sauce), 195

   as *rajasic* food, 2

   roasted eggplant with onions (*bharta*), 235

   sliced eggplants with onions and chickpea flour (*khalva*), 237

   sweet and sour bitter gourd with onions and potatoes (*karela, kandane bateta*), 266–67

   tomato and onion relish (*tametane kandani kachumber*), 86

# P

*pakora*
    battered vegetables (*pakora/bhajia*), 134–35
    chili *pakora* (*mirch pakora*), 136–37
    mashed banana *pakora* (*kela methi pakora*), 138
    *pakora* flour mix (*pakora atta*), 133
*palak aaloo* (spinach and potato "curry"), 273
*palak moglai* (spinach with split chickpeas), 276
*palak paneer* ("curried" spinach with *paneer*), 274
*palak vadi* (spinach dumplings), 193
*palak vatanana muthia* (steamed spinach and peas rounds), 171
*palakna muthia* (spinach kebabs), 169–70
pancakes, mixed flour savory pancakes (*handvana lotna puda*), 429–30
*panch dal* (five *dals*), 386–87
*Panchamrat* preparation, 54
*paneer. See* cheese
*paneer parotha* (*paneer*-stuffed *parotha*), 416
*panoo* (tamarind sauce), 394
*papad* (lentil wafers), 152
*papad* flour (*papadno lot*), **44**
*papadni kachumber* (*papadum* relish), 92
*papadno lot* (*papad* flour), **44**
*papadum* (lentil wafers), 152
*papadum* relish (*papadni kachumber*), 92
papaya (*paw paw/papayee*), **35**
    buttermilk with papaya (*papaya lassi*), 492
    green papaya relish (*kacha papayani kachumber*), 89
    papaya with cumin, 478
    spicy green papaya relish (*papayani chhin*), 90
*papayani chhin* (spicy green papaya relish), 90
*papdi* (rice wafers), 153–54
*papdi dhokli* (lima beans with dumplings), 220–21
*papdi muthia* (lima beans with spinach kebabs), 222–23

*papdi vengan* (lima beans with eggplant), 224
*papdinu shak* (lima beans with fresh spices), 219
paper-thin Gujarati bread (*fulka*/*chapati*), 404–05
*Parijat* flower, 1
*parotha,* 411–16
   cabbage-stuffed *parotha* (*kobijna parotha*), 414–15
   described, 399
   layered Indian bread, 411–12
   *paneer*-stuffed *parotha* (*paneer parotha*), 416
   potato-stuffed *parotha* (*aaloo parotha*), 413
   stuffing method, *425*
pastry. *See* desserts and sweetmeats
patties
   mixed bean patties with yogurt (*dahivada*), 146–47
   split chickpea patties (*chana dal vada*), 150
   split mung patties (*mung dal kachori*), 144–45
*paw paw*/*papayee* (papaya), **35**
*payas* (rice pudding with raisins), 444–45
peanuts (*moongphali*/*bhoyphali*), **37**
   potatoes with peanuts (*batetane shing*), 199
   sweet potatoes and potatoes with peanuts (*sakkaria bateta*), 208
   toasted peanuts (*shekeli shing*/*moongphali*), 184
peas (*vatana*)
   creamy cauliflower with potatoes and peas (*moglai gobi*), 213
   eggplant with peas (*vengan vatana*), 227
   green peas with cilantro-coconut sauce (*leela vatana*), 388
   green peas with potatoes (*vatana bateta*), 246
   honeydew melon with green peas (*khadbucha vatana*), 292
   peas and *paneer* in raisin sauce (*drakshawala matar paneer*), 247
   pumpkin with peas and tamarind (*kohlu vatana*), 260
   split peas (*vatanani dal*), **342**
   stuffed eggplants with peas (*vatana bharela vengan*), 233–34

peas (*vatana*) (*continued*)
    yellow peas in onion-yogurt sauce (*dopiaza matar*), 389–90
    yellow split peas with garlic and cloves (*vatanani dal*), 375
    zucchini with peas and tomatoes (zucchini *vatana*), 256
    *See also dals*
*peni*, 47
pepper (black, white and fresh green), **28–29**
persimmon chutney, 76
persimmon with cumin (*jeera* persimmon), 294
pickles
    about, 65–66, 114
    basic pickling spice (*athanano masalo*), 115–16
    dry fruit pickle (*suka mevanu athanu*), 122
    fresh carrot and cucumber pickle (*gajar kakdinu athanu*), 124
    hot and sweet chili pickle (*marchanu tikhune galu athanu*), 126
    hot chili pickle (*marchanu athanu*), 125
    mango pickle (*kerinu athanu/methia keri*), 117
    raisin pickle (*drakshnu athanu*), 127
    sweet and hot carrot pickle (*gajarnu athanu*), 119
    sweet and hot lemon pickle (*limbunu galu athanu*), 120–21
    sweet and hot mango pickle (*kerinu galune tikhu athanu*), 118
    unripe cherry pickle (*cherinu athanu*), 123
pickling spice (*athanano masalo*), 115–16
pigeon peas (*tuver*), **342**
    brown rice with *toor dal* (*karadni khichadi*), 309
    fresh pigeon peas (*leeli tuver*), 248
    Indian pasta with split pigeon peas (*dal dhokli*), 360–62
    rice and split pigeon peas with saffron (*beeranj*), 457
    split pigeon peas (*tuverni dall/arar dal*), **342**
    split pigeon peas with mung beans (*tuver mugni dal*), 358–59
    split pigeon peas with tomatoes and bulbous root (*suranwali dal*), 356–57
    whole pigeon peas with yogurt and spices (*toor kadhi*), 354–55

pilafs
  bulgur with vegetables (*lapsi pilaf*), 328
  dry peas pilaf (*suka vatanano pulav*), 317
  lentil pilaf (*masoorno pulav*), 310
  tricolor pilaf (*trirangi pulav*), 314–16
  vegetable pilaf (*shakno pulav*), 311–13
  wild rice pilaf (*jungli pulav*), 333
*pilla patodi* (chickpea flour rolls), 161–62
pineapple (*ananas*), **35**
  pineapple relish with cumin (*ananasno chhundo*), 96
*pista* (pistachios), **37**
pistachios (*pista*), **37**
*pitla* (onions with chickpea flour and yogurt), 197
*piyush* (buttermilk with saffron), 493
pomegranate seeds (*anardana/darukhatta*), **29**
*pongal* (South Indian sweet rice), 307–08
poppy seeds (*khus khus*), **29**
potatoes (*bateta*), **39**
  asparagus with potatoes (asparagus *bateta*), 209
  bottle gourd with potatoes (*doodhi bateta*), 249
  cabbage with potatoes and *garam masala* (*kobi bateta*), 240
  cauliflower with potatoes (*aaloo gobi*), 212
  coring potatoes illustrated, *202*
  creamy cauliflower with potatoes and peas (*moglai gobi*), 213
  green beans with potatoes (*fansi bateta*), 215
  green peas with potatoes (*vatana bateta*), 246
  ivy gourd with potatoes (*tindora bateta*), 268
  ivy gourd with spicy potatoes and onions (*tindora, bateta, kanda*), 269
  onions with potatoes (*kanda bateta*), 196
  pigeon peas consommé (*dalnu osaman*), 352–53
  potato chutney (*batetani chutney*), 72
  potato *raita* (*batetanu raitu*), 113

potatoes (*bateta*), **39** (*continued*)
  potato-stuffed *parotha* (*aaloo parotha*), 413
  potatoes with peanuts (*batetane shing*), 199
  spicy mashed potato rounds (*bateta vada*), 151
  spicy potatoes with *garam masala* (*suki bhaji*), 198
  spinach and potato "curry" (*palak aaloo*), 273
  stuffed potatoes in coconut-onion sauce (*kandana rasama bharela bateta*), 203–04
  stuffed potatoes in onion and yogurt sauce (*dum bateta*), 200–201
  stuffed potatoes in spinach and coconut sauce (*bhaji koprama bateta*), 205–06
  sweet and sour bitter gourd with onions and potatoes (*karela, kandane bateta*), 266–67
  sweet potatoes, potatoes, and peas with onions (*sakkaria bateta, vatana*), 207
  sweet potatoes and potatoes with peanuts (*sakkaria bateta*), 208
  tomatoes with potatoes (*tameta bateta*), 243–44
precooked rice with bell peppers and yogurt (*vagharelo bhat*), 300
*puda*
  mixed flour savory pancakes (*handvana lotna puda*), 429–30
  vegetarian omelettes (*puda*), 421
*pudino* (mint), **27**
*pulav. See* pilafs
*pulihara* (tamarind rice with nuts and *dal*), 305–06
pumpkin
  with peas and tamarind (*kohlu vatana*), 260
  with split lima beans and spinach (*kohlu, valdalne palak*), 261
*Punjabi bhindi* (okra with onions), 285
*Punjabi dal* (Indian black beans with *dals* and spices), 384–85
*puri*
  deep-fried Indian bread, 420
  festive *puri* (*Surti puri*), 421

*pyaz. See* onions
*pyazwali gucchi* (mushroom with green onions), 270

# Q
quinoa (*kodri*), **44**
  preparation of, 332

# R
*raab* (flour with jaggery and water), 489
radish (*mula*), **39**
*rai* (mustard seeds), **27–28**
*rai na kuria,* **28**
raisin and tamarind chutney (*draksh aamlini chutney*), 69
raisin *naan,* 423
raisin pickle (*drakshnu athanu*), 127
raisin sauce, peas and *paneer* in raisin sauce (*drakshawala matar paneer*), 247
*raitas*
  about, 65–66, 98
  banana *raita* (*kelanu raitu*), 108
  carrot *raita* (*gajarnu raitu*), 100
  cauliflower *raita* (*flowernu raitu*), 101
  cilantro *raita* (*kothmirnu raitu*), 103
  cucumber *raita* with green chilies (*kakdinu raitu*), 99
  dry fruit *raita* (*suka mevanu raitu*), 107
  dumpling *raita* (*bundi raita*), 106
  fresh fruit and nut *raita* (*durbari raita*), 109
  grains and spice *raita* (*methkoot*), 110–11
  mint *raita* (*fudinanu raitu*), 104
  onion *raita* (*kandanu raitu*), 105
  pairing with other foods, 98

raitas (*continued*)

    potato *raita* (*batetanu raitu*), 113

    spicy hot *raita* (*tikhari*), 112

    spinach *raita* (*bhajinu raitu*), 102

    *See also* yogurt

*rajagarani bhakhari* (amaranth flour bread), 438

*rajagarani kheer* (amaranth pudding), 464

*rajagarano lot* (amaranth flour), **40**

*rajagaro* (amaranth), **40**

*rajasic* foods, 2

*rajma* (kidney beans), **339**

*Ram tulsi* (basil), **10**

*ras malai* (*paneer* patty in sweet, cream sauce), 458–60

    shortcut, 461–62

*Rasayan hing,* **10**

*ratalu* (yams), **39**

*ravaiya vengan* (stuffed eggplants in spicy sauce), 229–30

*ravo* (semolina), **42**

recommendations and hints, 51–52

red black-eyed peas. *See* aduki beans (*choli*)

red daikon radish, **39**

    daikon relish (*muli kachumber*), 91

red lentils (*masoor dal*), **340**

red mung beans. *See* mung beans

red peppers, coconut and red pepper chutney (*koprune lal marchani chutney*), 73

relishes. *See* chutneys and relishes

Reshampatti chili powder brand, **13**

restricted diets

    cooking without salt, 48

    and sweeteners, 441–42

    *See also* low fat cooking

rice, bulgur and other grains, **43**, 295–333
  about, 296
  *basmati* rice (*bhat*), 298–99
  brown rice with *toor dal* (*karadni khichadi*), 309
  bulgur (*lapsi*), **40**
  bulgur dessert (*lapsi*), 477
  bulgur with milk and nuts (*fadano doodhpaak*), 456
  bulgur with spices (*khati lapsi*), 326
  bulgur with split mung beans and onions (*masala bhadku*), 327
  bulgur with vegetables (*lapsi pilaf*), 328
  cashew and saffron *khichadi* (*kesarwali khichadi*), 321–22
  coconut rice (*koprano bhat*), 303
  cumin and pepper *khichadi* (*masalawali khichadi*), 323
  dry peas pilaf (*suka vatanano pulav*), 317
  eggplant rice (*vangi bhat*), 302
  grains and flours described and listed, **40–45**
  lentil pilaf (*masoorno pulav*), 310
  Lucknowi rice with vegetables (*tahri*), 304
  precooked rice with bell peppers and yogurt (*vagharelo bhat*), 300
  quinoa (*kodri*), 332
  saffron rice (*kesarwalo bhat*), 301
  sorghum *khichadi* (*juwarni khichadi*), 324
  South Indian sweet rice (*pongal*), 307–08
  split lima bean *khichadi* (*valdalni khichadi*), 318–19
  tamarind rice with nuts and *dal* (*pulihara*), 305–06
  three grain savory porridge (*bajri*, mung, *chokhanu bhadku*), 325
  tricolor pilaf (*trirangi pulav*), 314–16
  unhulled split mung *khichadi* (*kathiawadi khichadi*), 320
  vegetable *biryani* (*shakni biryani*), 329–31
  vegetable pilaf (*shakno pulav*), 311–13
  wild rice pilaf (*jungli pulav*), 333

rice flour (*chokhano lot*), **43**
  rice flour bread (*chokhani rotli*), 432
  rice flour curls (*chakri*), 172–73
rice pudding with coconut (*kopra doodhpaak*), 474
rice pudding with raisins (*payas*), 444–45
rice wafers (*papdi*), 153–54
ricotta cheese (part-skim) as dessert substitute, 441
ridge gourd. *See* bottle gourd and ridge gourd
roasted eggplant with onions (*bharta*), 235
roasted eggplant with yogurt (*bharta*), 236
rolling pin, 47
root vegetables, described and listed, **38–39**
rose essence, **46**
rose *lassi* (*gulab lassi*), 494
rose milk (*gulabnu doodh*), 497
rose *sherbat* (*gulabnu sherbat*), 496
rose syrup, 450–51, 496
*rotla*
  described, 399
  shaping with hands, *436*

# S

*sabudana* (tapioca), **44**
*sabut lal mirch* (red chilies), **12**
*sabut val* (lima beans with tamarind), 382–83
*sada dosa* (South Indian crepes), 426–27
*safarjan* (apple), **33**
*safed jeera* (cumin seeds), **15**
*safed mari*, **28–29**

saffron (*kesar*), **29**
  buttermilk with saffron (*kesar lassi/piyush*), 493
  cashew and saffron *khichadi* (*kesarwali khichadi*), 321–22
  milk with saffron and nuts (*kesar mevanu doodh*), 497
  saffron rice (*kesarwalo bhat*), 301
*sai bhaji* (spinach with carrots), 277
*sakkar/khand* (sugar), **30–31**
  cooking without, 48–49
*sakkaria. See* sweet potatoes
*sakkaria bateta* (sweet potatoes and potatoes with peanuts), 208
*sakkaria bateta, vatana* (sweet potatoes, potatoes, and peas with onions), 207
*sakkarteti* (cantaloupe), 478
salt (*namak*), **30**
  black salt (*kala namak*), **30**
  cooking without, 48
  sea salt (*sindhav*), **30**
*sambar*, 376–77
  onion *sambar*, 378–79
*samosa*
  flour tortillas for, 139
  tortilla shortcut method, 140–41
  traditional *samosa*, 142–43
*sangavela mug* (sprouted mung beans with garlic), 371
*sangavela muth* (sprouted brown mung beans), 372
*sapola* (*chickoo*), **34**
*sattvic* foods, 2
  milk as the most perfect, 54
sauces
  cilantro-coconut sauce, 388
  coconut-onion sauce, 203–04
  coconut sauce, 211

sauces (*continued*)
   cream sauce, 459, 461–62
   onion and yogurt sauce, 200, 389–90
   onion sauce, 252–53, 391–92
   raisin sauce, 247
   spicy yogurt sauce, 214
   spinach and coconut sauce, 205–06
   tamarind sauce (*panoo*), 394
   yogurt-chili sauce (*kadhi*), 393
*saunf* (fennel), **9**
*saunfwale karele* (stuffed bitter gourd with anise), 264–65
savory cabbage cake (*kobijno bhakhar*), 167–68
screw pine (*kewra* essence), **46**
sea salt (*sindhav*), **30**
semolina (*ravo*), **42**
sesame oil, 47
sesame seeds (*till/tal*), **30**
   spiced spinach with sesame (*bhaji ragad*), 275
*sev* (chickpea flour noodles), 174
*sevno sancho* (noodle press), 47, *175*
*shah jeera* (black cumin seeds), **15**
*shahi firnee* (ground rice with nuts), 446
*shakni biryani* (vegetable *biryani*), 329–31
*shakno masalo* (vegetable *masala*), 23–24
*shakno pulav* (vegetable pilaf), 311–13
*shekeli badam* (toasted almonds), 184
*shekeli shing/moongphali* (toasted peanuts), 184
*shreekhand* (sweetened yogurt dessert), 452
sieve, 47, *50*
silver or gold leaves (*varak/vark*), **30**
*sindhav* (sea salt), **30**
sliced eggplants with onions and chickpea flour (*khalva*), 237

snacks
  about, 130, 172
  Bombay snack mix (*bhelpuri*), 178–79
  butter biscuits (*Surti khari biscuit*), 182
  cardamom cookies (*nankhatai*), 183
  chickpea flour noodles (*sev*), 174
  Cream of Wheat with yogurt and cashew nuts (*upama*), 180–81
  rice flour curls (*chakri*), 172–73
  stuffed crispy rounds (*mathdi*), 176–77
  toasted almonds (*shekeli badam*), 184
  toasted peanuts (*shekeli shing/moongphali*), 184
solidified milk (*khoya/mavo*), 62
  in desserts, 441
*sonth* (ginger, powdered), **26**
*sooji. See* Cream of Wheat
*sooji kheer/galvanu* (Cream of Wheat pudding), 443
sorghum (*juwar*), **43**
  sorghum *khichadi* (*juwarni khichadi*), 324
sorghum flour (*juwarno lot*), **44**
  sorghum flour bread (*juwarna rotla*), 435
South Indian crepes (*sada dosa*), 426–27
South Indian *sambar*, 376–77
South Indian sweet rice (*pongal*), 307–08
soybeans, **342**
spaghetti squash with dumplings (spaghetti squash *ne vadi*), 262–63
spiced aduki beans (*lal choli*), 346
spiced black-eyed peas (*chola*), 344–45
spiced spinach with sesame (*bhaji ragad*), 275
spices and herbs
  coriander and cumin mix (*dhania jeera*), 26
  described and listed, **9–32**
  flour *masala* (*lotwalo masalo*), 25

spices and herbs (*continued*)
  *garam masalas,* 21–22
  mortar and pestle for grinding/crushing, *28*
  toasting spices, 9, 48
  vegetable *masala* (*shakno masalo*), 23–24
spicy cabbage, stir-cooked with mustard seeds (*vaghareli kobij*), 242
spicy hot *raita* (*tikhari*), 112
spicy mashed potato rounds (*bateta vada*), 151
spicy *naan* (*masala naan*), 423
spicy potatoes with *garam masala* (*suki bhaji*), 198
spicy spinach squares (*bhajina dhokla*), 166
spinach
  bean and spinach cake (*chola chanano handvo*), 165
  "curried" spinach with *paneer* (*palak paneer*), 274
  lima beans with spinach kebabs (*papdi muthia*), 222–23
  *masala* mushrooms with spinach (*gucchi palak*), 271
  pumpkin with split lima beans and spinach (*kohlu, valdalne palak*), 261
  spiced spinach with sesame (*bhaji ragad*), 275
  spicy spinach squares (*bhajina dhokla*), 166
  spinach and coconut sauce, 205–06
  spinach and potato "curry" (*palak aaloo*), 273
  spinach dumplings (*palak vadi*), 193
  spinach kebabs (*palakna muthia*), 169–70
  spinach *raita* (*bhajinu raitu*), 102
  spinach with carrots (*sai bhaji*), 277
  spinach with split chickpeas (*palak moglai*), 276
  steamed spinach and peas rounds (*palak vatanana muthia*), 171
split and whole Indian black beans (*moglai dal*), 380–81
split black bean flour (*adadno lot*), **45**
split black beans (*urid dal*), **339**, 368

split chickpeas (*chana dal*), **338–39**
  with cinnamon and green chili, 351
  patties (*chana dal vada*), 150
  *See also* chickpeas
split lima beans (*valni dal*), **340**, 373–74
split mung beans (*mugni dal*), **341**, 366
  patties (*mung dal kachori*), 144–45
  split pigeon peas with mung beans (*tuver mugni dal*), 358–59
  with zucchini (zucchini *mugni dal*), 367
split peas (*vatanani dal*), **342**
split pigeon peas (*tuverni dal/arar dal*), **342**
  with mung beans (*tuver mugni dal*), 358–59
  with tomatoes and bulbous root (*suranwali dal*), 356–57
sprouted beans, **343**
sprouted brown mung beans (*sangavela muth*), 372
  with dumplings (*muth dhokli*), 372
sprouted mung beans with garlic (*sangavela mug*), 371
squash
  *bhakhari* with squash and spices (*doodhini bhakhari*), 409
  *See also* bitter gourd and tinde (ivy gourd); bottle gourd and ridge
    gourd; zucchini
stainless steel sieve, 47, *50*
star anise (*badiyan*), **9**
star fruit. *See* carambola or star fruit (*kamrakh*)
steamed savory cake (*dhokla*), 155–56
steamed savory rounds (*idlee*), 159–60
steamed spinach and peas rounds (*palak vatanana muthia*), 171
steaming techniques, 50
strawberry *lassi,* 493
stuffed bananas
  with chickpea flour and spices (*kelana ravaiya*), 291
  with fresh spices (*bharela kela*), 289–90

stuffed bitter gourd with anise (*saunfwale karele*), 264–65

stuffed crispy rounds (*mathdi*), 176–77

stuffed eggplants

    in cilantro sauce (*kothnirma ravaiya*), 231–32

    with peas (*vatana bharela vengan*), 233–34

    in spicy sauce (*ravaiya vengan*), 229–30

stuffed half-moon shaped pastry (*ghughra*), 466–67, *468*

stuffed okra (*bhindi masala*), 283–84

stuffed potatoes

    in coconut-onion sauce (*kandana rasama bharela bateta*), 203–04

    in onion and yogurt sauce (*dum bateta*), 200–201

    in spinach and coconut sauce (*bhaji koprama bateta*), 205–06

stuffed round pastry (*ghari*), 469–70

stuffed zucchini (*bhareli* zucchini), 257–58

stuffing method illustrated, *259*

sugar (*sakkar/khand*), **30–31**

    cooking without, 48–49

    sweeteners and restricted diets, 441–42

sugar syrup, 459–60

*suka mevanu athanu* (dry fruit pickle), 122

*suka mevanu raitu* (dry fruit *raita*), 107

*suka vatanano pulav* (dry peas pilaf), 317

*suki bhaji* (spicy potatoes with *garam masala*), 198

*Suphala* (coconut), **14**

*suran* (elephant's foot or bulbous root), **38**

*suranwali dal* (split pigeon peas with tomatoes and bulbous root), 356–57

*Surti khari biscuit* (butter biscuits), 182

*Surti puri* (festive *puri*), 421

sweet, sour and hot mung beans (*mugno ragdo*), 364–65

sweet and hot carrot pickle (*gajarnu athanu*), 119

sweet and hot lemon pickle (*limbunu galu athanu*), 120–21

sweet and hot mango pickle (*kerinu galune tikhu athanu*), 118 sweet and sour bitter gourd with onions and potatoes (*karela, kandane bateta*), 266–67

sweet and spicy green tomatoes (*kacha tameta khalva*), 245

sweet basil seeds (*tukmaria*), **31**

sweet potatoes (*sakkaria*), **39**

    sweet potatoes, potatoes, and peas with onions (*sakkaria bateta, vatana*), 207

    sweet potatoes and potatoes with peanuts (*sakkaria bateta*), 208

sweetened yogurt dessert (*shreekhand*), 452

sweetened yogurt dessert with black pepper (*matho*), 453

sweeteners and restricted diets, 441–42

sweetmeats. *See* desserts and sweetmeats

## T

*tadka,* 51

*tahri* (Lucknowi rice with vegetables), 304

*taj* (cinnamon), **13**

*tal* (sesame seeds), **30**

tamarind (*aamli/imli*), **31**

    lima beans with tamarind (*sabut val*), 382–83

    pumpkin with peas and tamarind (*kohlu vatana*), 260

    raisin and tamarind chutney (*draksh aamlini chutney*), 69

    tamarind aperitif (*jaljeera/jeerapani*), 501

    tamarind rice with nuts and *dal* (*pulihara*), 305–06

    tamarind sauce (*panoo*), 394

*tamasic* foods, 2

*tameta bateta* (tomatoes with potatoes), 243–44

*tametane kandani kachumber* (tomato and onion relish), 86

*tametani chutney* (tomato chutney), 74

tapioca (*sabudana*), **44**

    milk with rose, tapioca and vermicelli (*falooda*), 499–500

*tapkir no lot* (arrow root flour), **40**

*tarbuch* (watermelon), 479

*tarbuchno ras* (watermelon juice), 498

*tava*, 47

tea. *See chai*

tea without tea leaves (*ukalo*), 488

*tejpatta* (bay leaves), **11**

*thali* serving plate, 190

*thandai* (Mahashivratri drink), 495

*thepla* (wheat and millet bread), 417–18

thick Gujarati bread (*bhakhari*), 408–10

thick mango juice (*kerino ras*), 480

thickened yogurt (*maska*), 58

*tikhari* (spicy hot *raita*), 112

*till/tal* (sesame seeds), **30**

*tinde. See* bitter gourd and tinde (ivy gourd)

*tindora, bateta, kanda* (ivy gourd with spicy potatoes and onions), 269

*tindora bateta* (ivy gourd with potatoes), 268

toasted almonds (*shekeli badam*), 184

toasted peanuts (*shekeli shing/moongphali*), 184

toasted split chickpea chutney (*chana dal chutney*), 83

*toddy*, 483

tomatoes

split pigeon peas with tomatoes and bulbous root (*suranwali dal*), 356–57

sweet and spicy green tomatoes (*kacha tameta khalva*), 245

tomato and onion relish (*tametane kandani kachumber*), 86

tomato chutney (*tametani chutney*), 74

tomatoes with potatoes (*tameta bateta*), 243–44

zucchini with peas and tomatoes (zucchini *vatana*), 256

*toor dal*, brown rice with *toor dal* (*karadni khichadi*), 309

*toor kadhi* (whole pigeon peas with yogurt and spices), 354–55

tortillas, *samosa* preparation with, *139*
tricolor pilaf (*trirangi pulav*), 314–16
*trirangi pulav* (tricolor pilaf), 314–16
*tukmaria* (sweet basil seeds), **31**
*tulsi* seeds (sweet basil seeds), **31**
*tulsi/tulasi* (basil), **10–11**
*turia* (ridge gourd with mustard and lemon), 254
*turia kakdi* (ridge gourd with cucumber and yam), 255
turmeric (*haldi/haldar*), **31–32**
turmeric, fresh (*leeli haldar*), **32**
turmeric, mango (*amba haldar*), **32**
*tuver. See* pigeon peas
*tuver mugni dal* (split pigeon peas with mung beans), 358–59
*tuverni dal* (split pigeon peas), **342**

U

*ukalo* (tea without tea leaves), 488
unhulled split mung *khichadi* (*kathiawadi khichadi*), 320
unripe cherry pickle (*cherinu athanu*), 123
unripe mango dessert (*khandkeri*), 471
unsalted butter, 47
*upama* (Cream of Wheat with yogurt and cashew nuts), 180–81
*urid* (black beans), **339**
*urid dal* (split black beans), **339**, 368
*urid dal* flour, **45**
utensils for cooking, 47

V

*vadi. See* dumplings (*vadi*)
*vaghar,* 51
*vaghareli chhash* (buttermilk with cumin and mustard), 491
*vaghareli kobij* (spicy cabbage, stir-cooked with mustard seeds), 242

*vagharelo bhat* (precooked rice with bell peppers and yogurt), 300

*Vaishnavs*

  *Panchamrat* preparation, 54

  *rajasic* foods and, 2

*val. See* lima beans

*valdalni khichadi* (split lima bean *khichadi*), 318–19

*valni dal* (split lima beans), **340**, 373–74

*vangi bhat* (eggplant rice), 302

*varak/vark* (silver or gold leaves), **30**

*variali/badi saunf* (fennel seeds), **19**

*vatana. See* peas

*vatana bateta* (green peas with potatoes), 246

*vatana bharela vengan* (stuffed eggplants with peas), 233–34

*vatanani dal* (split peas), **342**, 375

Veganism as Western practice, 54

vegetable *biryani* (*shakni biryani*), 329–31

vegetable casserole (*dum shak*), 287–88

vegetable *masala* (*shakno masalo*), 23–24

vegetables

  amaranth greens, 281–82

  asparagus, 209–10

  bitter gourd and tinde (ivy gourd), 264–69

  bottle gourd and ridge gourd, 249–55

  cabbage, 240–42

  cauliflower, 211–14

  collard greens, 278–80

  dumplings, 192–94

  eggplant, 227–39

  fruits as, 289–94

  green beans and long beans, 215–18

  lima beans and cluster beans, 219–26

  mixed vegetables, 287–88

vegetables (*continued*)
  mushrooms, 270–72
  okra, 283–86
  onions, 195–97
  peas and pigeon peas, 246–47
  potatoes and sweet potatoes, 198–208
  pumpkin, 260–61
  root vegetables, **38–39**
  serving of, 190
  spaghetti squash with dumplings, 262–63
  spinach, collard, and amaranth greens, 273–82
  stuffing method illustrated, *259*
  tomatoes, 243–45
  zucchini, 256–58
  *See also specific vegetable entries*
vegetarian "gumbo" (*bhinda, kandane paneer*), 286
vegetarian omelettes (*puda*), 421
vegetarianism
  Hindu practice and, 2
  sweeteners and, 441–42
*vengan valni dal* (eggplant with split Indian lima beans), 228
*vengan vatana* (eggplant with peas), 227


## W

walnuts (*akhrot*), **37**
  walnut pudding (*akhrotni basudi*), 463
watermelon (*tarbuch*), 479
watermelon juice (*tarbuchno ras*), 498
wheat (*ghaun*), **44**
wheat and millet bread (*dhebral thepla*), 417–18
wheat flour (*ghaunno lot*), **44**
  American wheat flour, 397
  coarsely ground (*ghavno kakario lot*), **45**

whole pigeon peas with yogurt and spices (*toor kadhi*), 354–55

whole-wheat flours and *chapati* flour, 397

wild rice pilaf (*jungli pulav*), 333

## Y

yams (*ratalu*), **39**

    ridge gourd with cucumber and yam (*turia kakdi*), 255

yellow peas in onion-yogurt sauce (*dopiaza matar*), 389–90

yellow split peas with garlic and cloves (*vatanani dal*), 375

yogurt

    homemade (*dahi*), 56–57

    homemade yogurt described, 54–55

    thickened yogurt (*maska*), 58

    yogurt-chili sauce (*kadhi*), 393

    yogurt with milk (*golvo*), 494

    *See also raitas*

## Z

zucchini

    split mung beans with zucchini (zucchini *mugni dal*), 367

    stuffed zucchini (*bhareli* zucchini), 257–58

    zucchini with mushrooms (zucchini *gucchi*), 272

    zucchini with peas and tomatoes (zucchini *vatana*), 256

    *See also* squash

0-595-24422-X

8508683R0

Made in the USA
Lexington, KY
10 February 2011